# Banya
## the explosive delivery man

STORY AND ART BY

# KIM YOUNG-OH

LETTERING **STEVE DUTRO**

TRANSLATION **TAESOON KANG** & **DEREK KIRK KIM**

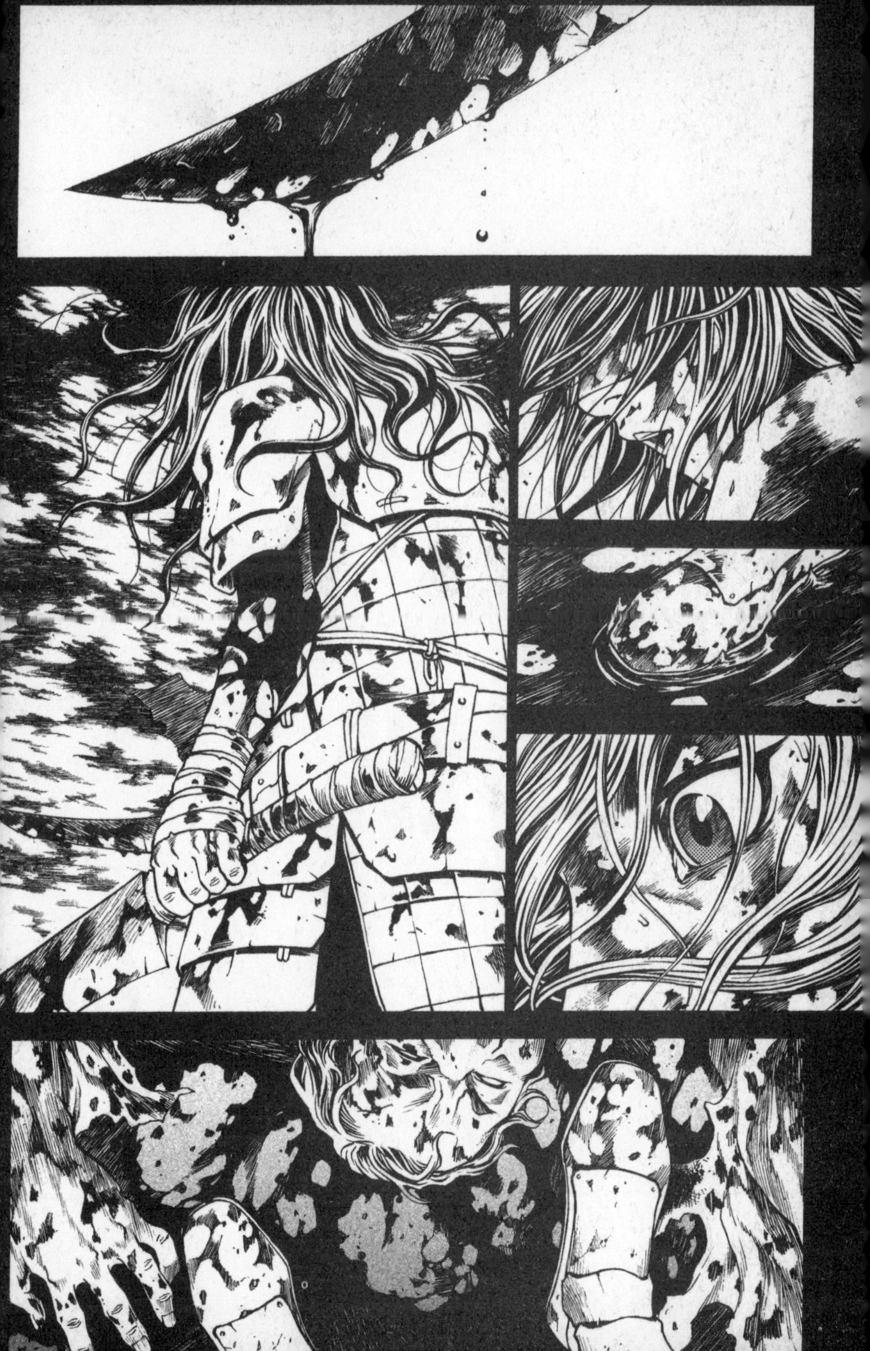

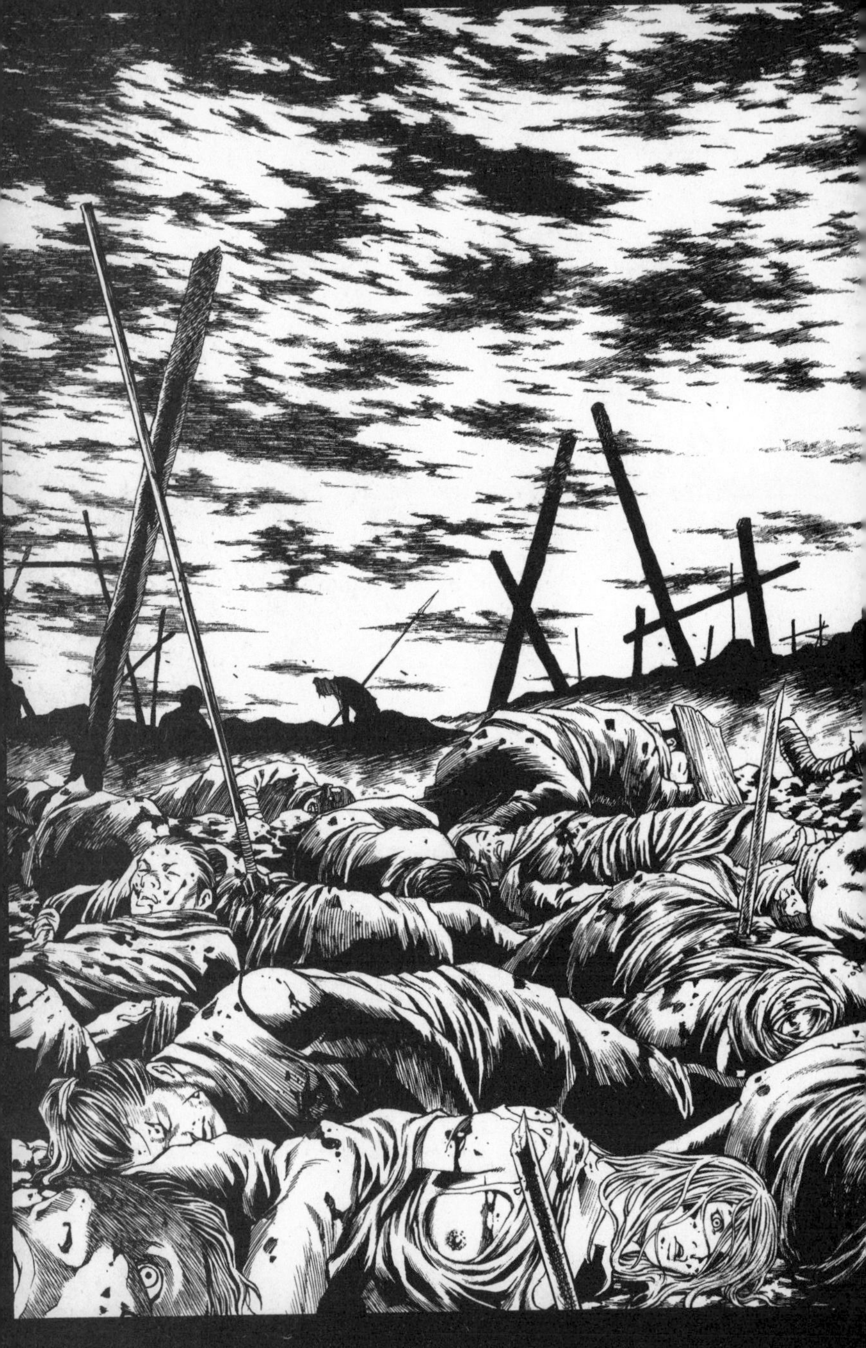

## Chapter 22
# PEOPLE FROM THE PAST, PART 1

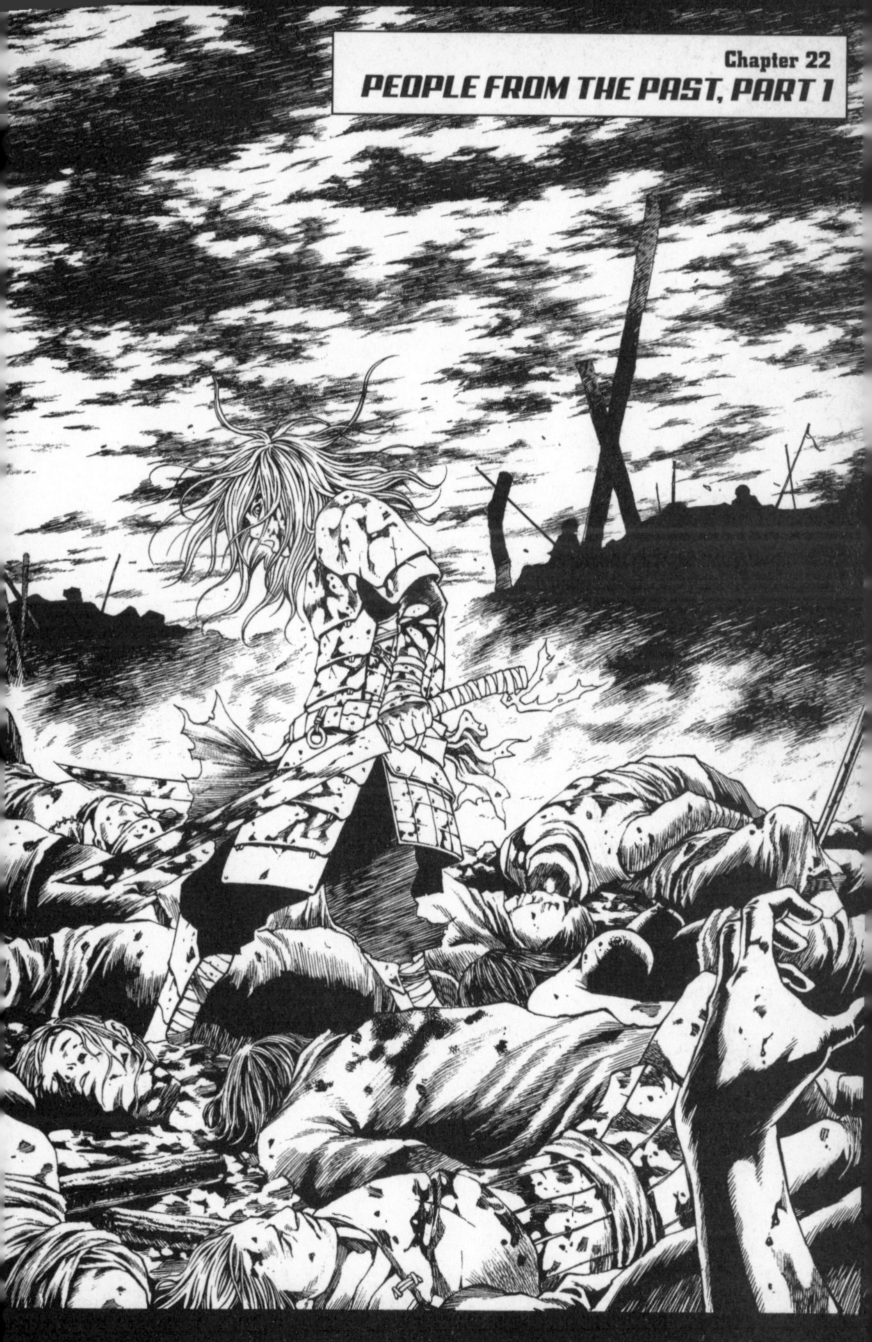

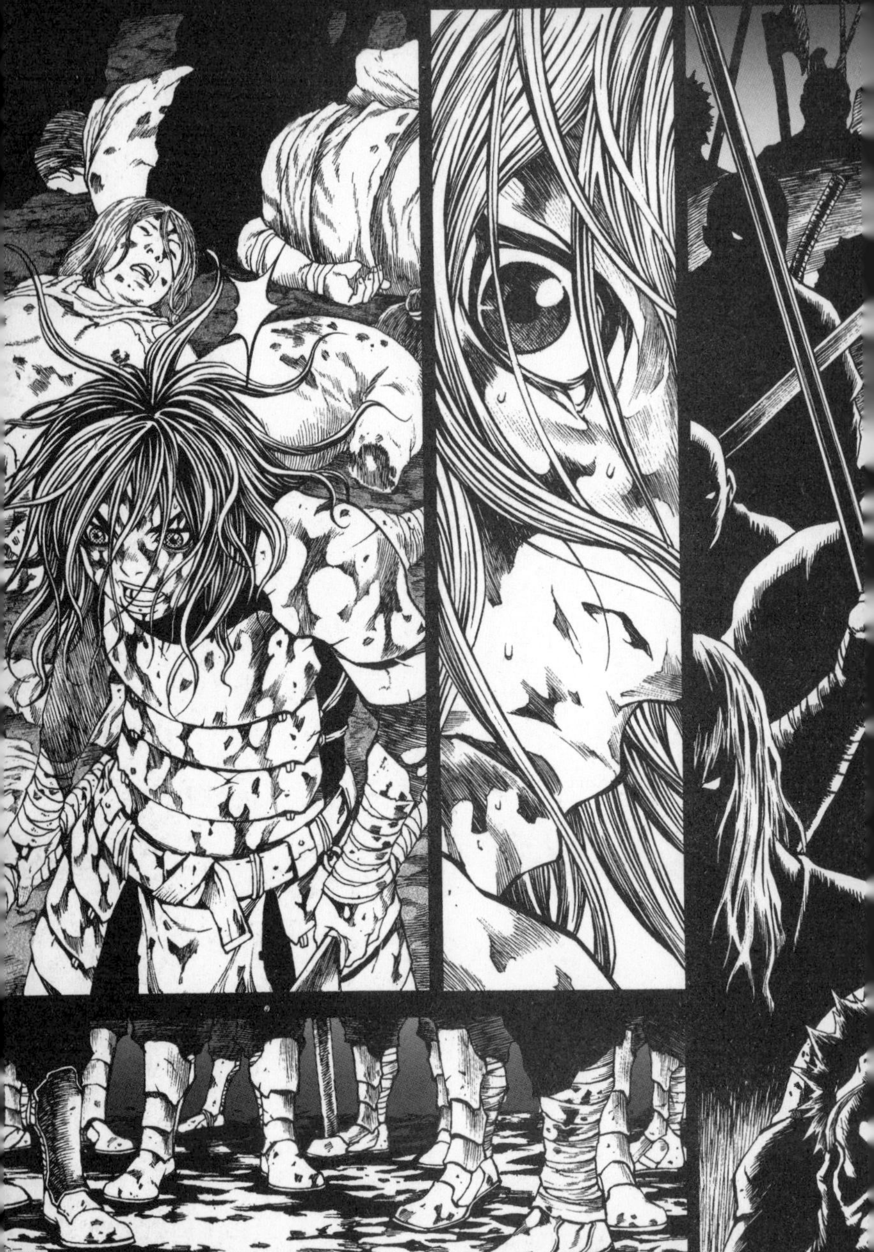

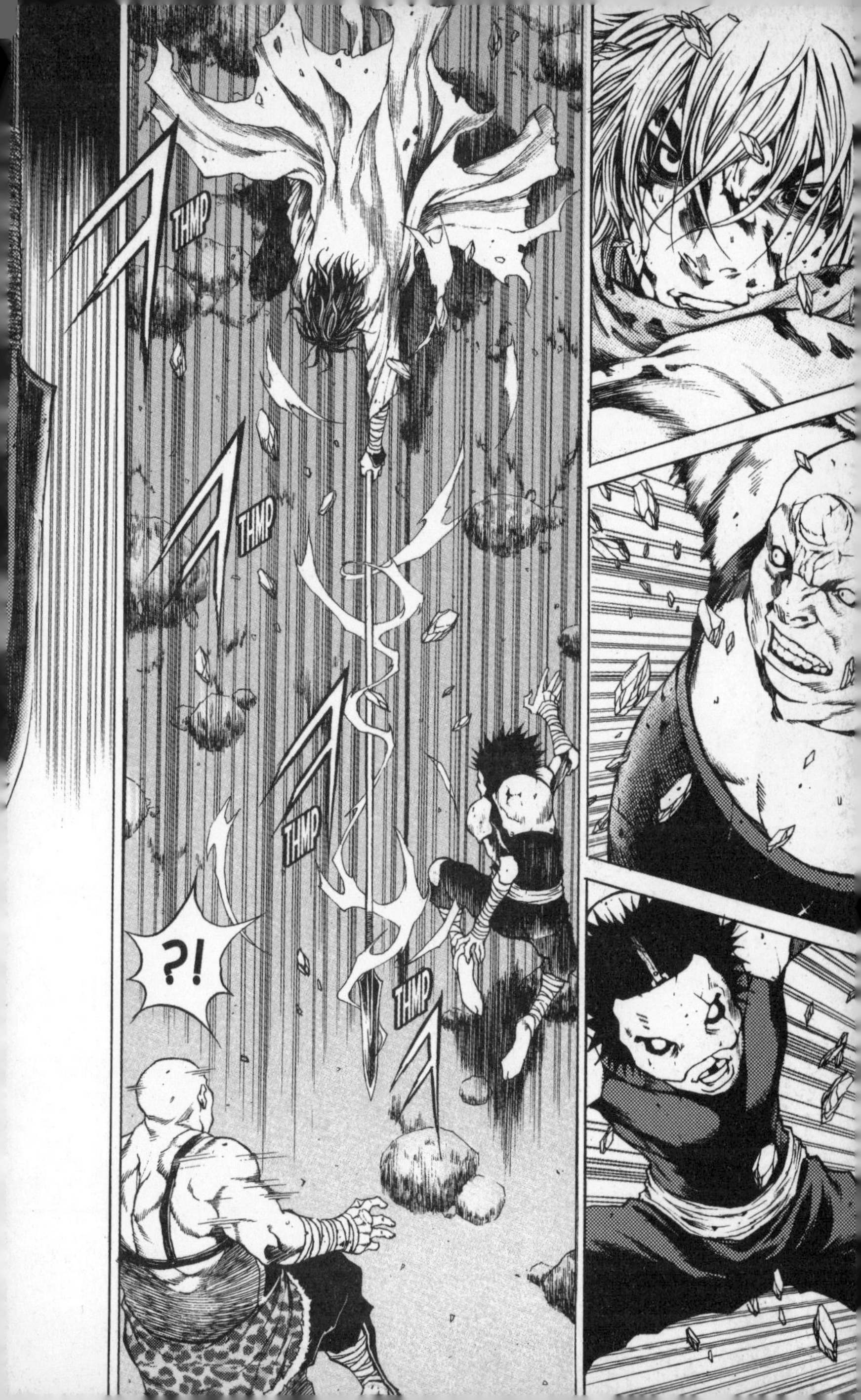
THMP
THMP
THMP
THMP
?!

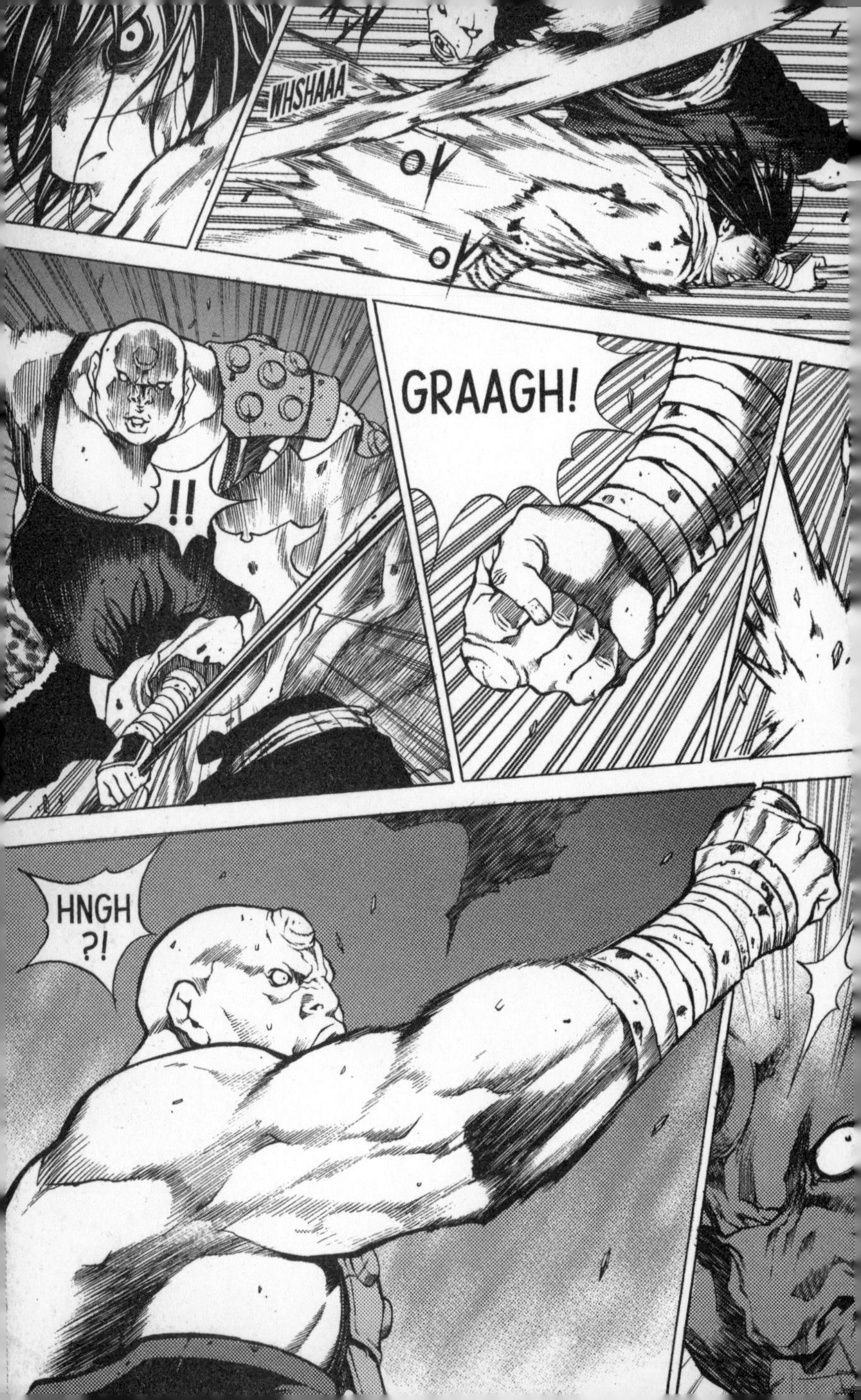
WHSHAAA
GRAAGH!
!!
HNGH ?!

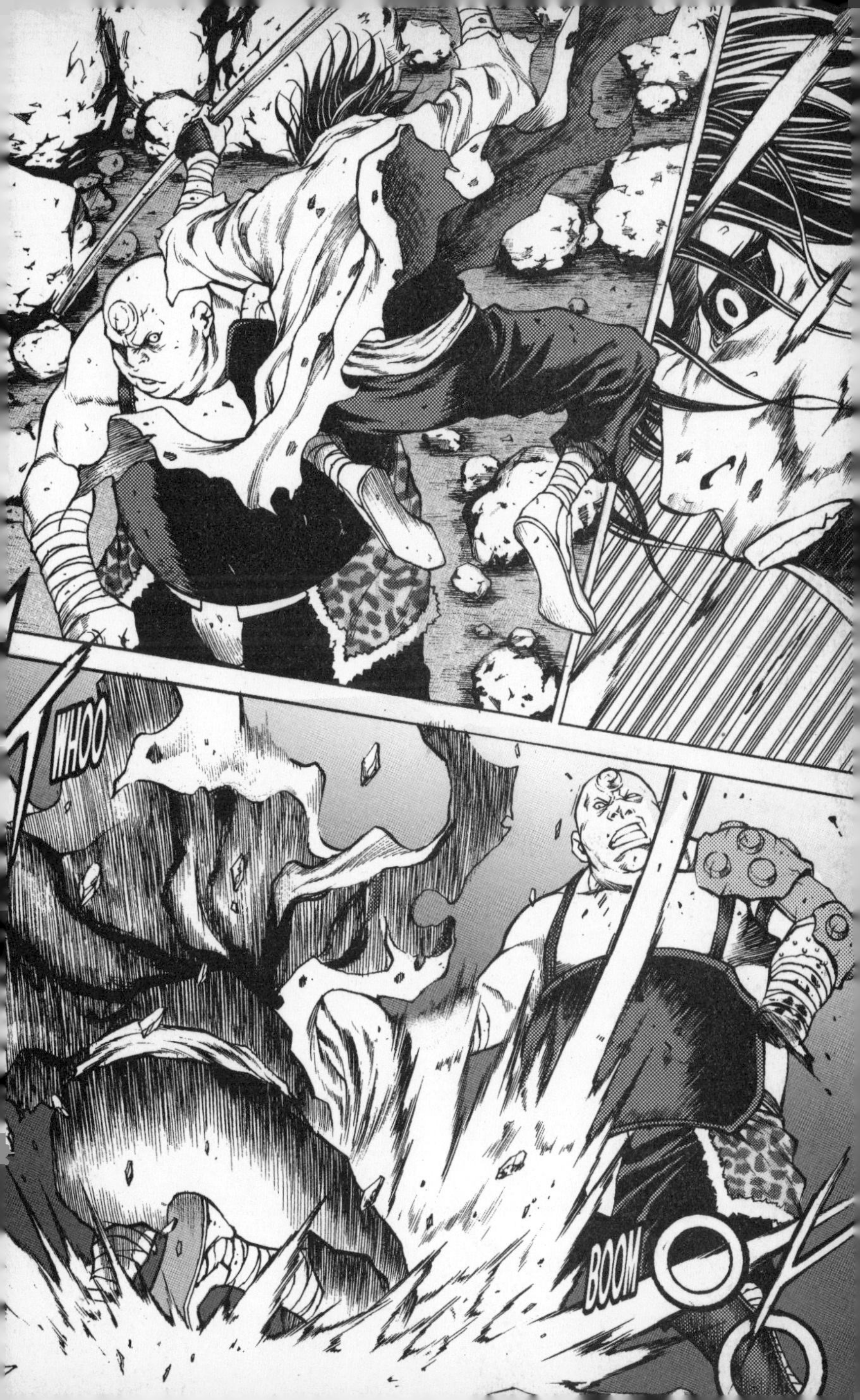
WHOO
BOOM

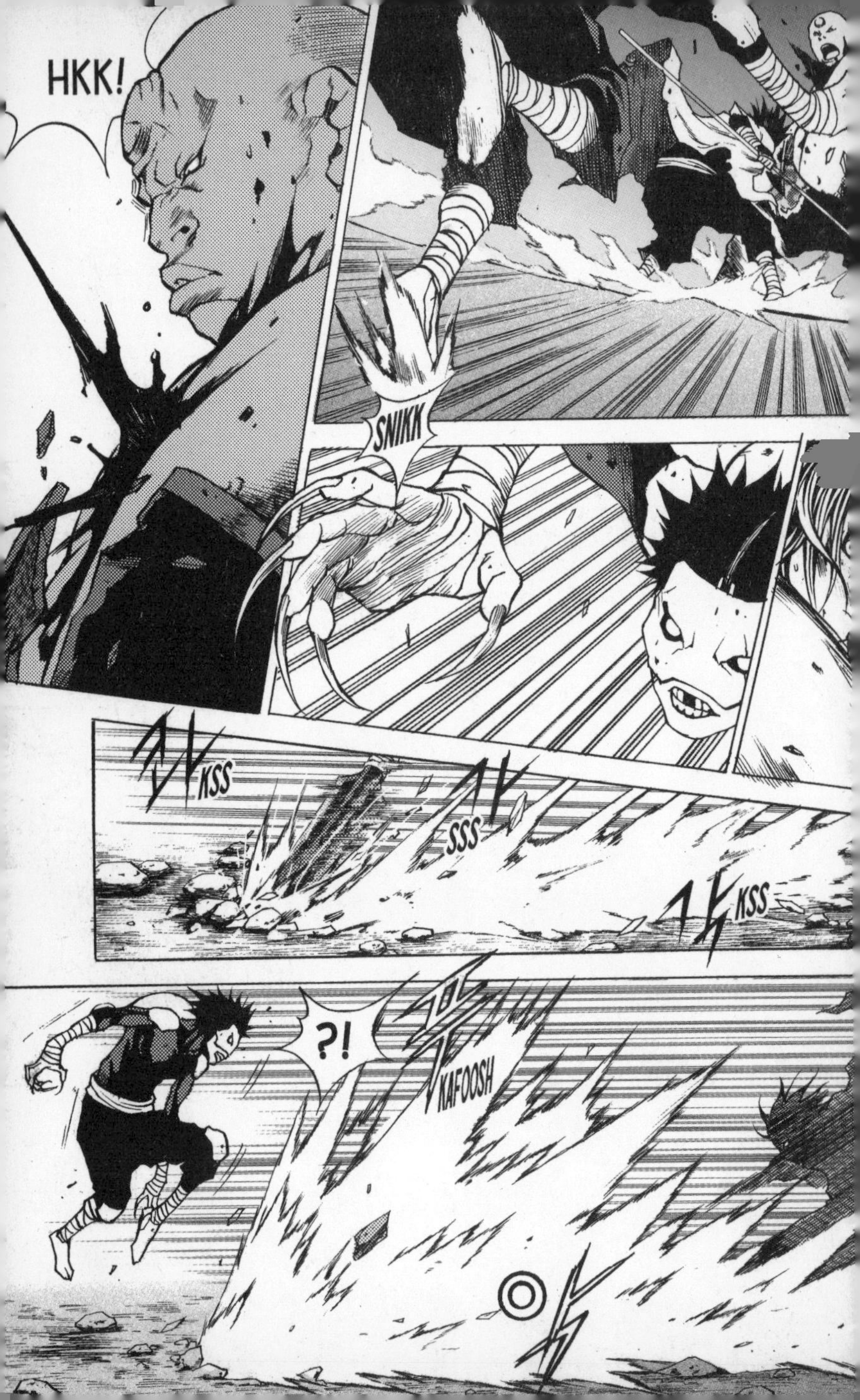
SNIKK
HKK!
KSS
SSS
KSS
?!
KAFOOSH

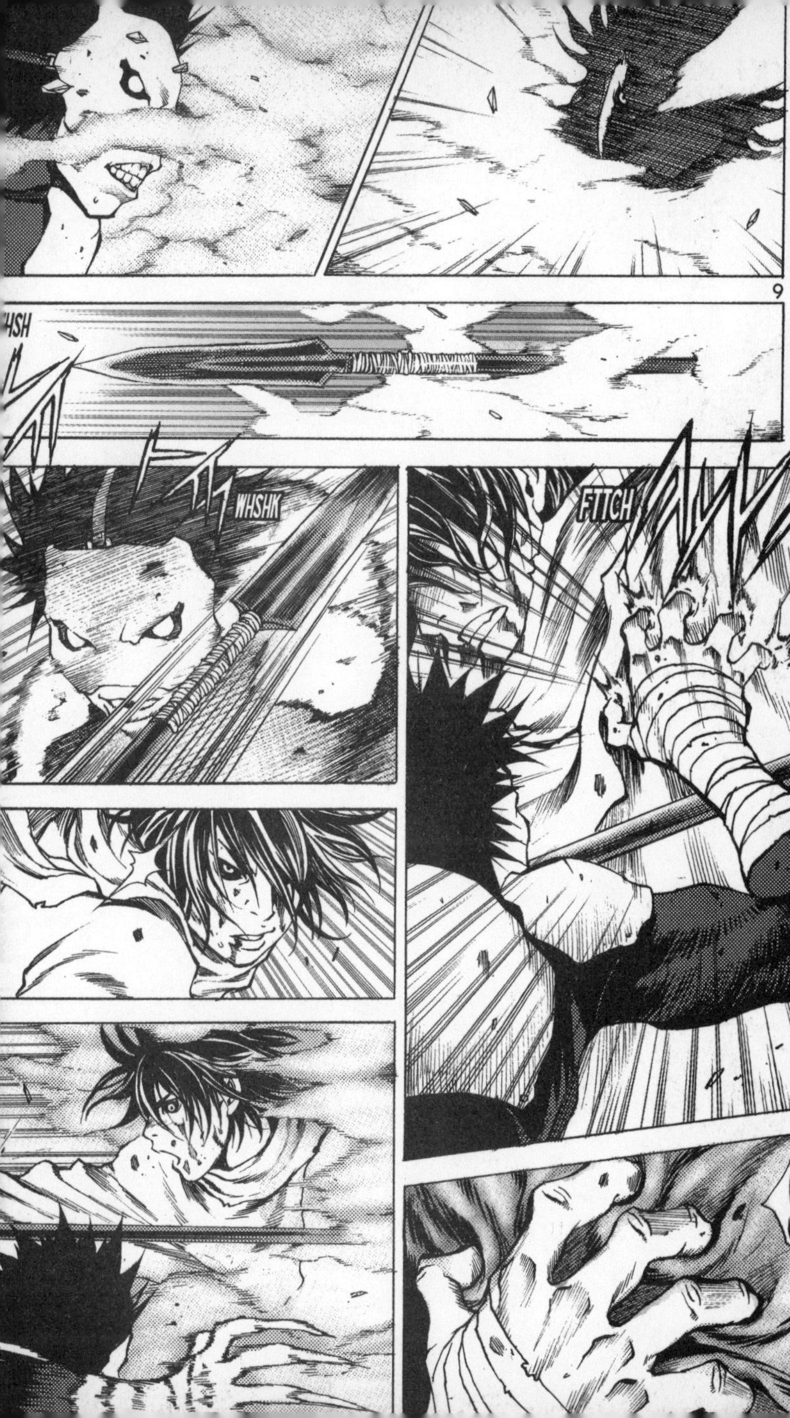
HSH
WHSHK
FTTCH
SKRNCH

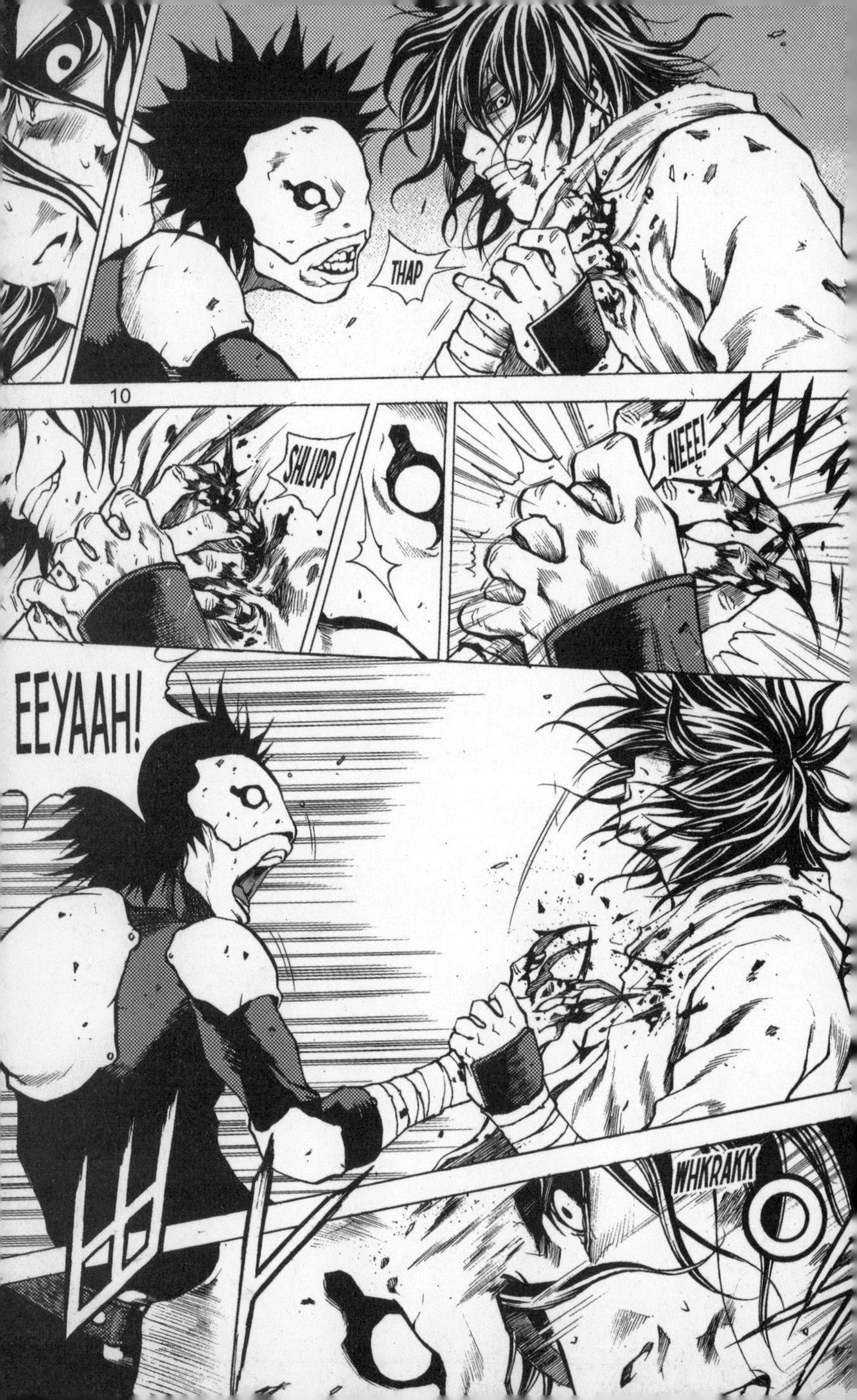

THAP
10
AIEEE!
SHLUPP
EEYAAH!
WHKRAKK

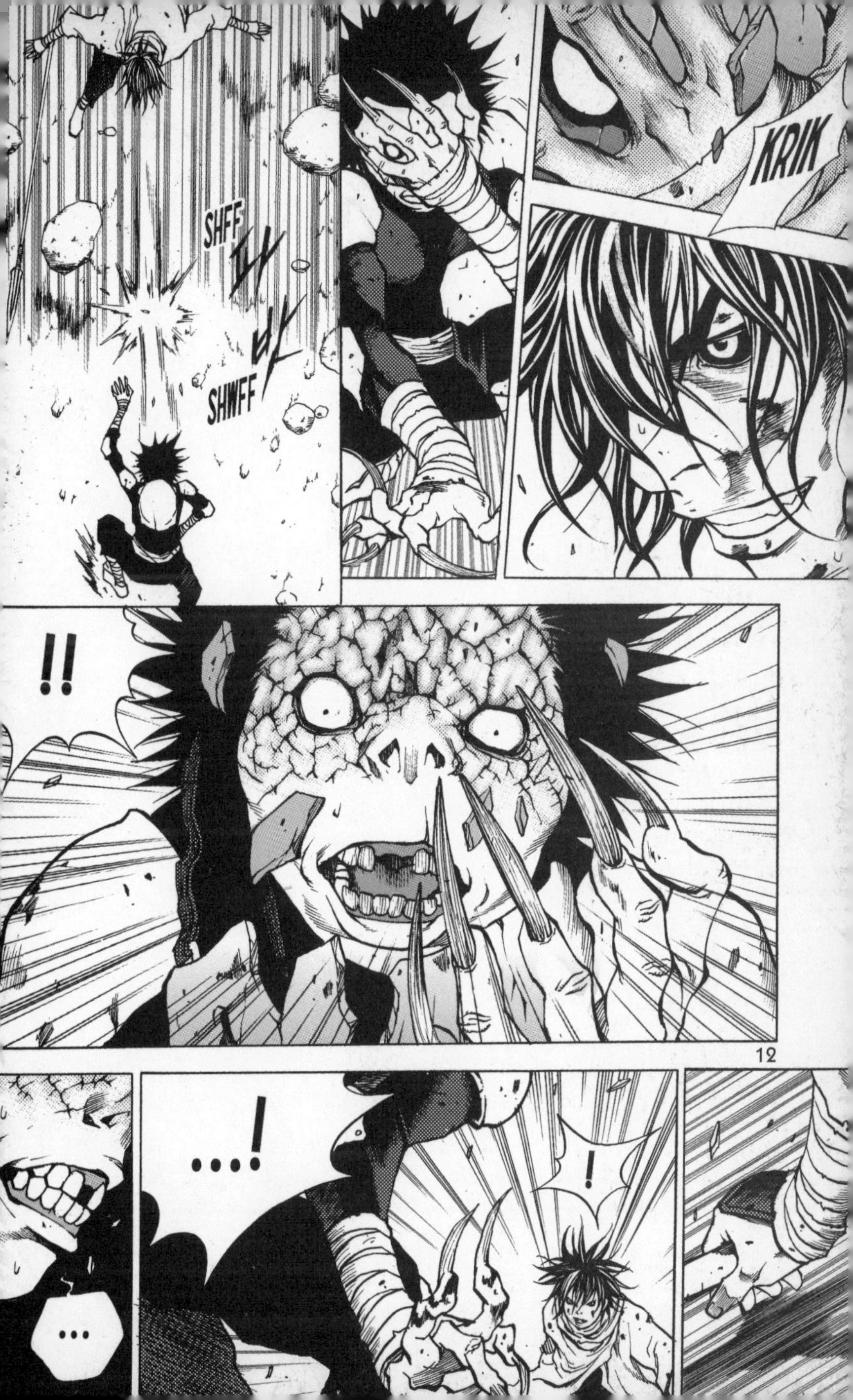
KRIK
SHFF
SHWFF
!!
!
...!
...

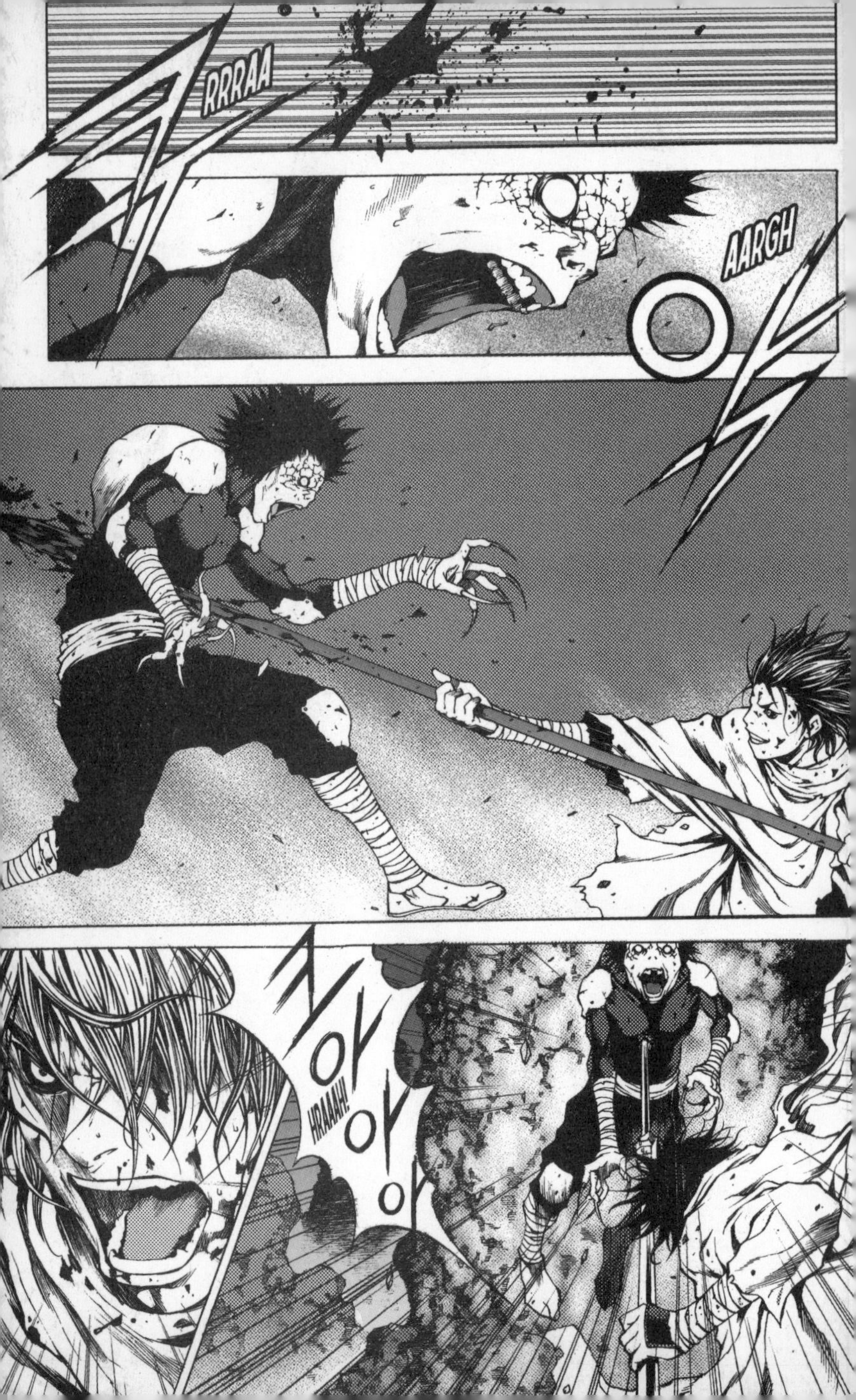
RRRAA
AARGH
HRAAAH!

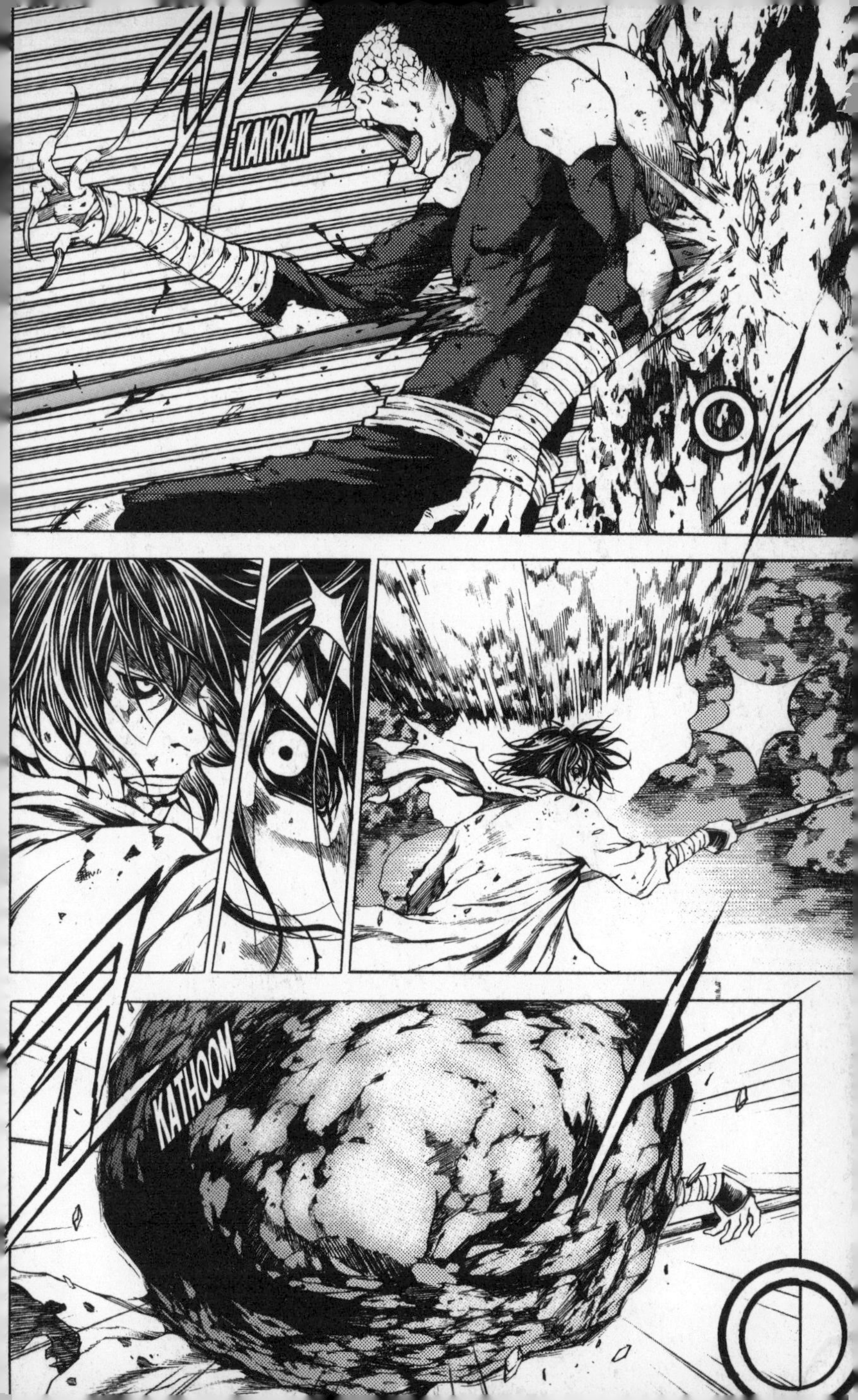
KAKRAK
KATHOOM

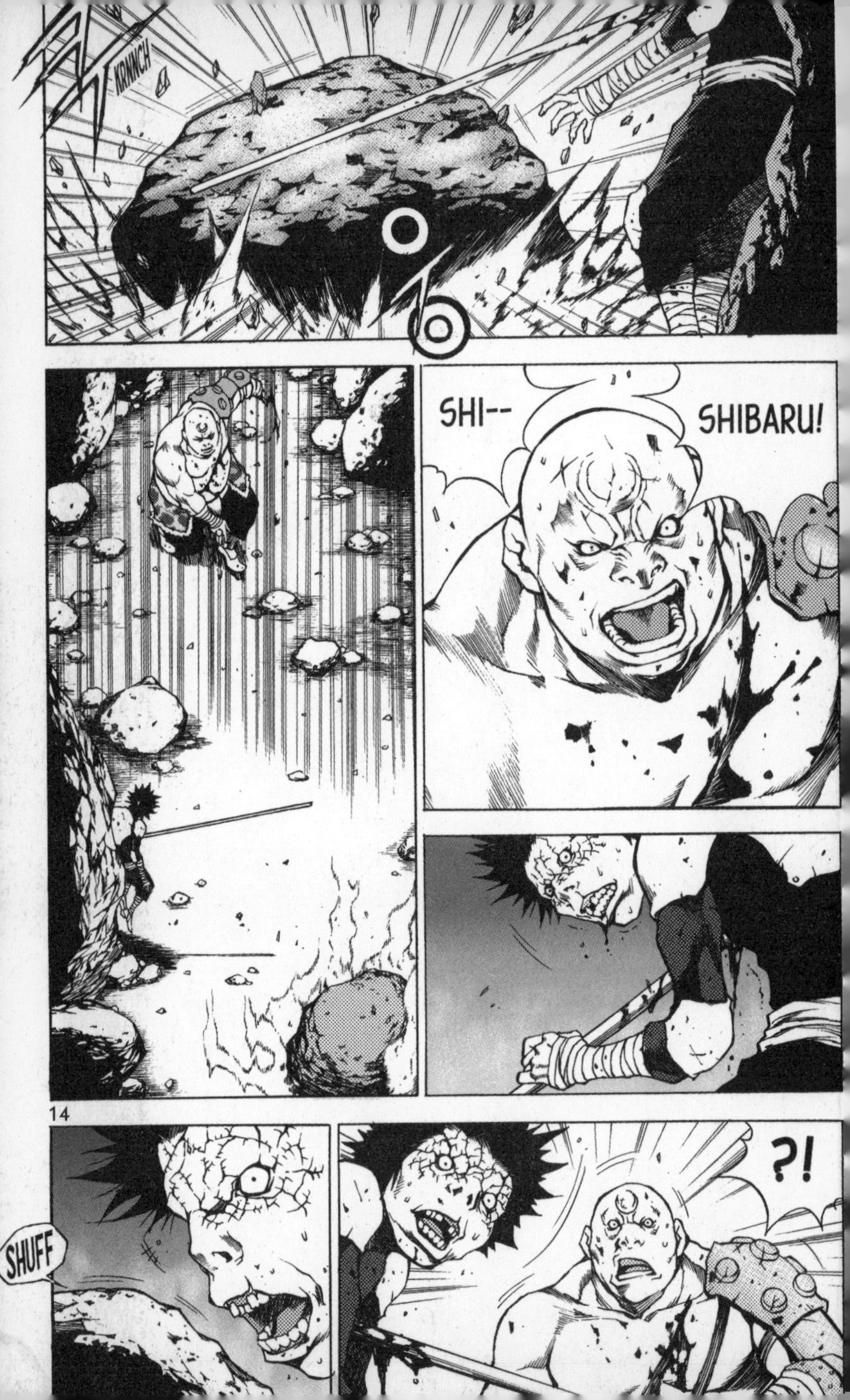
KRNNCH
SHI--
SHIBARU!
SHUFF
?!

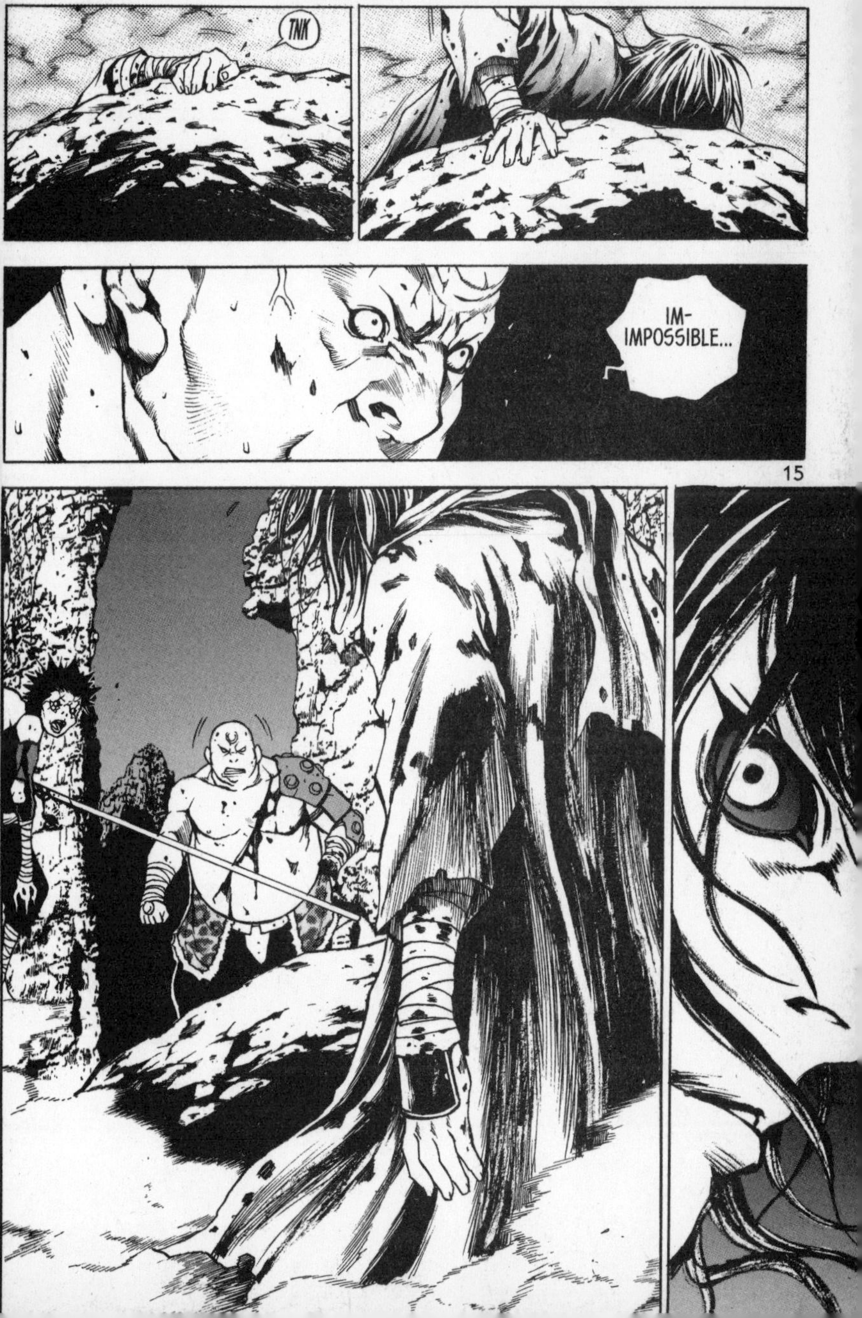
TNK
IM-
IMPOSSIBLE...

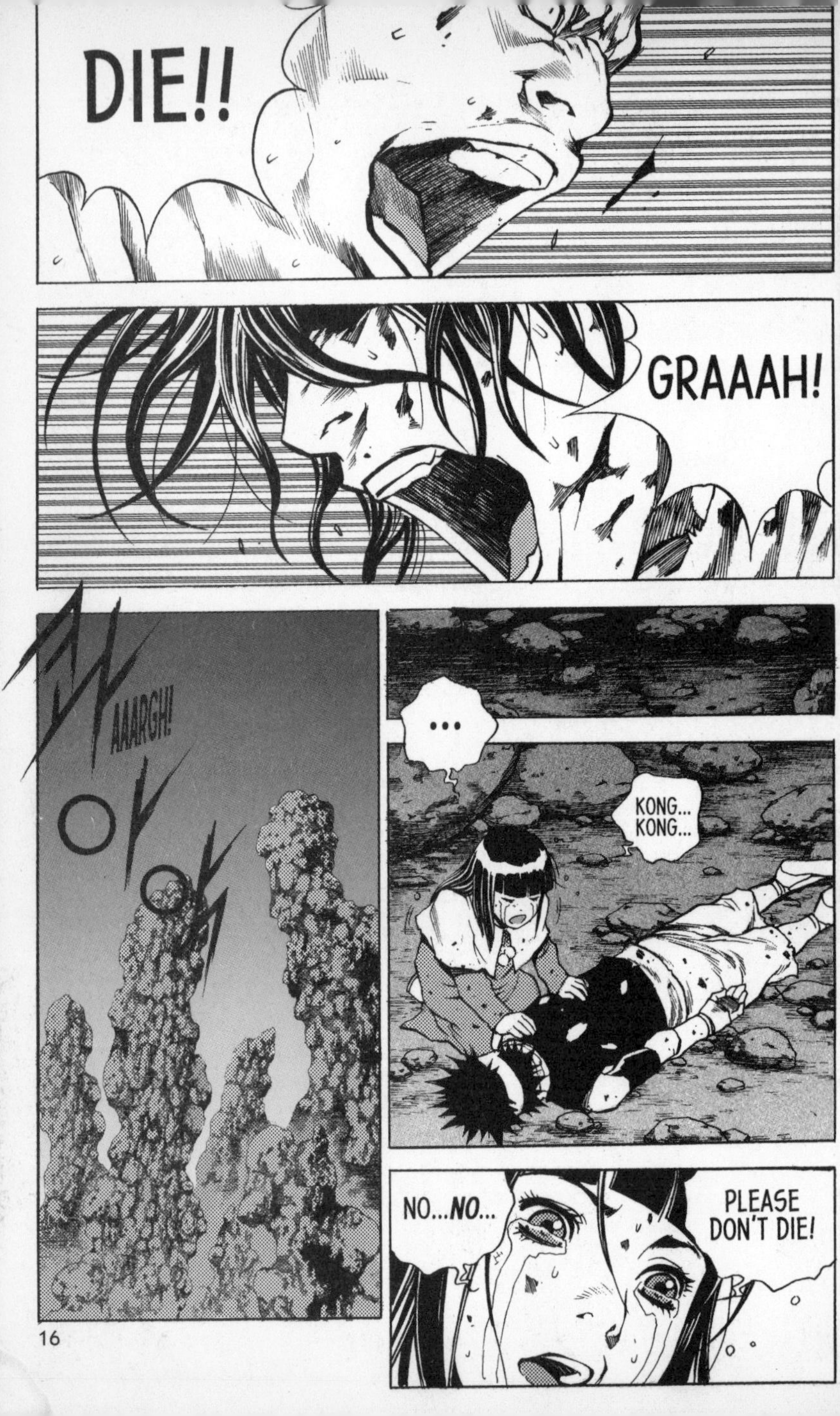
DIE!!
GRAAAH!
AAARGH!
...
KONG... KONG...
NO...NO...
PLEASE DON'T DIE!

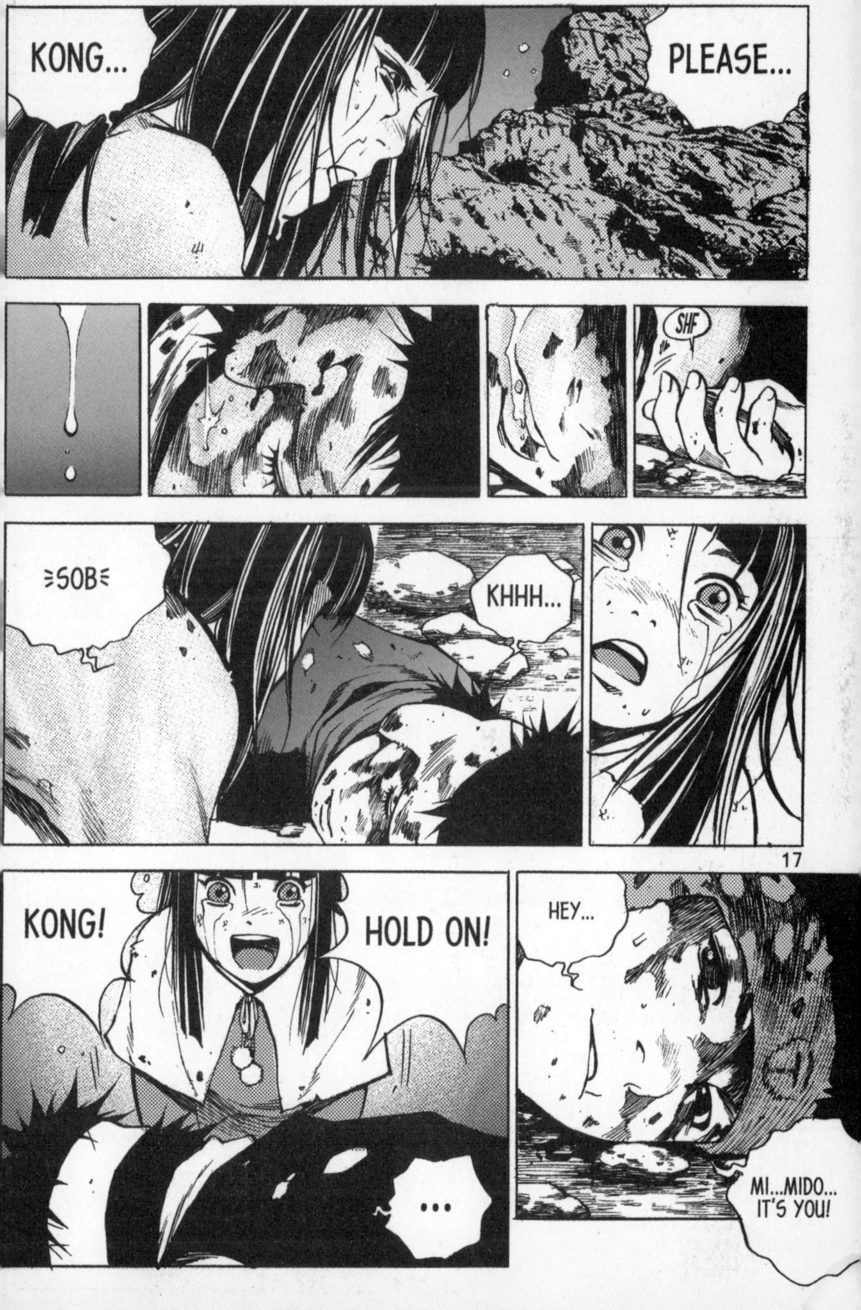
KONG...
PLEASE...
SHF
SOB
KHHH...
KONG!
HOLD ON!
...
HEY...
MI...MIDO... IT'S YOU!

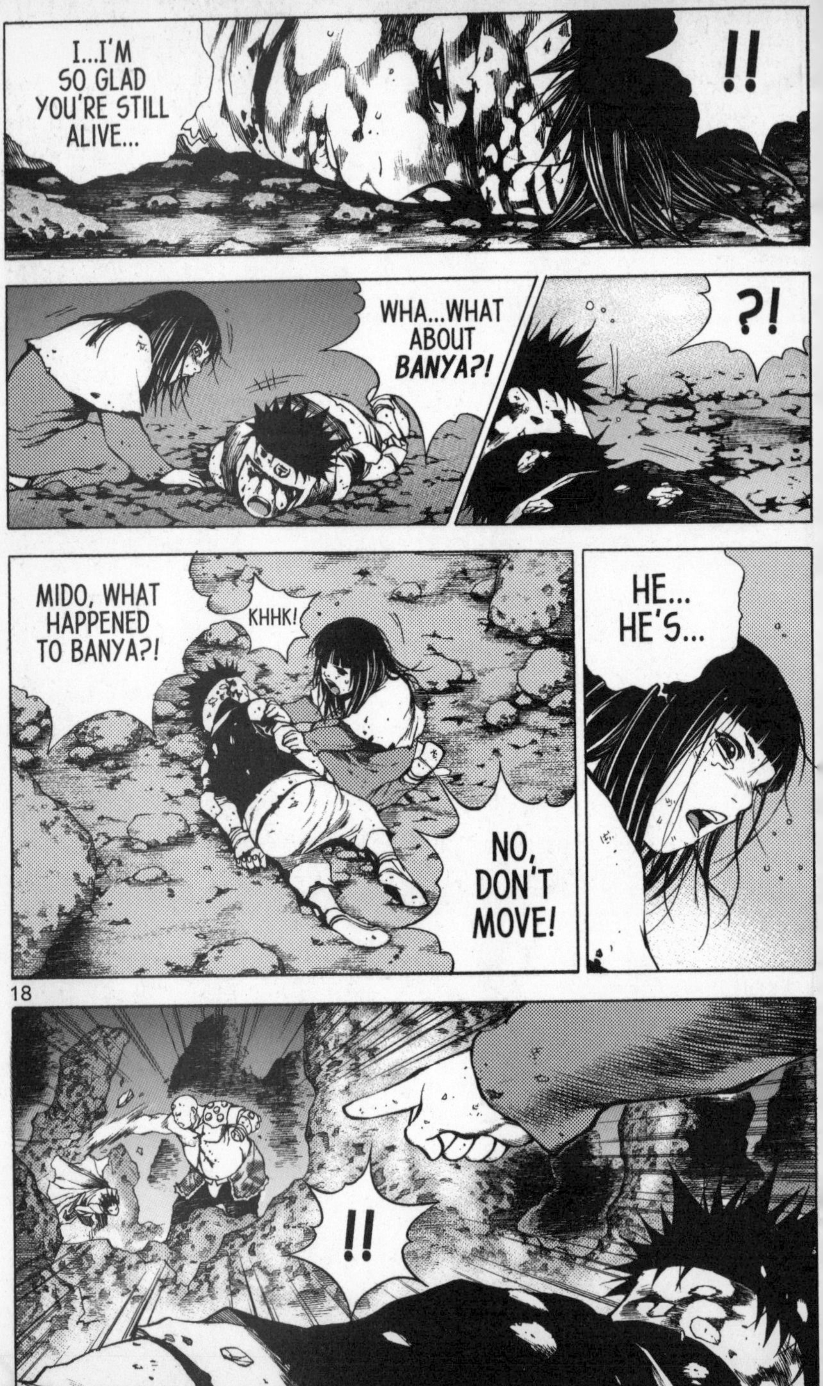
!!
I...I'M SO GLAD YOU'RE STILL ALIVE...
?!
WHA...WHAT ABOUT BANYA?!
HE... HE'S...
KHHK!
MIDO, WHAT HAPPENED TO BANYA?!
NO, DON'T MOVE!
!!

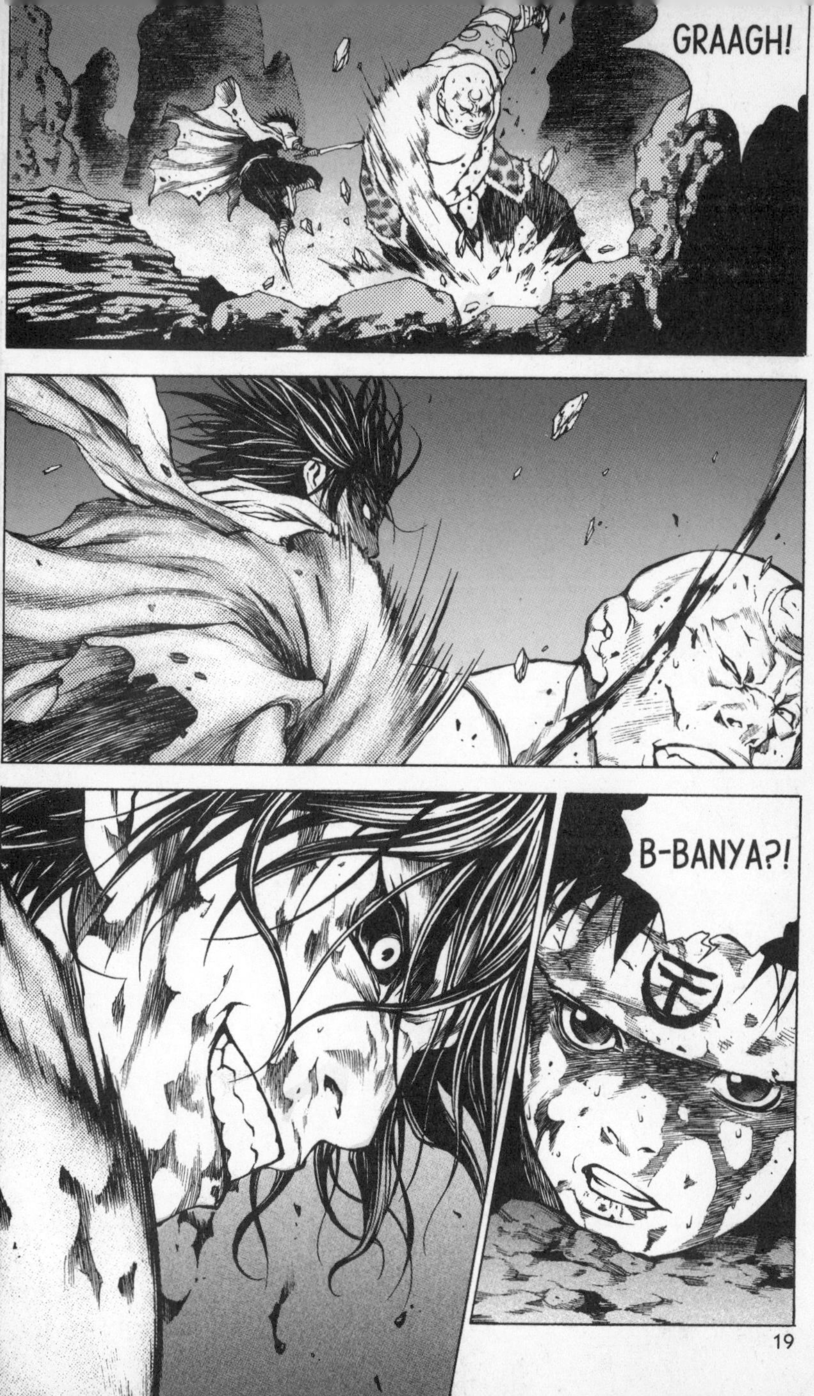
GRAAGH!
B-BANYA?!

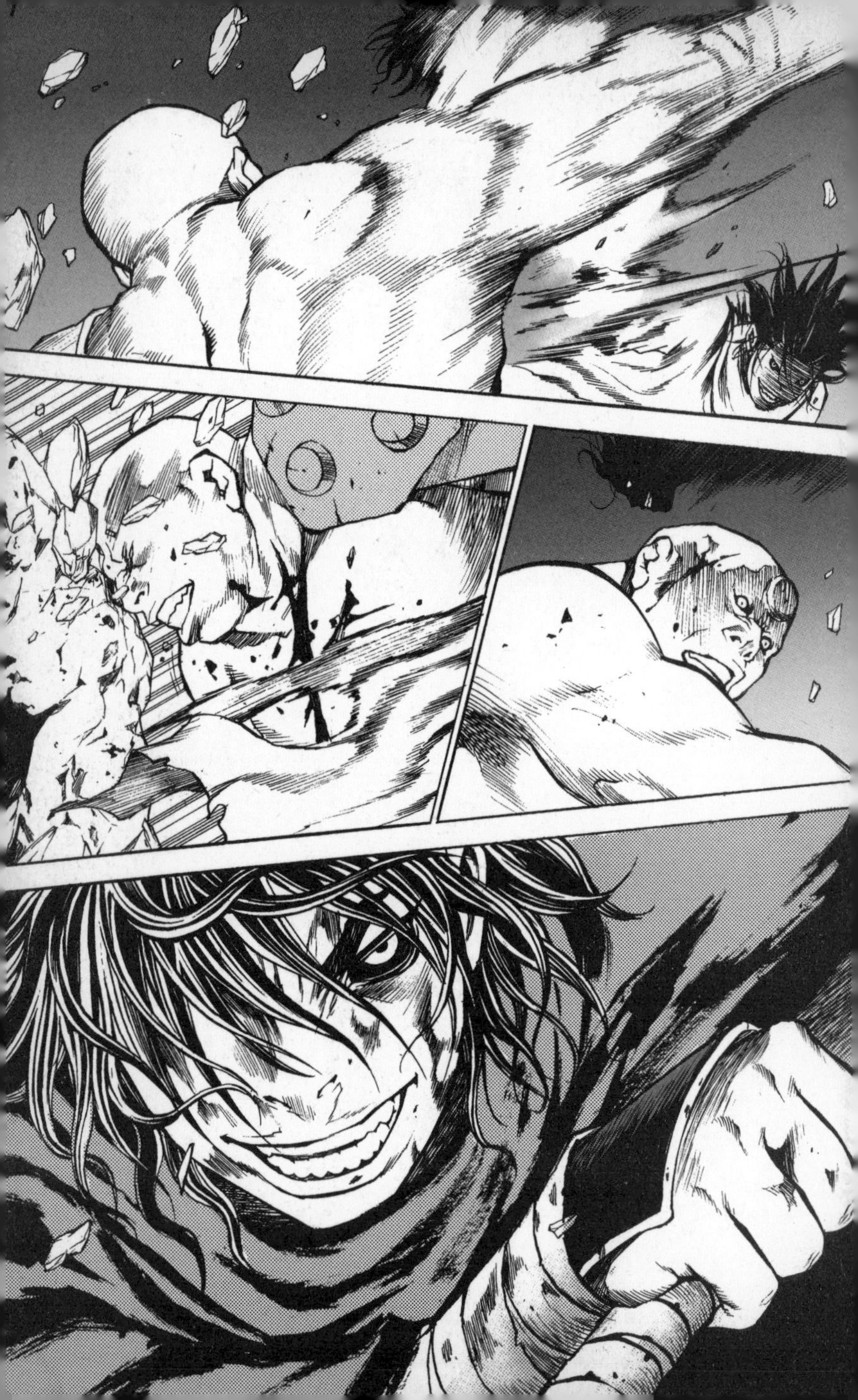

## Chapter 23
# PEOPLE FROM THE PAST, PART 2

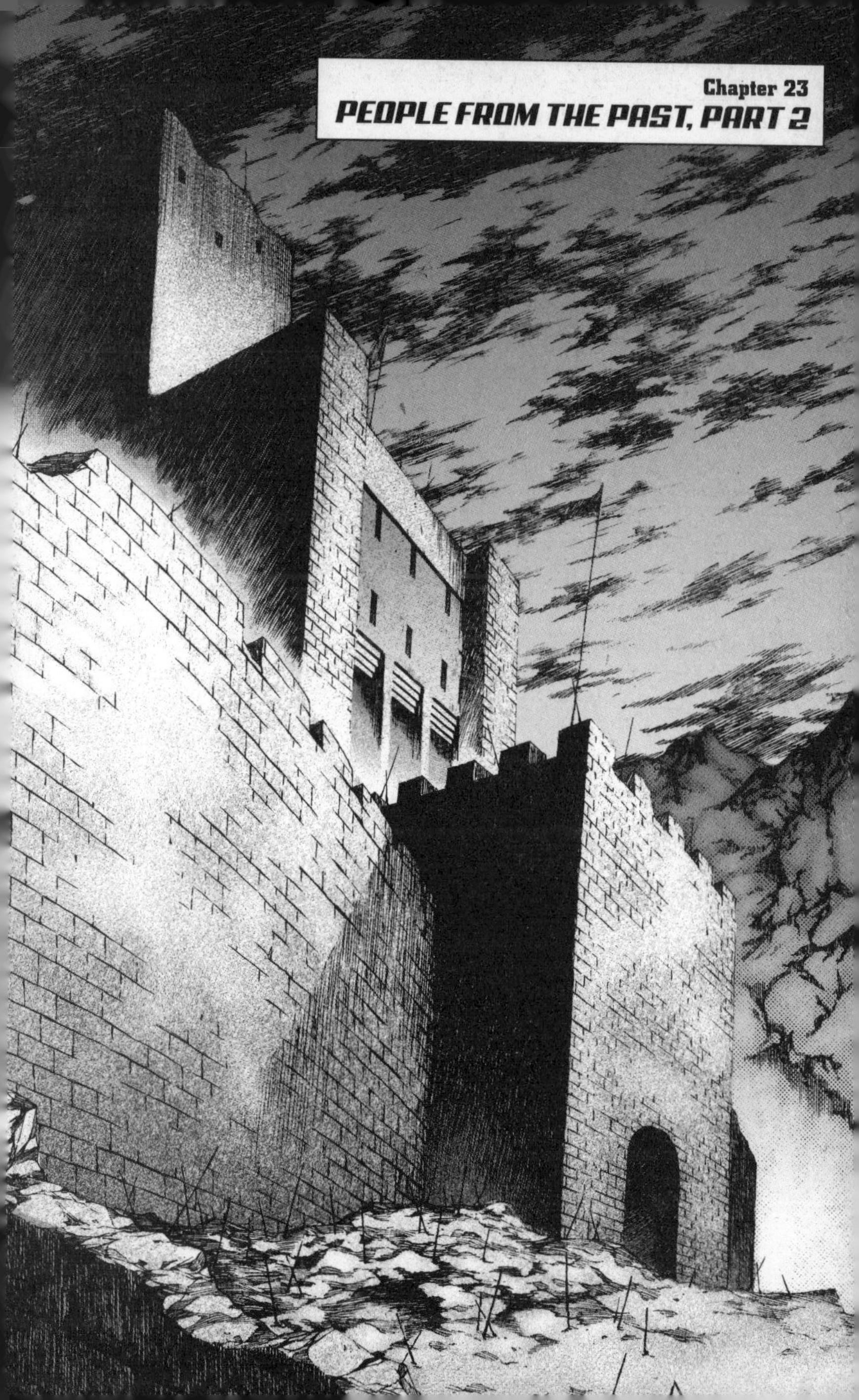

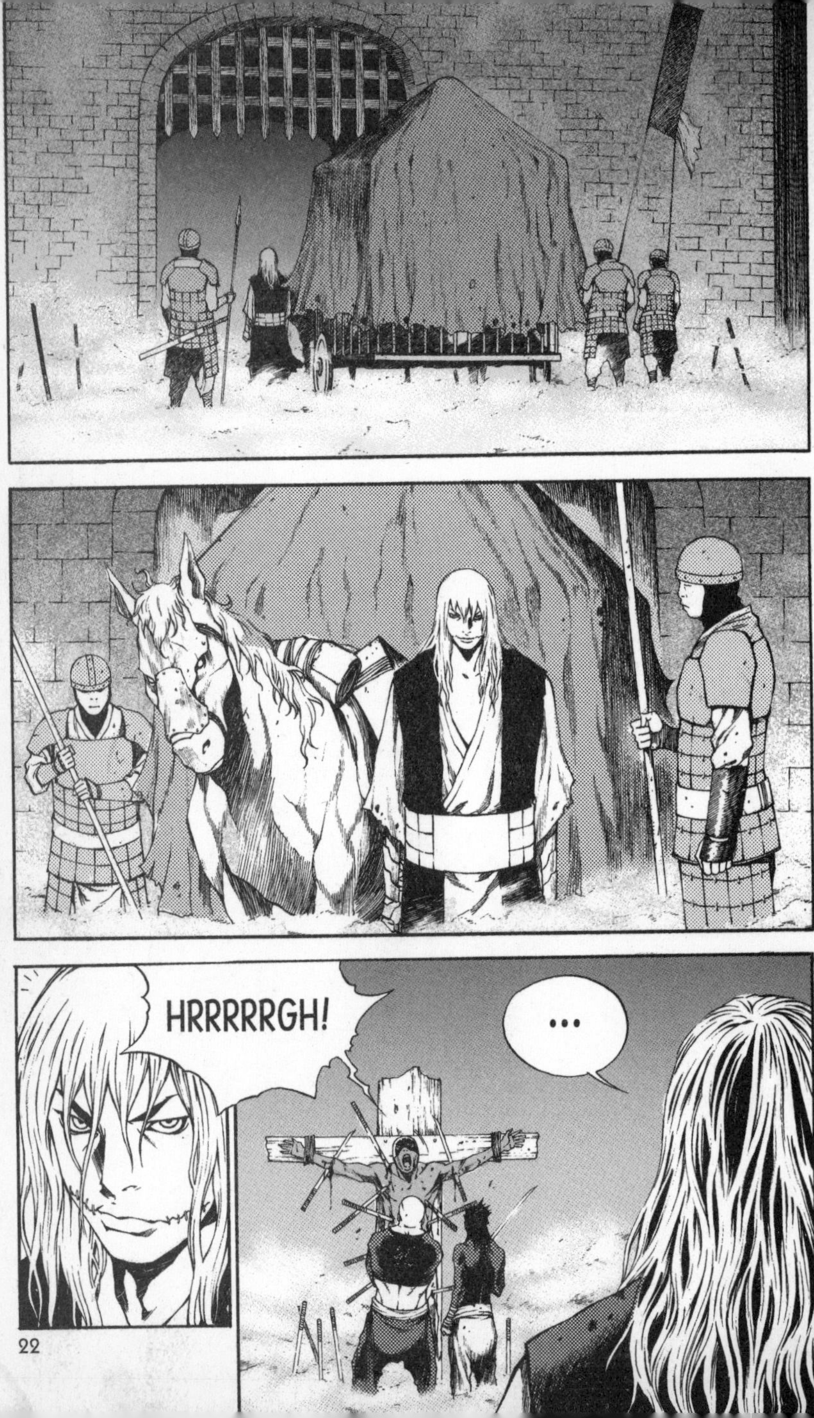
HRRRRRGH!
...

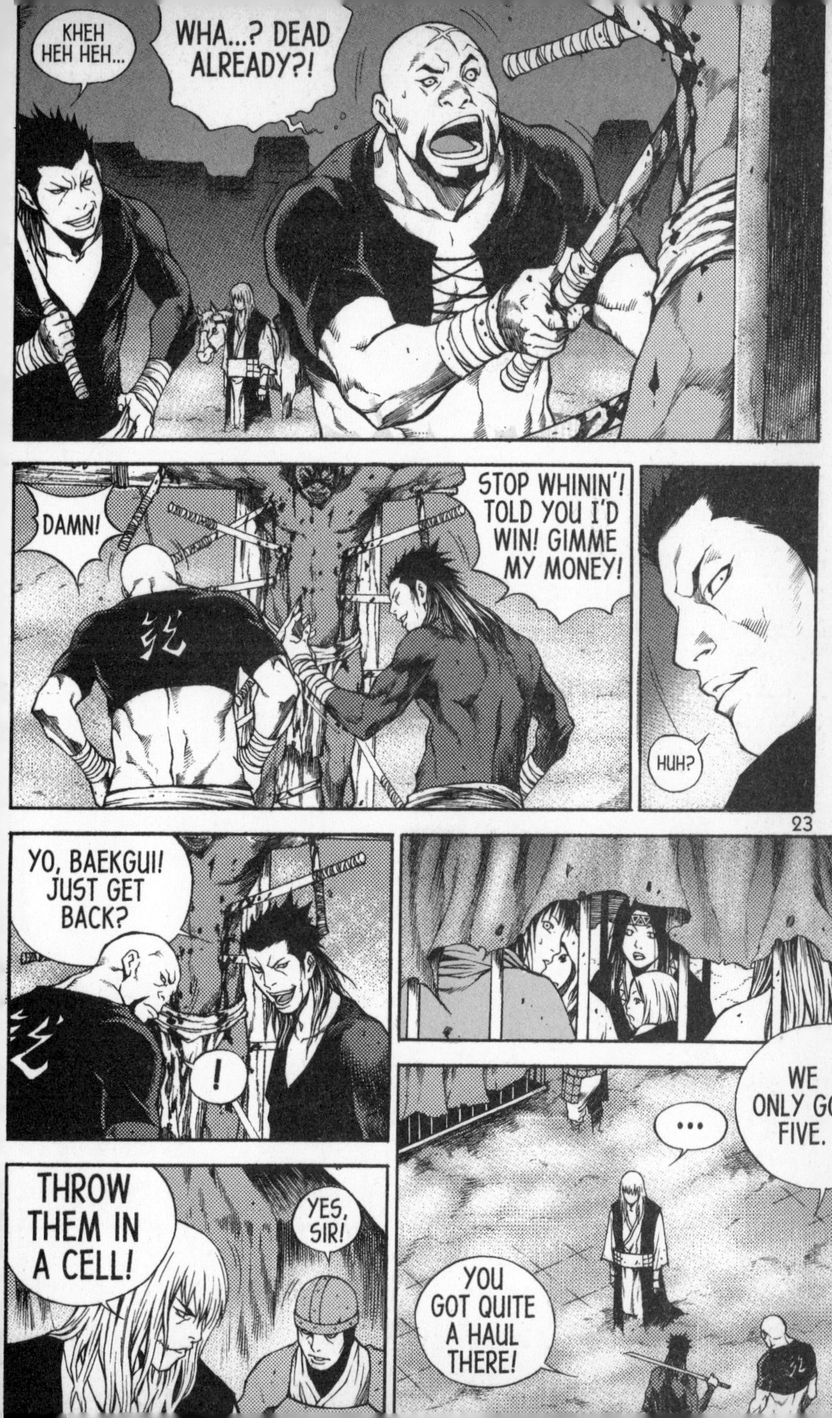
KHEH HEH HEH...
WHA...? DEAD ALREADY?!
DAMN!
STOP WHININ'! TOLD YOU I'D WIN! GIMME MY MONEY!
HUH?
YO, BAEKGUI! JUST GET BACK?
!
THROW THEM IN A CELL!
YES, SIR!
YOU GOT QUITE A HAUL THERE!
...
WE ONLY GOT FIVE.

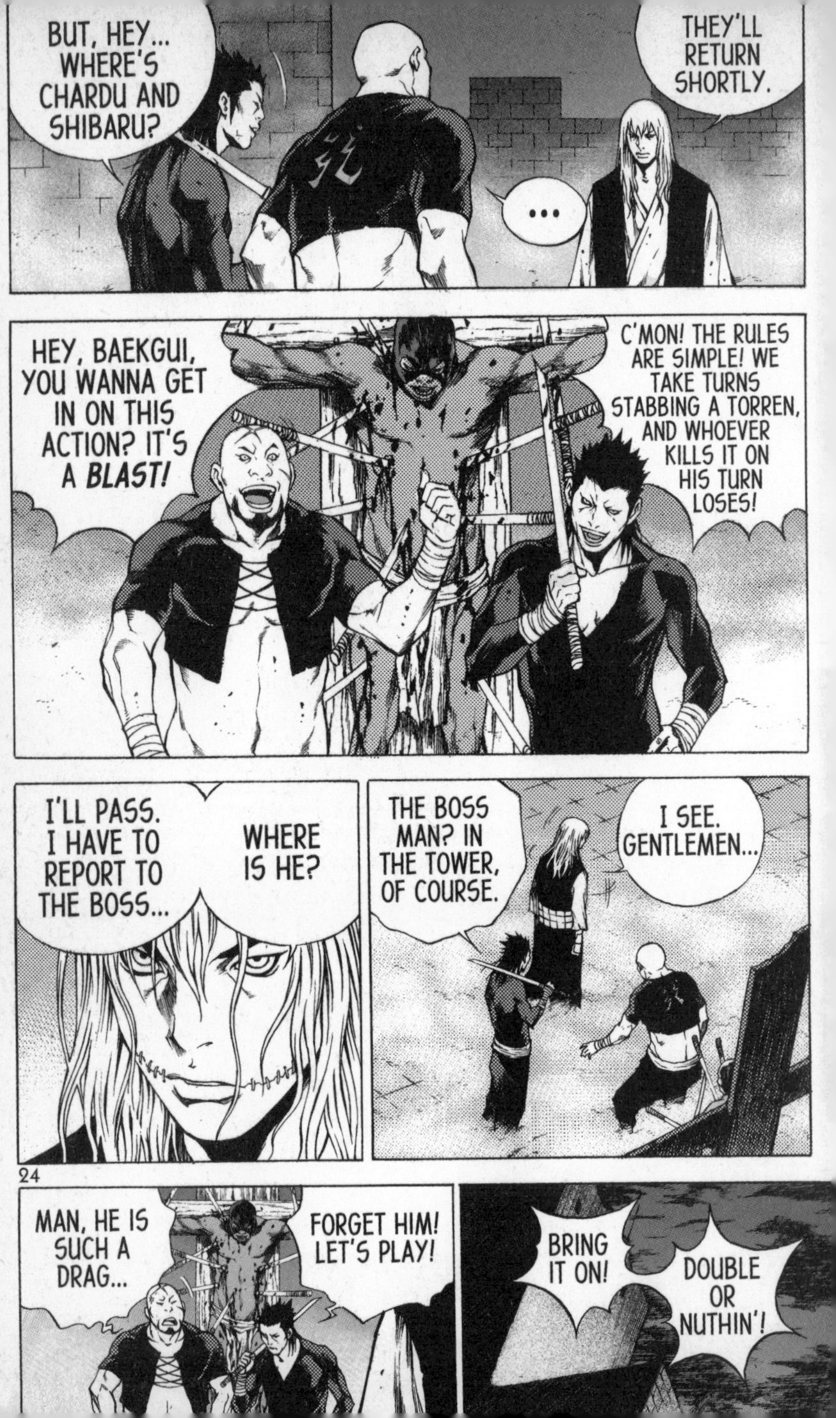
BUT, HEY... WHERE'S CHARDU AND SHIBARU?
THEY'LL RETURN SHORTLY.
...
HEY, BAEKGUI, YOU WANNA GET IN ON THIS ACTION? IT'S A BLAST!
C'MON! THE RULES ARE SIMPLE! WE TAKE TURNS STABBING A TORREN, AND WHOEVER KILLS IT ON HIS TURN LOSES!
I'LL PASS. I HAVE TO REPORT TO THE BOSS...
WHERE IS HE?
THE BOSS MAN? IN THE TOWER, OF COURSE.
I SEE. GENTLEMEN...
MAN, HE IS SUCH A DRAG...
FORGET HIM! LET'S PLAY!
BRING IT ON!
DOUBLE OR NUTHIN'!

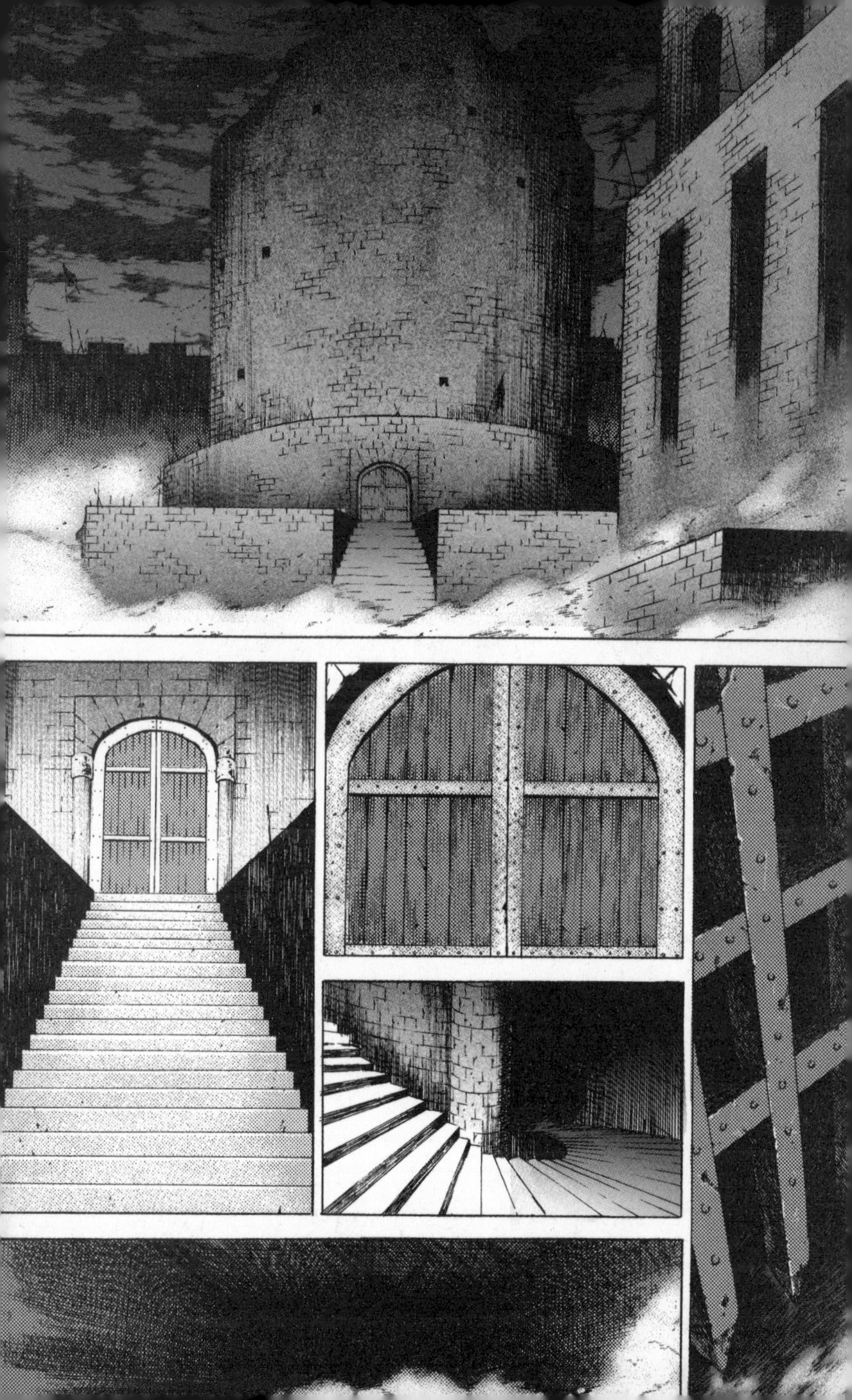

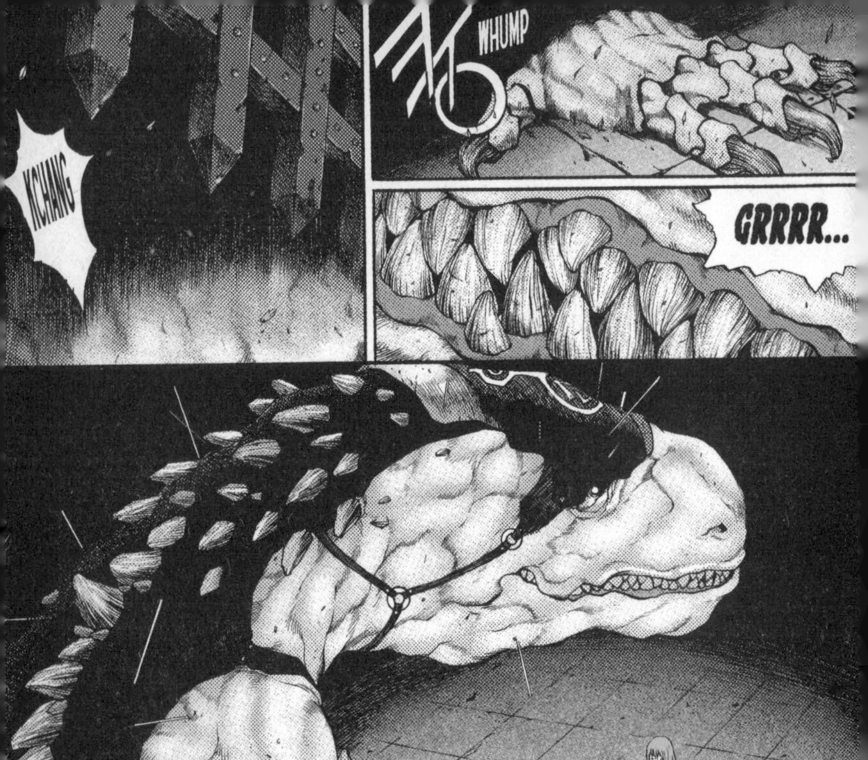
KCHANG
WHUMP
GRRRR...

26

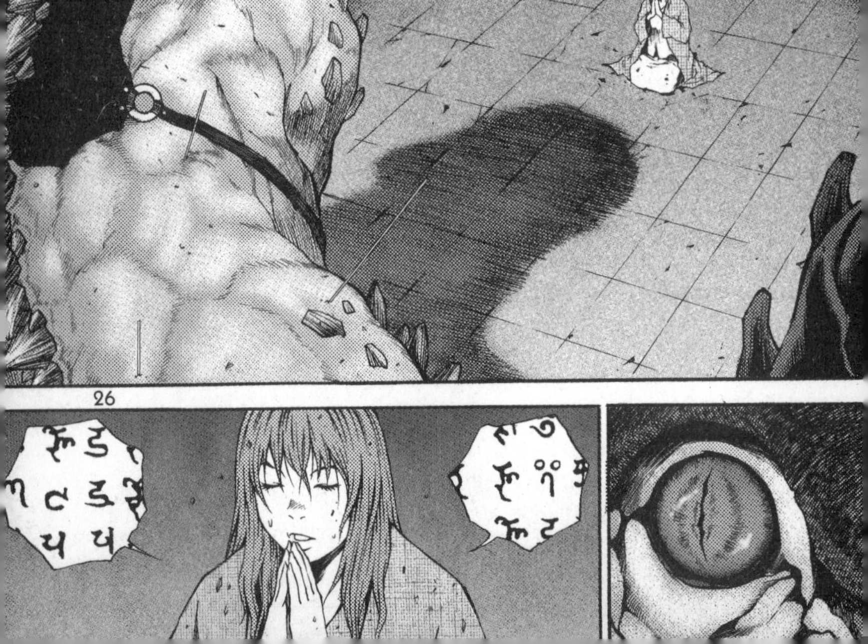

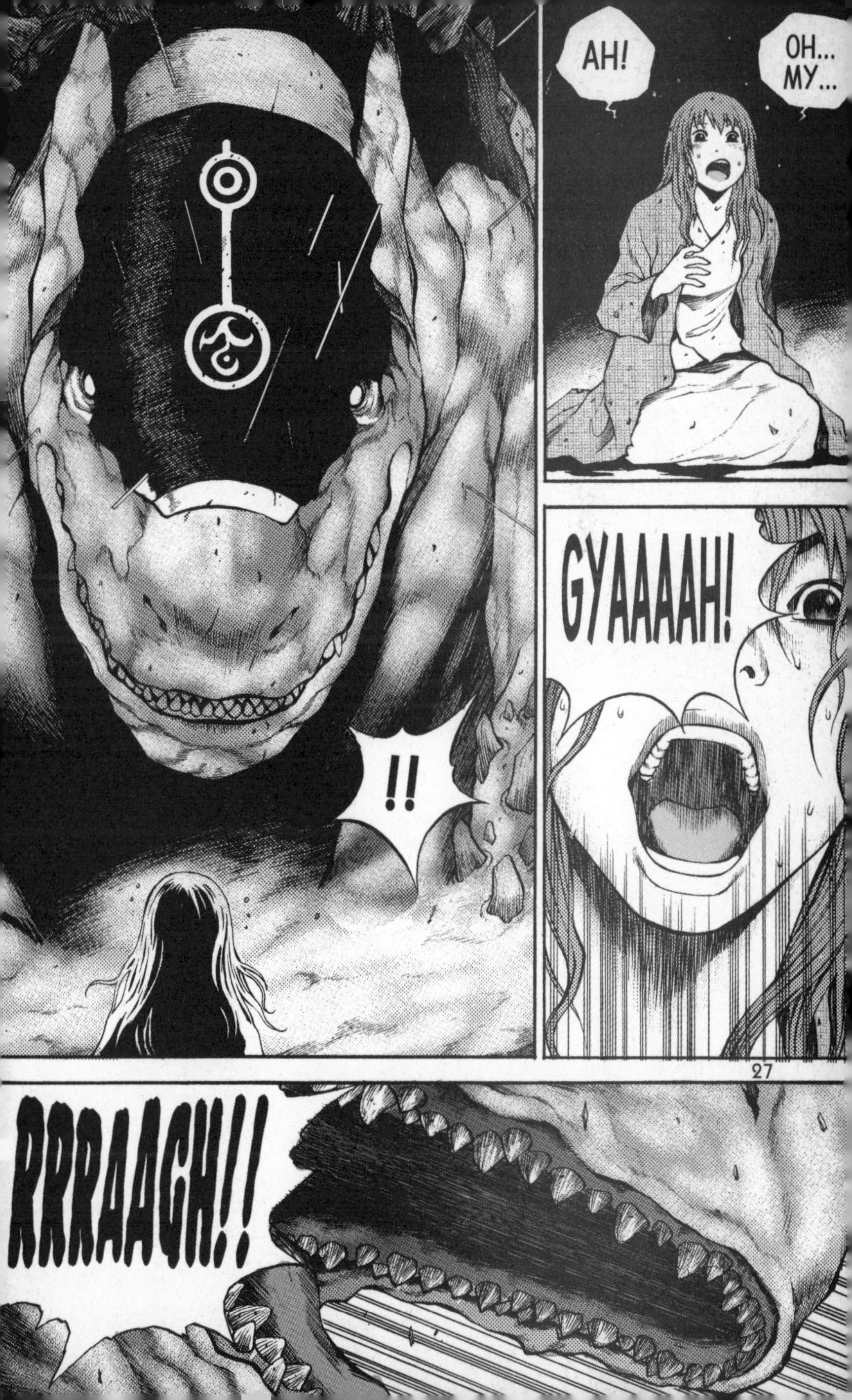
OH... MY...
AH!
GYAAAAH!
!!
RRRAAGH!!

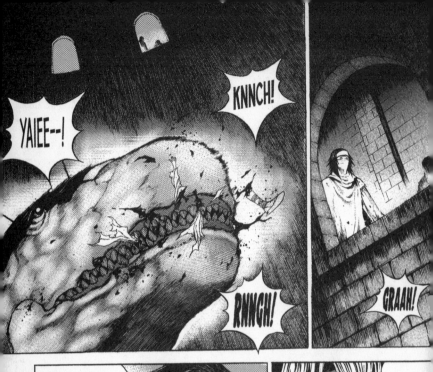

YAIEE--!

KNNCH!

RNNGH!

GRAAH!

MY LORD, ANOTHER FAILURE!

...

28

IF SHE CAN'T CONTROL THIS PUNY EXCUSE FOR A MONSTER, WE HAVE NO NEED FOR HER ANYWAY!

...

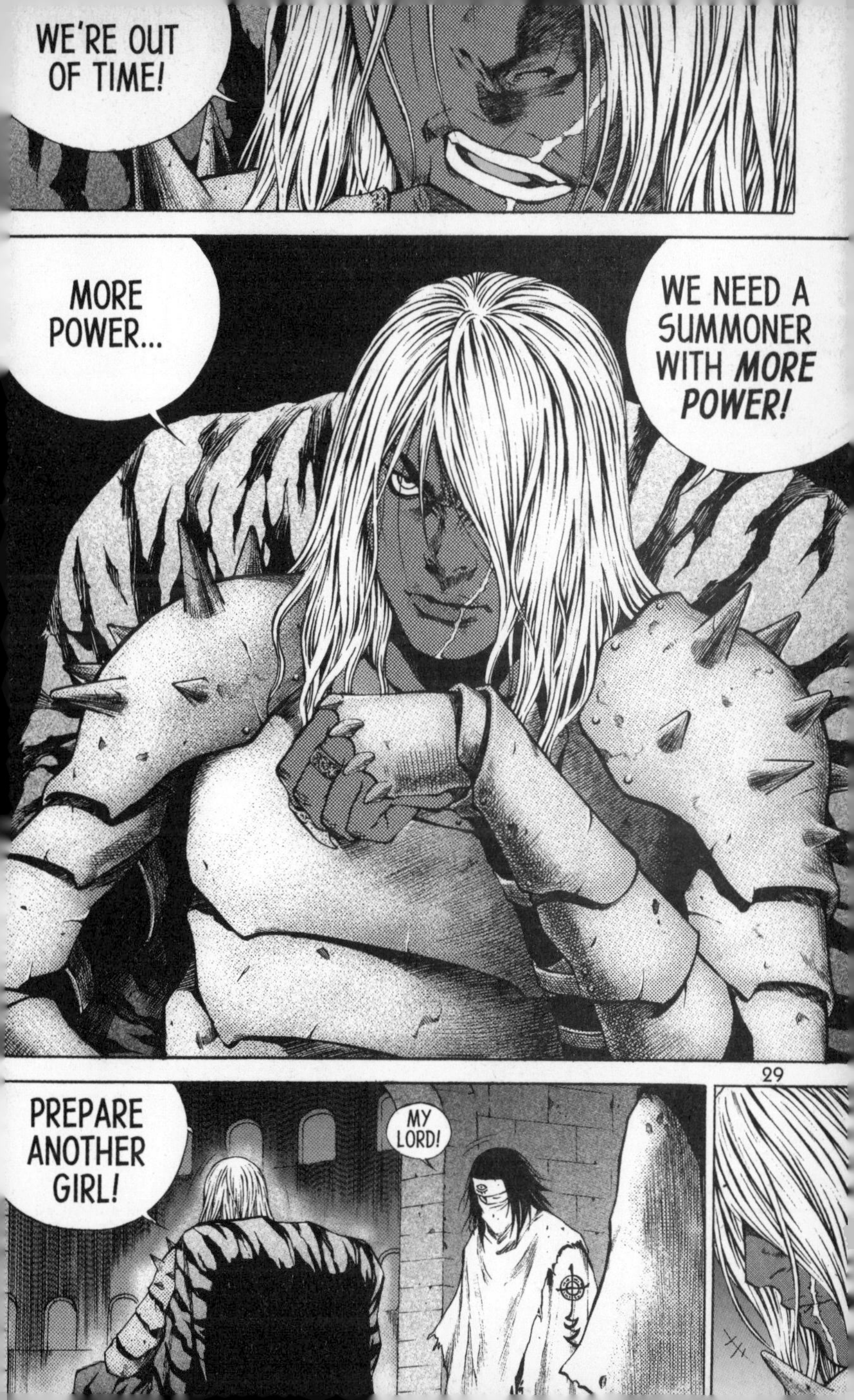
WE'RE OUT OF TIME!
MORE POWER...
WE NEED A SUMMONER WITH MORE POWER!
PREPARE ANOTHER GIRL!
MY LORD!

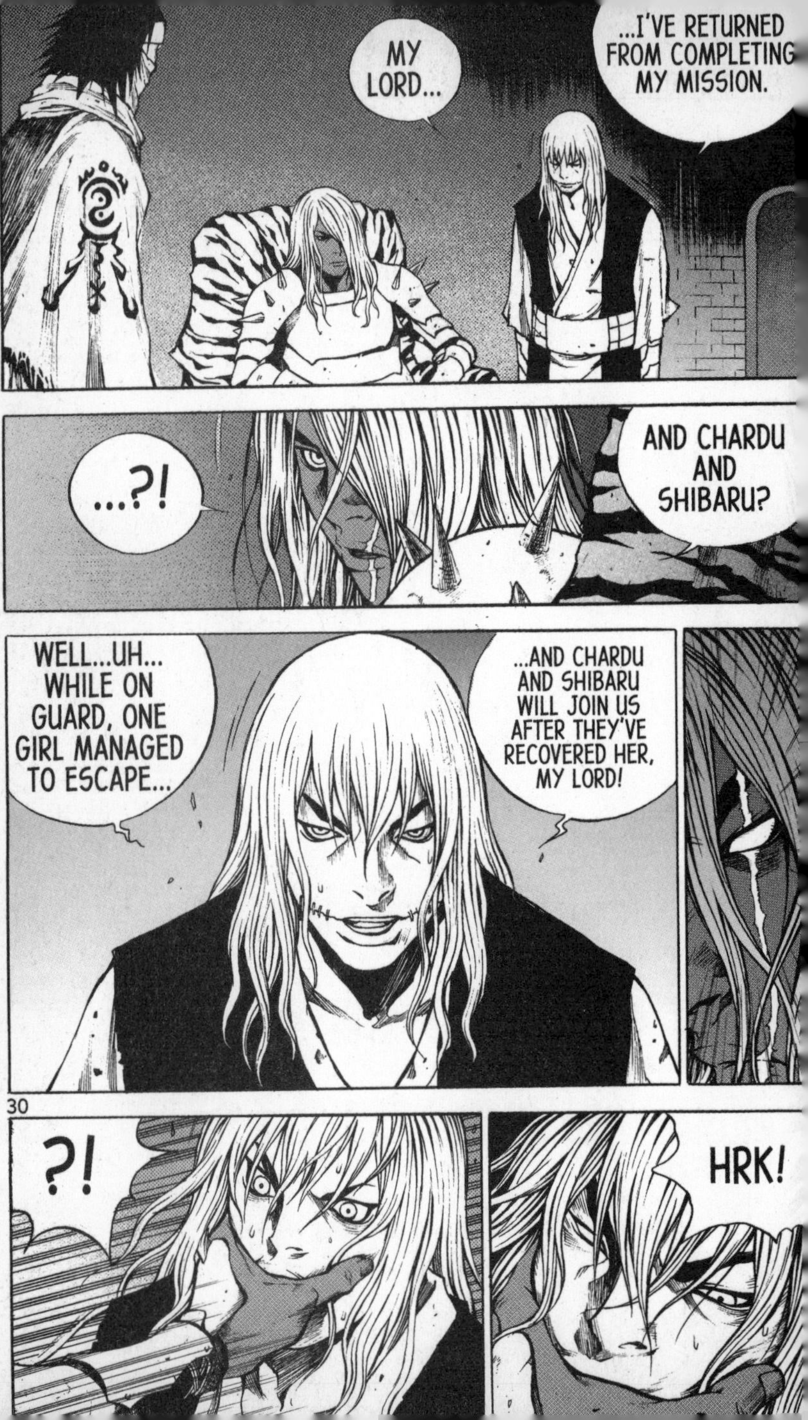
MY LORD...
...I'VE RETURNED FROM COMPLETING MY MISSION.
...?!
AND CHARDU AND SHIBARU?
WELL...UH... WHILE ON GUARD, ONE GIRL MANAGED TO ESCAPE...
...AND CHARDU AND SHIBARU WILL JOIN US AFTER THEY'VE RECOVERED HER, MY LORD!
?!
HRK!

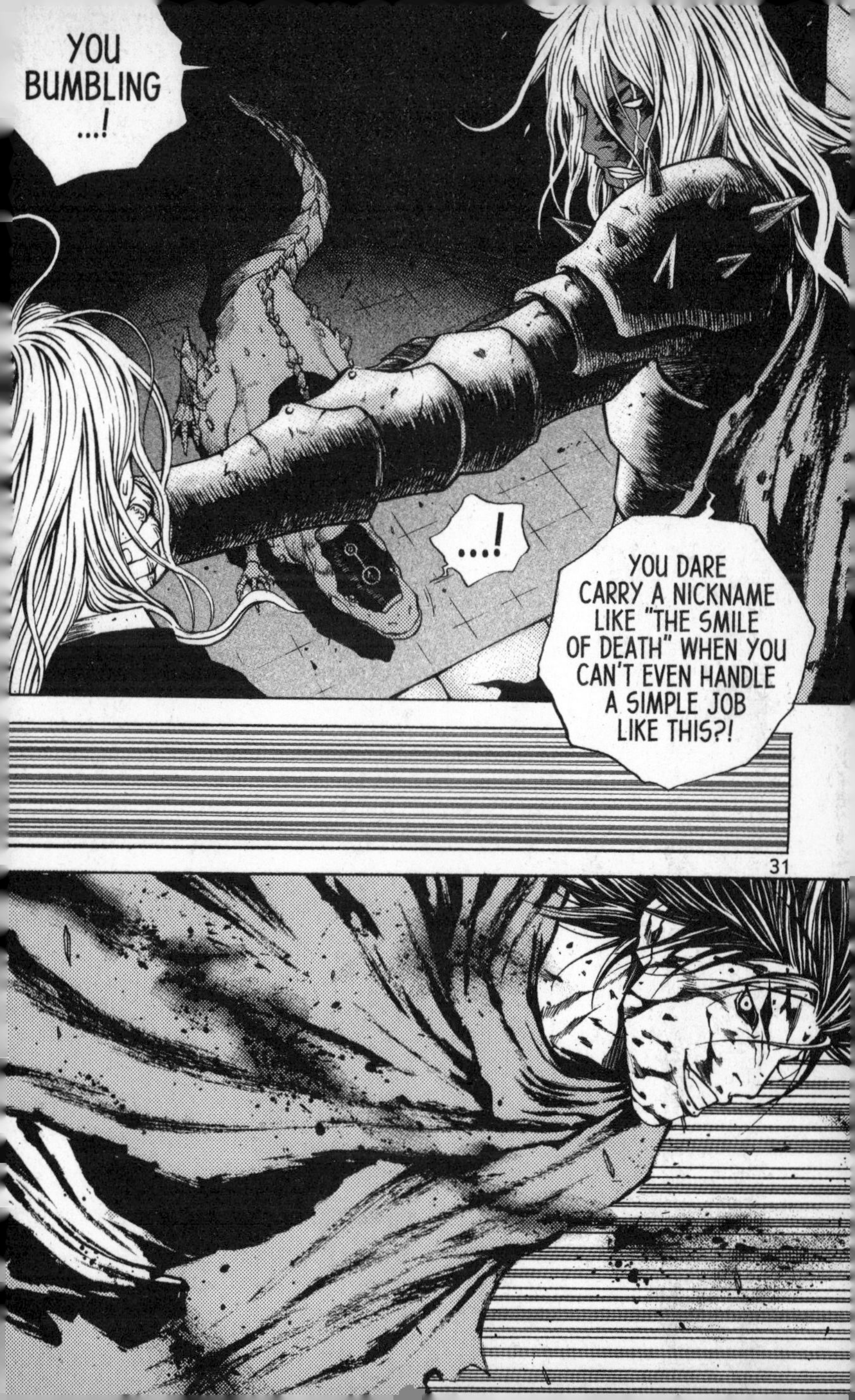
YOU BUMBLING ...!
...!
YOU DARE CARRY A NICKNAME LIKE "THE SMILE OF DEATH" WHEN YOU CAN'T EVEN HANDLE A SIMPLE JOB LIKE THIS?!

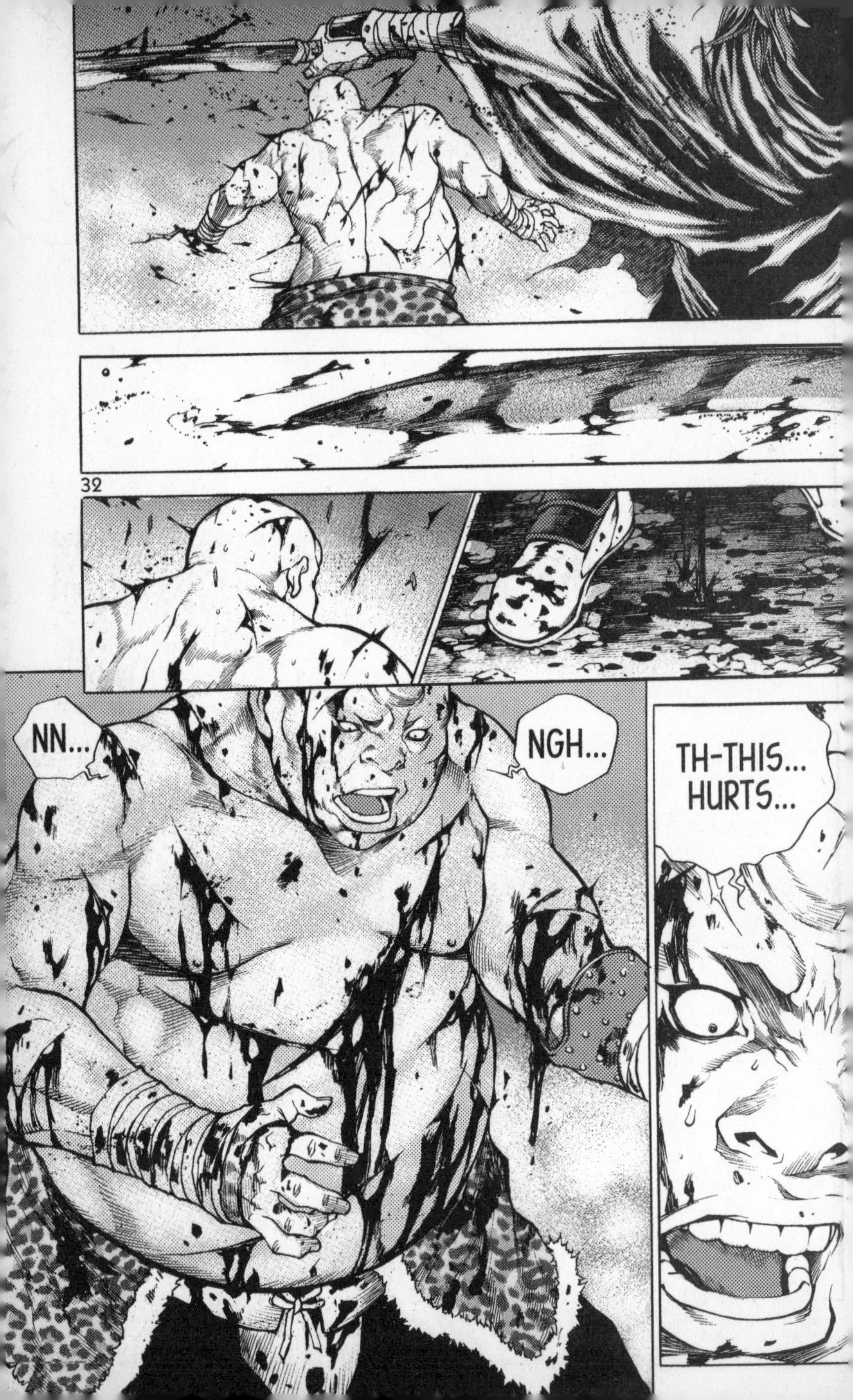
NN...
NGH...
TH-THIS... HURTS...

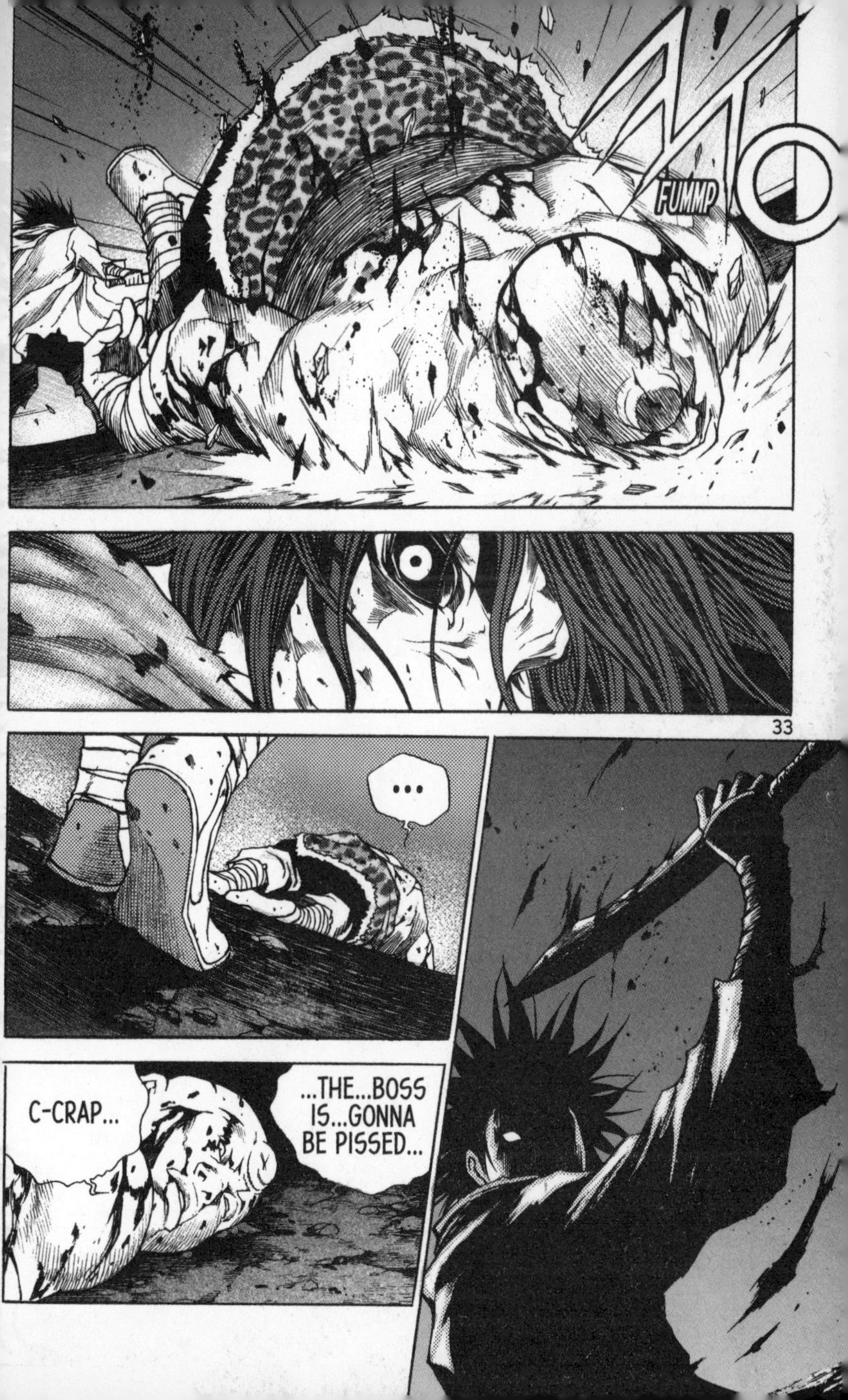
FUMMP
...
C-CRAP...
...THE...BOSS IS...GONNA BE PISSED...

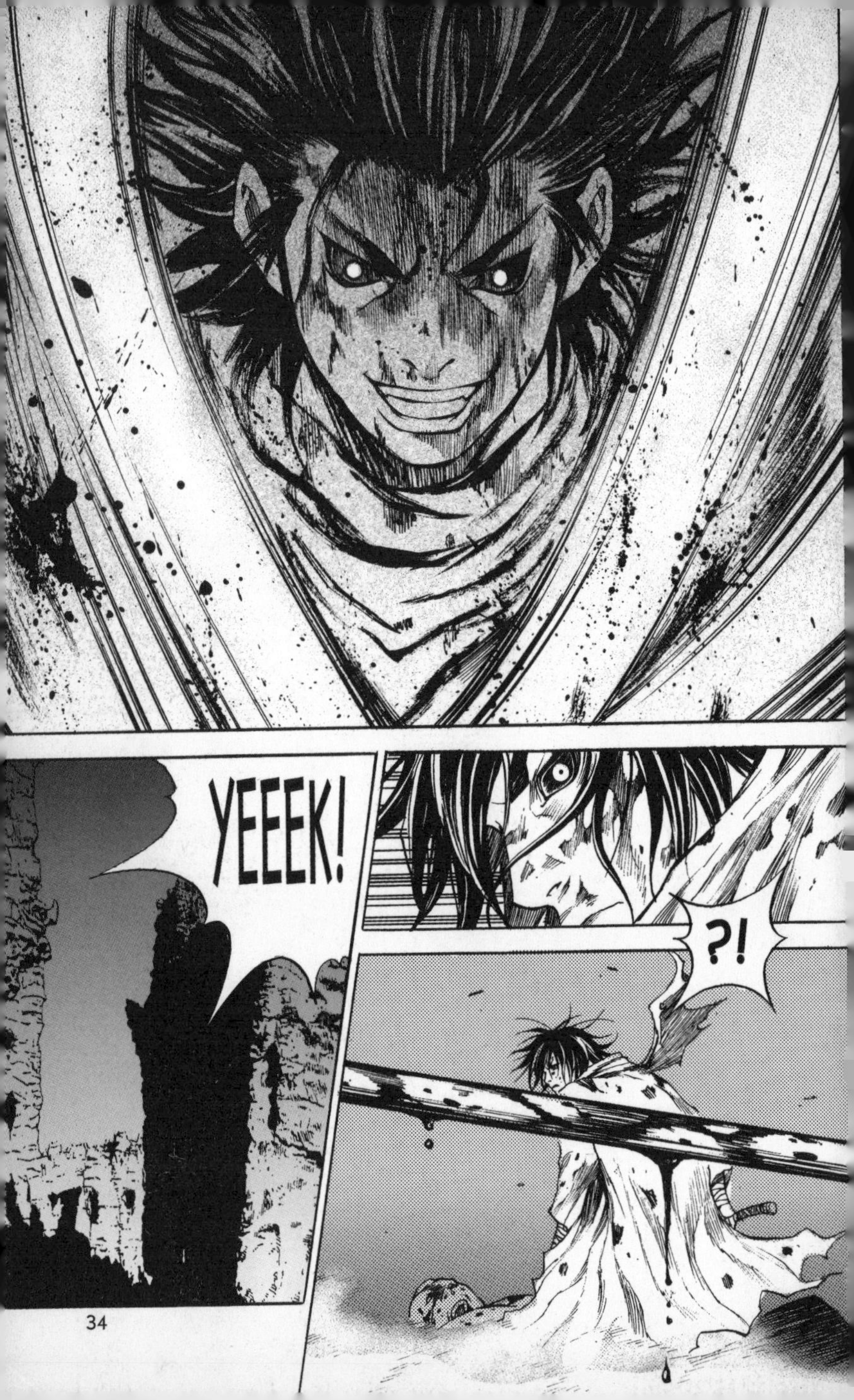
YEEEK!
?!

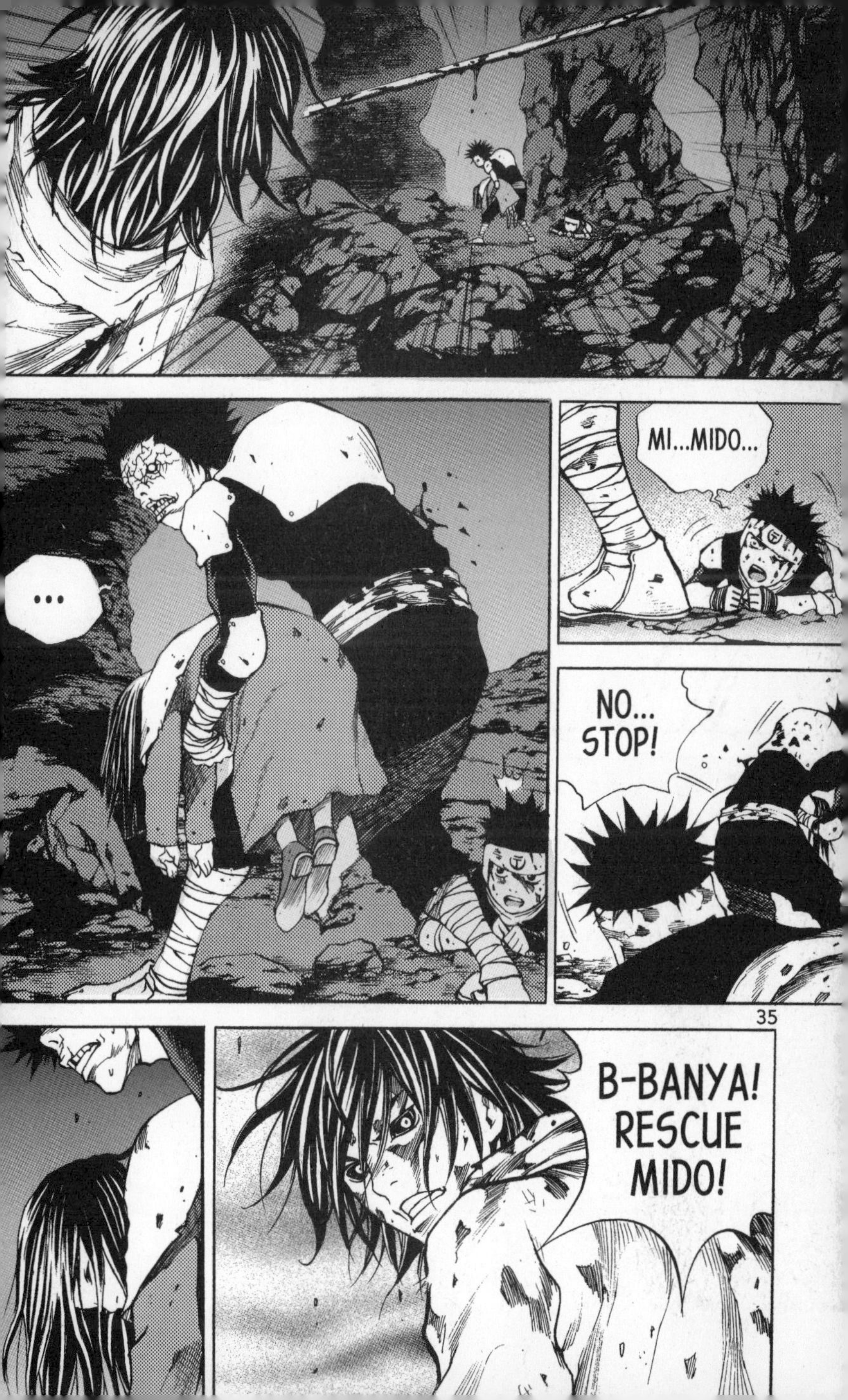
MI...MIDO...
NO... STOP!
...
B-BANYA! RESCUE MIDO!

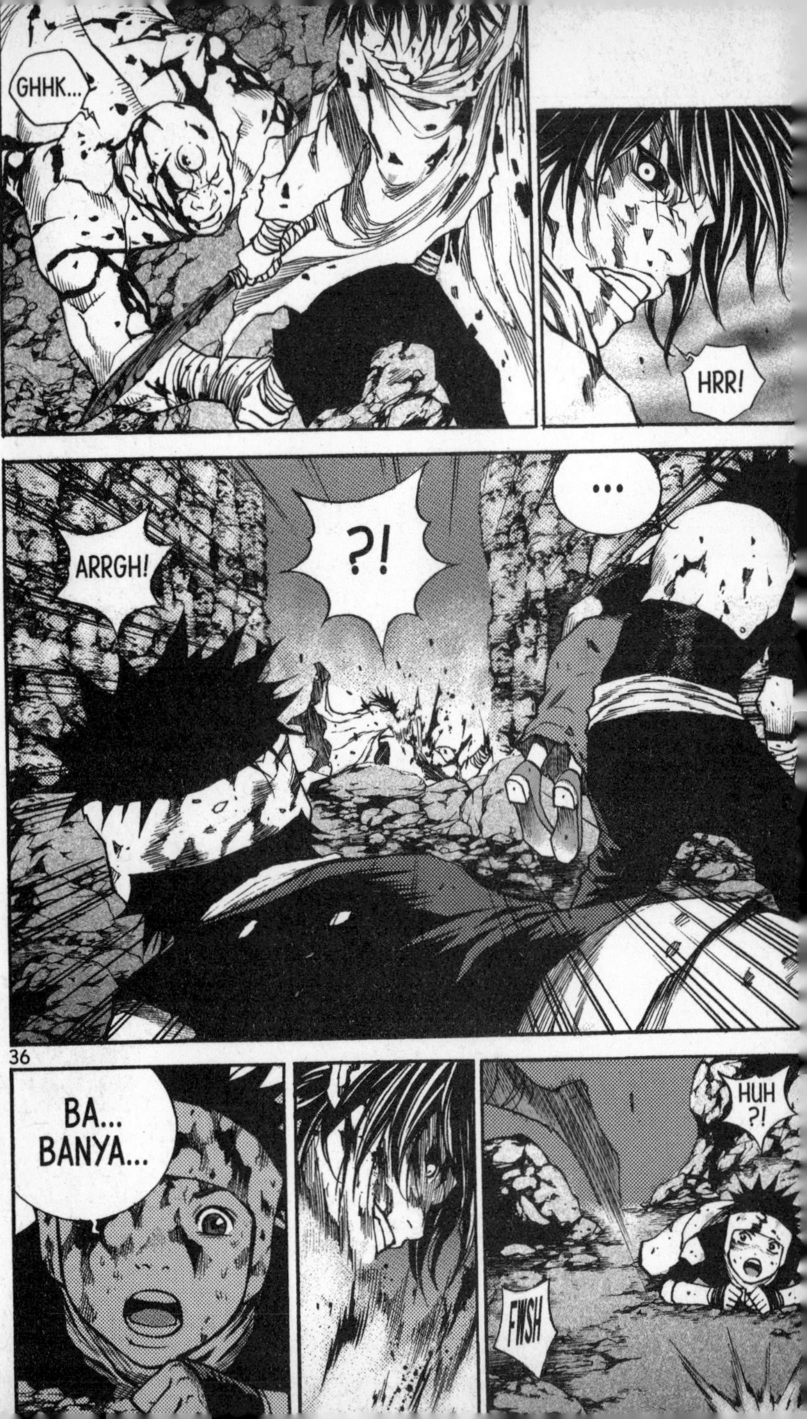
GHHK...
HRR!
ARRGH!
?!
...
BA... BANYA...
HUH ?!
FWSH

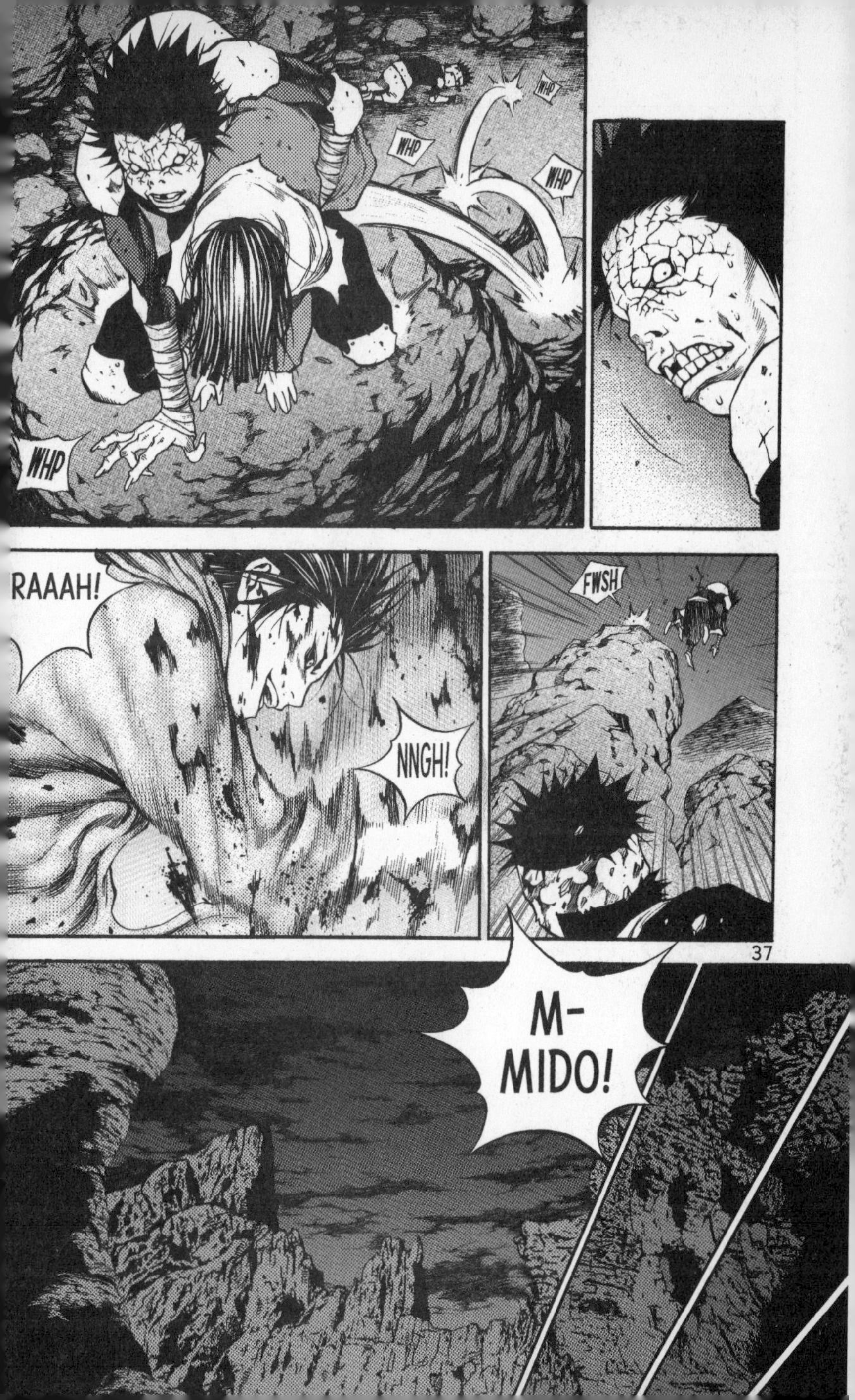
WHP
WHP
WHP
WHP
RAAAH!
NNGH!
FWSH
M-
MIDO!

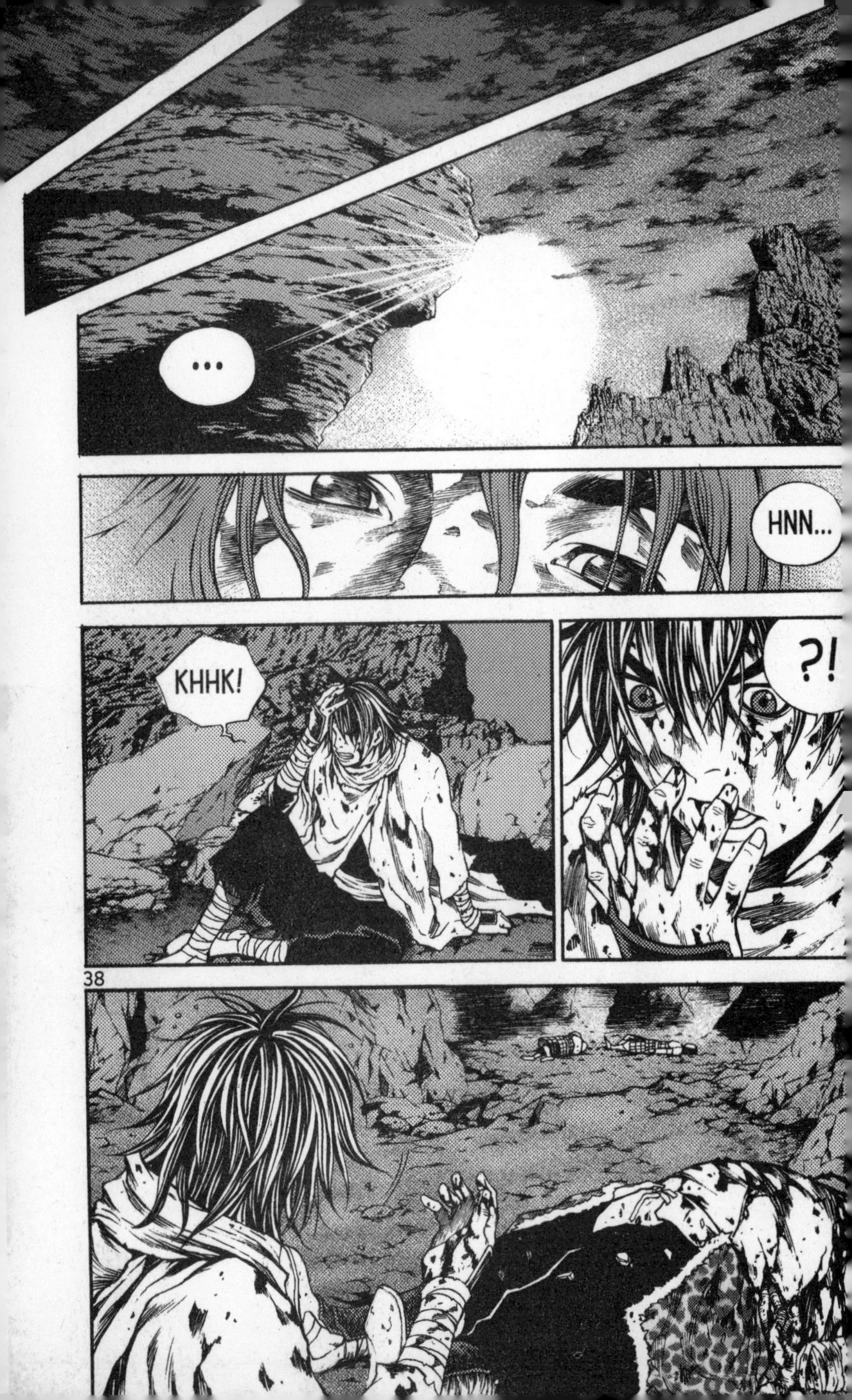
...
HNN...
?!
KHHK!

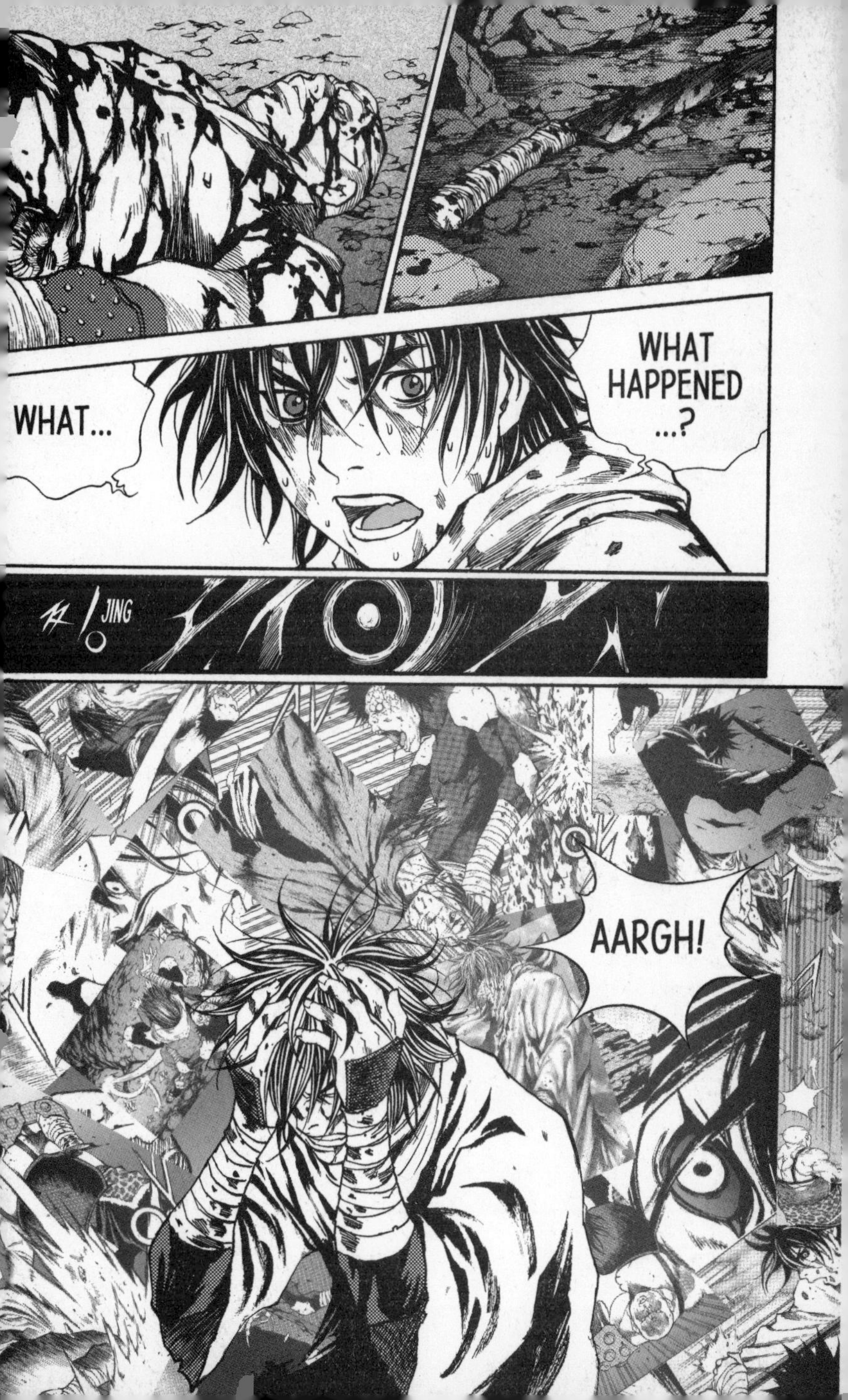
WHAT...
WHAT HAPPENED ...?
JING
AARGH!

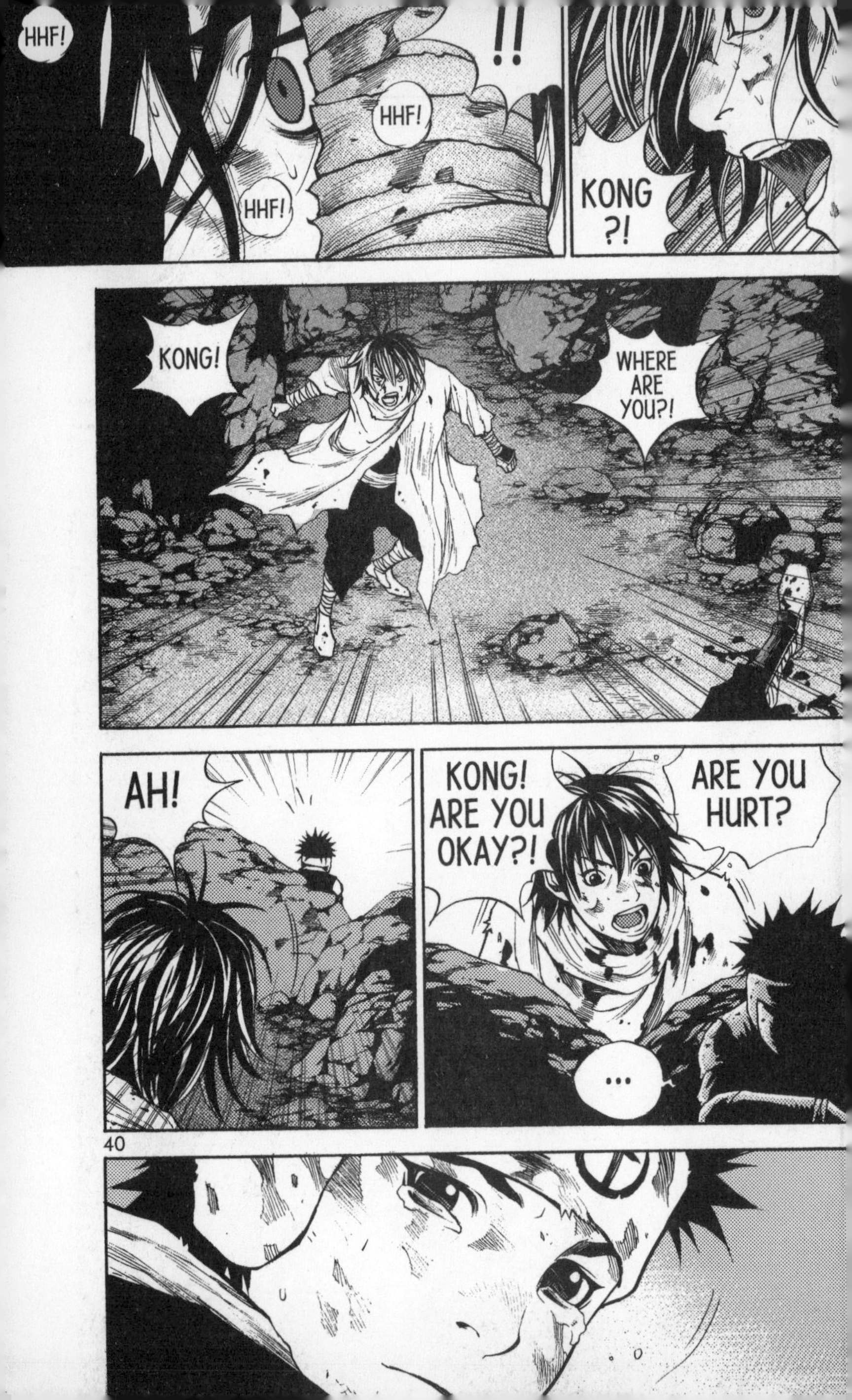
HHF!
HHF!
HHF!
!!
KONG ?!
KONG!
WHERE ARE YOU?!
AH!
KONG! ARE YOU OKAY?!
ARE YOU HURT?
...

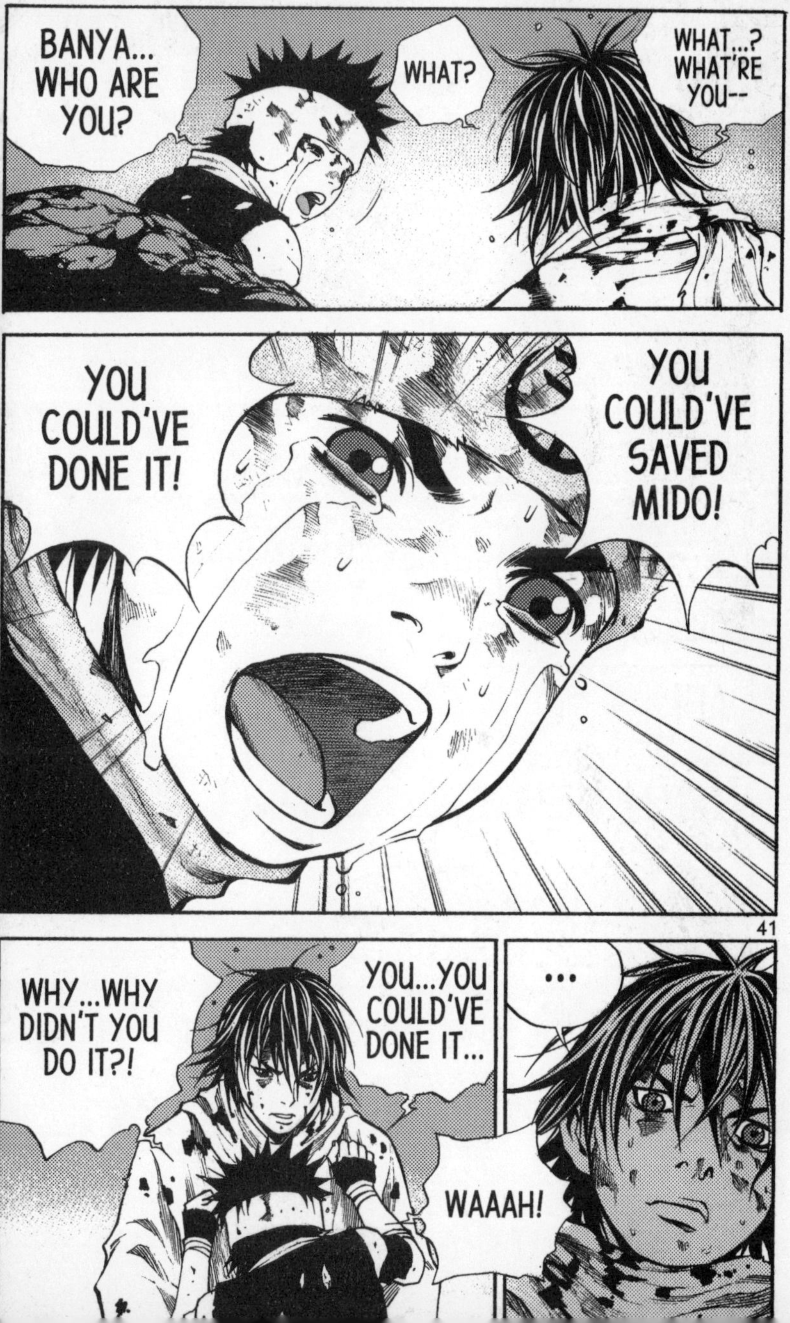
WHAT...? WHAT'RE YOU--
WHAT?
BANYA... WHO ARE YOU?
YOU COULD'VE SAVED MIDO!
YOU COULD'VE DONE IT!
YOU...YOU COULD'VE DONE IT...
WHY...WHY DIDN'T YOU DO IT?!
...
WAAAH!

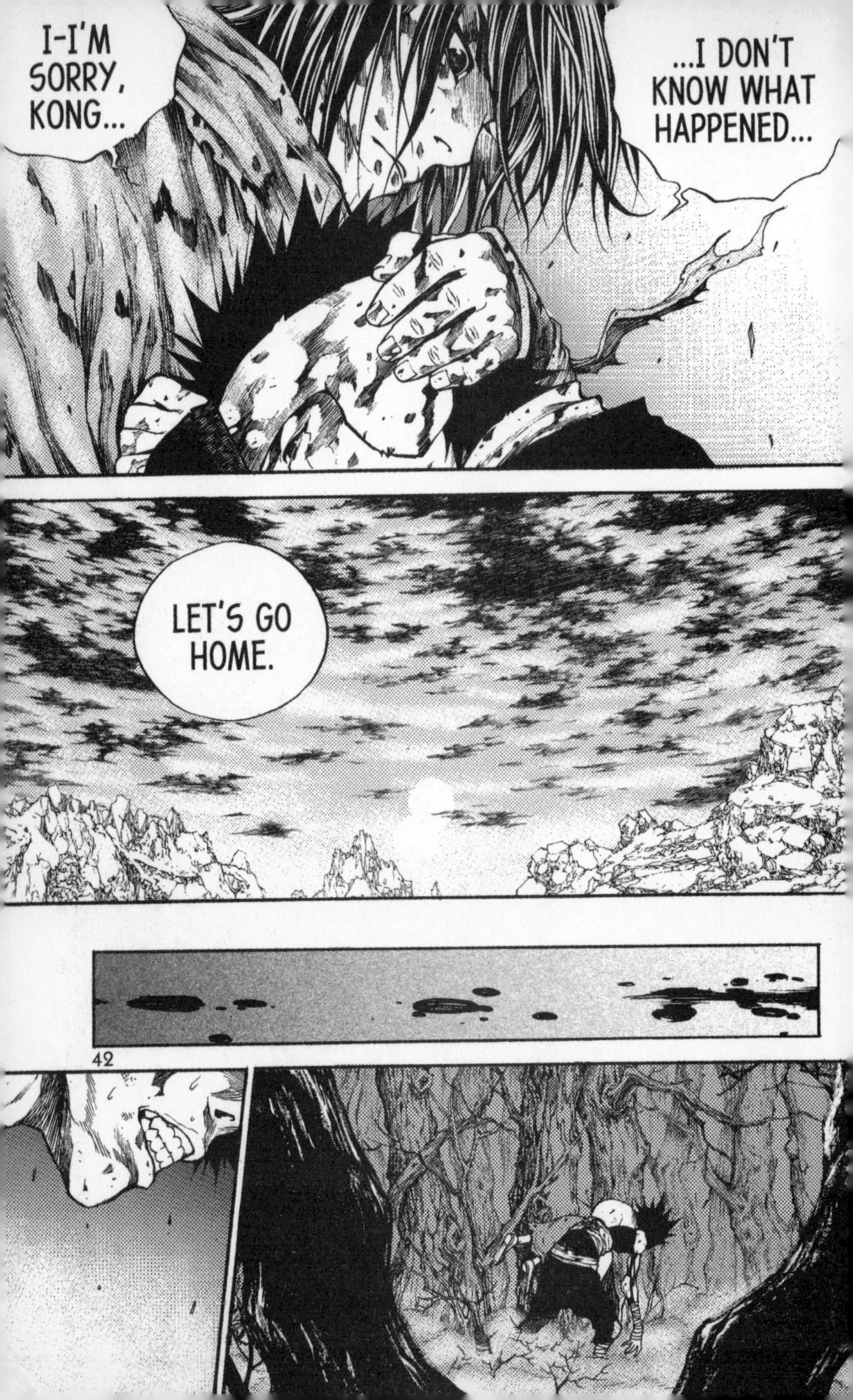

...I DON'T KNOW WHAT HAPPENED...
I-I'M SORRY, KONG...
LET'S GO HOME.

Banya
the explosive delivery man

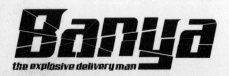

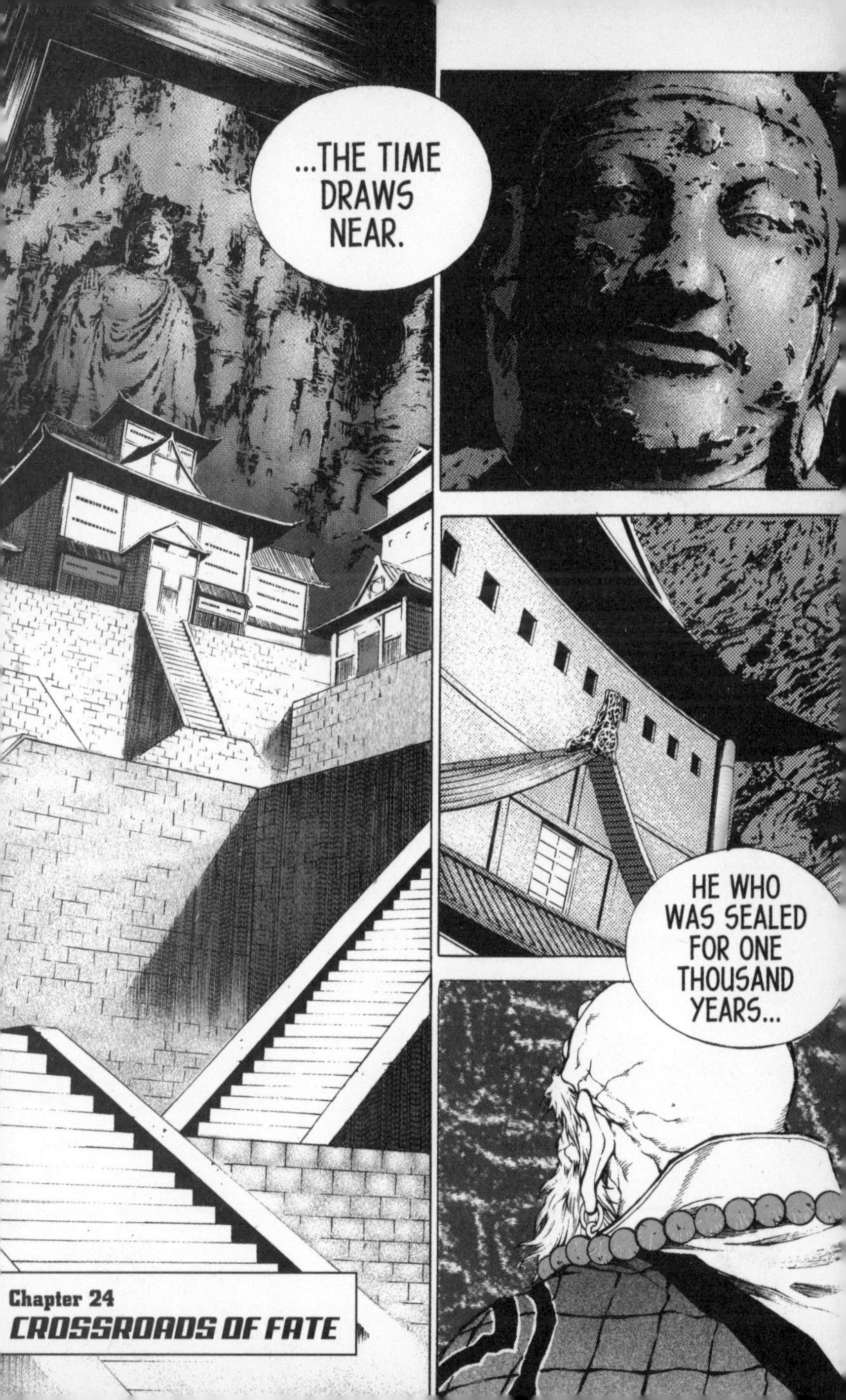
Chapter 24
CROSSROADS OF FATE
HE WHO WAS SEALED FOR ONE THOUSAND YEARS...
...THE TIME DRAWS NEAR.

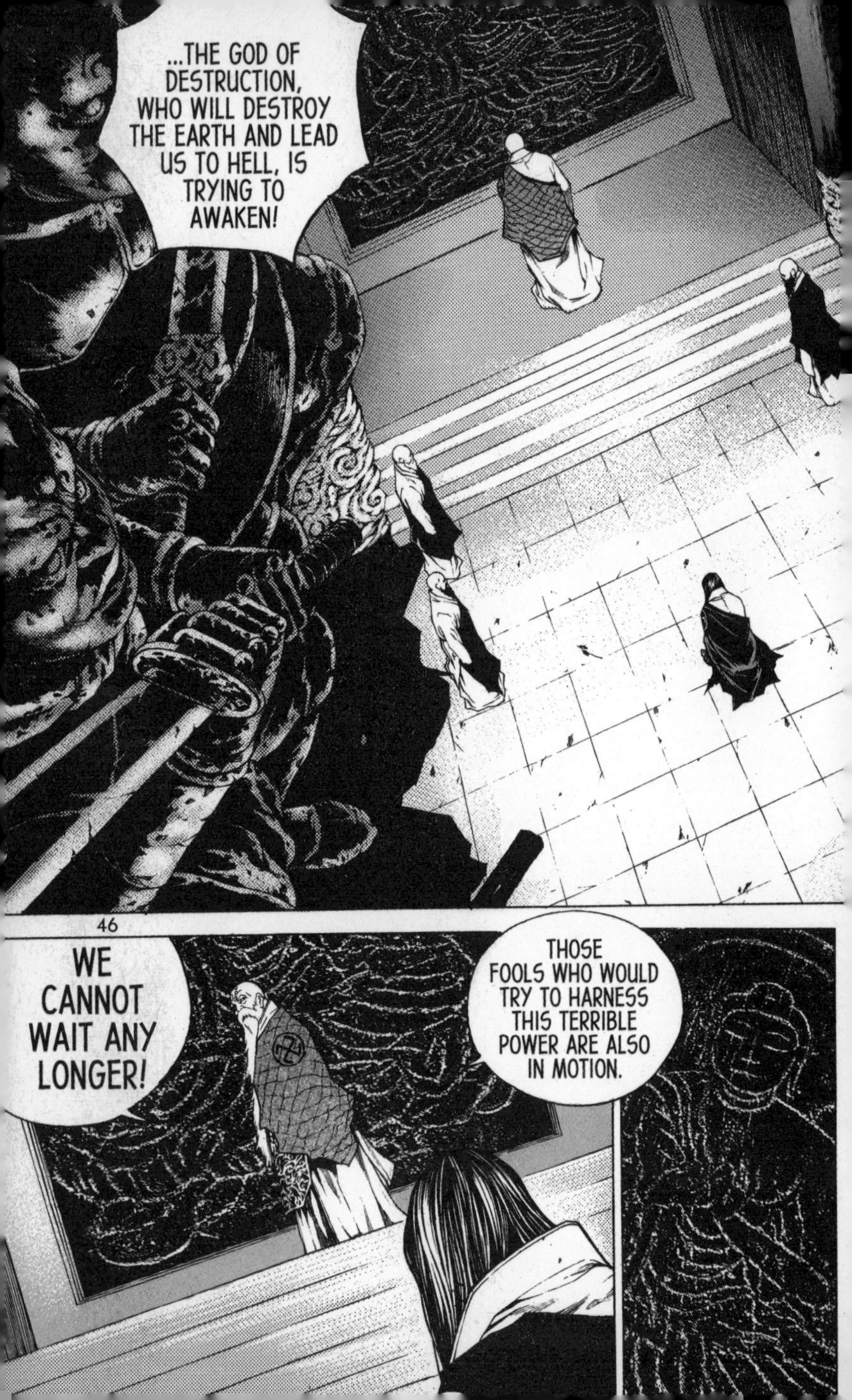
...THE GOD OF DESTRUCTION, WHO WILL DESTROY THE EARTH AND LEAD US TO HELL, IS TRYING TO AWAKEN!
THOSE FOOLS WHO WOULD TRY TO HARNESS THIS TERRIBLE POWER ARE ALSO IN MOTION.
WE CANNOT WAIT ANY LONGER!

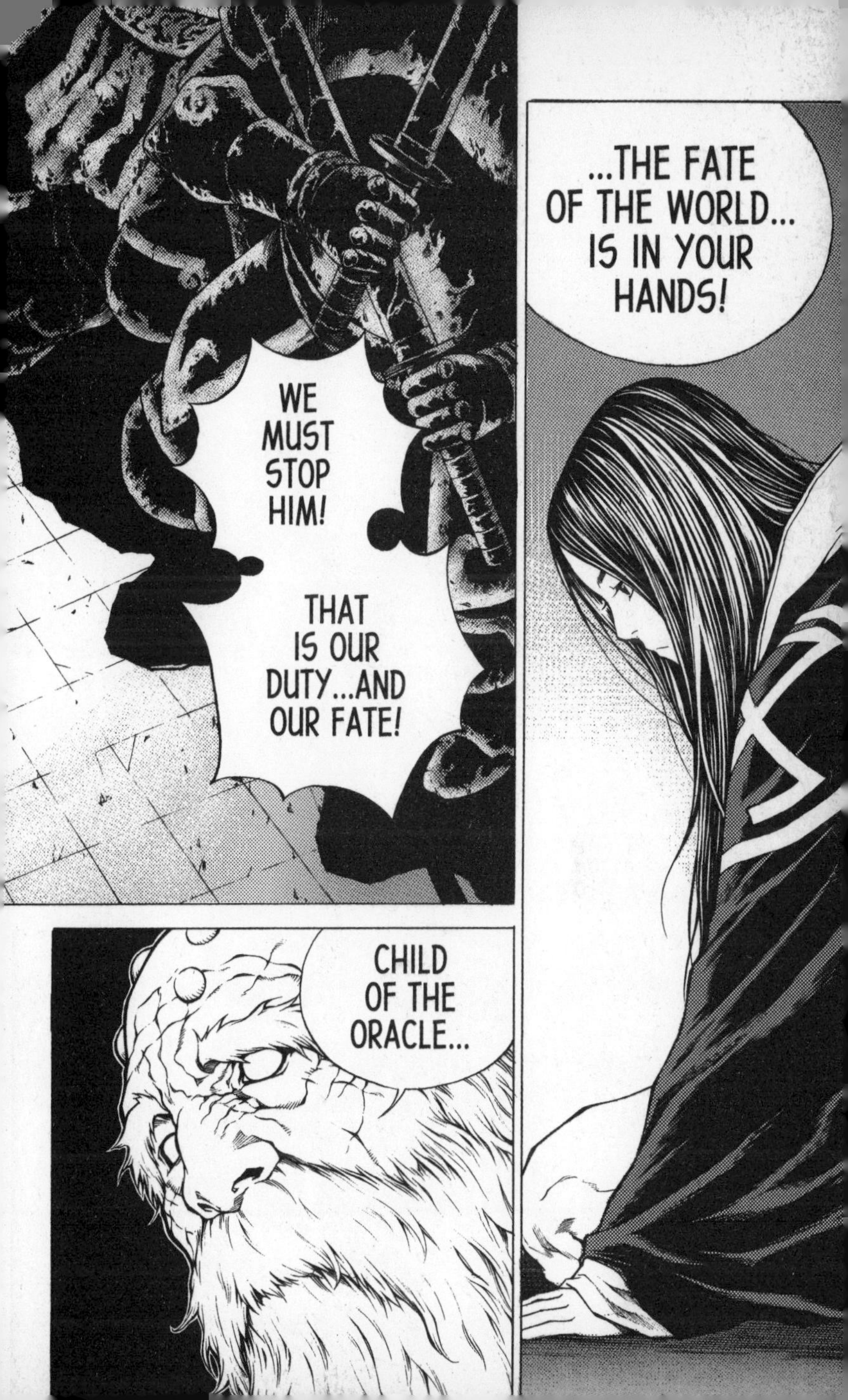
WE MUST STOP HIM!
THAT IS OUR DUTY...AND OUR FATE!
CHILD OF THE ORACLE...
...THE FATE OF THE WORLD... IS IN YOUR HANDS!

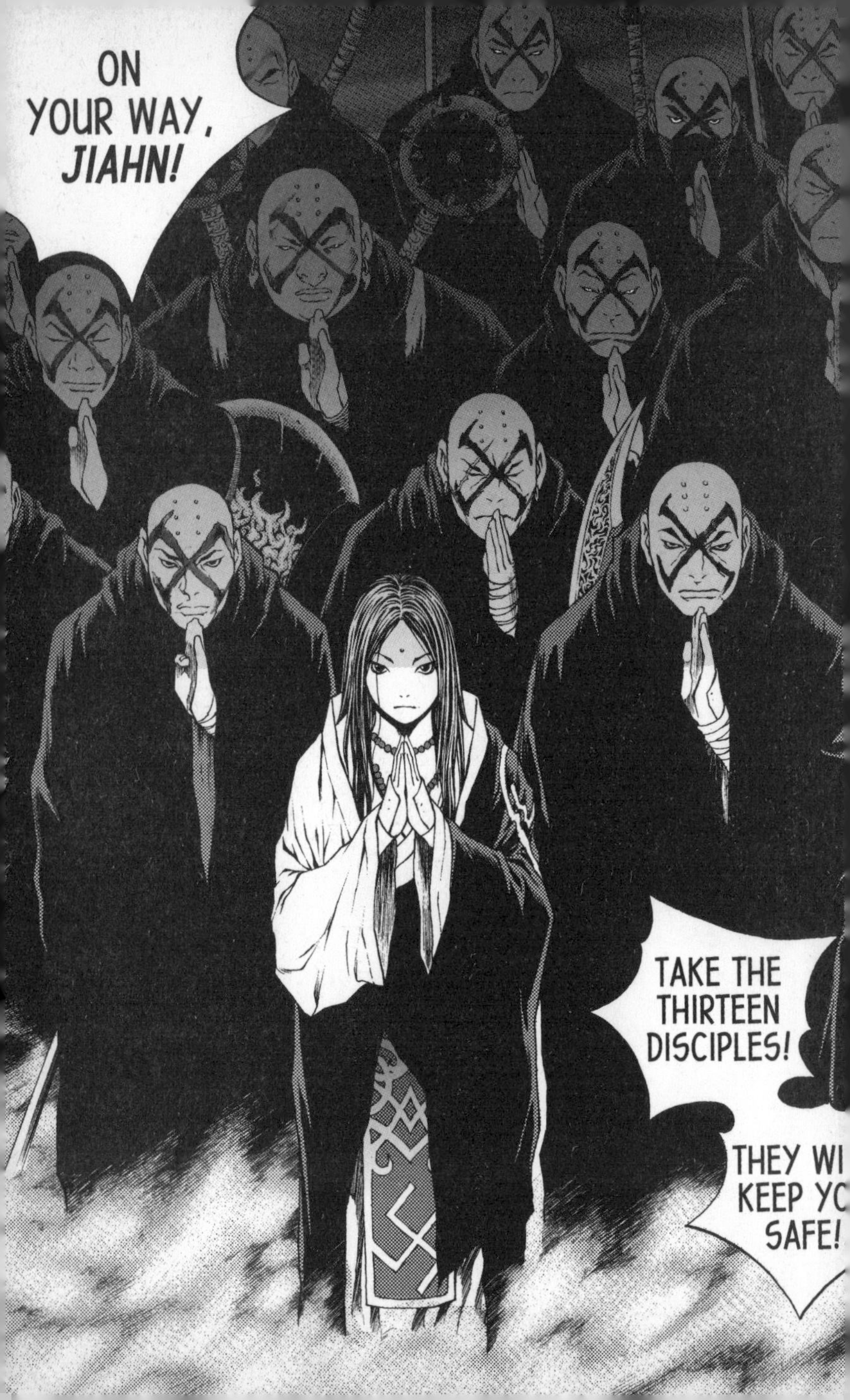
ON YOUR WAY, JIAHN!
TAKE THE THIRTEEN DISCIPLES!
THEY WI KEEP YO SAFE!

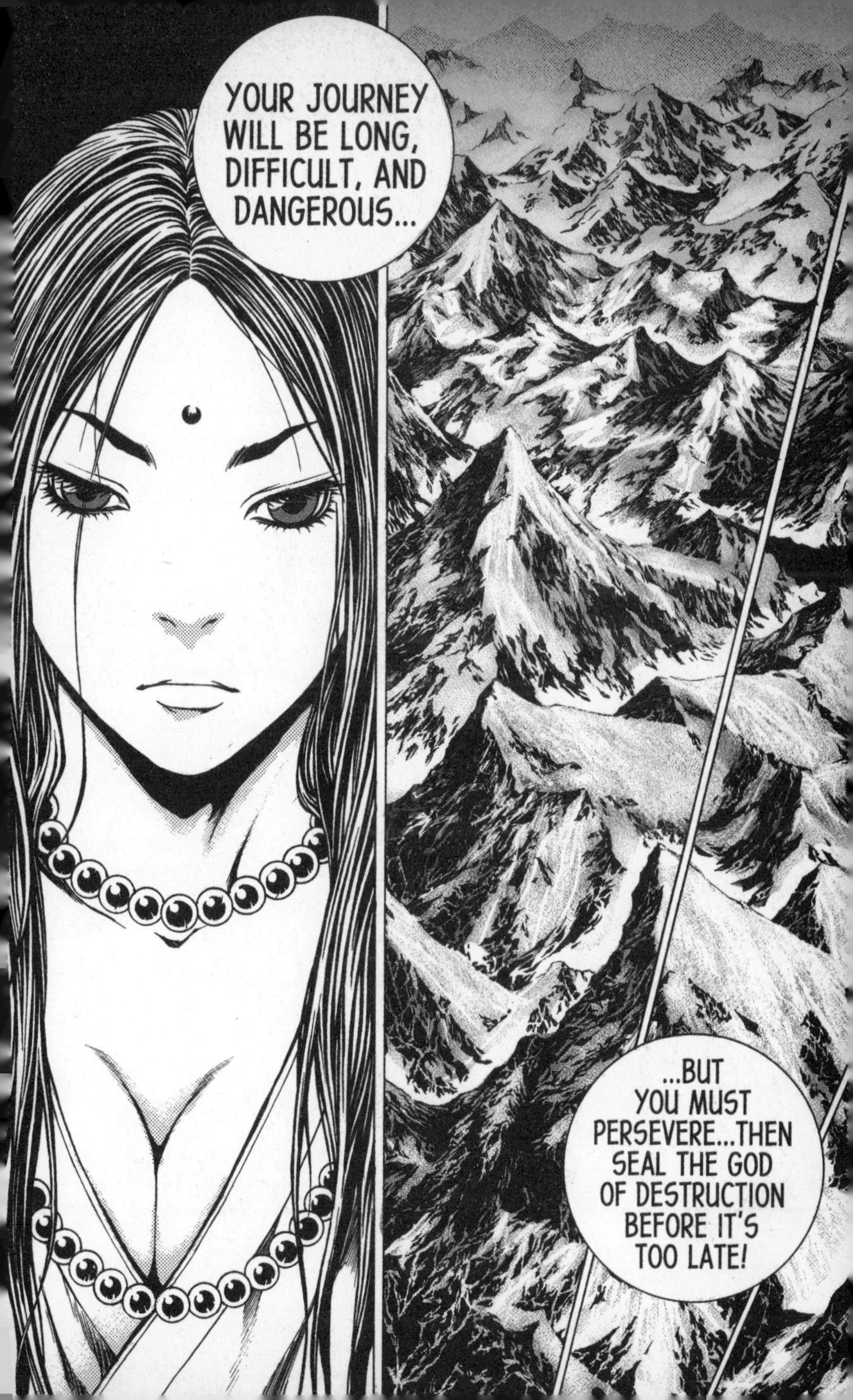
YOUR JOURNEY WILL BE LONG, DIFFICULT, AND DANGEROUS...
...BUT YOU MUST PERSEVERE...THEN SEAL THE GOD OF DESTRUCTION BEFORE IT'S TOO LATE!

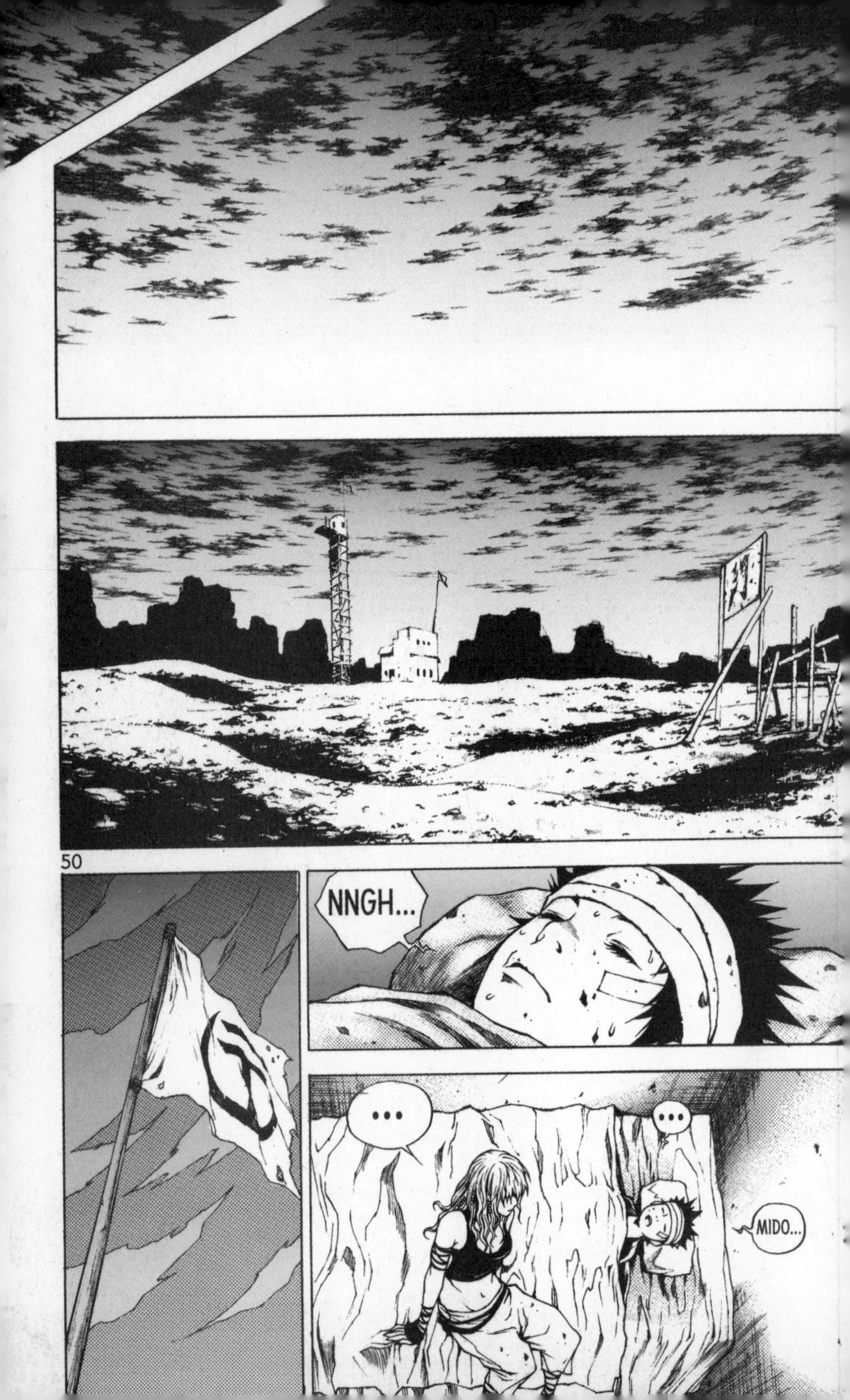

NNGH...
...
...
MIDO...

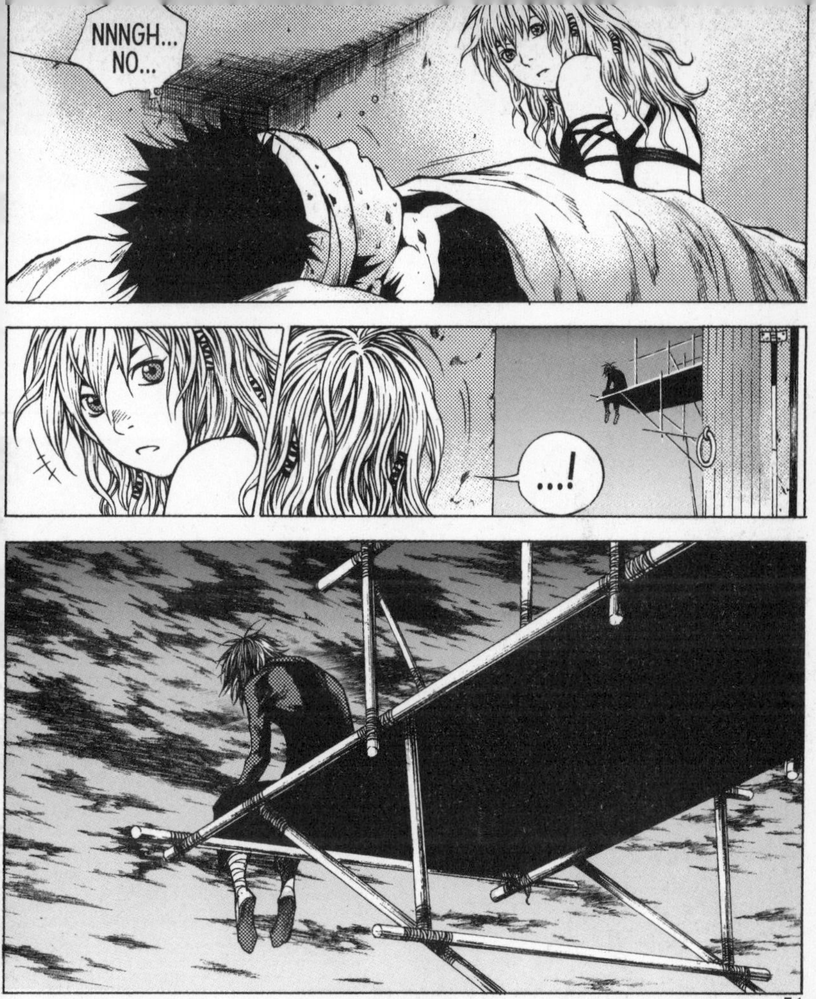
NNNGH... NO...
...!



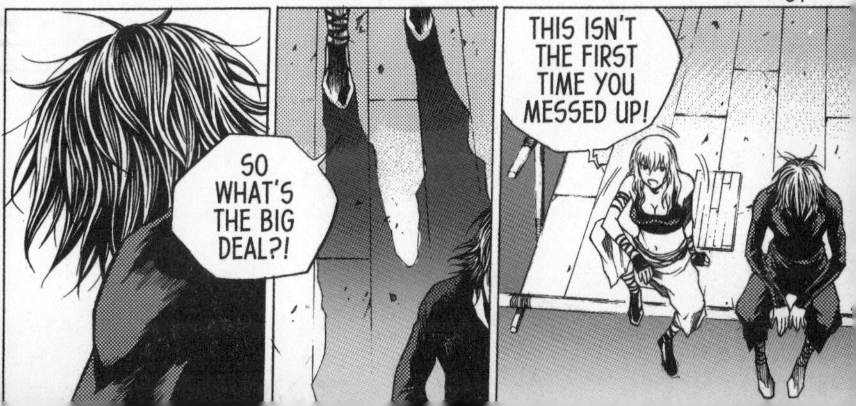
THIS ISN'T THE FIRST TIME YOU MESSED UP!
SO WHAT'S THE BIG DEAL?!

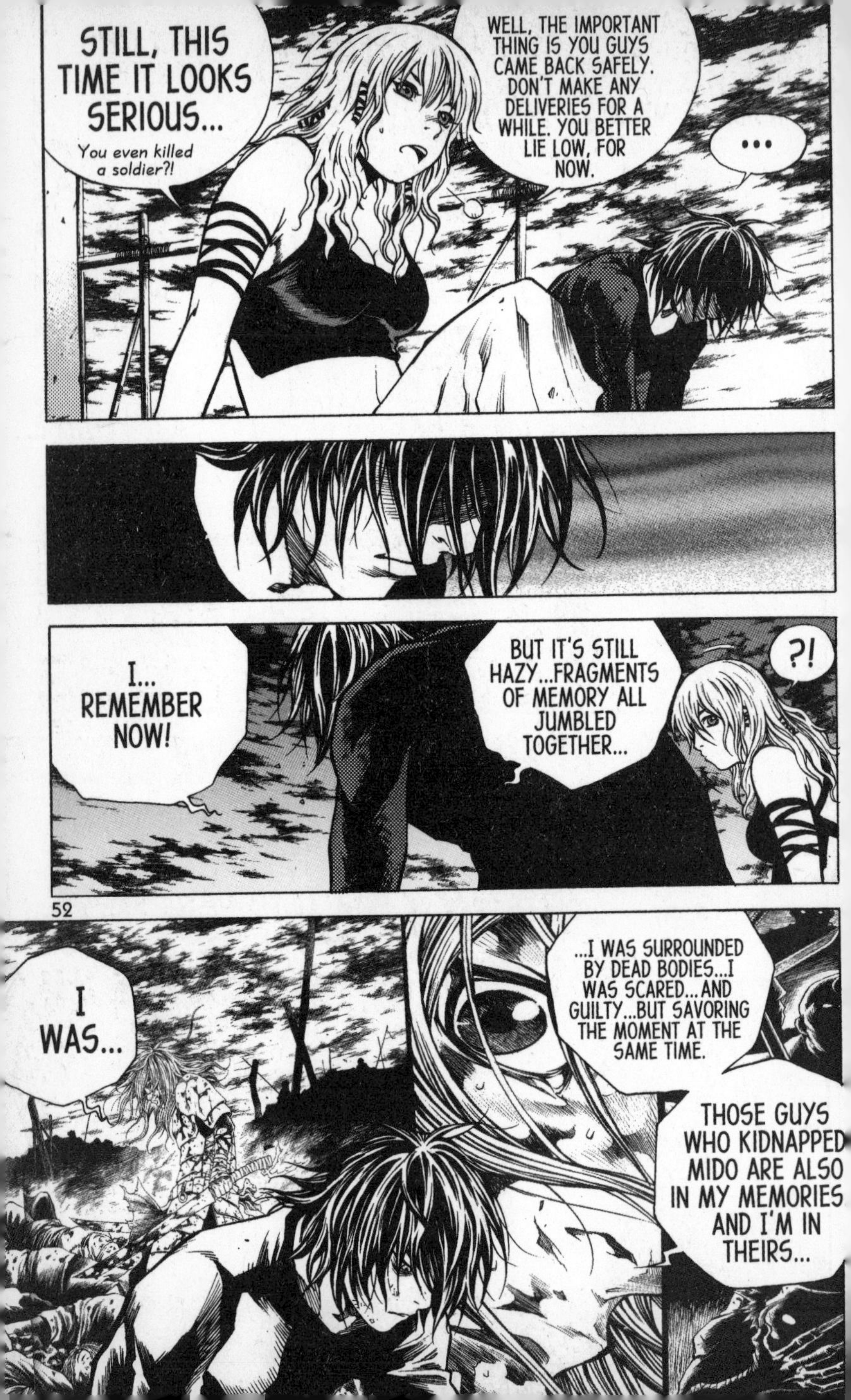
STILL, THIS TIME IT LOOKS SERIOUS...
You even killed a soldier?!
WELL, THE IMPORTANT THING IS YOU GUYS CAME BACK SAFELY. DON'T MAKE ANY DELIVERIES FOR A WHILE. YOU BETTER LIE LOW, FOR NOW.
...
I... REMEMBER NOW!
BUT IT'S STILL HAZY...FRAGMENTS OF MEMORY ALL JUMBLED TOGETHER...
?!
I WAS...
...I WAS SURROUNDED BY DEAD BODIES...I WAS SCARED...AND GUILTY...BUT SAVORING THE MOMENT AT THE SAME TIME.
THOSE GUYS WHO KIDNAPPED MIDO ARE ALSO IN MY MEMORIES AND I'M IN THEIRS...

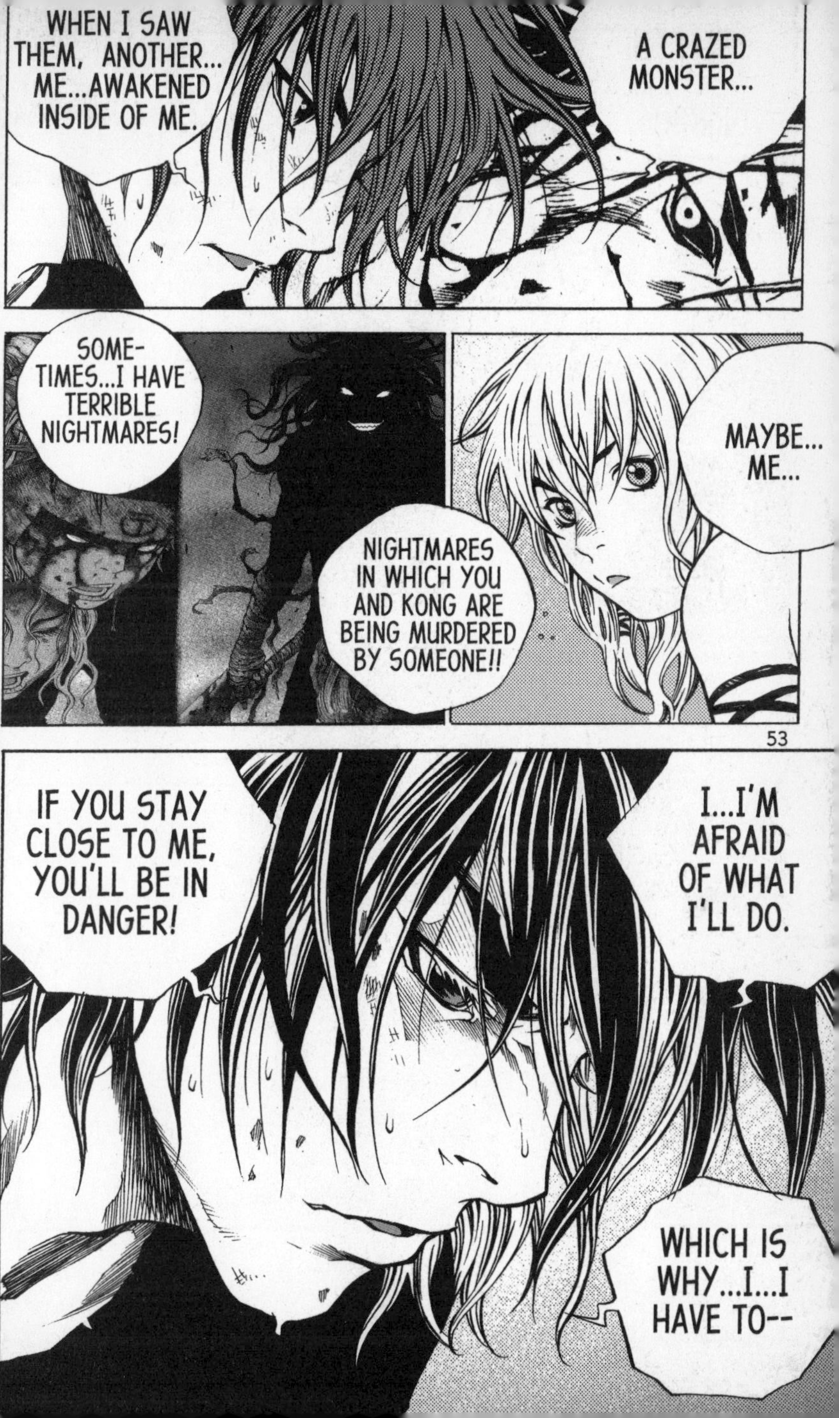
WHEN I SAW THEM, ANOTHER... ME...AWAKENED INSIDE OF ME.
A CRAZED MONSTER...
SOME-TIMES...I HAVE TERRIBLE NIGHTMARES!
NIGHTMARES IN WHICH YOU AND KONG ARE BEING MURDERED BY SOMEONE!!
MAYBE... ME...
I...I'M AFRAID OF WHAT I'LL DO.
IF YOU STAY CLOSE TO ME, YOU'LL BE IN DANGER!
WHICH IS WHY...I...I HAVE TO--

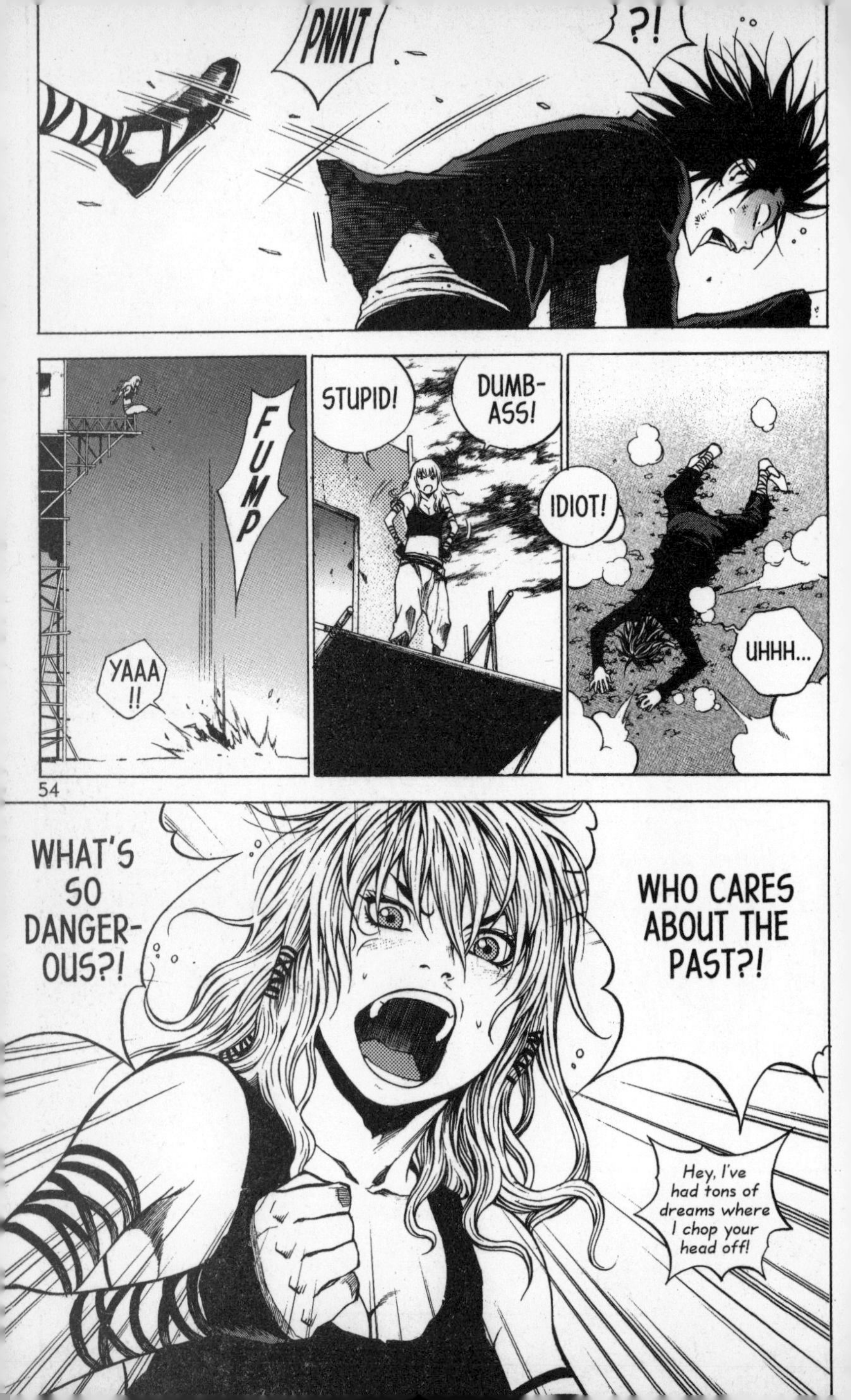
PNNT
?!
FUMP
YAAA !!
STUPID!
DUMB-ASS!
IDIOT!
UHHH...
WHAT'S SO DANGER-OUS?!
WHO CARES ABOUT THE PAST?!
Hey, I've had tons of dreams where I chop your head off!

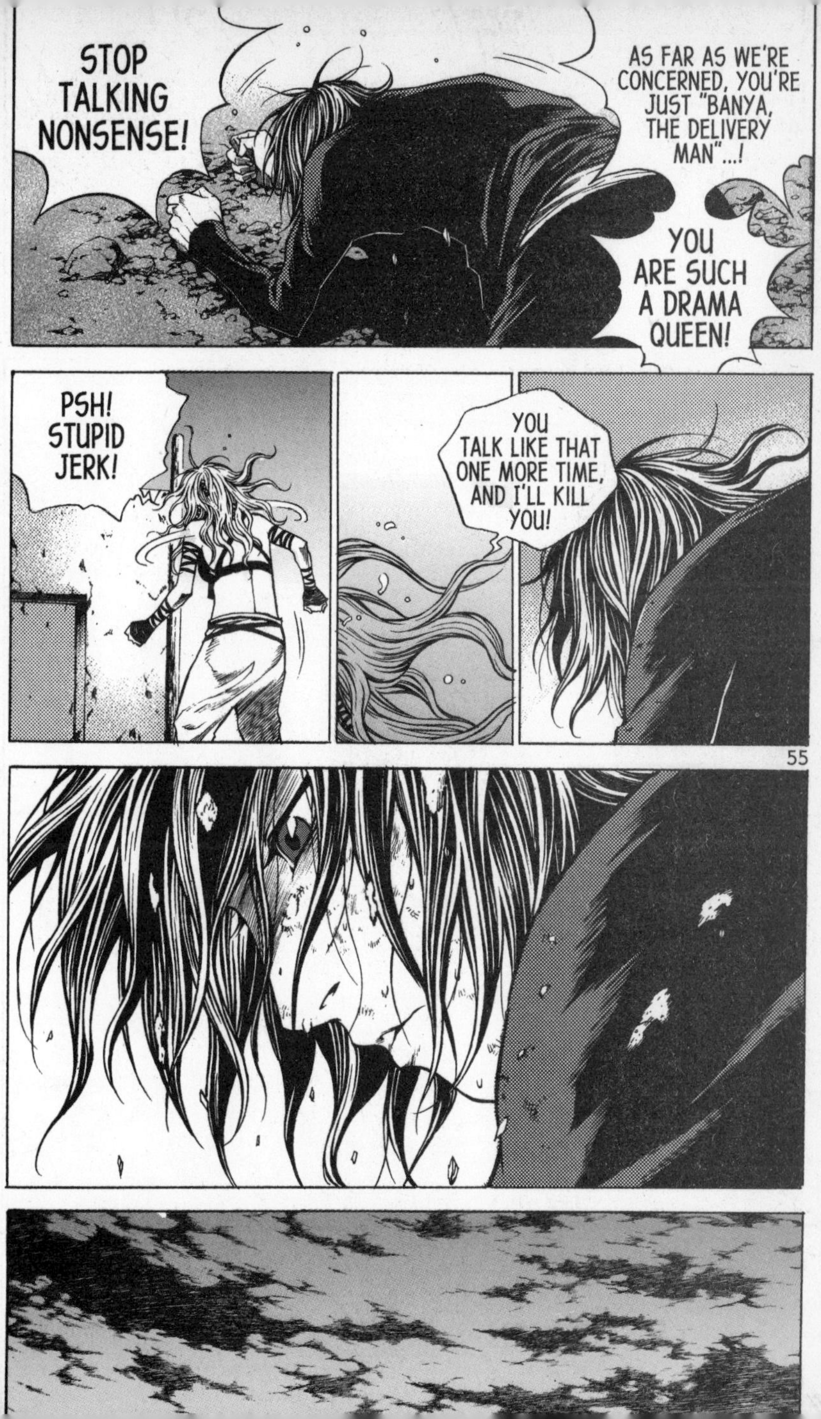
STOP TALKING NONSENSE!
AS FAR AS WE'RE CONCERNED, YOU'RE JUST "BANYA, THE DELIVERY MAN"...!
YOU ARE SUCH A DRAMA QUEEN!
PSH! STUPID JERK!
YOU TALK LIKE THAT ONE MORE TIME, AND I'LL KILL YOU!

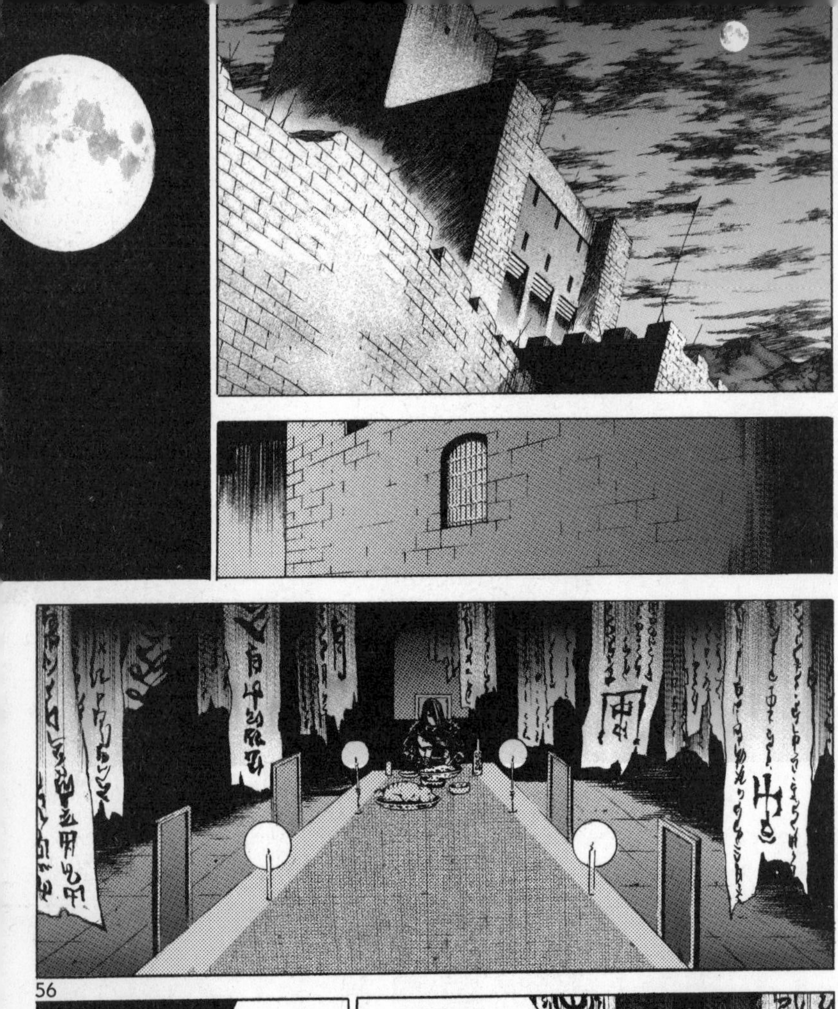



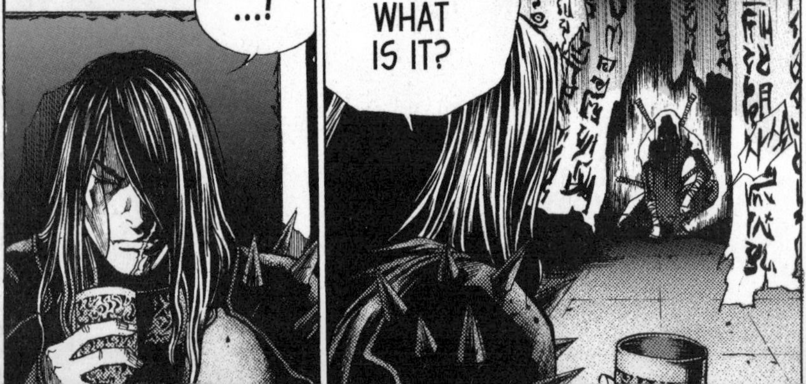

...!
WHAT IS IT?

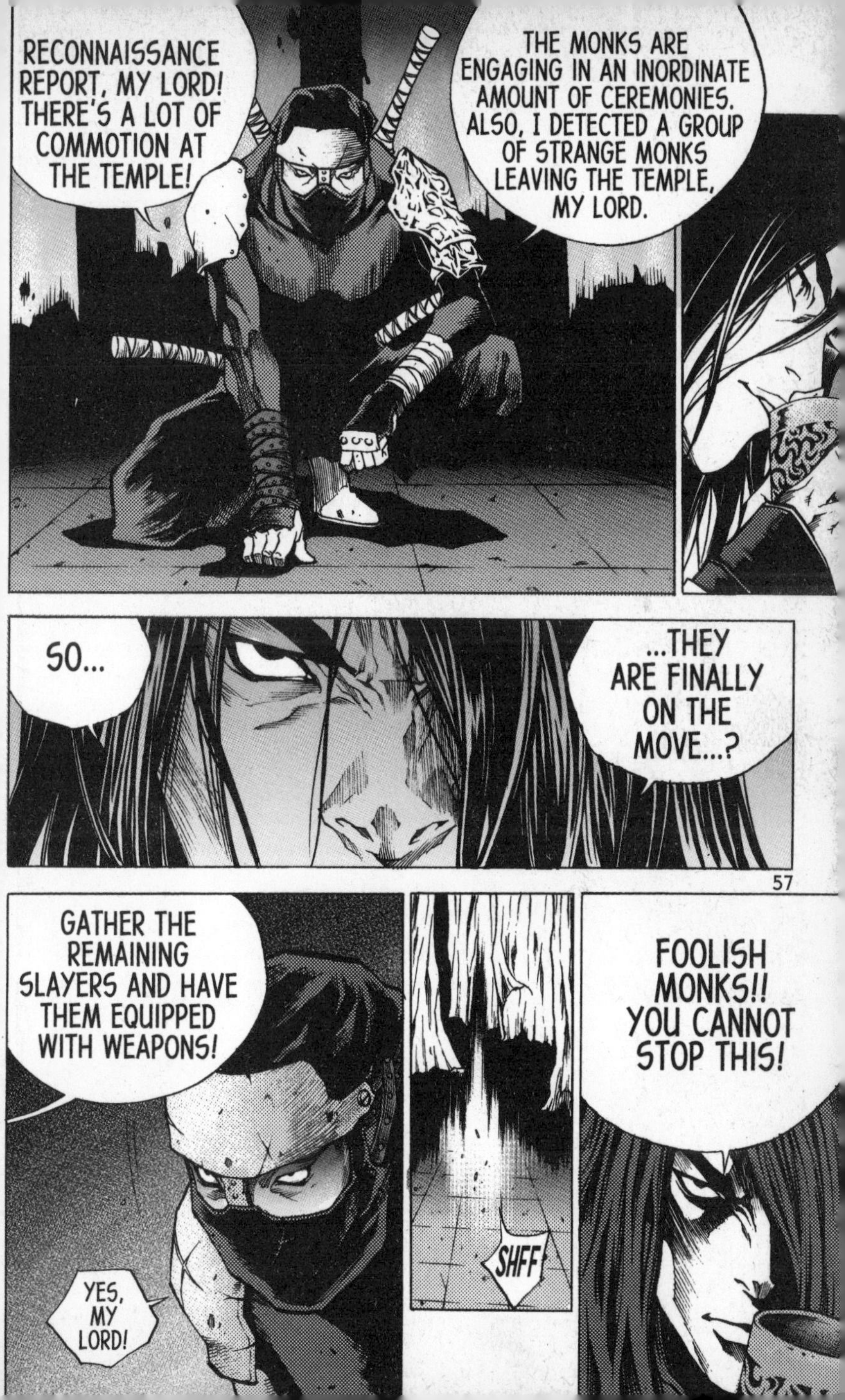
RECONNAISSANCE REPORT, MY LORD! THERE'S A LOT OF COMMOTION AT THE TEMPLE!
THE MONKS ARE ENGAGING IN AN INORDINATE AMOUNT OF CEREMONIES. ALSO, I DETECTED A GROUP OF STRANGE MONKS LEAVING THE TEMPLE, MY LORD.
SO...
...THEY ARE FINALLY ON THE MOVE...?
GATHER THE REMAINING SLAYERS AND HAVE THEM EQUIPPED WITH WEAPONS!
YES, MY LORD!
SHFF
FOOLISH MONKS!! YOU CANNOT STOP THIS!

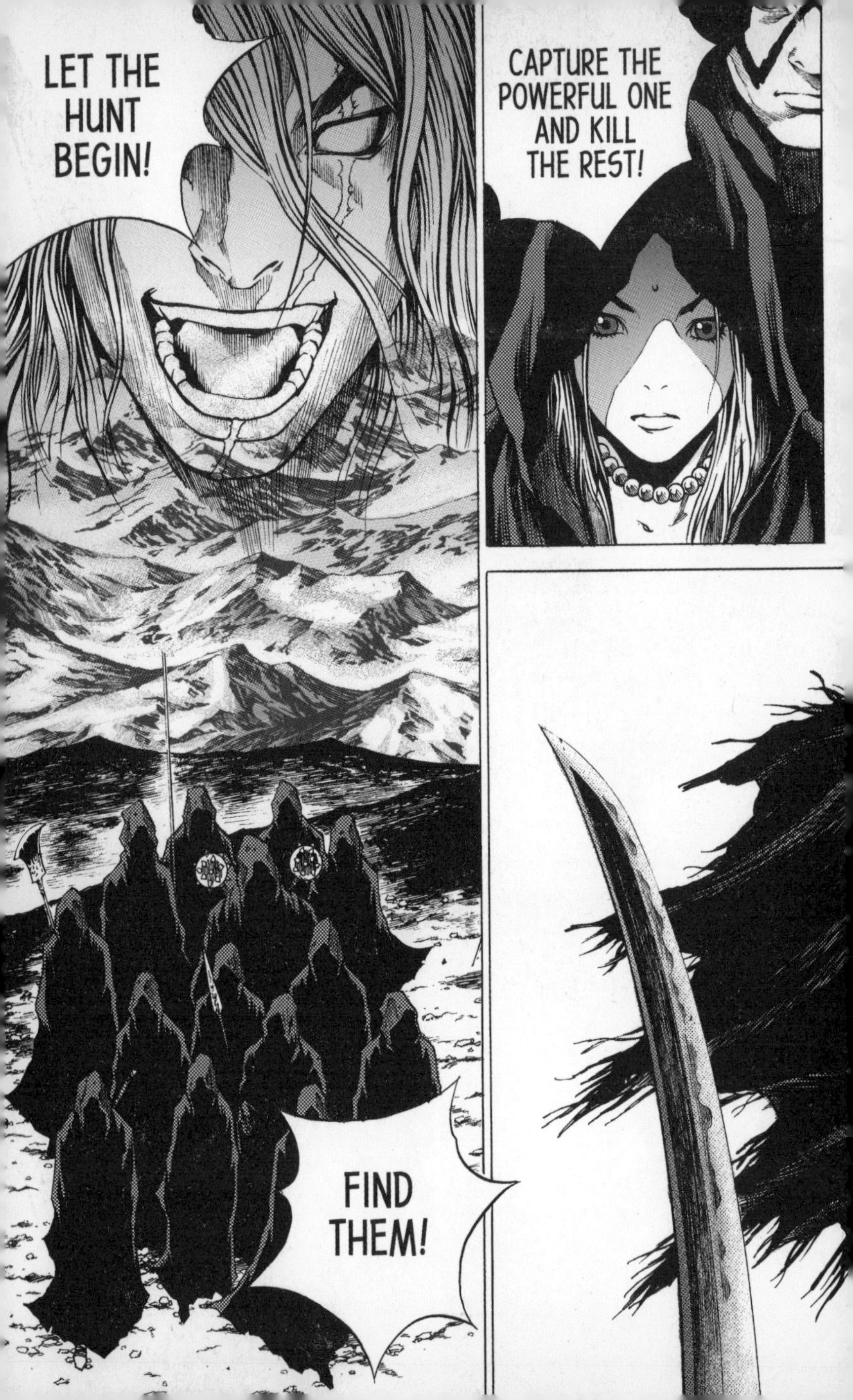
CAPTURE THE POWERFUL ONE AND KILL THE REST!
LET THE HUNT BEGIN!
FIND THEM!

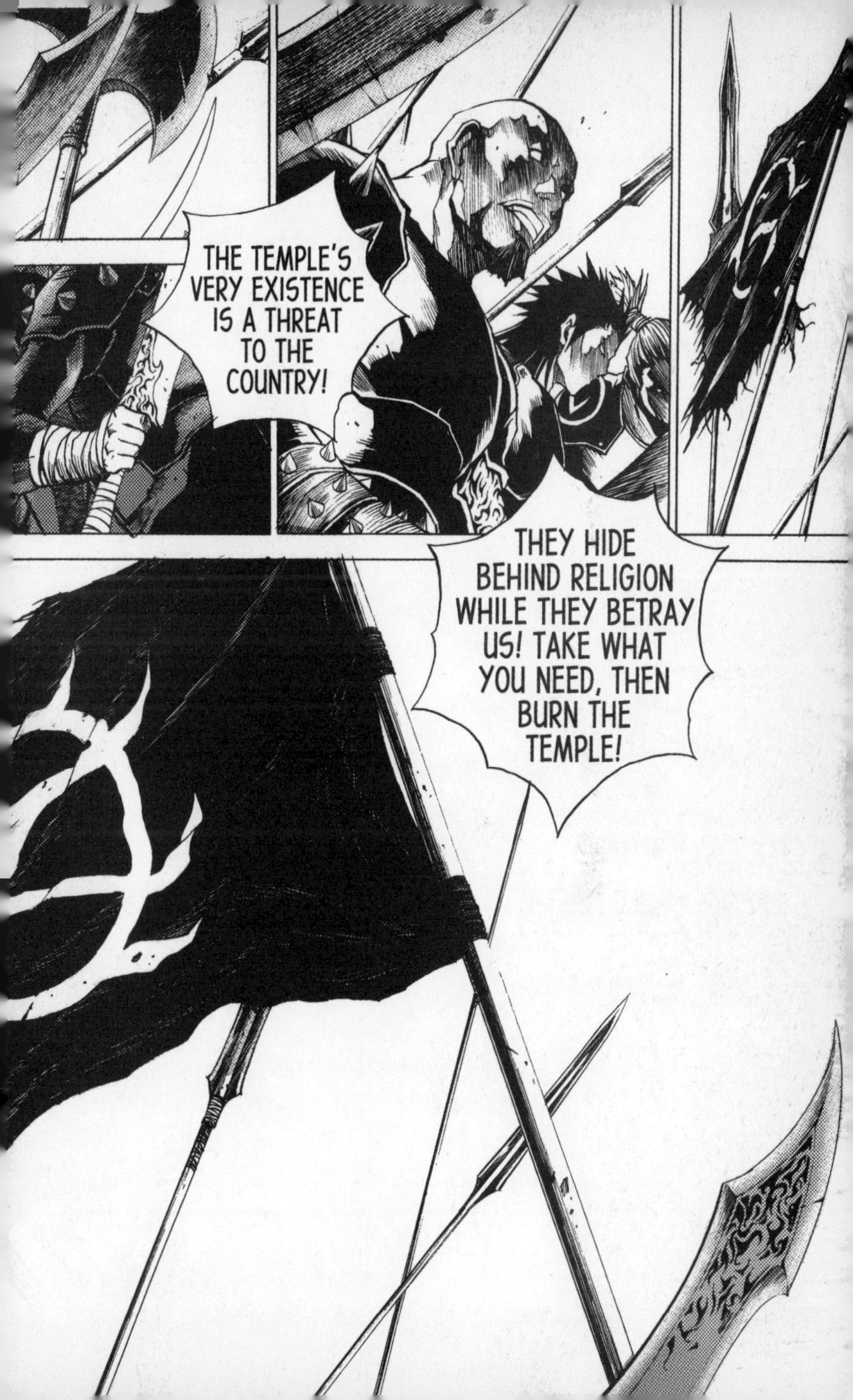
THE TEMPLE'S VERY EXISTENCE IS A THREAT TO THE COUNTRY!
THEY HIDE BEHIND RELIGION WHILE THEY BETRAY US! TAKE WHAT YOU NEED, THEN BURN THE TEMPLE!

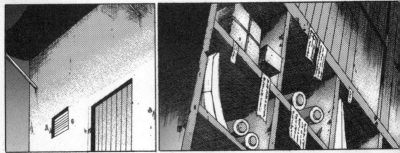

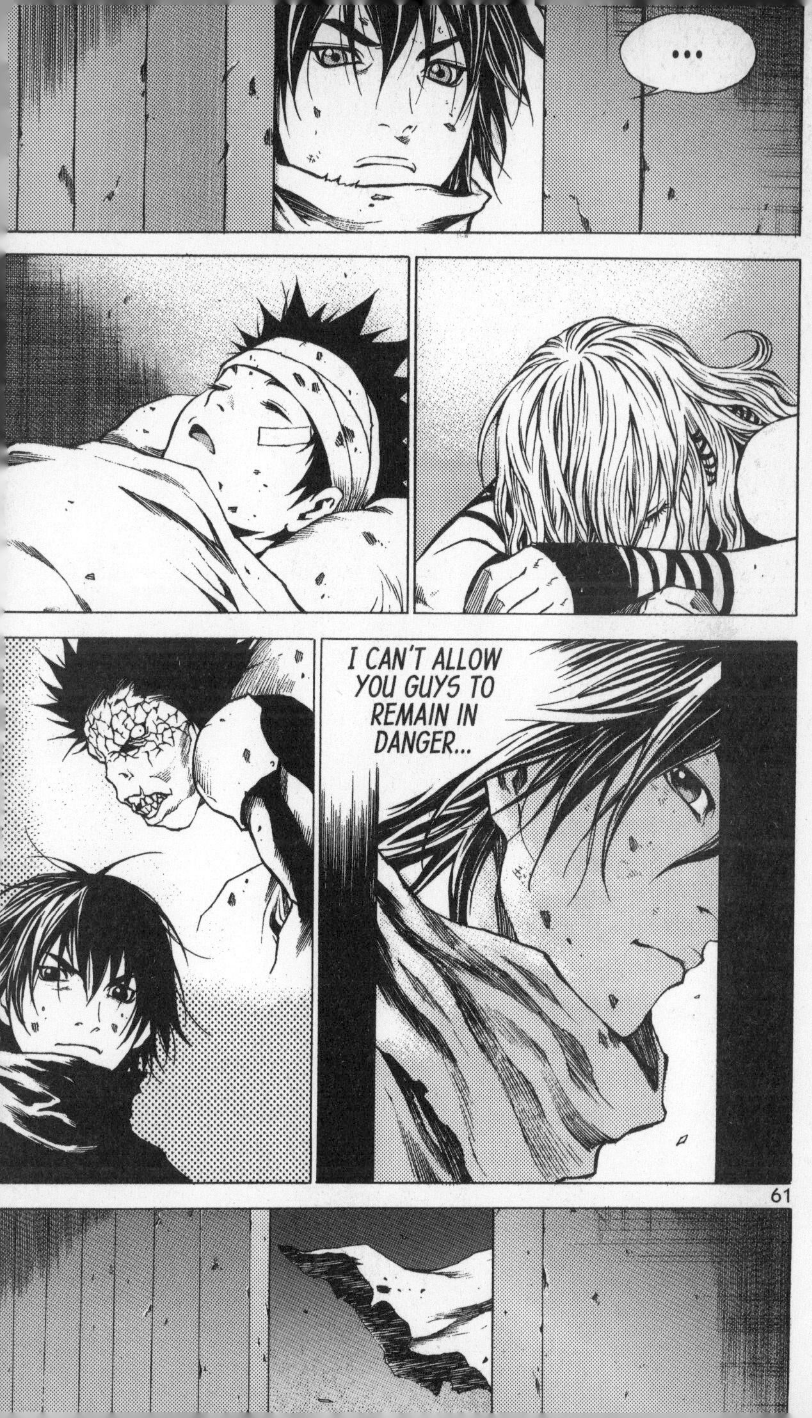
...
I CAN'T ALLOW YOU GUYS TO REMAIN IN DANGER...

...

STUPID...
FOOL...

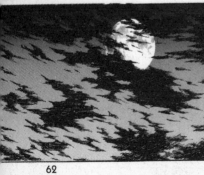

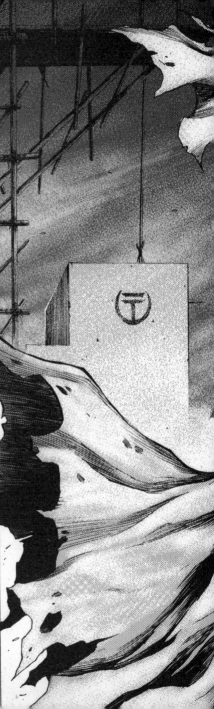

62

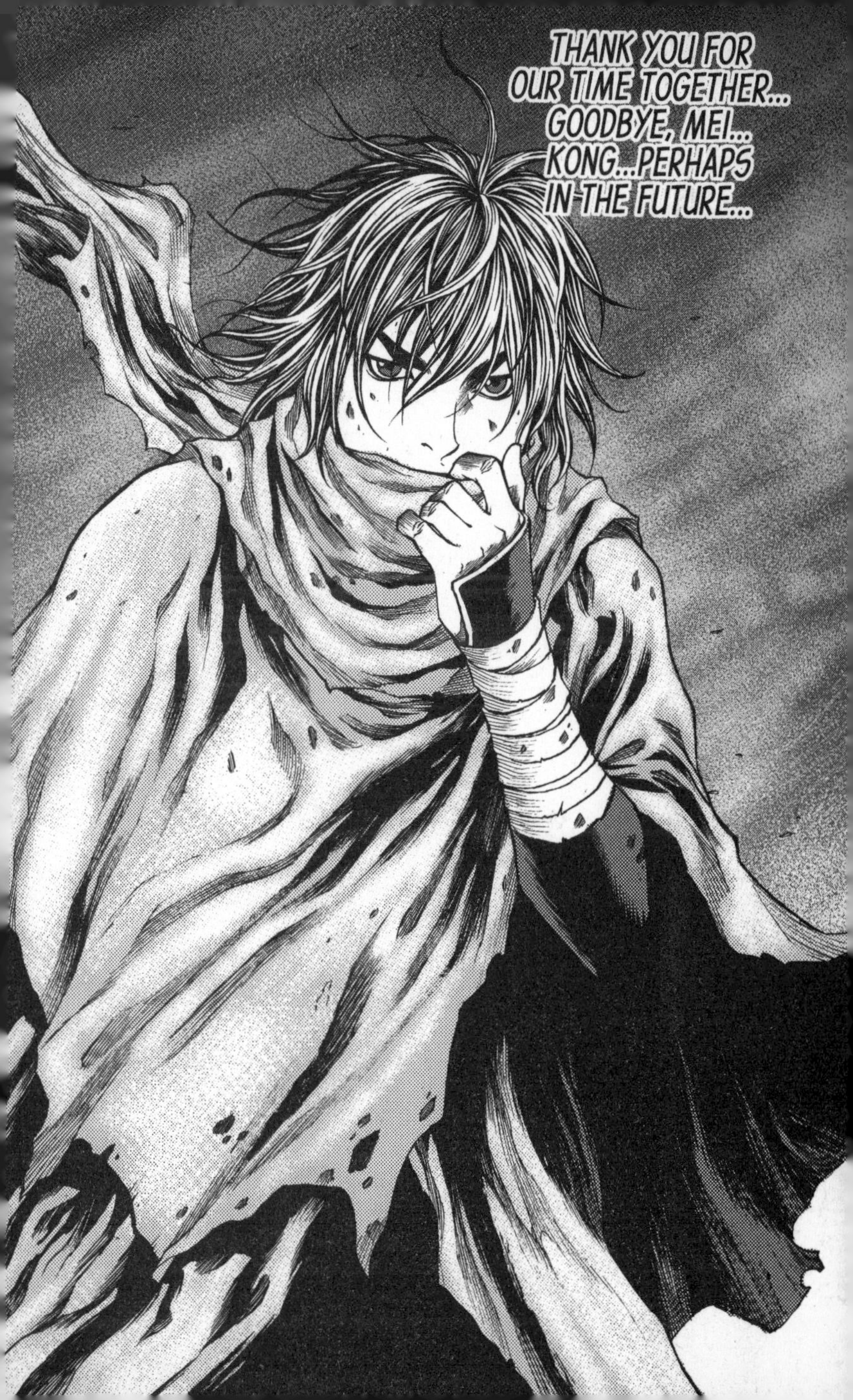
THANK YOU FOR OUR TIME TOGETHER... GOODBYE, MEI... KONG...PERHAPS IN THE FUTURE...

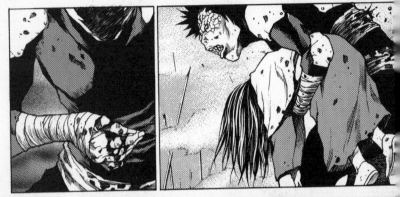

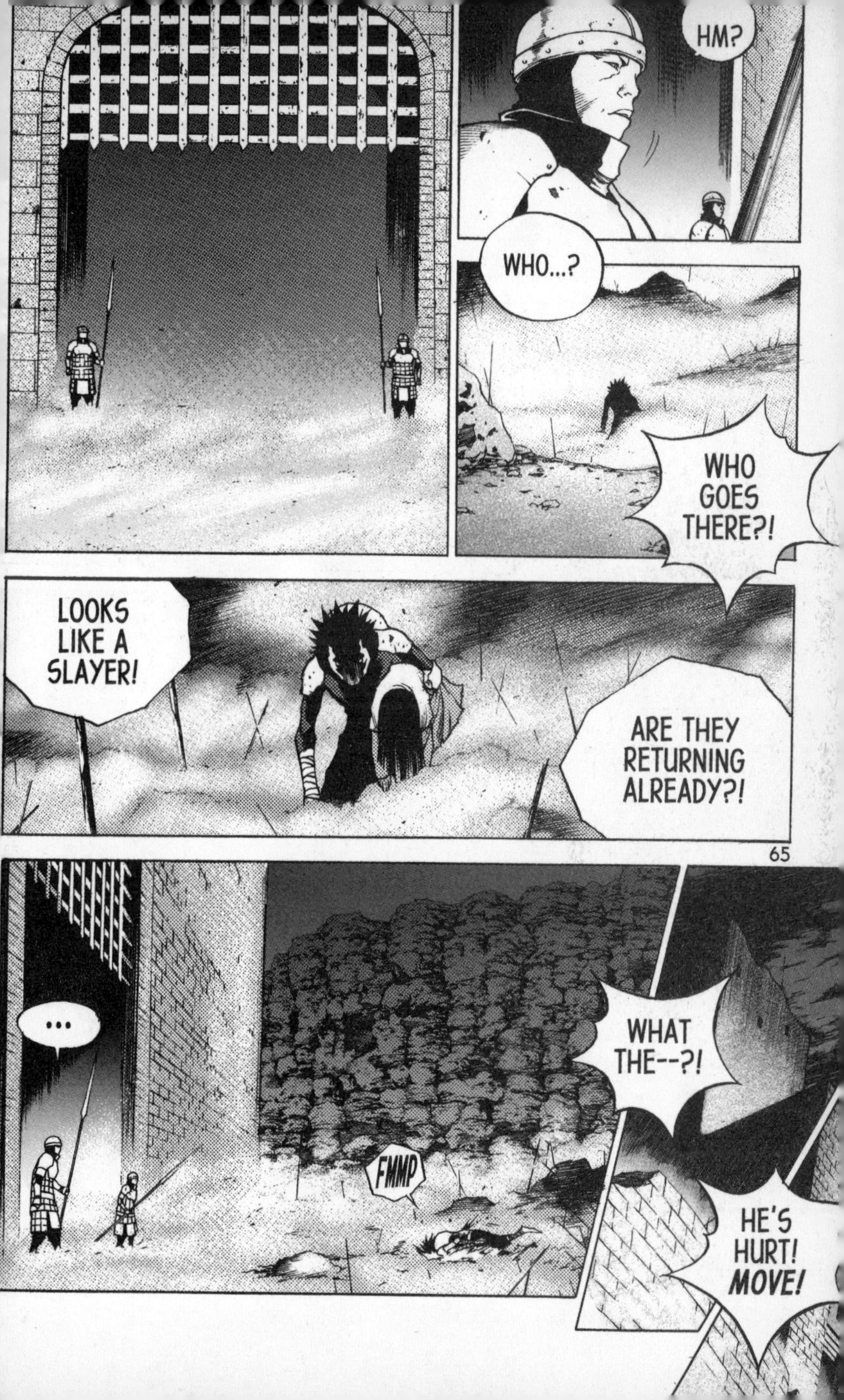
HM?
WHO...?
WHO GOES THERE?!
LOOKS LIKE A SLAYER!
ARE THEY RETURNING ALREADY?!
...
FMMP
WHAT THE--?!
HE'S HURT! *MOVE!*

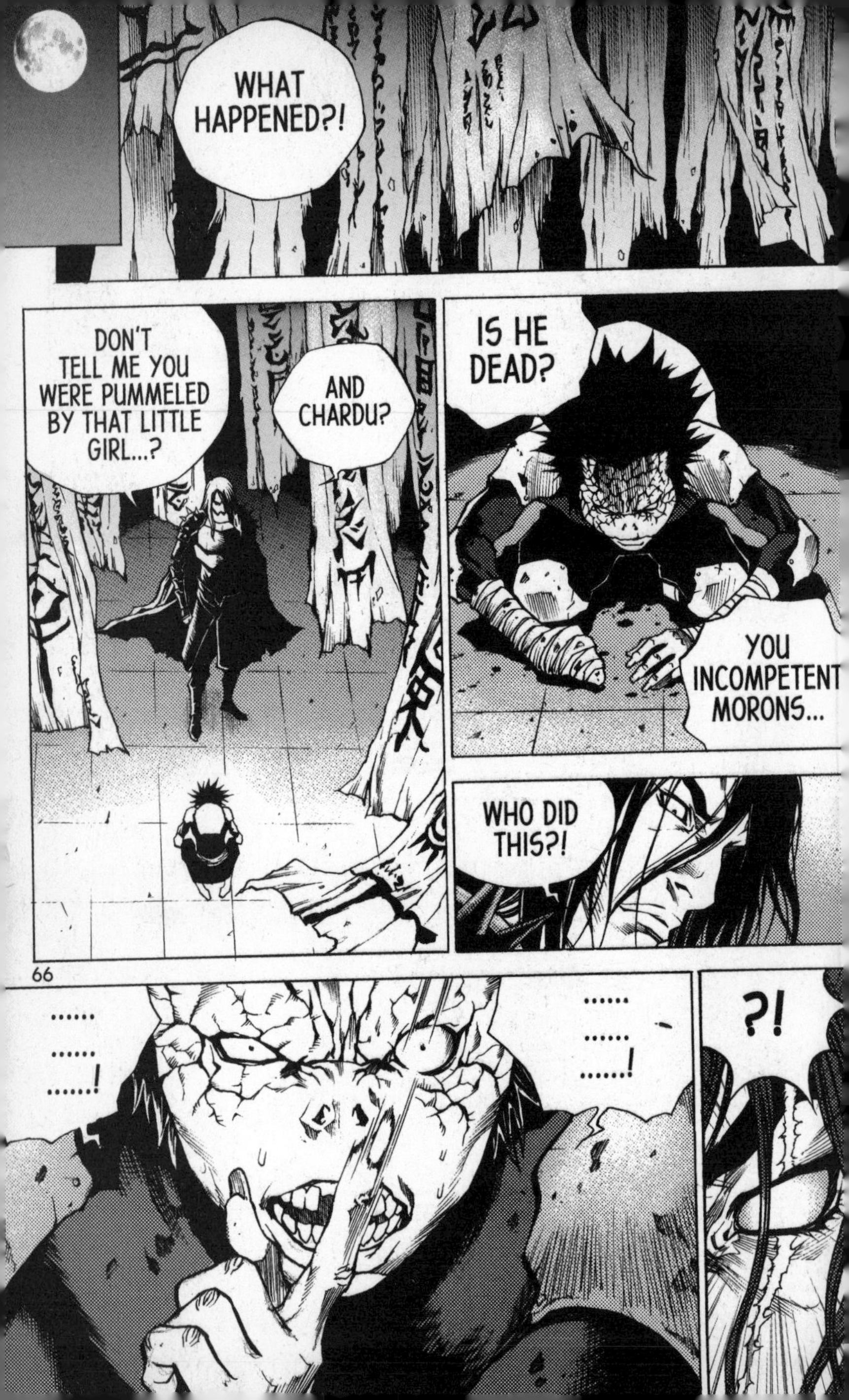
WHAT HAPPENED?!
DON'T TELL ME YOU WERE PUMMELED BY THAT LITTLE GIRL...?
AND CHARDU?
IS HE DEAD?
YOU INCOMPETENT MORONS...
WHO DID THIS?!
...... ...... ......!
...... ...... ......!
?!

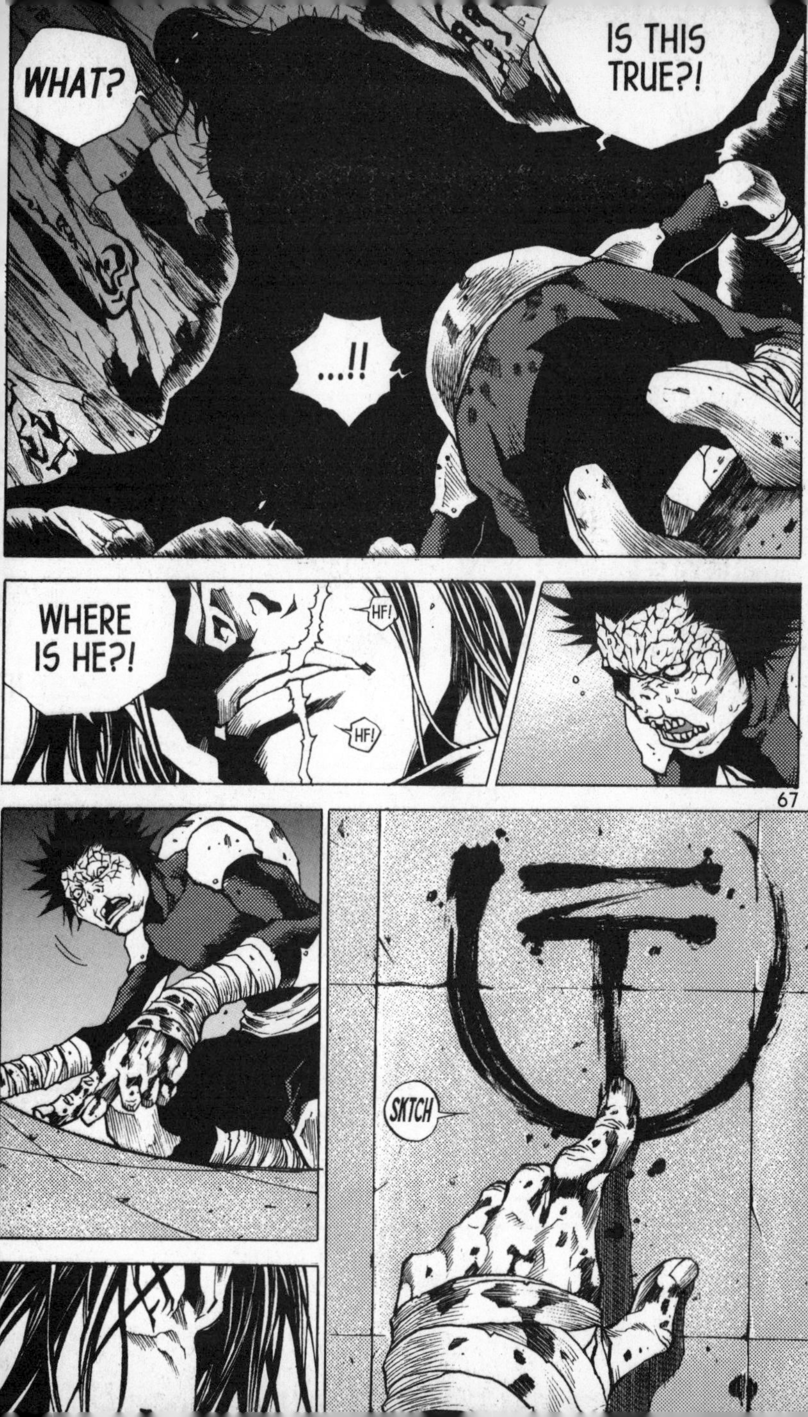
WHAT?
IS THIS TRUE?!
...!!
WHERE IS HE?!
HF!
HF!
SKTCH

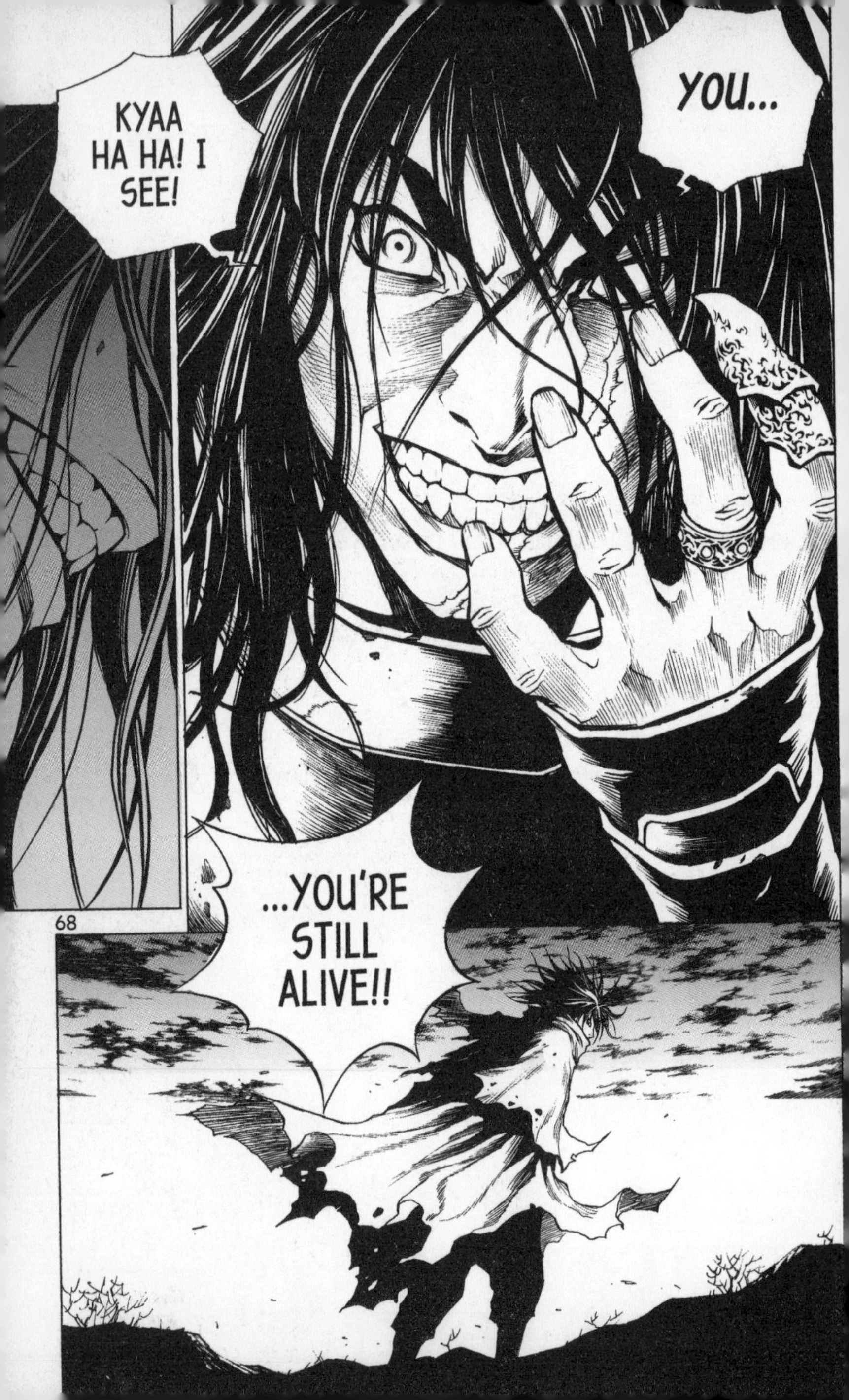
YOU...
KYAA
HA HA! I
SEE!
...YOU'RE
STILL
ALIVE!!

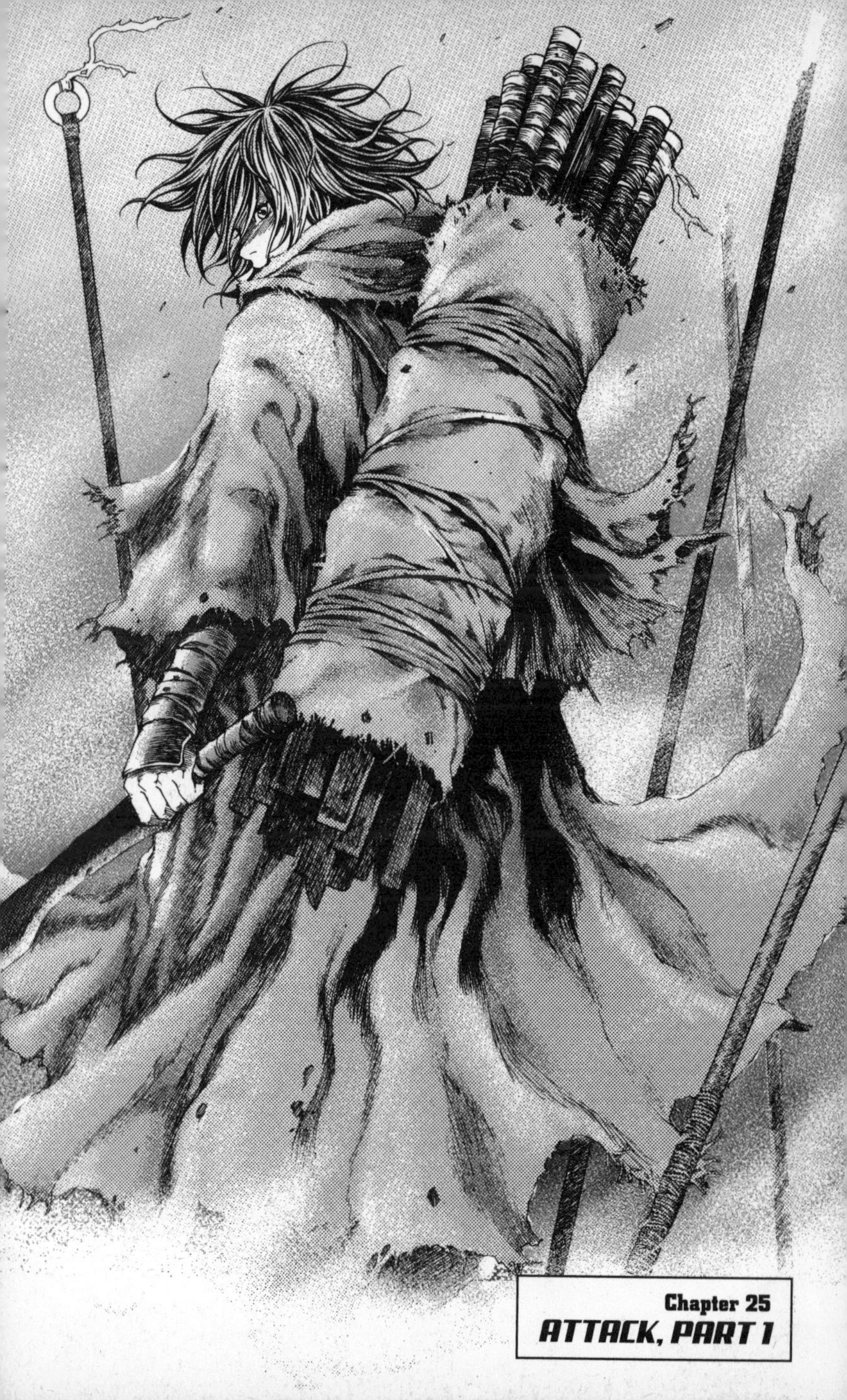

## Chapter 25
## ATTACK, PART 1

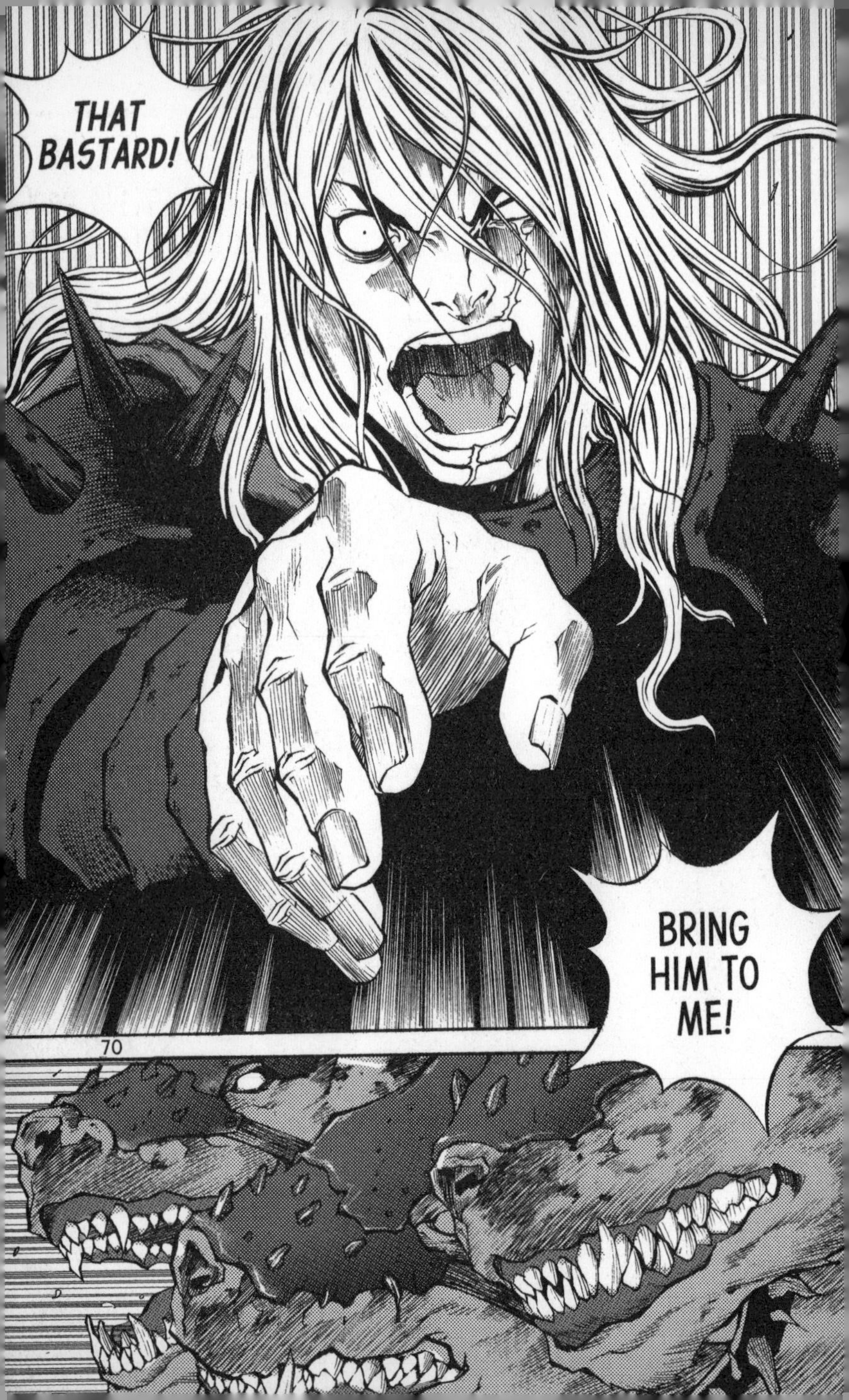
THAT BASTARD!
BRING HIM TO ME!

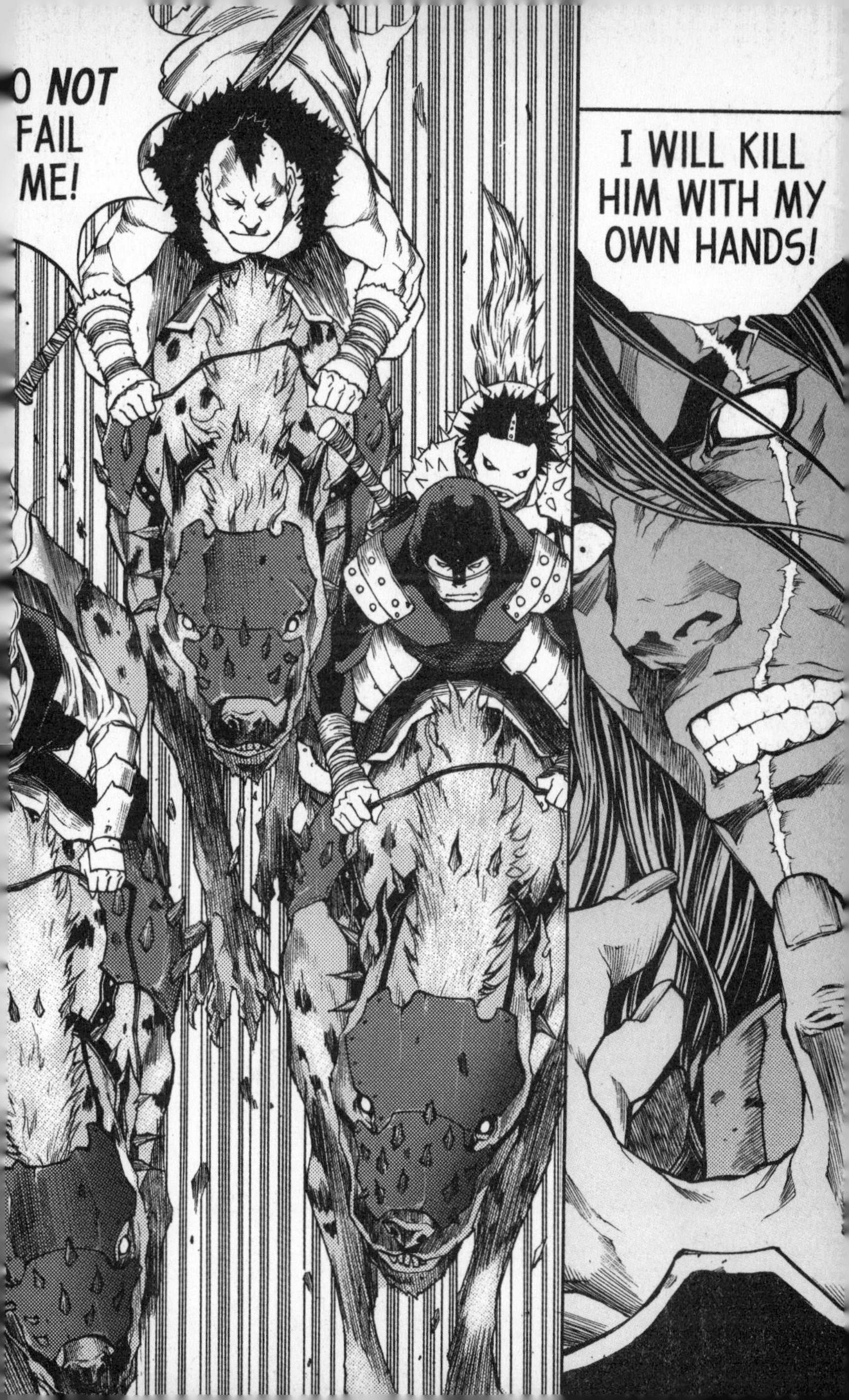
O NOT FAIL ME!
I WILL KILL HIM WITH MY OWN HANDS!

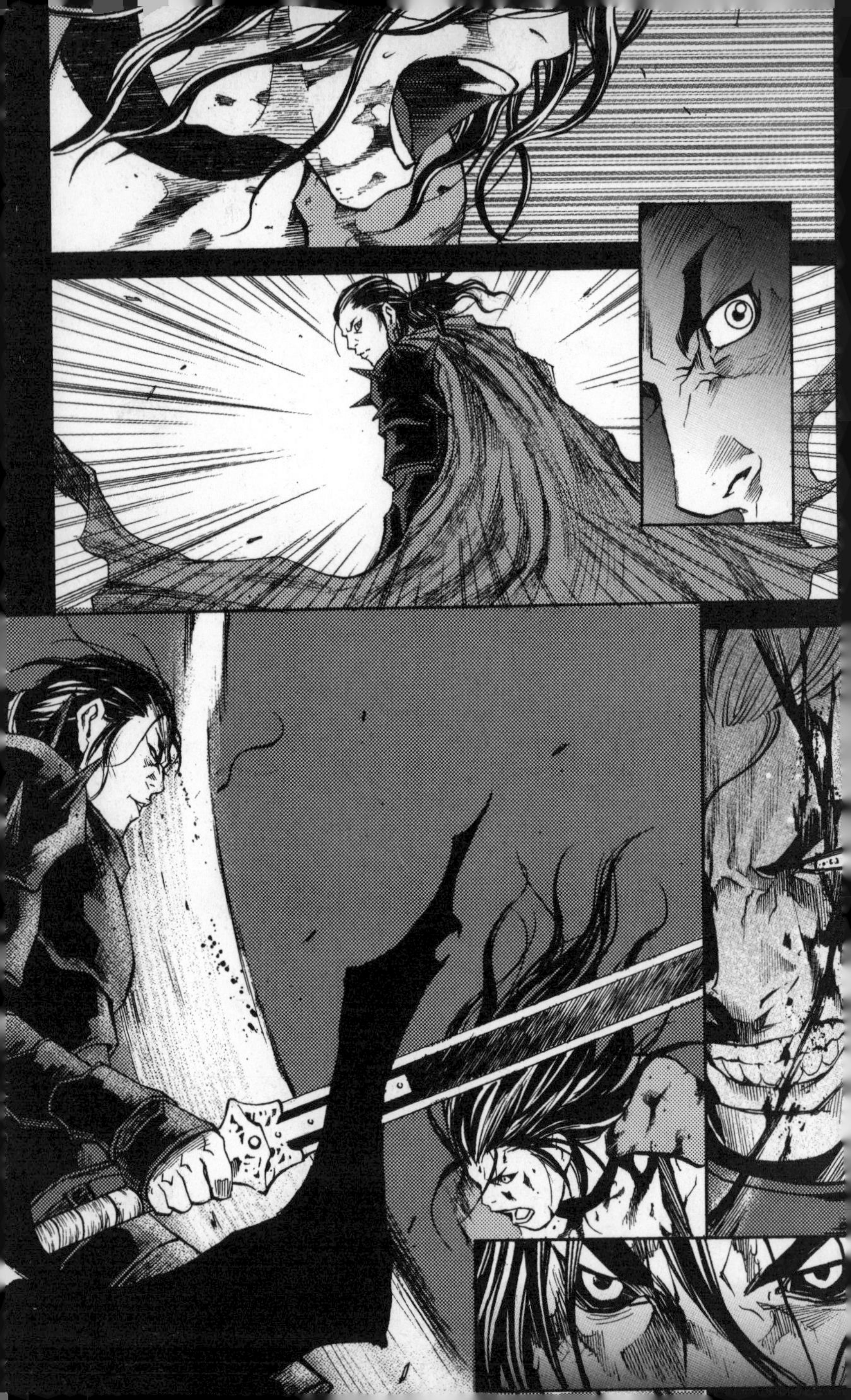

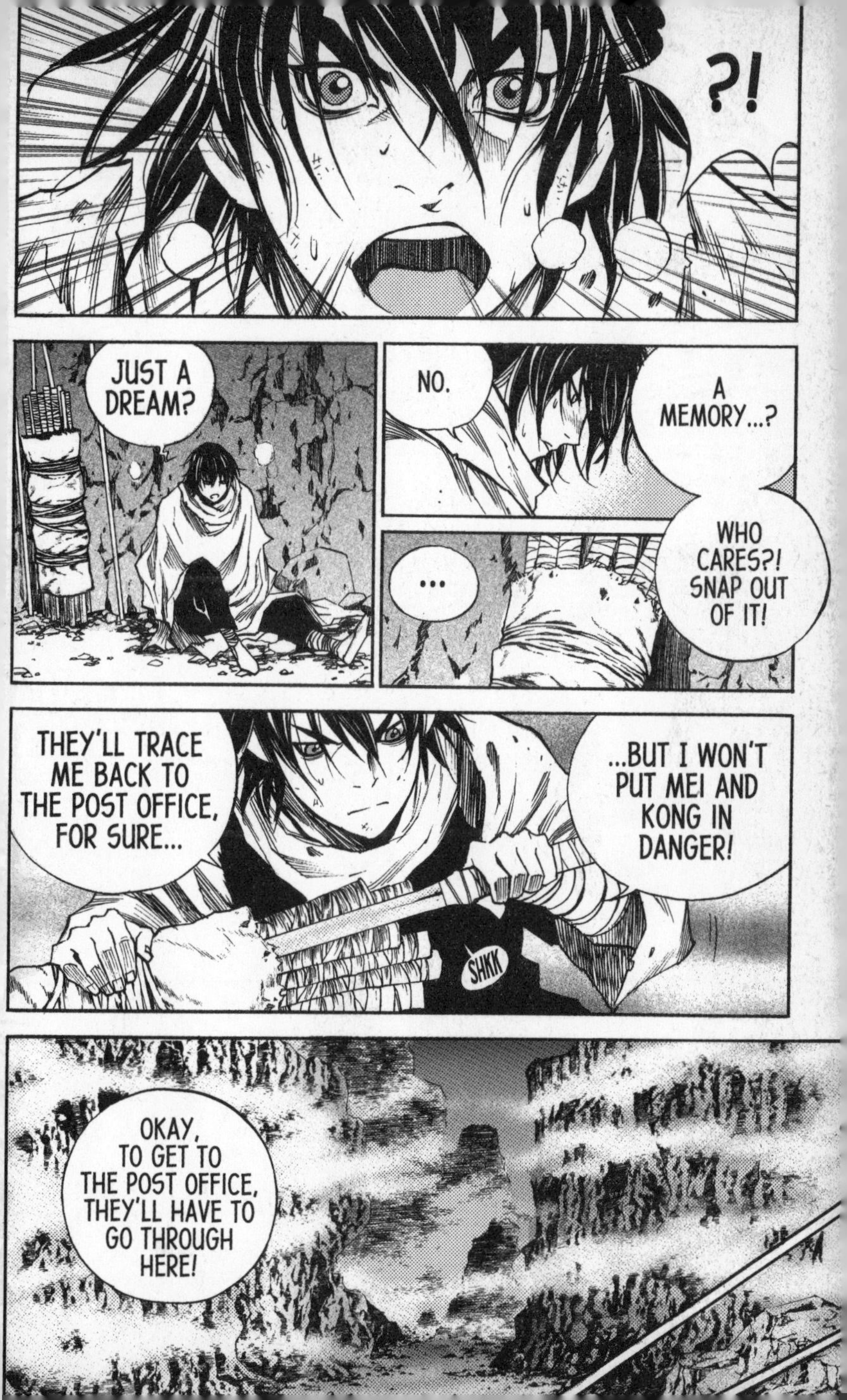
?!
JUST A DREAM?
NO.
A MEMORY...?
...
WHO CARES?! SNAP OUT OF IT!
THEY'LL TRACE ME BACK TO THE POST OFFICE, FOR SURE...
...BUT I WON'T PUT MEI AND KONG IN DANGER!
SHKK
OKAY, TO GET TO THE POST OFFICE, THEY'LL HAVE TO GO THROUGH HERE!

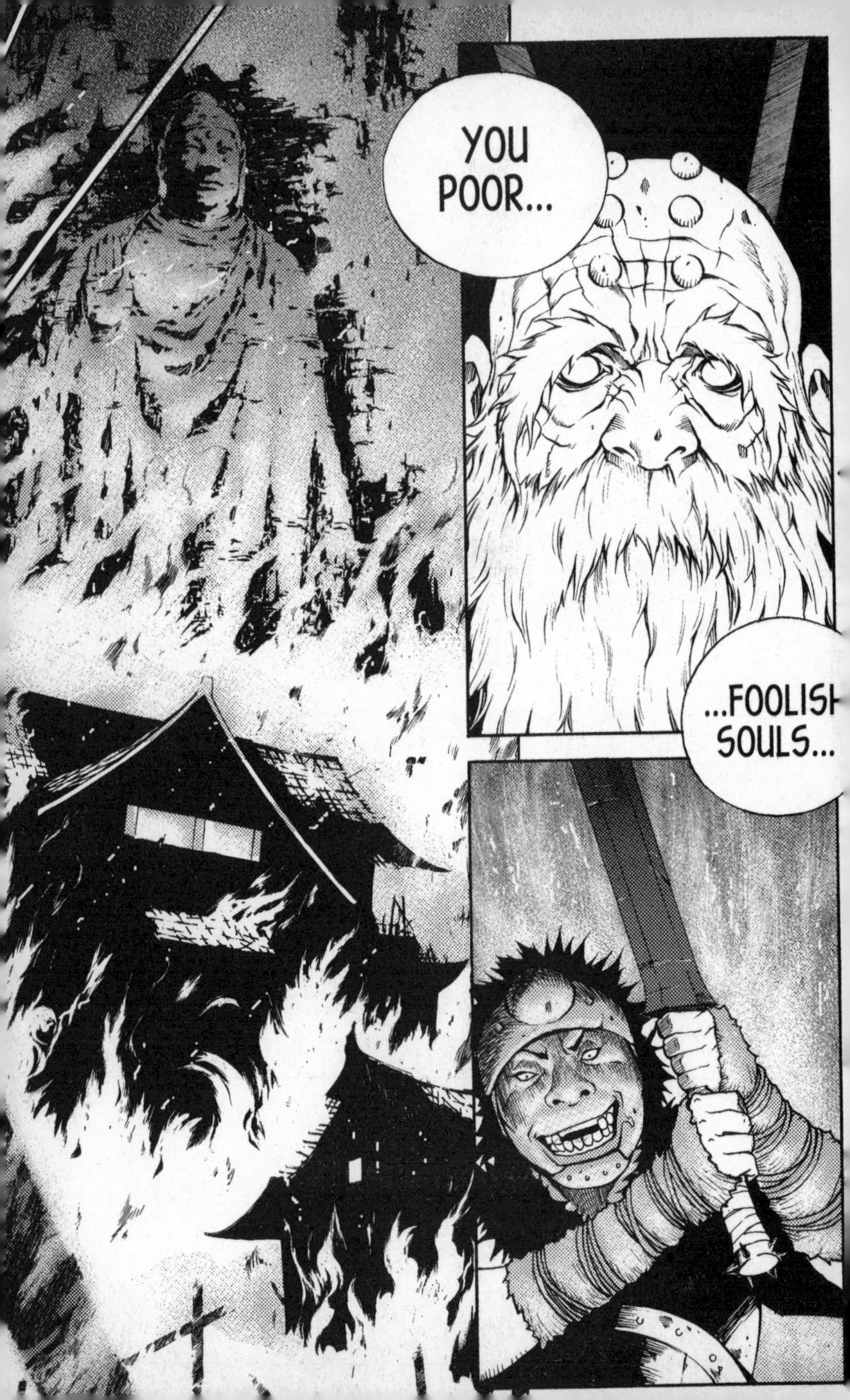

YOU POOR...
...FOOLISH SOULS...

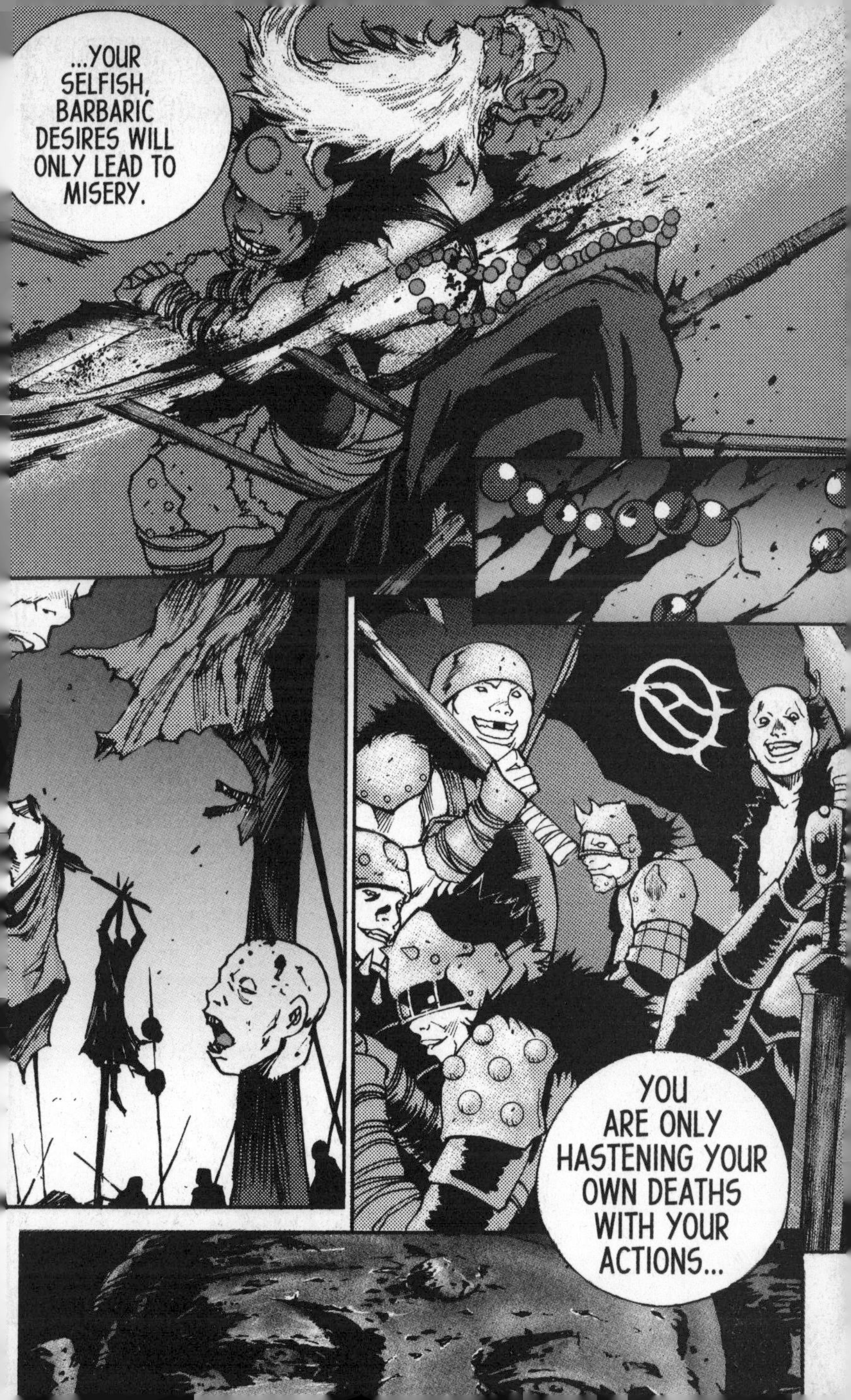
...YOUR SELFISH, BARBARIC DESIRES WILL ONLY LEAD TO MISERY.
YOU ARE ONLY HASTENING YOUR OWN DEATHS WITH YOUR ACTIONS...

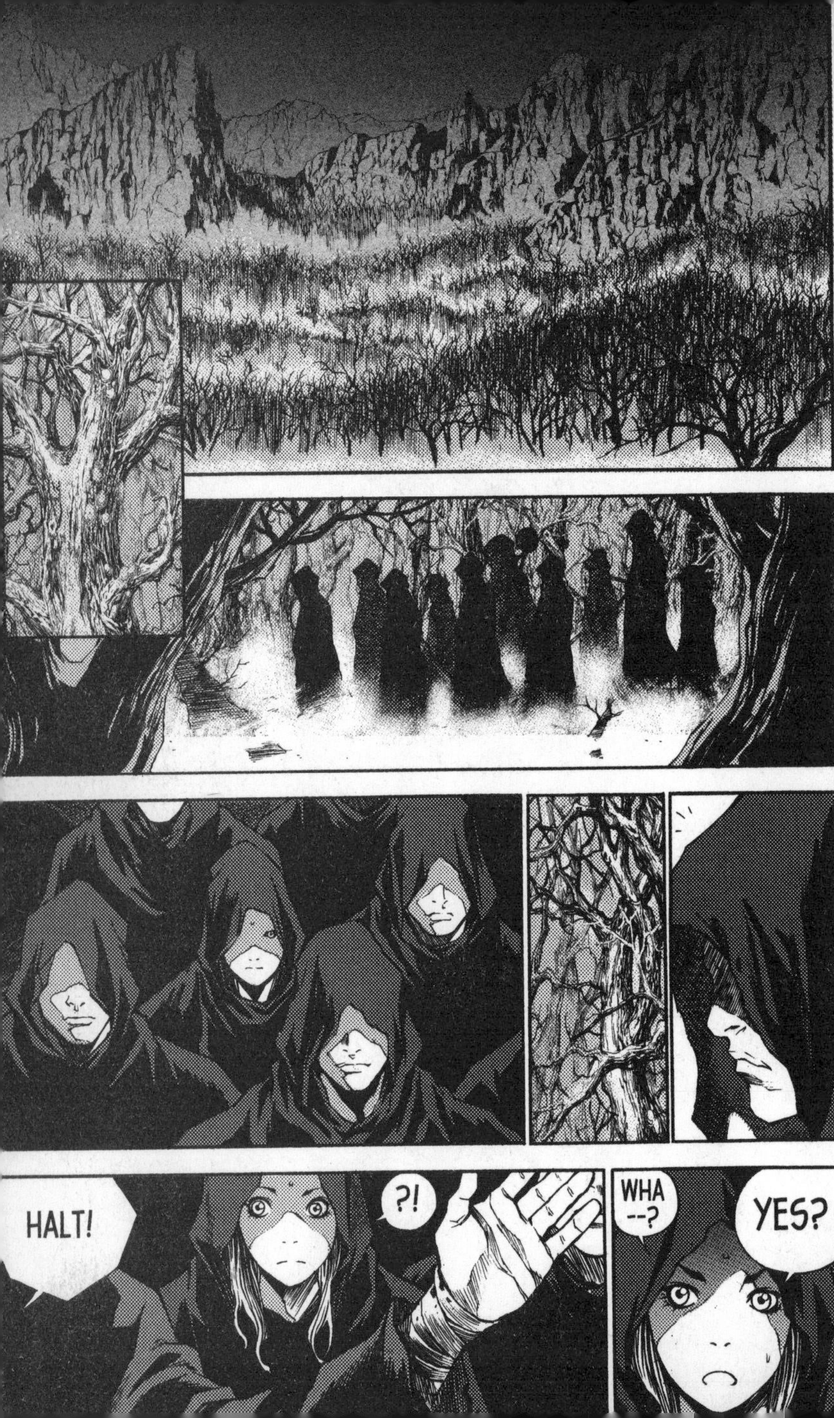
HALT!
?!
WHA --?
YES?

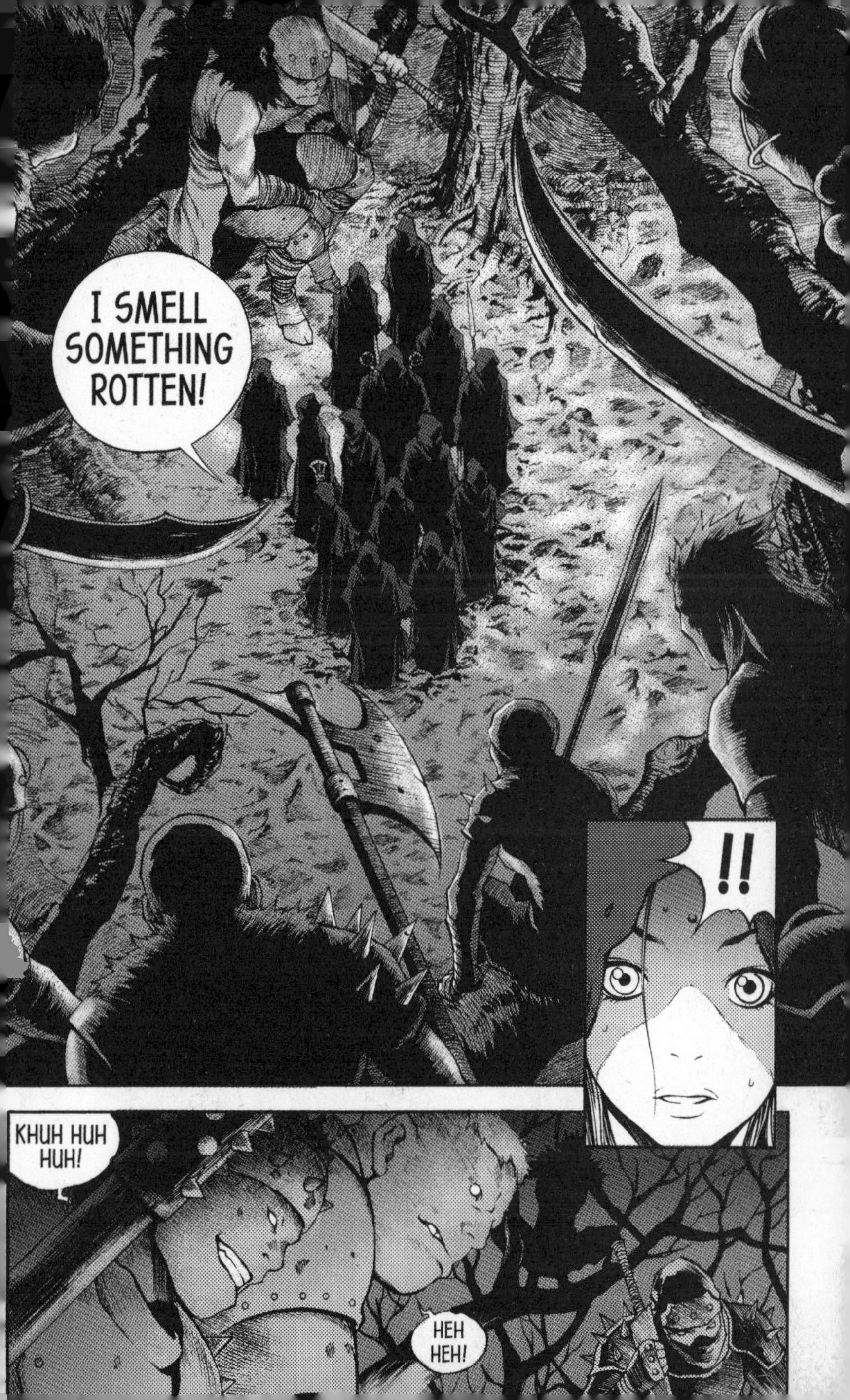
I SMELL SOMETHING ROTTEN!
!!
KHUH HUH HUH!
HEH HEH!

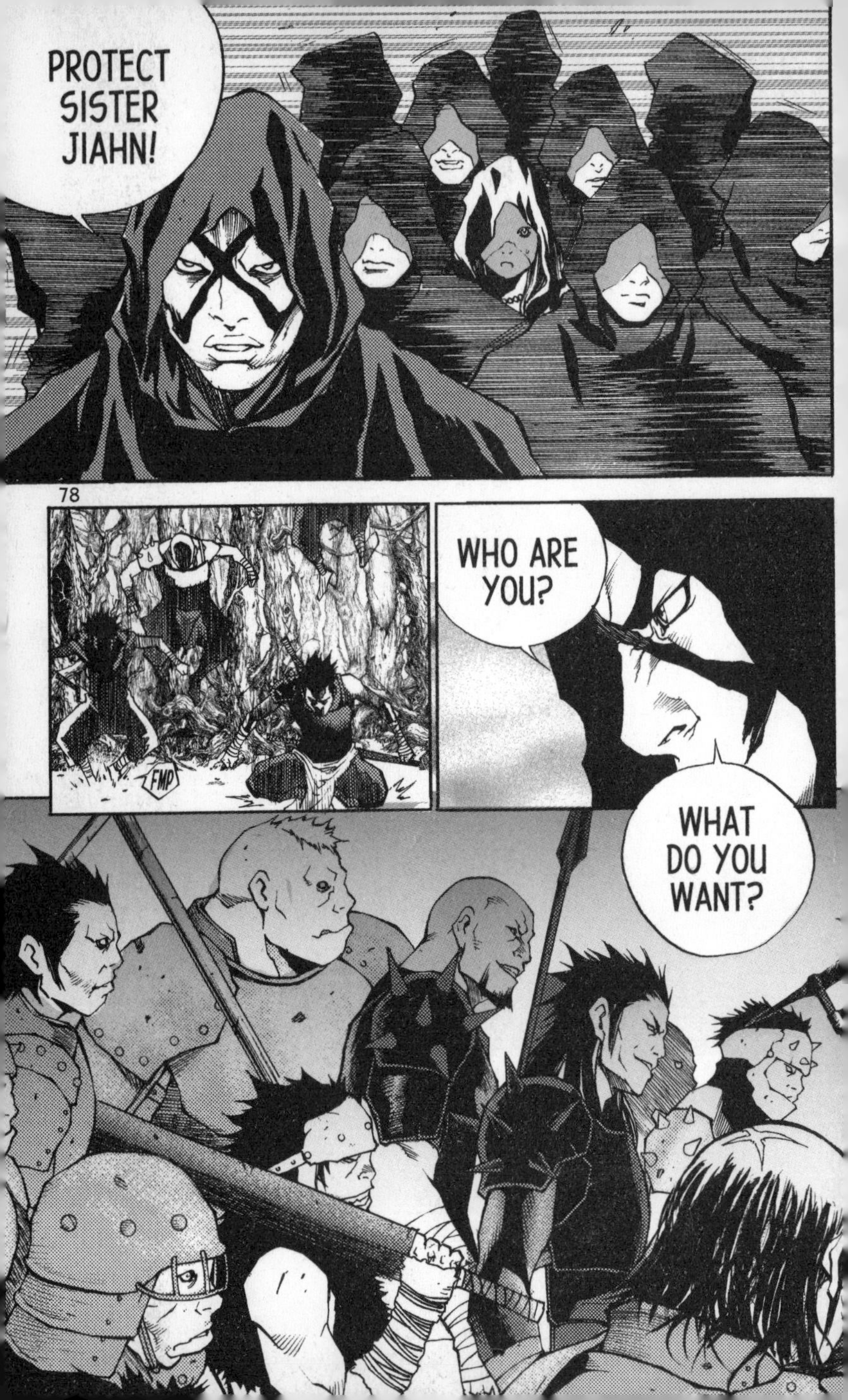
PROTECT SISTER JIAHN!
78
FMP
WHO ARE YOU?
WHAT DO YOU WANT?

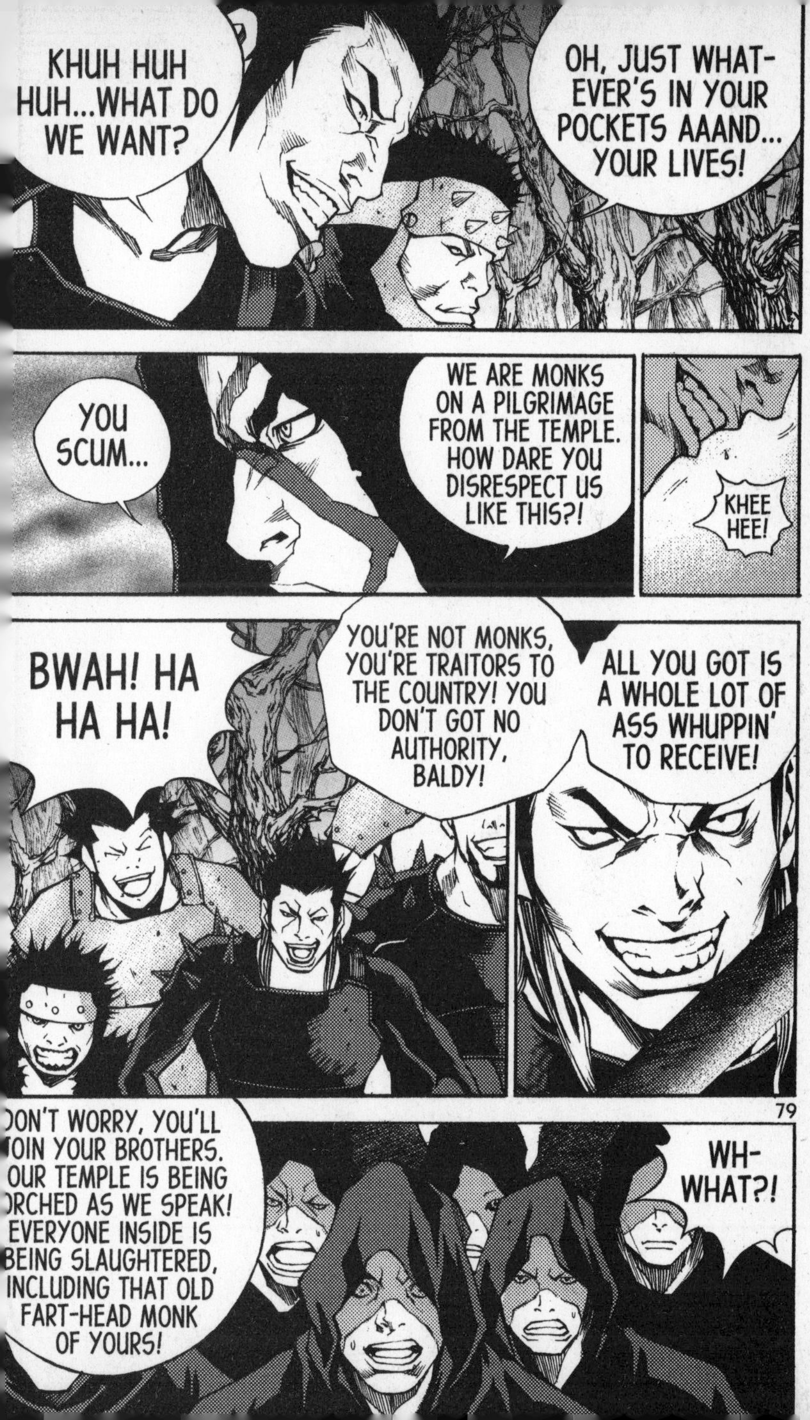
KHUH HUH HUH...WHAT DO WE WANT?
OH, JUST WHAT-EVER'S IN YOUR POCKETS AAAND... YOUR LIVES!
YOU SCUM...
WE ARE MONKS ON A PILGRIMAGE FROM THE TEMPLE. HOW DARE YOU DISRESPECT US LIKE THIS?!
KHEE HEE!
BWAH! HA HA HA!
YOU'RE NOT MONKS, YOU'RE TRAITORS TO THE COUNTRY! YOU DON'T GOT NO AUTHORITY, BALDY!
ALL YOU GOT IS A WHOLE LOT OF ASS WHUPPIN' TO RECEIVE!
DON'T WORRY, YOU'LL JOIN YOUR BROTHERS. YOUR TEMPLE IS BEING TORCHED AS WE SPEAK! EVERYONE INSIDE IS BEING SLAUGHTERED, INCLUDING THAT OLD FART-HEAD MONK OF YOURS!
WH-WHAT?!

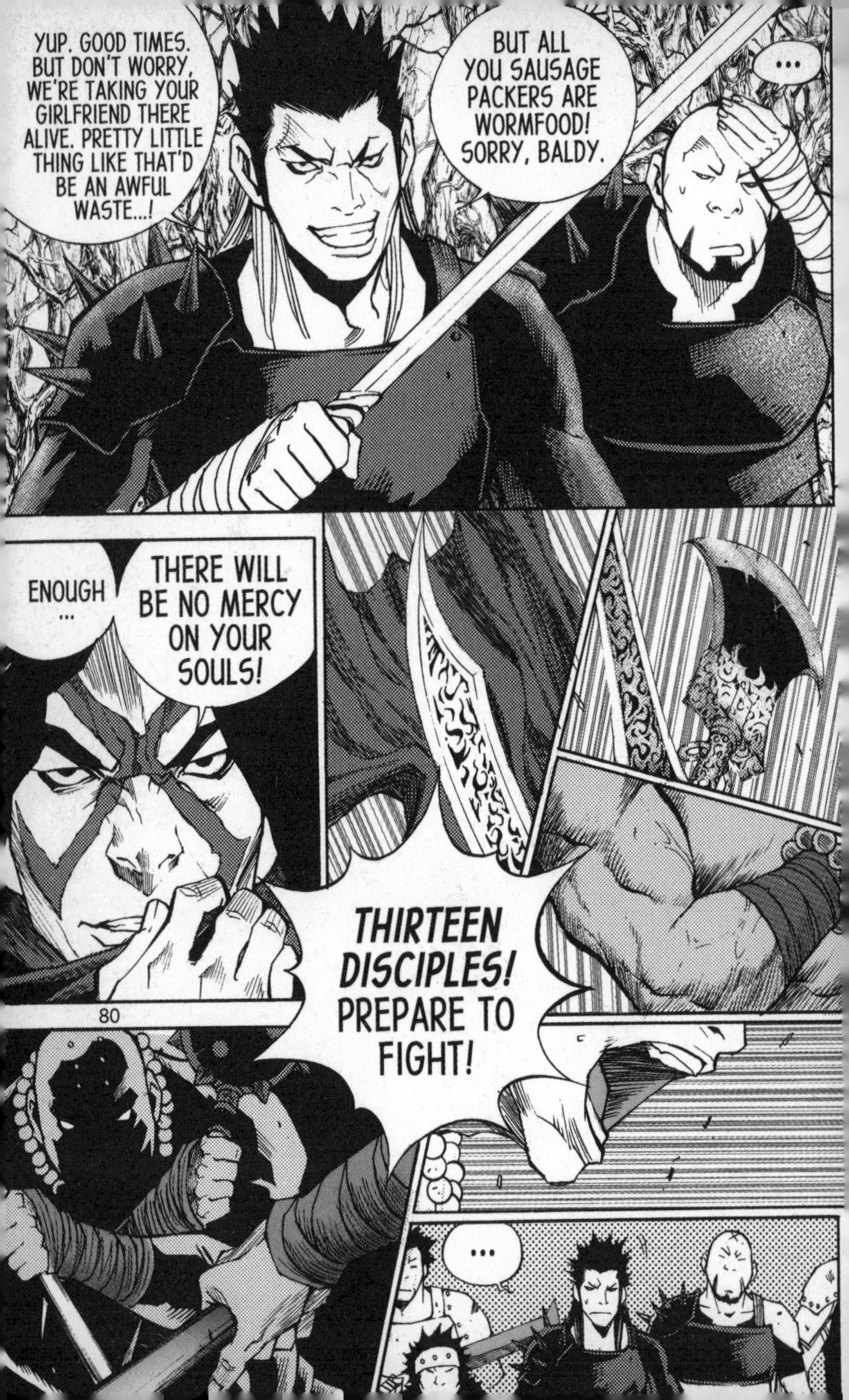
YUP. GOOD TIMES. BUT DON'T WORRY, WE'RE TAKING YOUR GIRLFRIEND THERE ALIVE. PRETTY LITTLE THING LIKE THAT'D BE AN AWFUL WASTE...!
BUT ALL YOU SAUSAGE PACKERS ARE WORMFOOD! SORRY, BALDY.
...
ENOUGH ...
THERE WILL BE NO MERCY ON YOUR SOULS!
THIRTEEN DISCIPLES! PREPARE TO FIGHT!
...

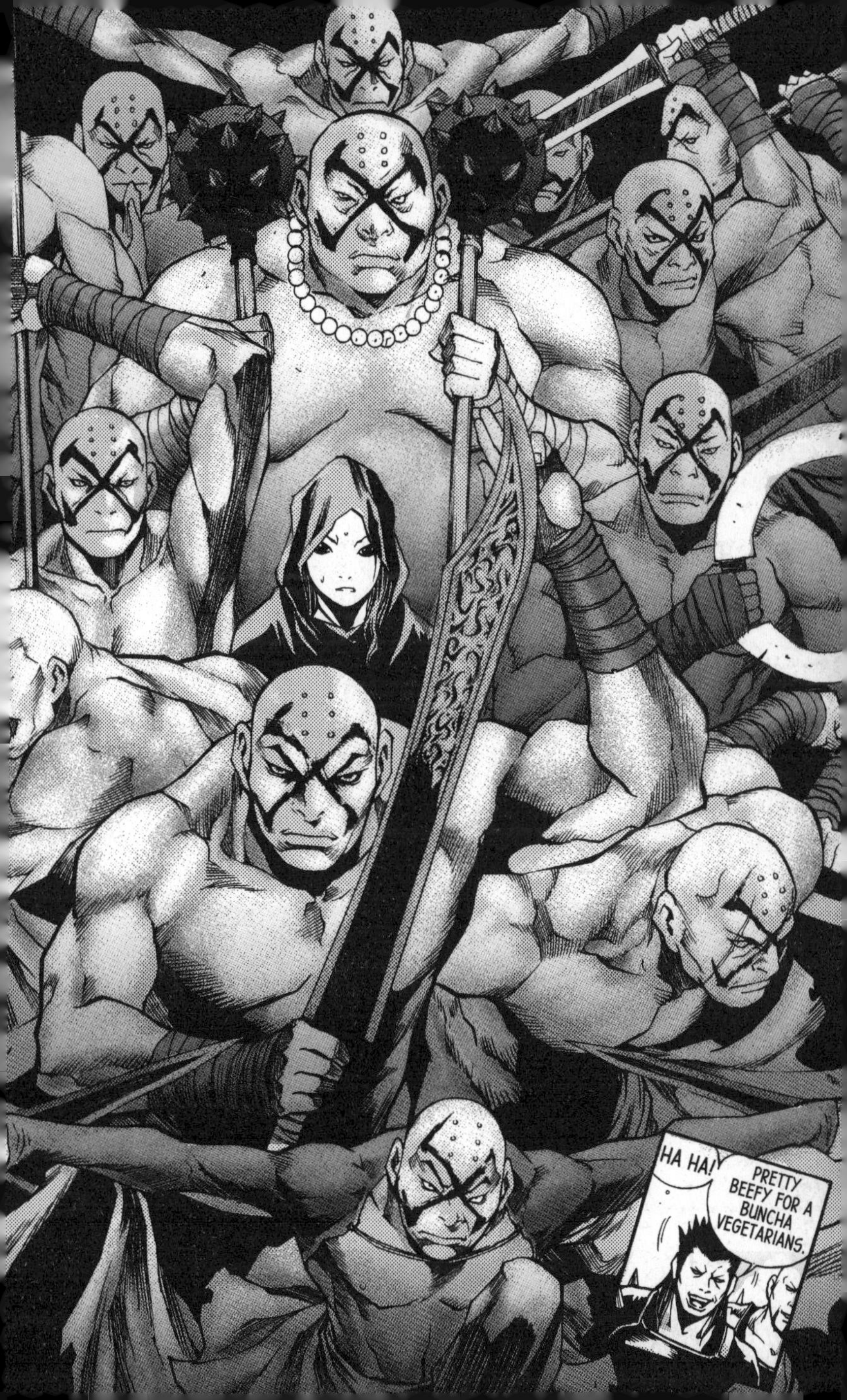
HA HA!
PRETTY BEEFY FOR A BUNCHA VEGETARIANS.

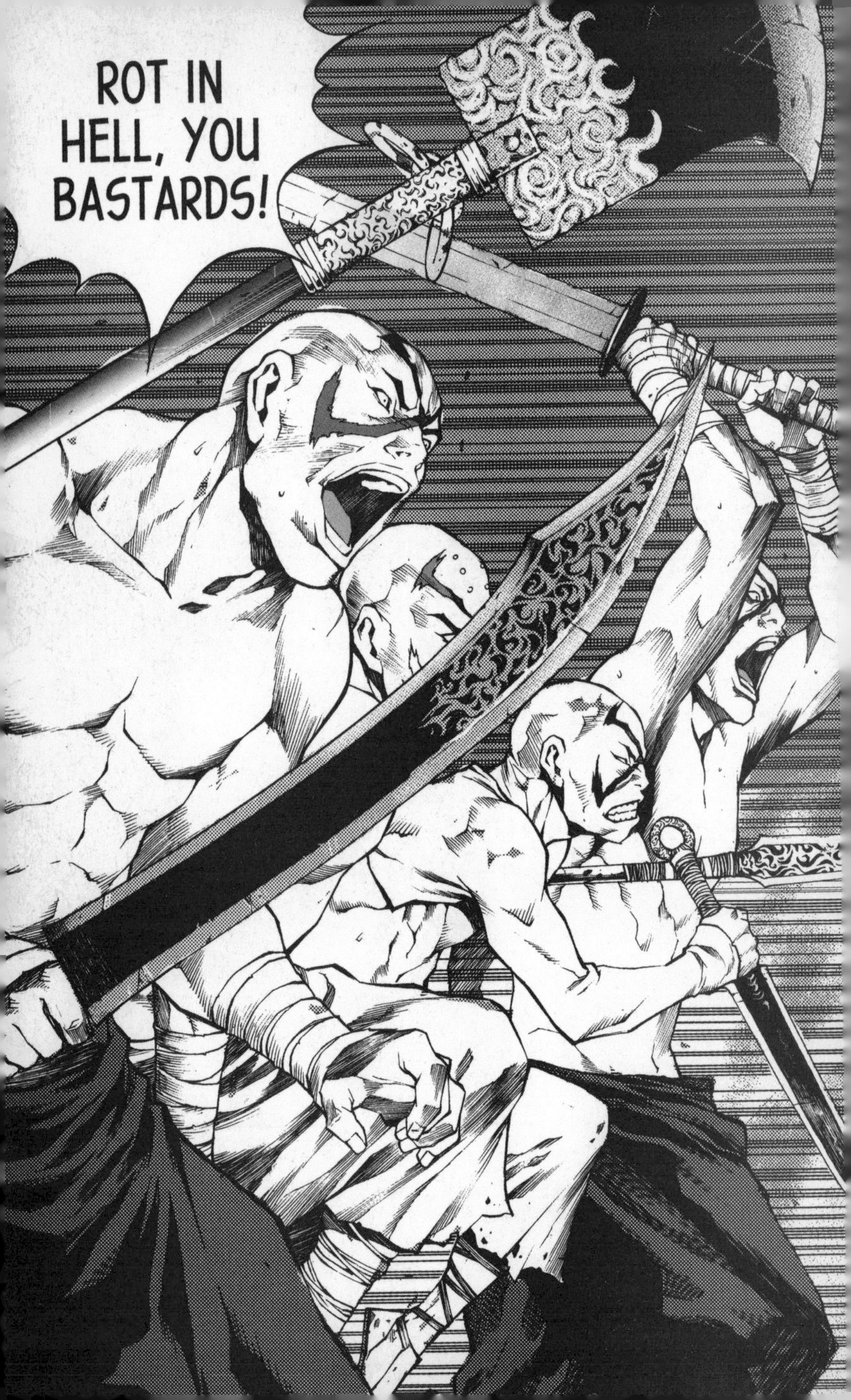
ROT IN HELL, YOU BASTARDS!

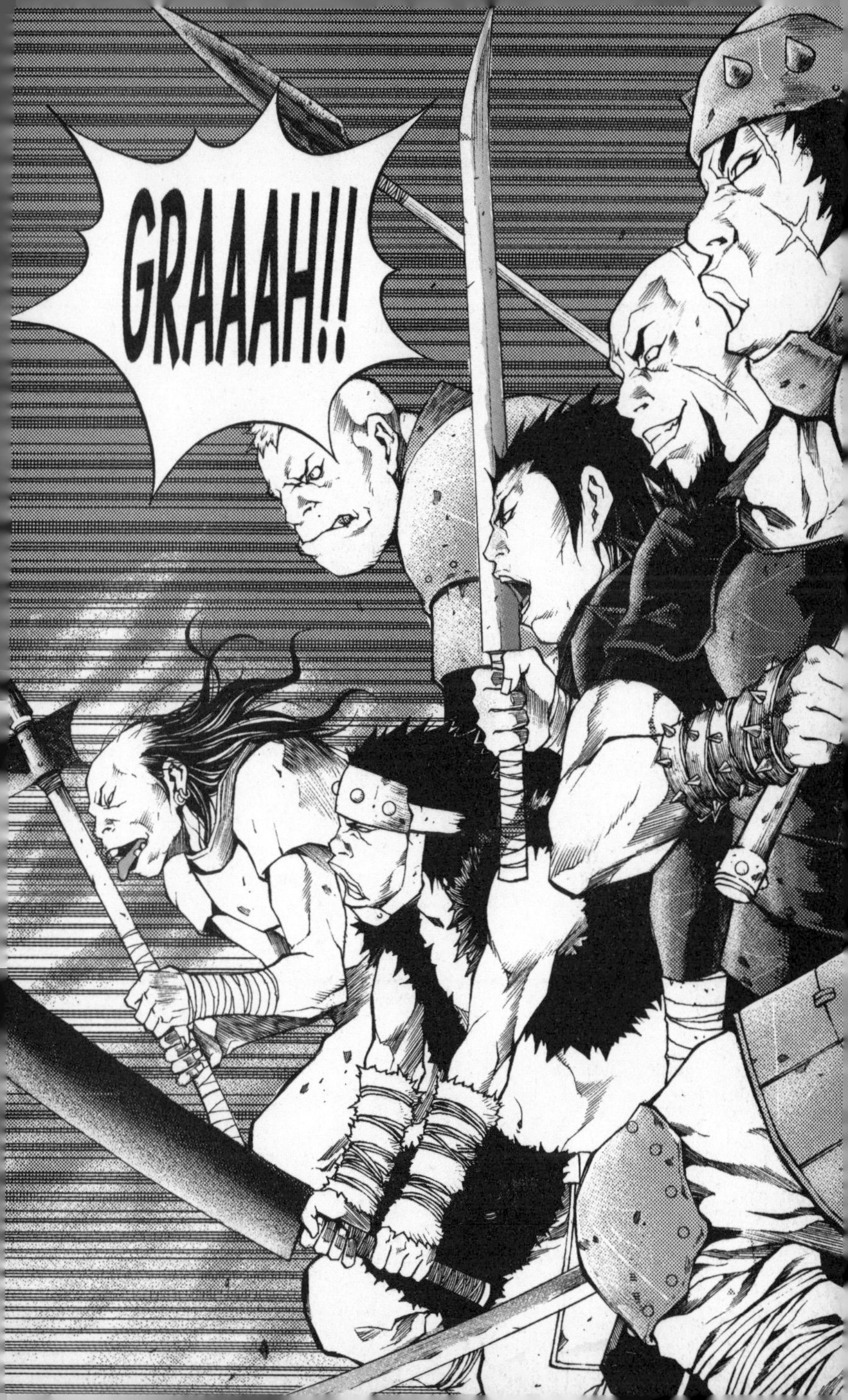
GRAAAH!!

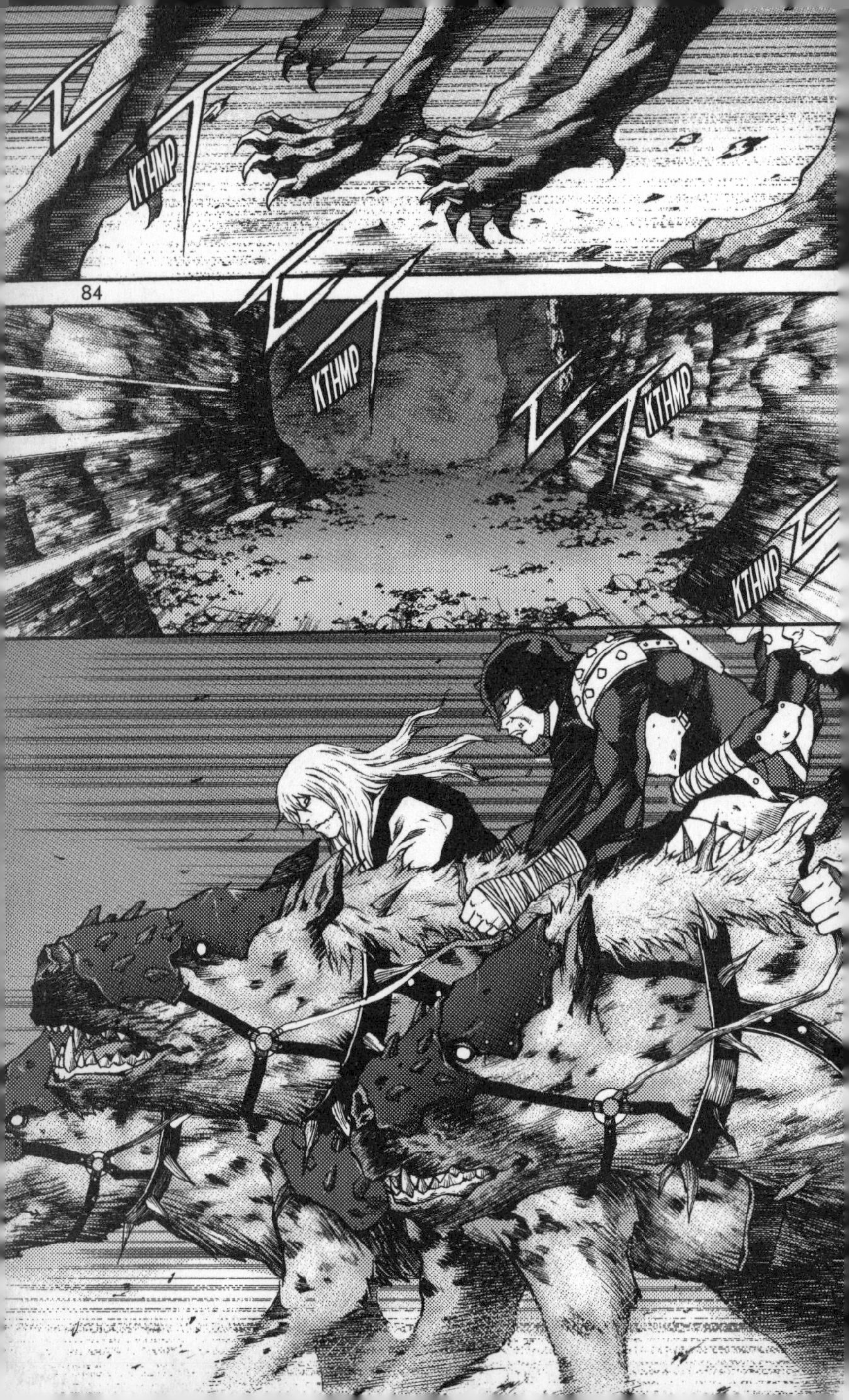
KTHMP
KTHMP
KTHMP
KTHMP

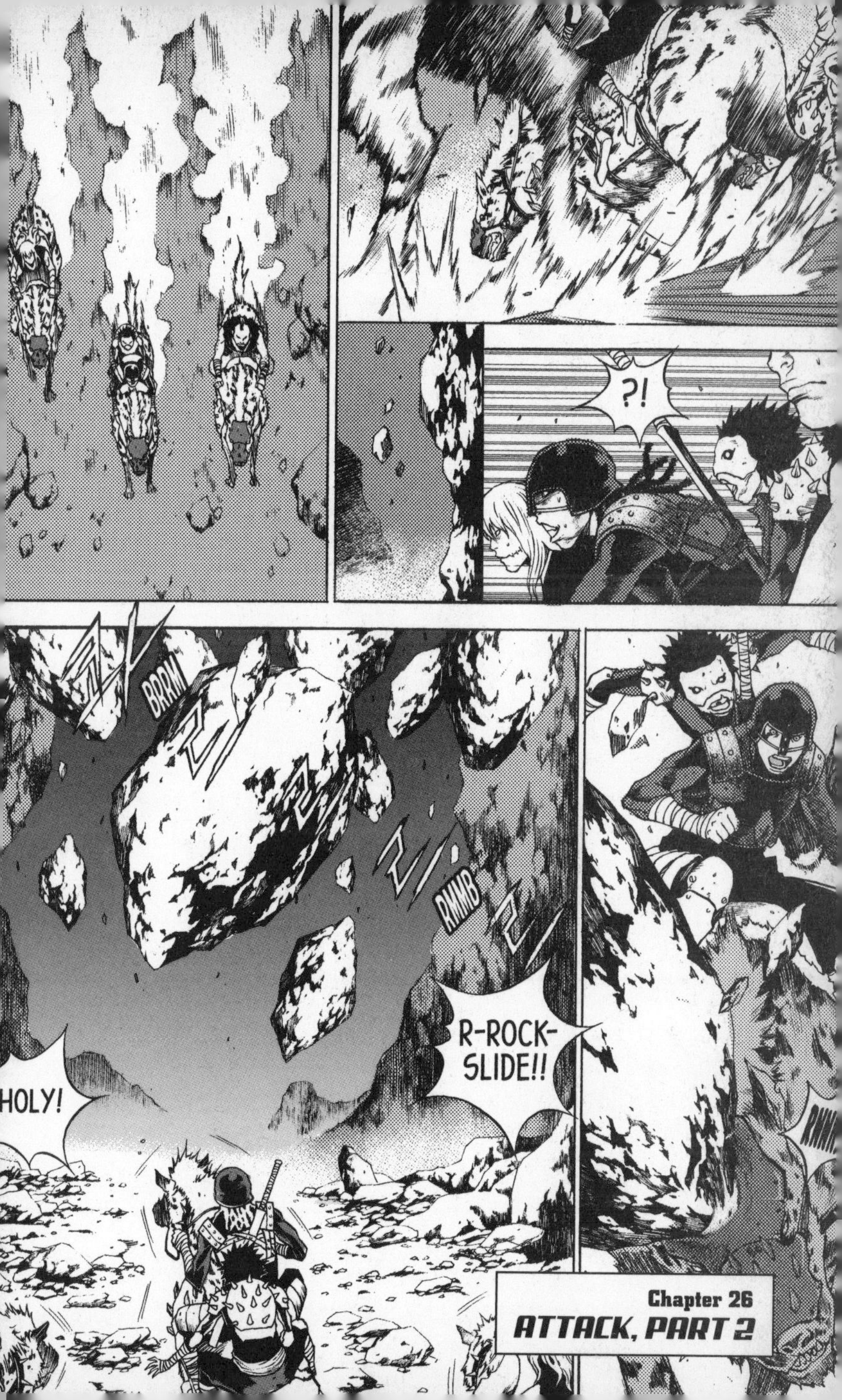
?!
BRRM
RMMB
R-ROCK-SLIDE!!
HOLY!
Chapter 26
ATTACK, PART 2

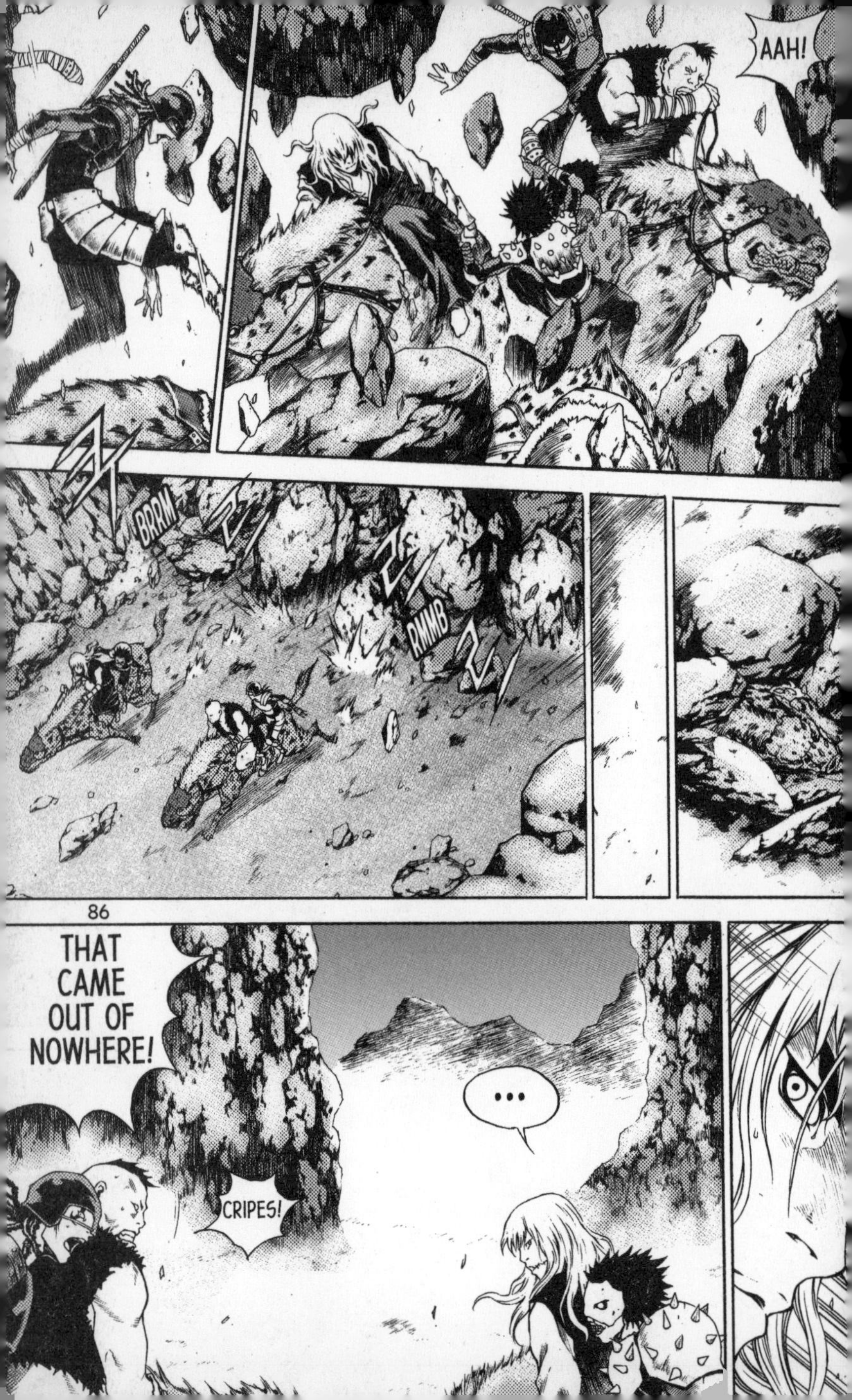
AAH!
BRRM
RMMB
THAT CAME OUT OF NOWHERE!
CRIPES!
...

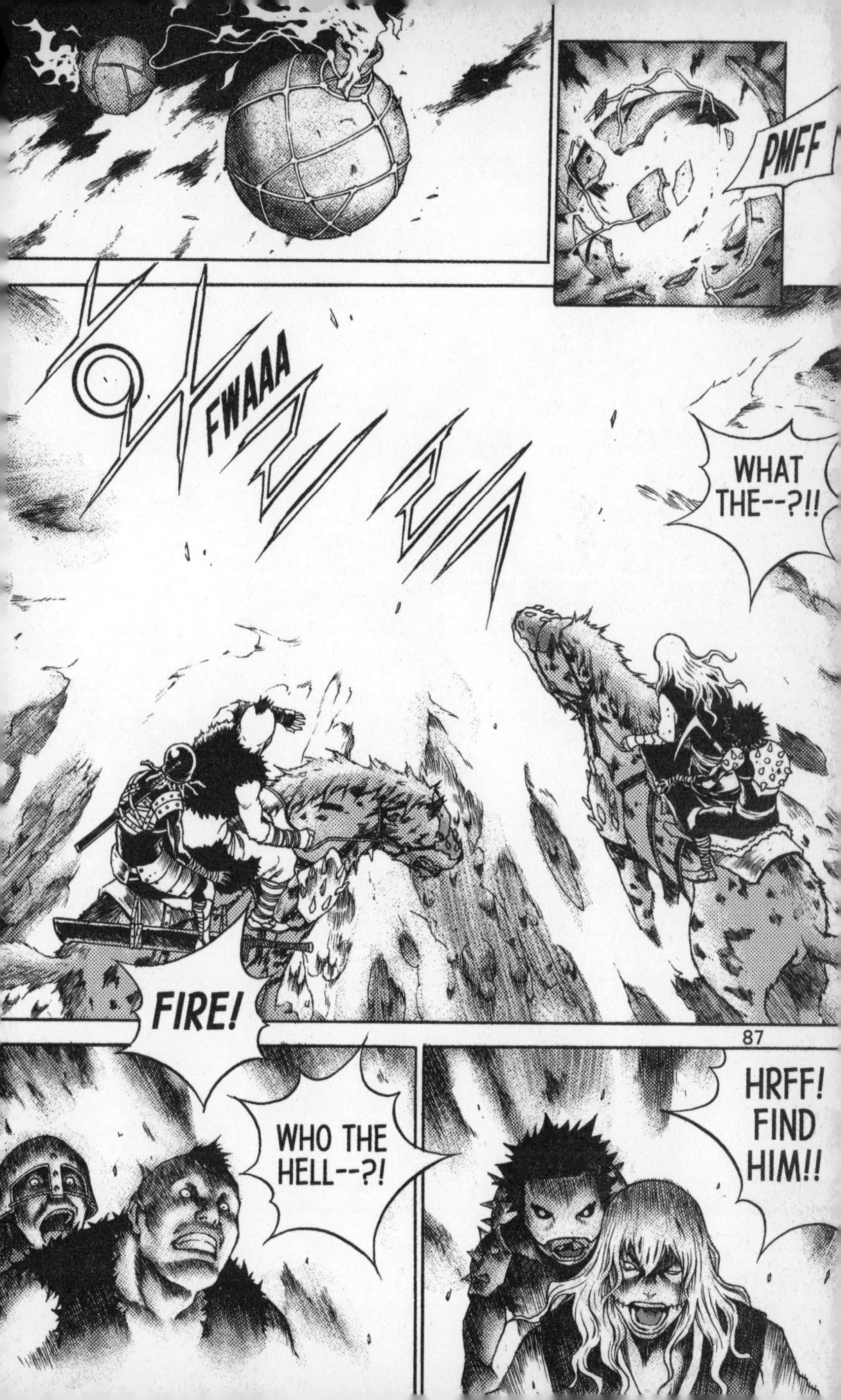
PMFF
FWAAA
WHAT THE--?!!
FIRE!
WHO THE HELL--?!
HRFF! FIND HIM!!

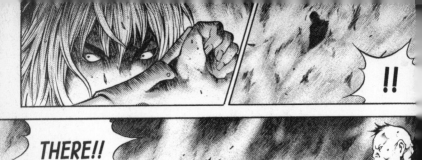

THERE!!

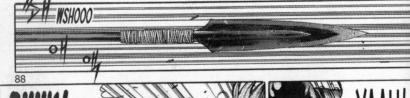

WSHOOO

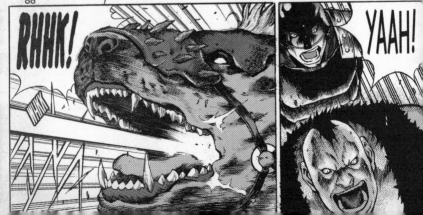

RHHK!

YAAH!

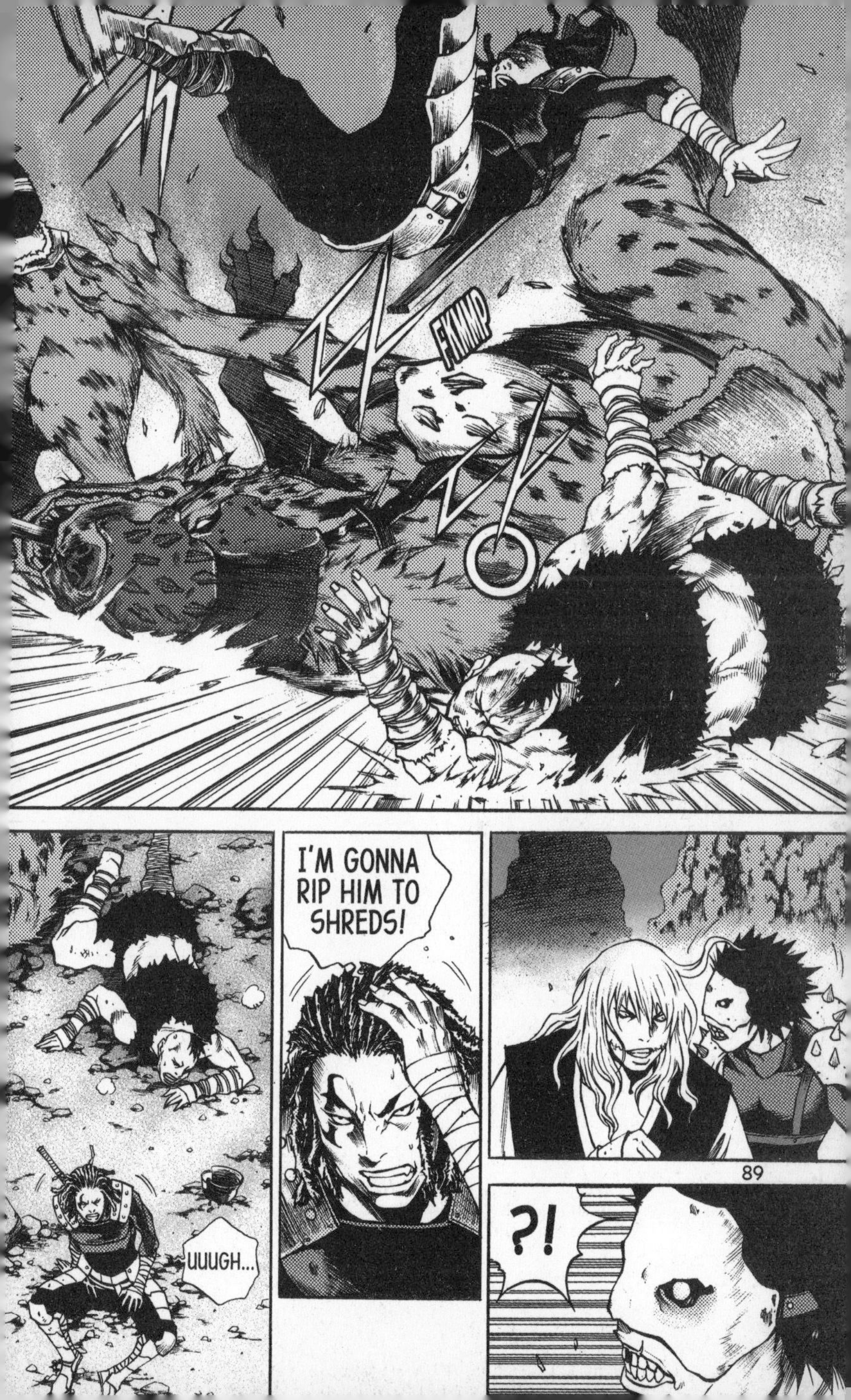
FKMMP
UUUGH...
I'M GONNA RIP HIM TO SHREDS!
?!

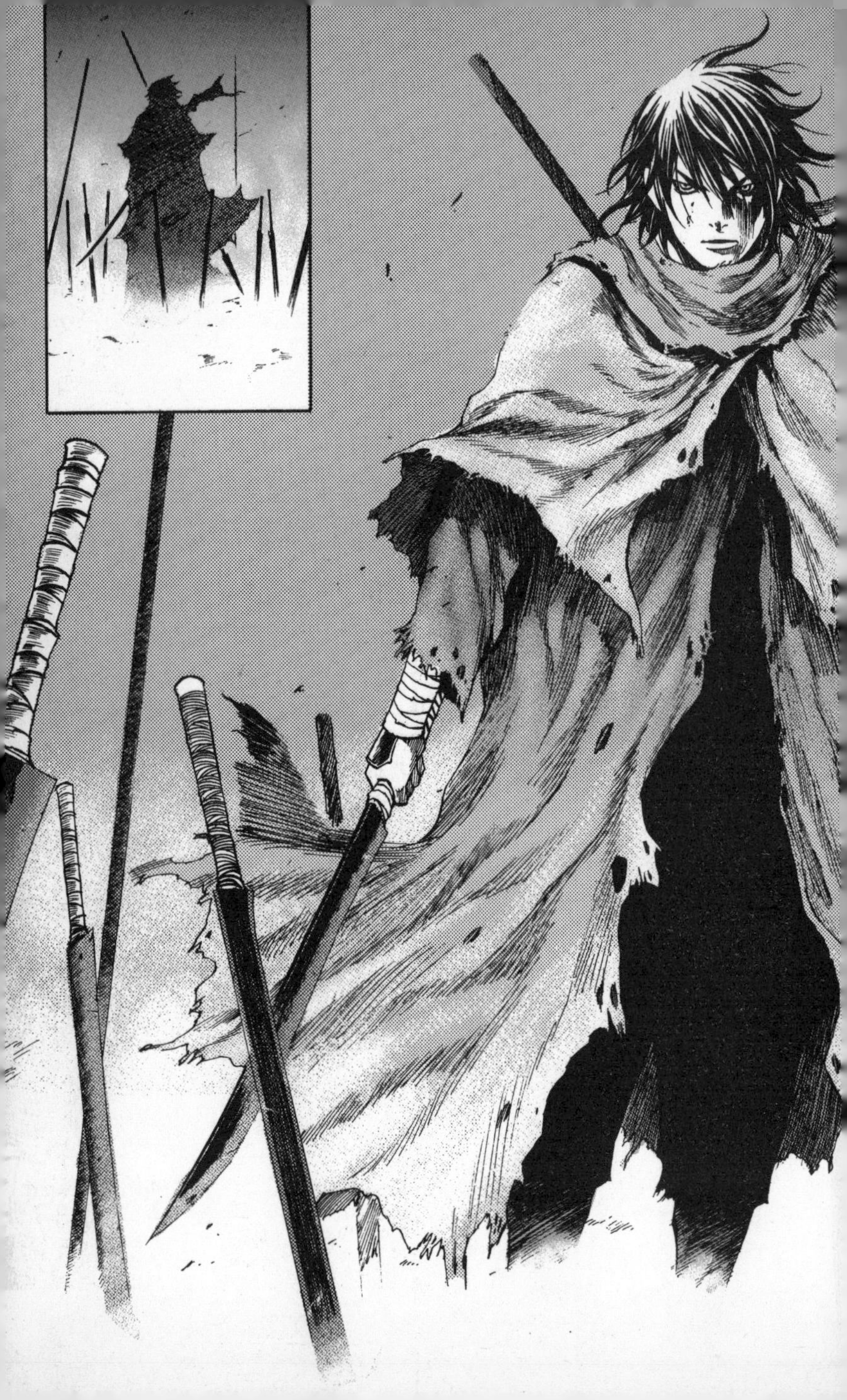

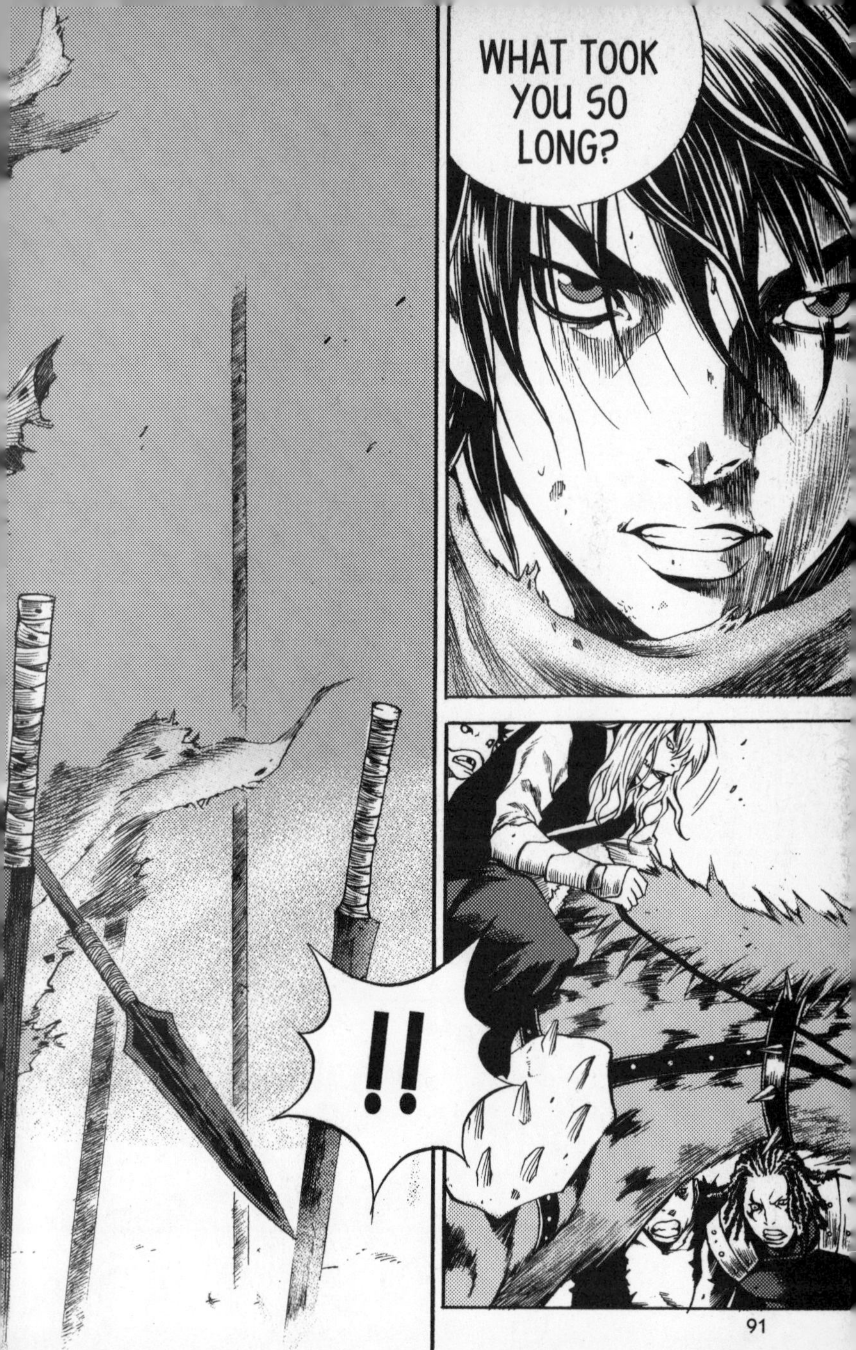
WHAT TOOK YOU SO LONG?
!!

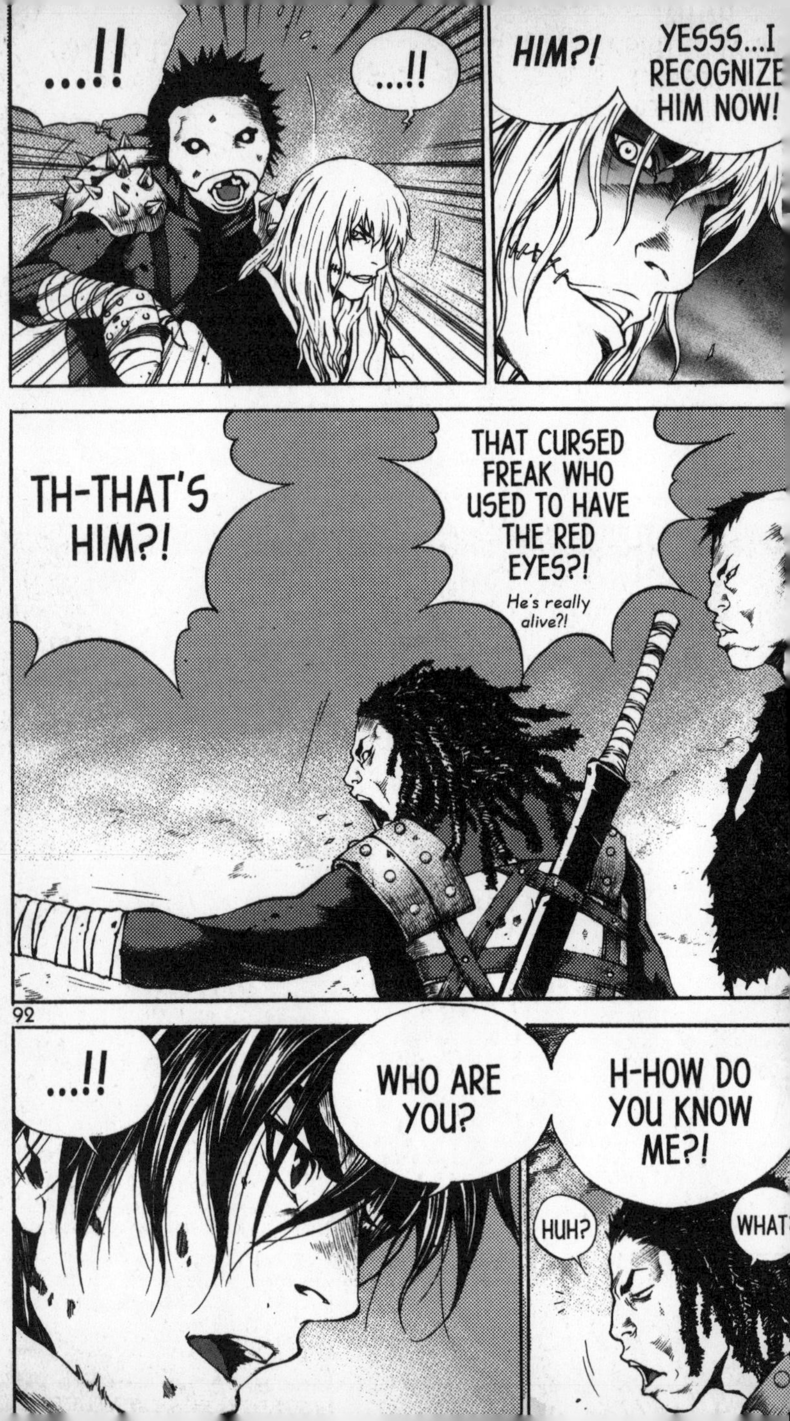
...!!
...!!
HIM?!
YESSS...I RECOGNIZE HIM NOW!
TH-THAT'S HIM?!
THAT CURSED FREAK WHO USED TO HAVE THE RED EYES?!
He's really alive?!
...!!
WHO ARE YOU?
H-HOW DO YOU KNOW ME?!
HUH?
WHAT

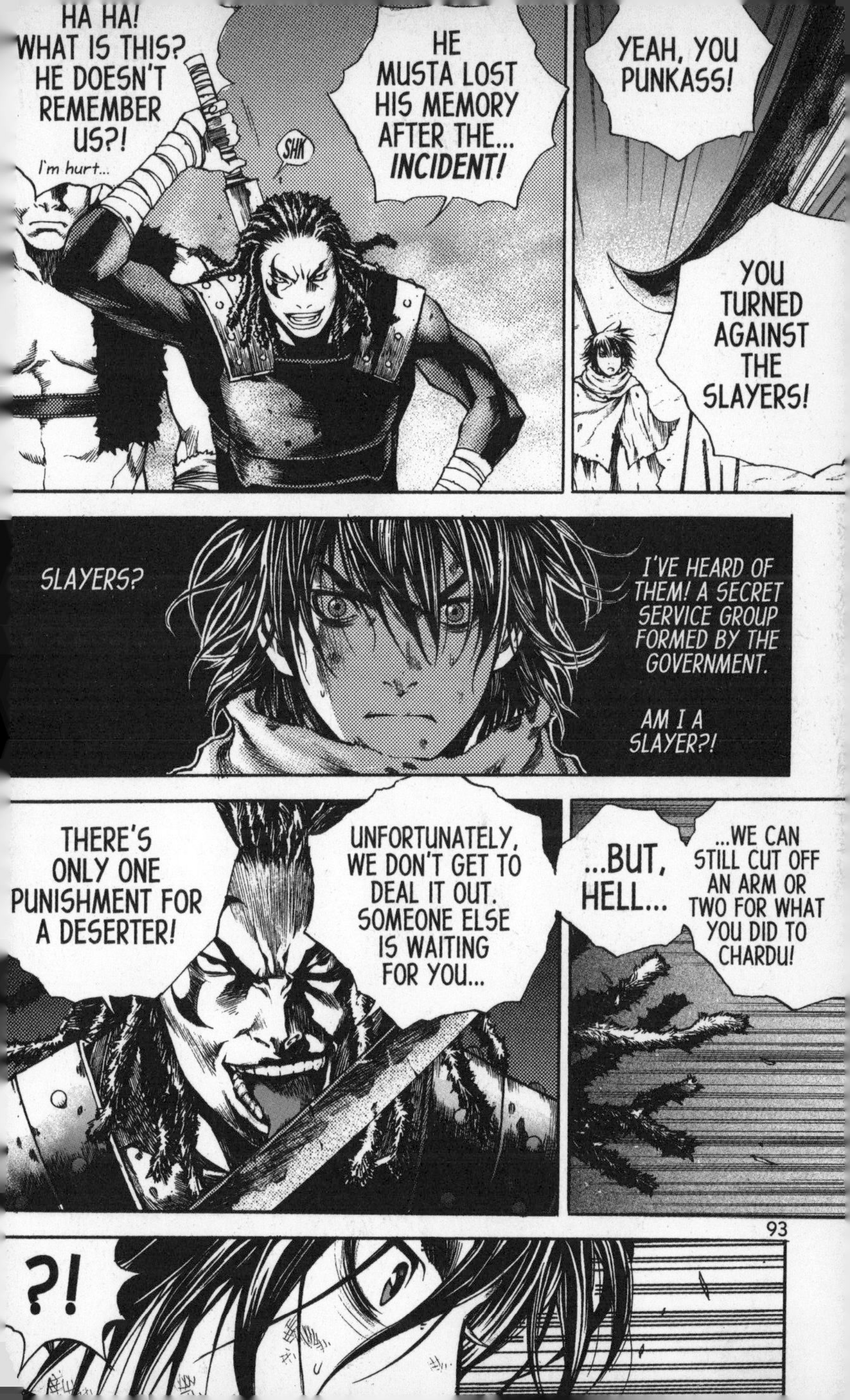
HA HA! WHAT IS THIS? HE DOESN'T REMEMBER US?!
I'm hurt...
SHK
HE MUSTA LOST HIS MEMORY AFTER THE... INCIDENT!
YEAH, YOU PUNKASS!
YOU TURNED AGAINST THE SLAYERS!
SLAYERS?
I'VE HEARD OF THEM! A SECRET SERVICE GROUP FORMED BY THE GOVERNMENT.
AM I A SLAYER?!
THERE'S ONLY ONE PUNISHMENT FOR A DESERTER!
UNFORTUNATELY, WE DON'T GET TO DEAL IT OUT. SOMEONE ELSE IS WAITING FOR YOU...
...BUT, HELL...
...WE CAN STILL CUT OFF AN ARM OR TWO FOR WHAT YOU DID TO CHARDU!
?!

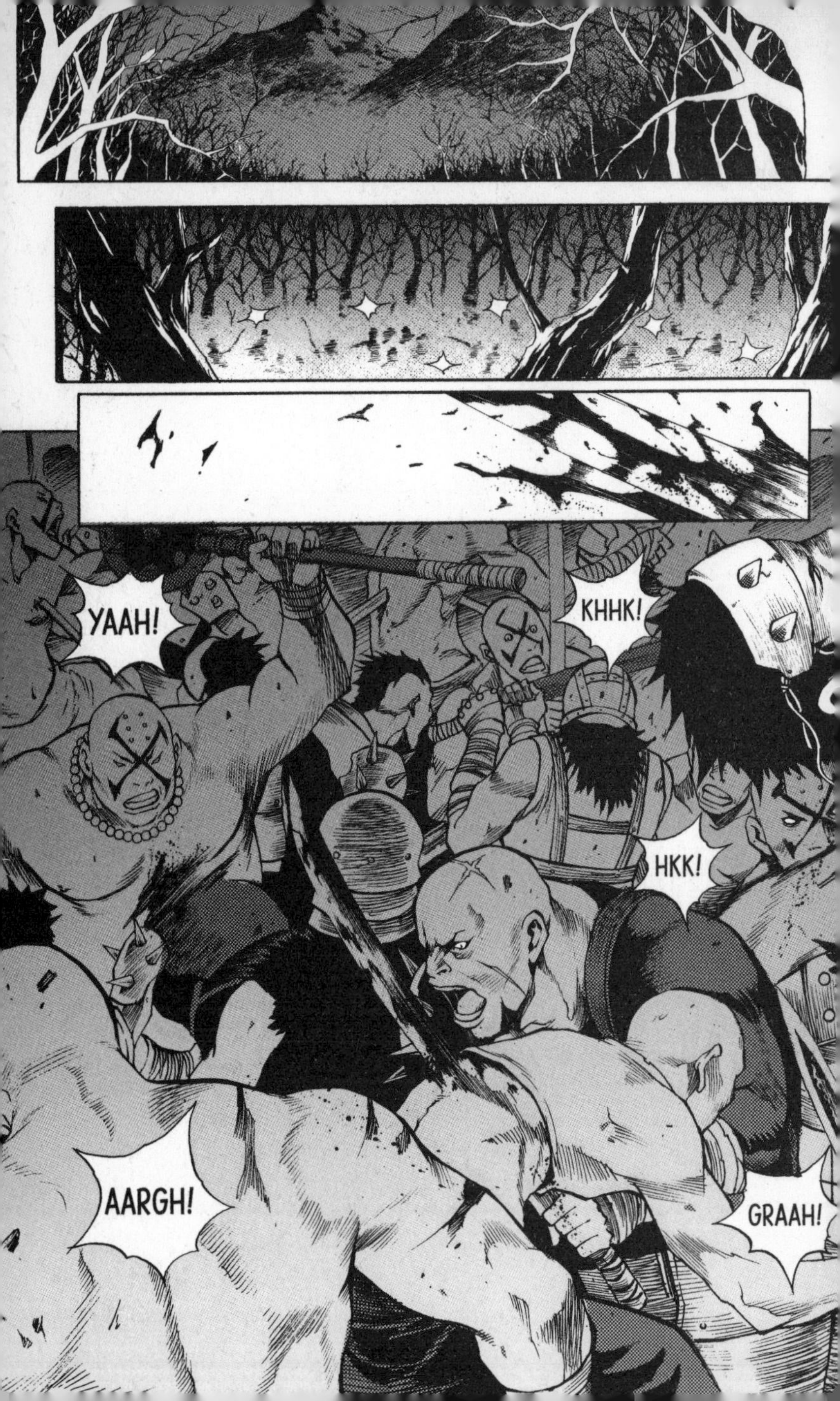
YAAH!
KHHK!
HKK!
AARGH!
GRAAH!

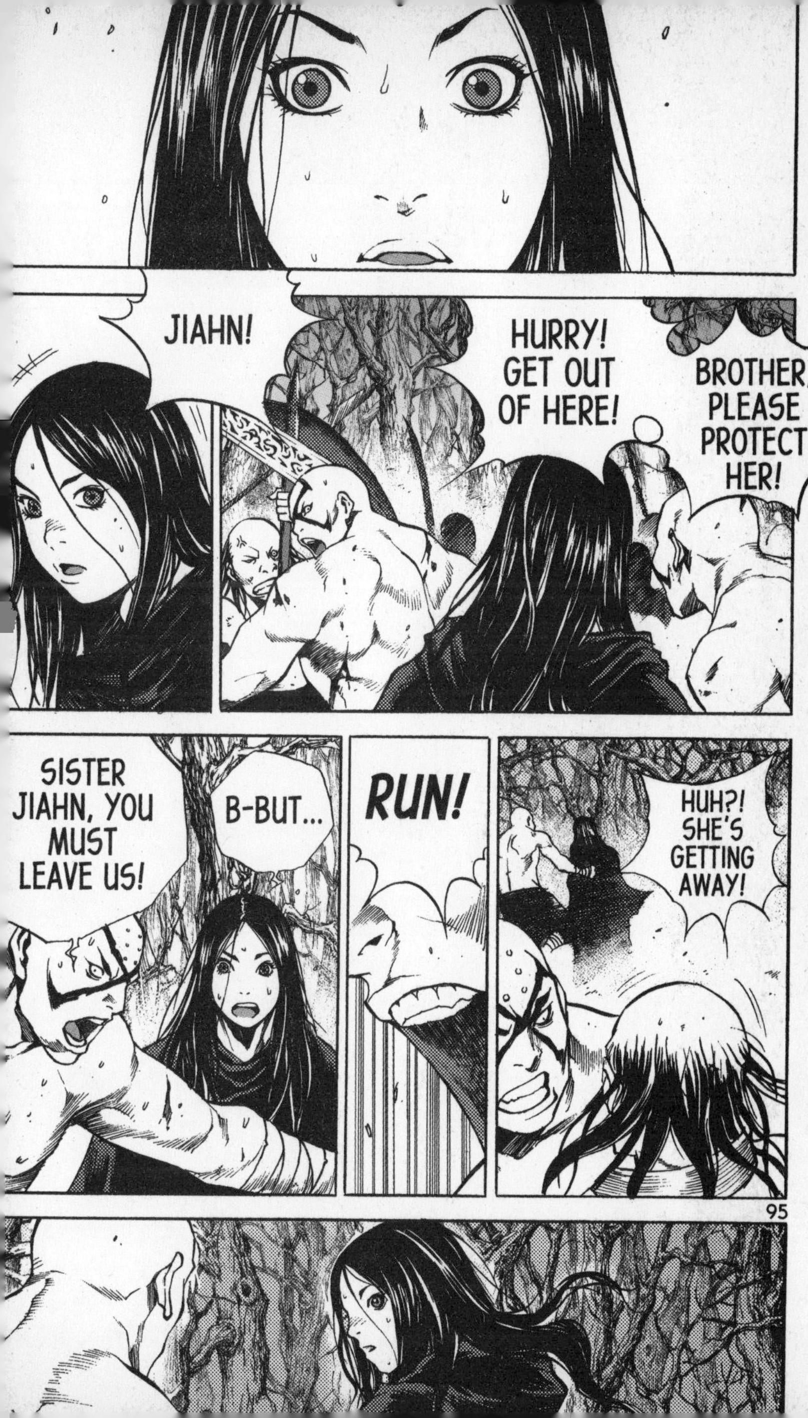
JIAHN!
HURRY! GET OUT OF HERE!
BROTHER, PLEASE PROTECT HER!
SISTER JIAHN, YOU MUST LEAVE US!
B-BUT...
RUN!
HUH?! SHE'S GETTING AWAY!

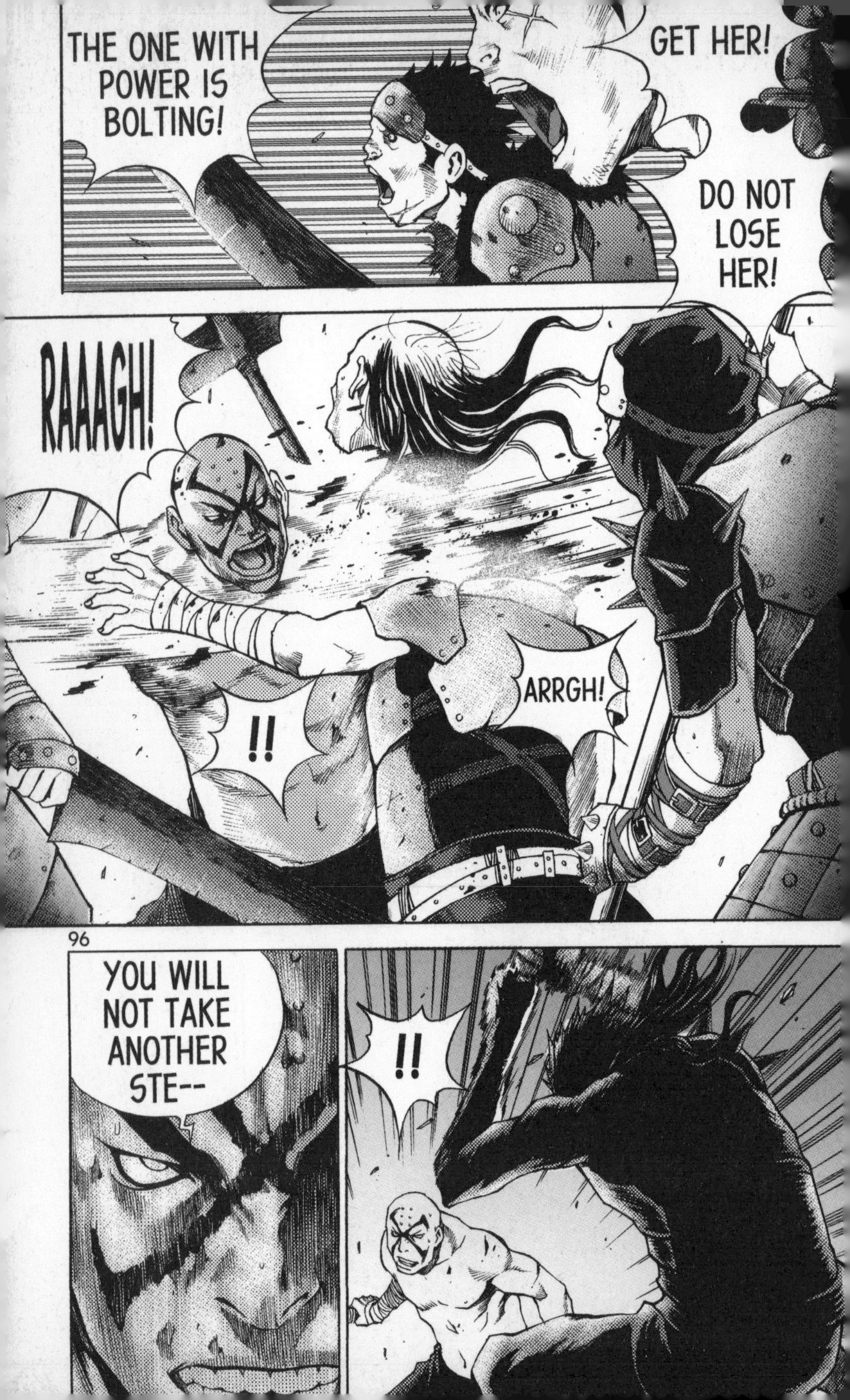
THE ONE WITH POWER IS BOLTING!
GET HER!
DO NOT LOSE HER!
RAAAGH!
ARRGH!
!!
YOU WILL NOT TAKE ANOTHER STE--
!!

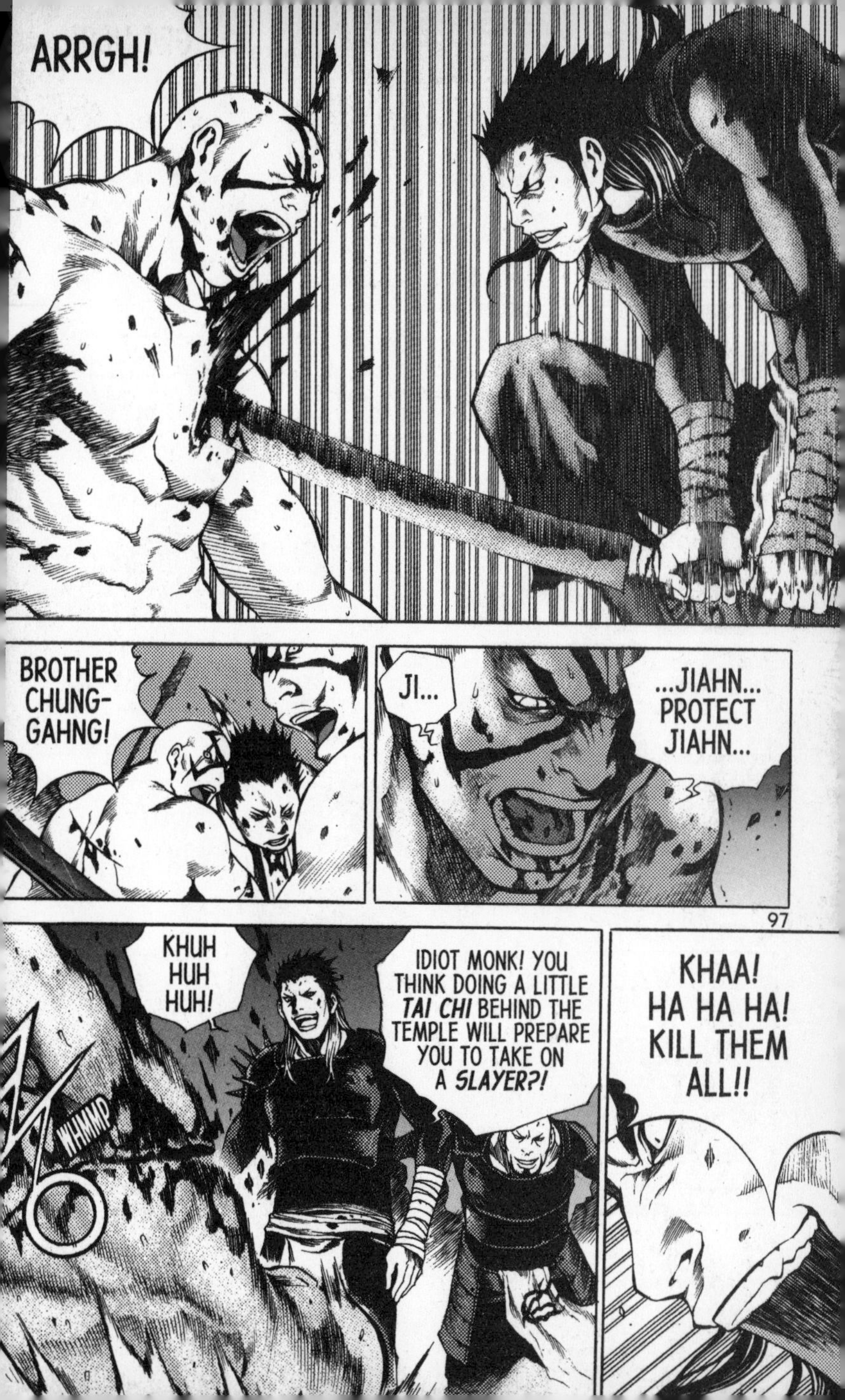
ARRGH!
BROTHER CHUNG-GAHNG!
JI...
...JIAHN... PROTECT JIAHN...
KHUH HUH HUH!
IDIOT MONK! YOU THINK DOING A LITTLE *TAI CHI* BEHIND THE TEMPLE WILL PREPARE YOU TO TAKE ON A *SLAYER?!*
WHMMP
KHAA! HA HA HA! KILL THEM ALL!!

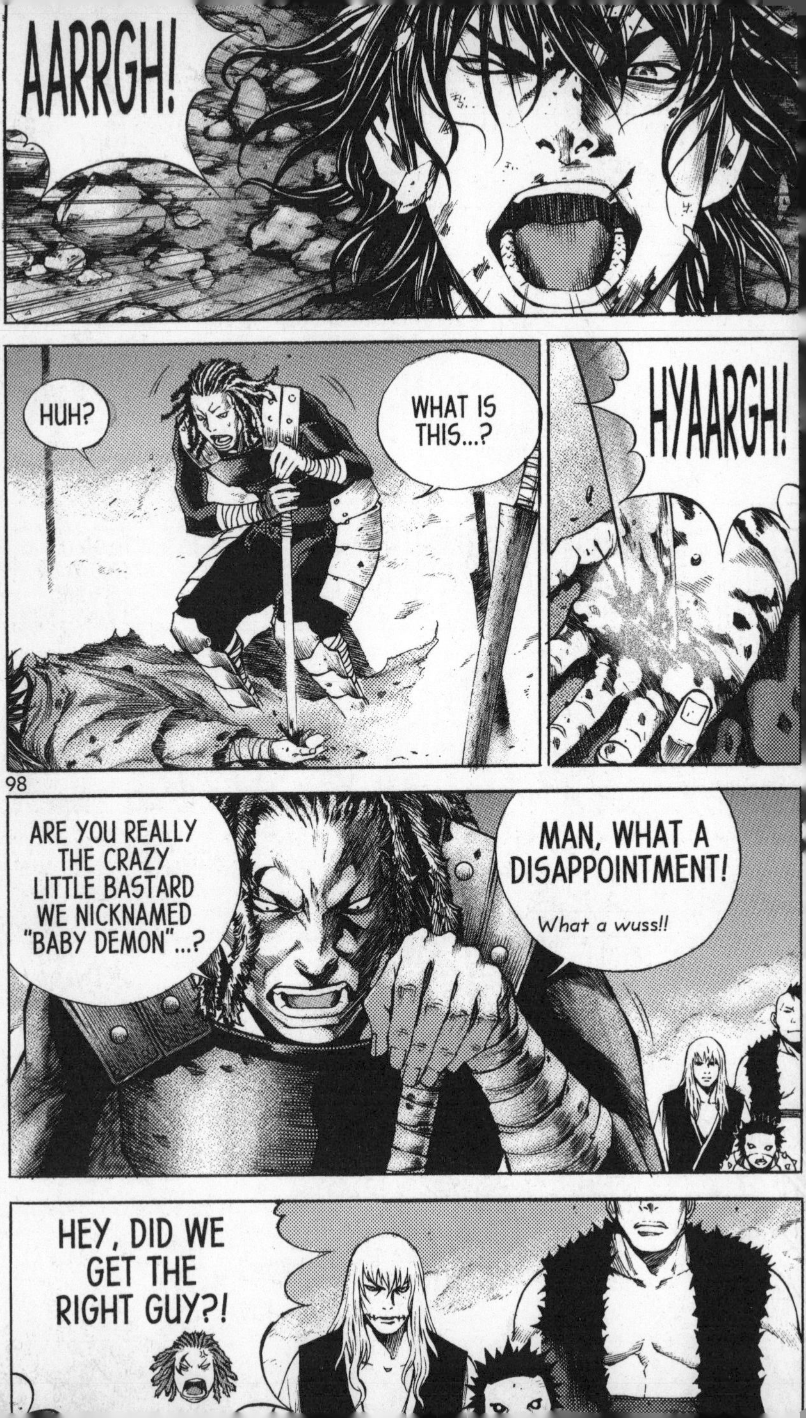
AARRGH!
HUH?
WHAT IS THIS...?
HYAARGH!
ARE YOU REALLY THE CRAZY LITTLE BASTARD WE NICKNAMED "BABY DEMON"...?
MAN, WHAT A DISAPPOINTMENT!
What a wuss!!
HEY, DID WE GET THE RIGHT GUY?!

98

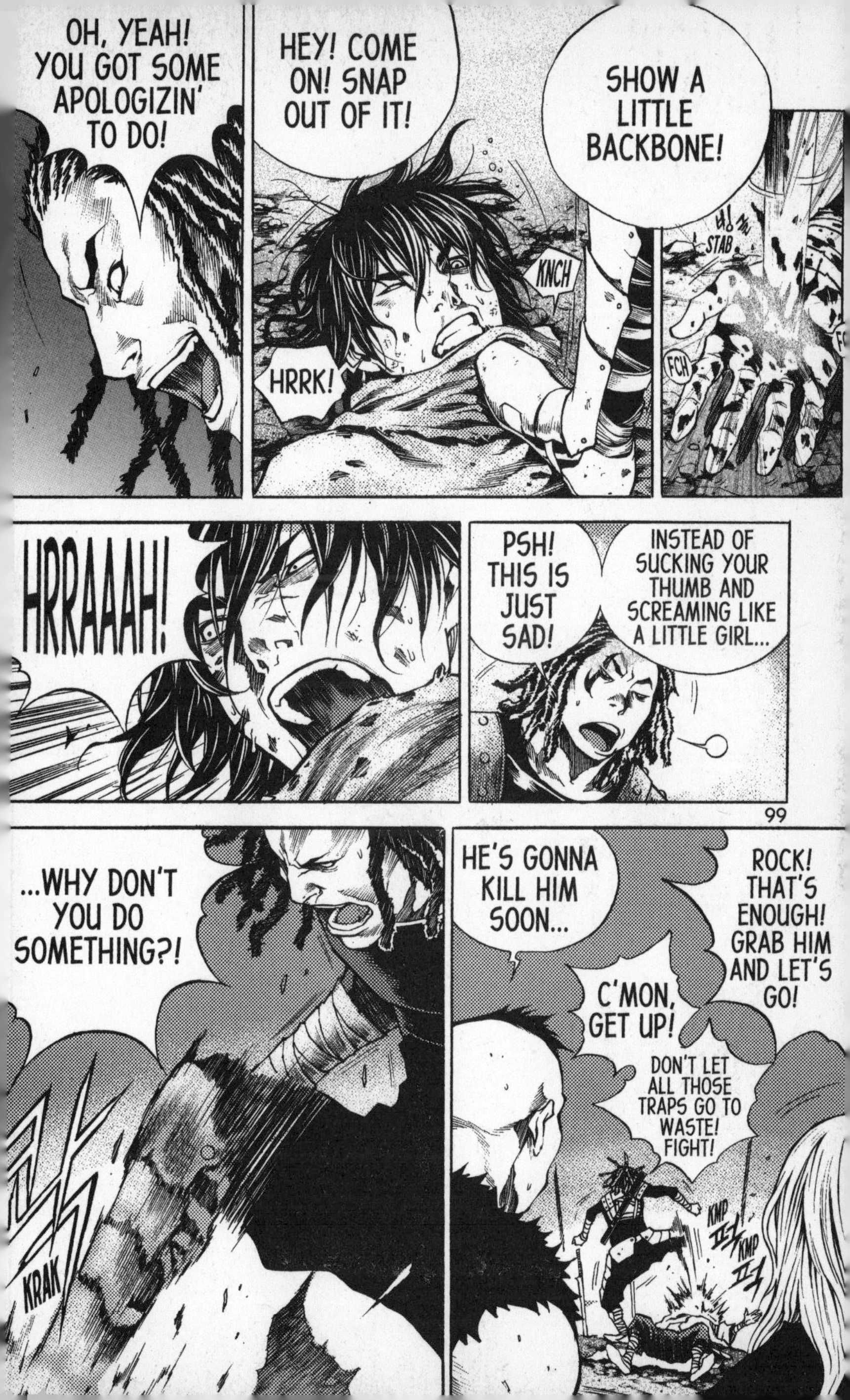
OH, YEAH! YOU GOT SOME APOLOGIZIN' TO DO!
HEY! COME ON! SNAP OUT OF IT!
KNCH
HRRK!
SHOW A LITTLE BACKBONE!
STAB
FCH
HRRAAAH!
PSH! THIS IS JUST SAD!
INSTEAD OF SUCKING YOUR THUMB AND SCREAMING LIKE A LITTLE GIRL...
...WHY DON'T YOU DO SOMETHING?!
KRAK
HE'S GONNA KILL HIM SOON...
ROCK! THAT'S ENOUGH! GRAB HIM AND LET'S GO!
C'MON, GET UP!
DON'T LET ALL THOSE TRAPS GO TO WASTE! FIGHT!
KMP
KMP

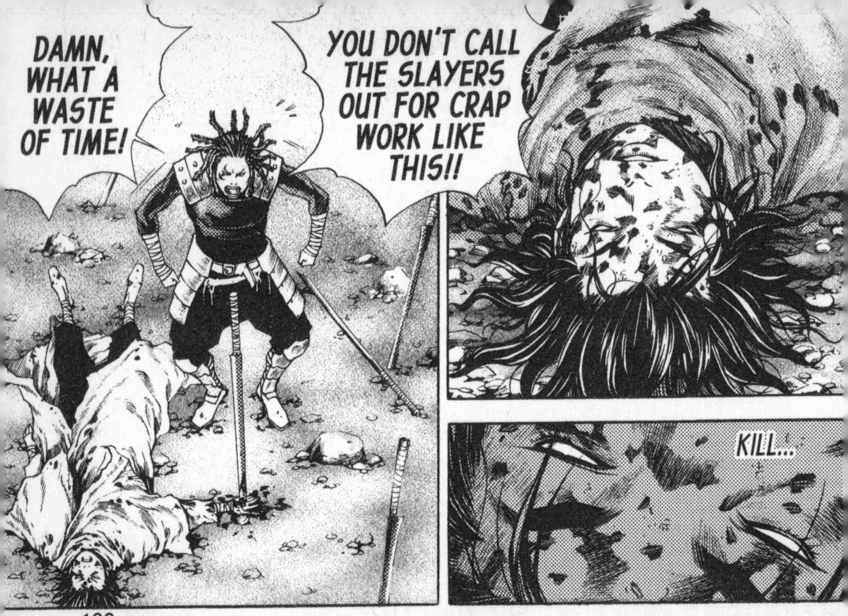
DAMN, WHAT A WASTE OF TIME!
YOU DON'T CALL THE SLAYERS OUT FOR CRAP WORK LIKE THIS!!
KILL...

100

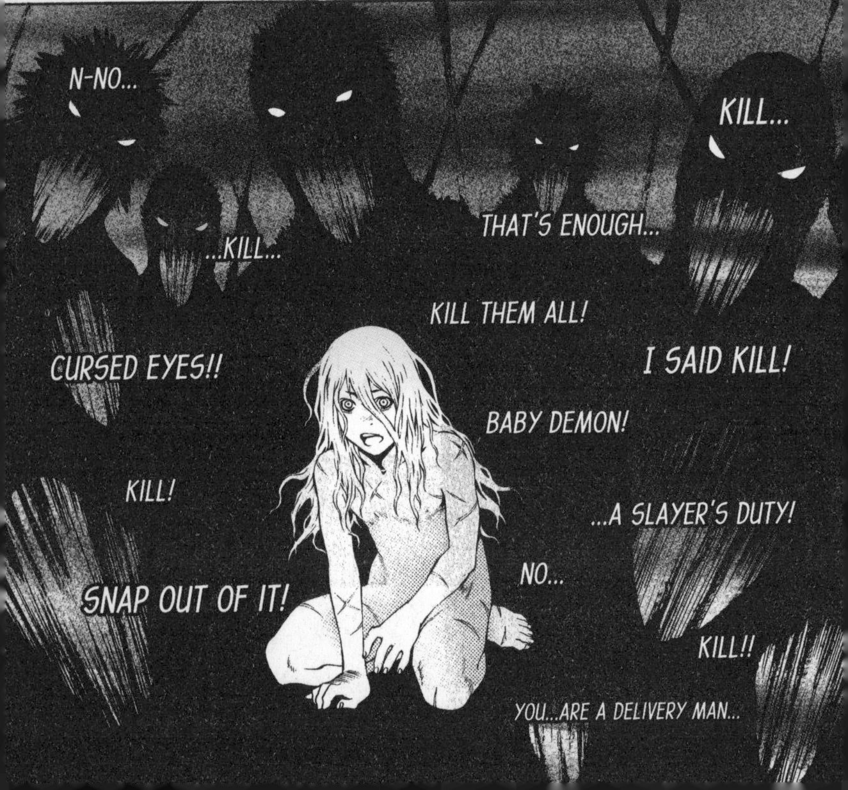
N-NO...
KILL...
THAT'S ENOUGH...
...KILL...
KILL THEM ALL!
I SAID KILL!
CURSED EYES!!
BABY DEMON!
KILL!
...A SLAYER'S DUTY!
NO...
SNAP OUT OF IT!
KILL!!
YOU...ARE A DELIVERY MAN...

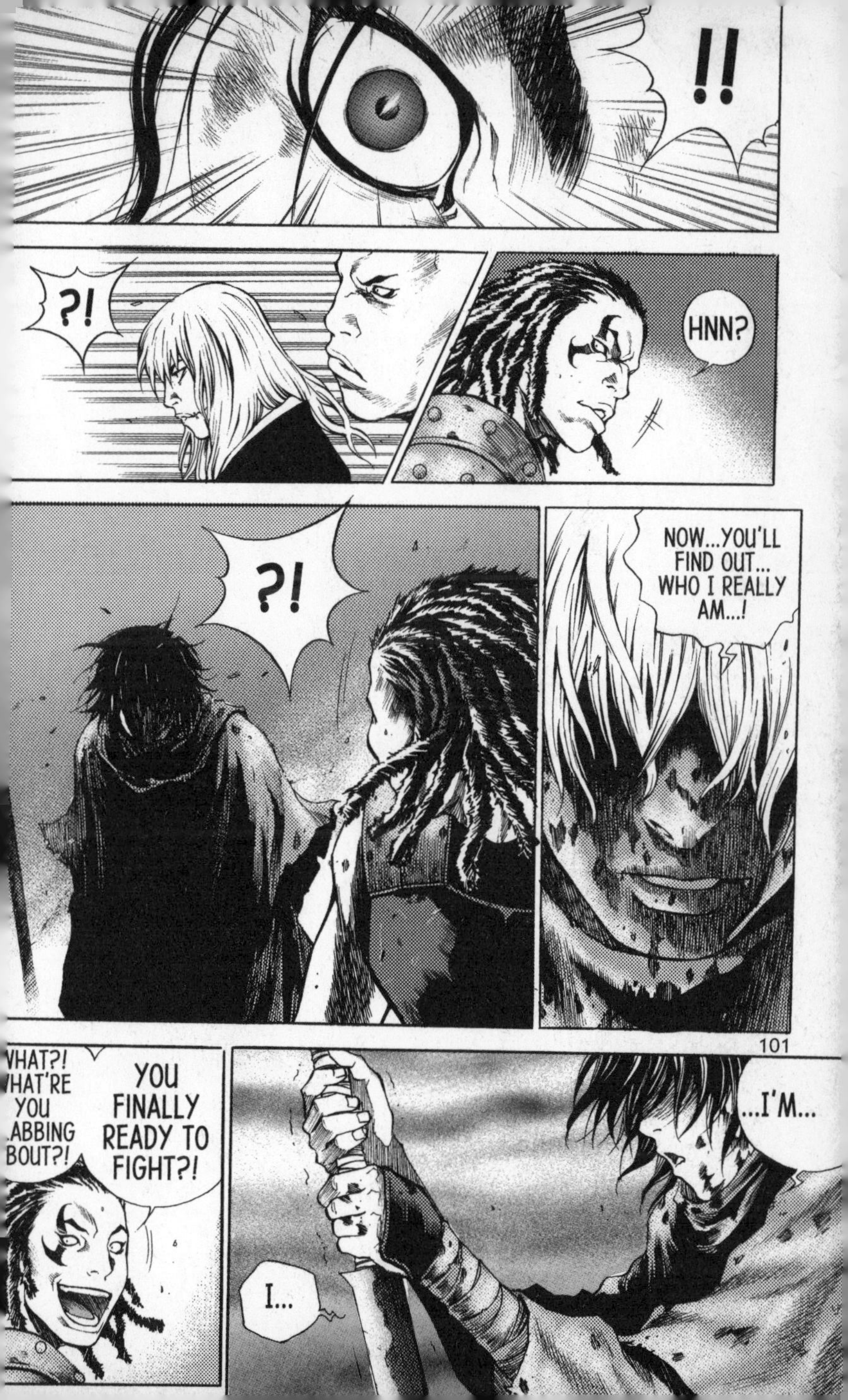
!!
?!
HNN?
?!
NOW...YOU'LL FIND OUT... WHO I REALLY AM...!
VHAT?! VHAT'RE YOU ABBING BOUT?!
YOU FINALLY READY TO FIGHT?!
I...
...I'M...

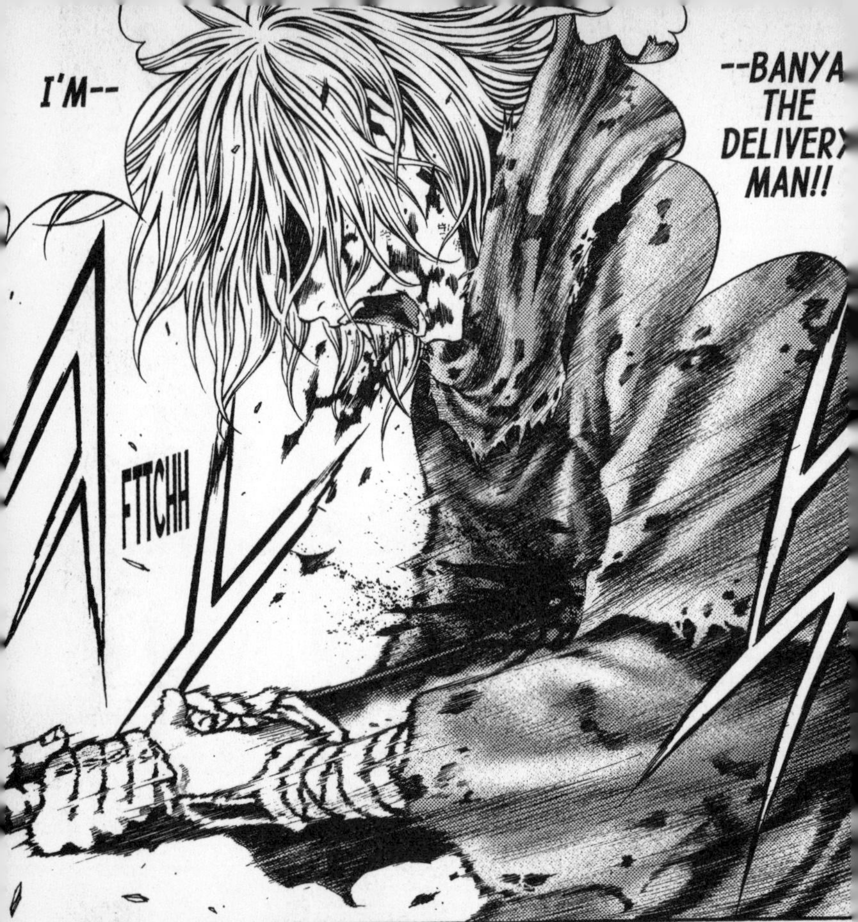
I'M--
--BANYA THE DELIVERY MAN!!
FTTCHH

102

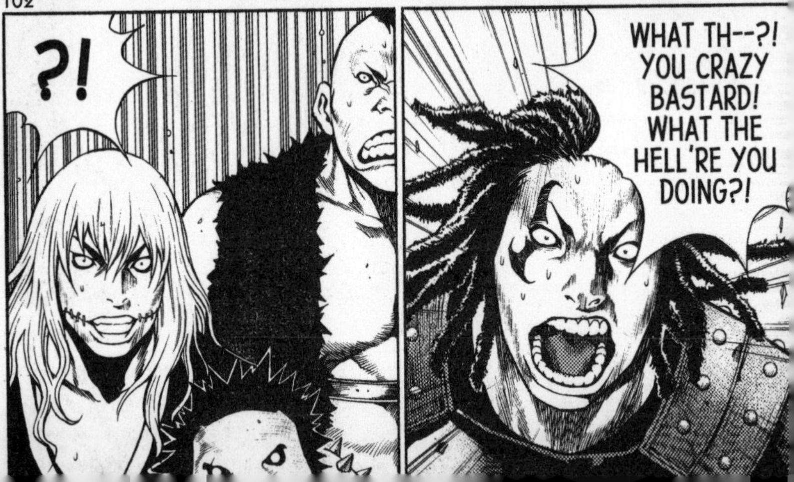
WHAT TH--?! YOU CRAZY BASTARD! WHAT THE HELL'RE YOU DOING?!
?!

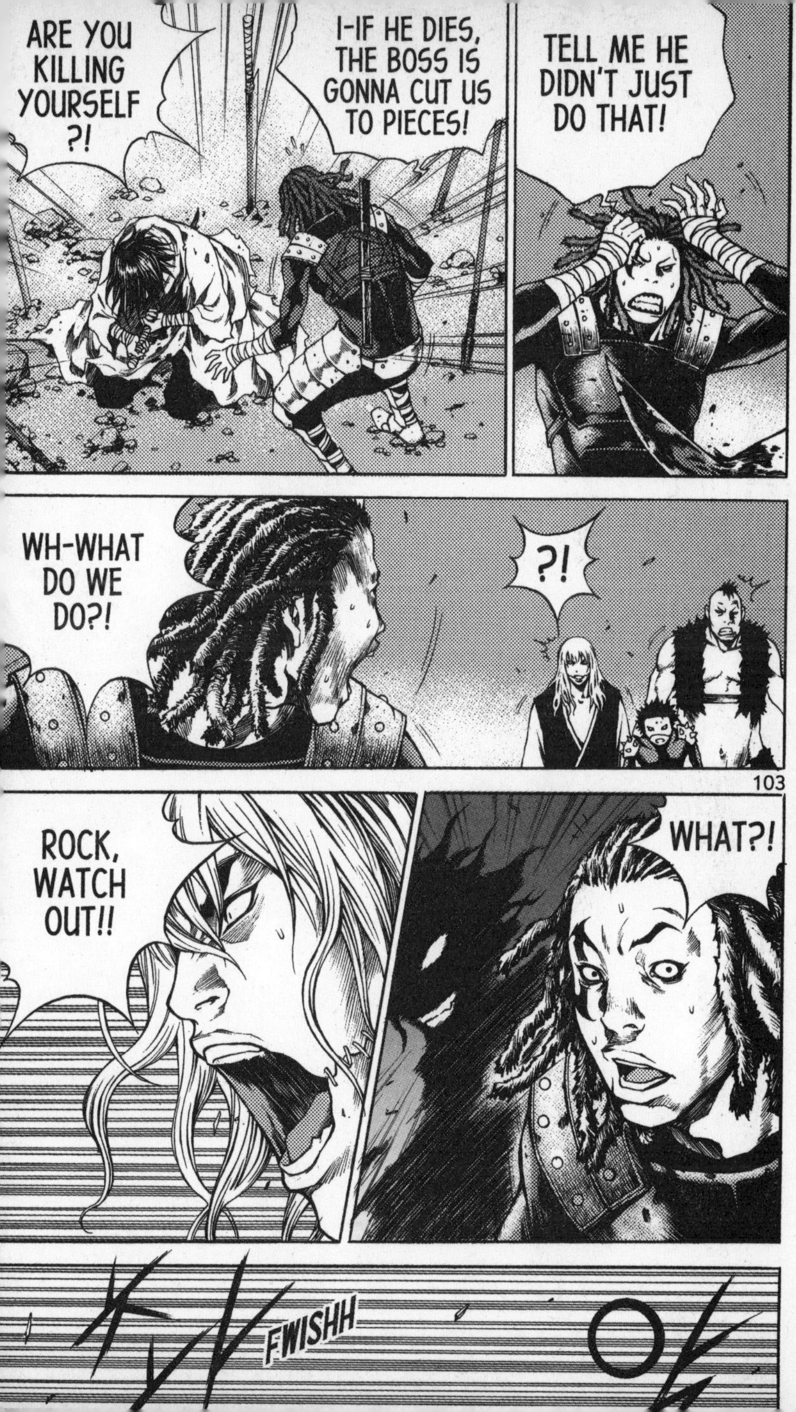
ARE YOU KILLING YOURSELF ?!
I-IF HE DIES, THE BOSS IS GONNA CUT US TO PIECES!
TELL ME HE DIDN'T JUST DO THAT!
WH-WHAT DO WE DO?!
?!
ROCK, WATCH OUT!!
WHAT?!
FWISHH

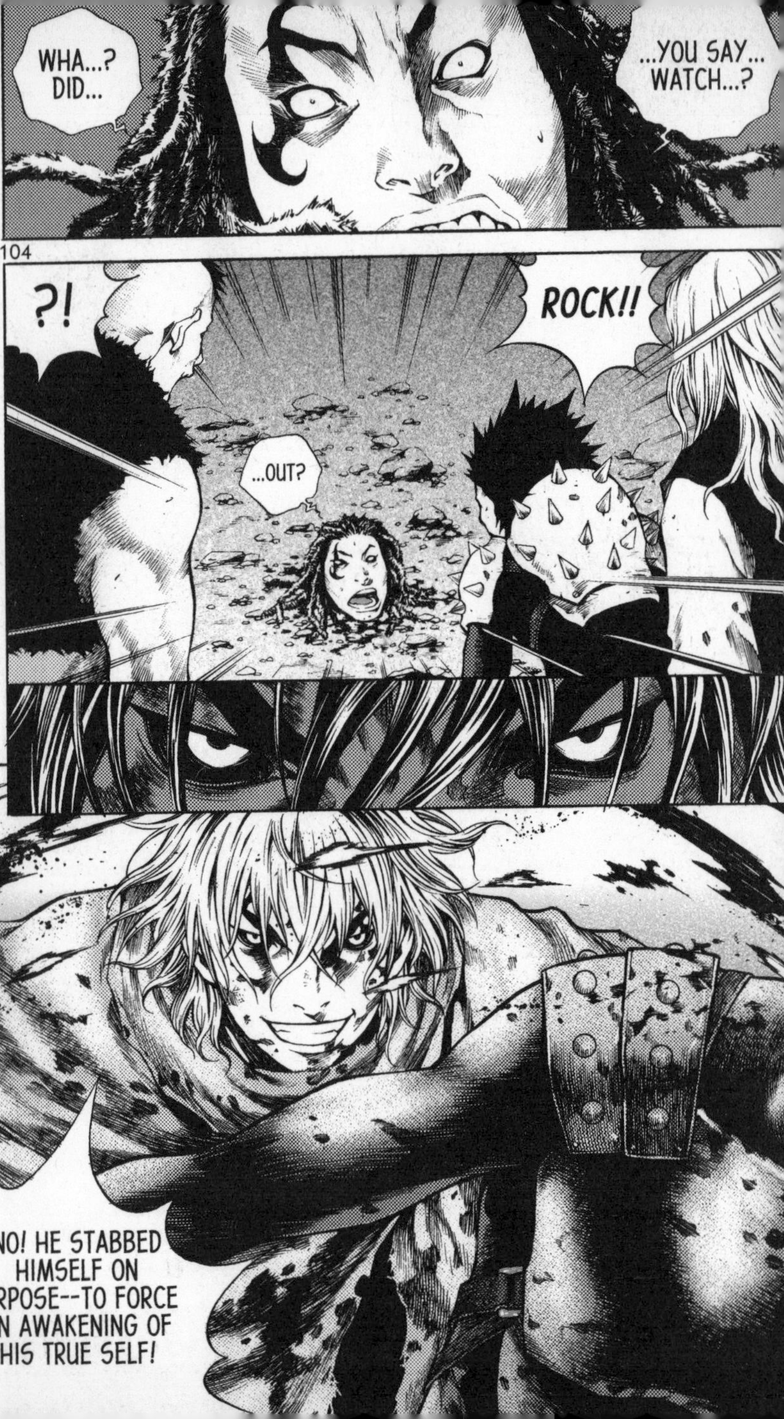
WHA...? DID...
...YOU SAY... WATCH...?
?!
ROCK!!
...OUT?
NO! HE STABBED HIMSELF ON PURPOSE--TO FORCE AN AWAKENING OF HIS TRUE SELF!

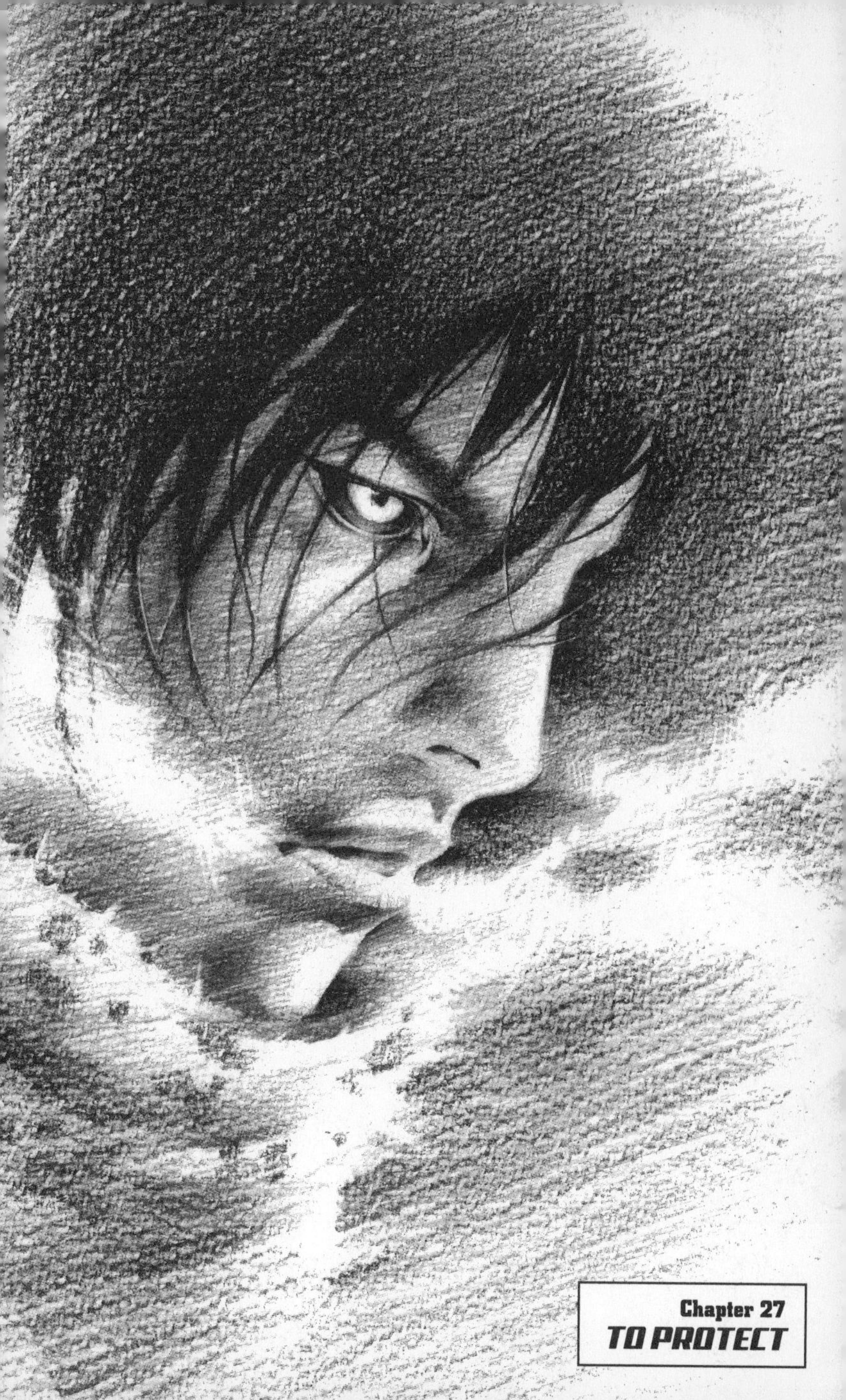

## Chapter 27
## TO PROTECT

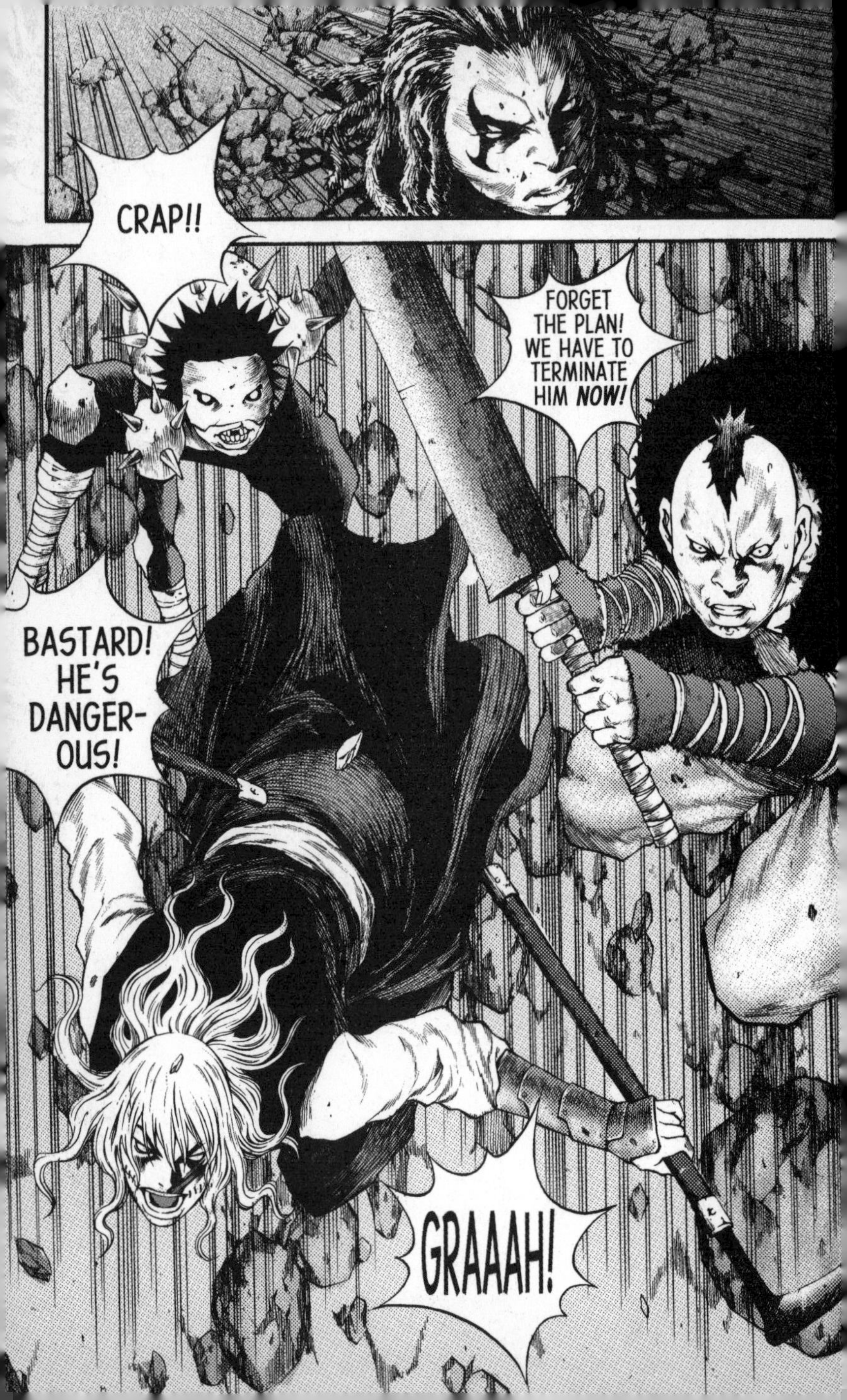
CRAP!!
FORGET THE PLAN! WE HAVE TO TERMINATE HIM NOW!
BASTARD! HE'S DANGER-OUS!
GRAAAH!

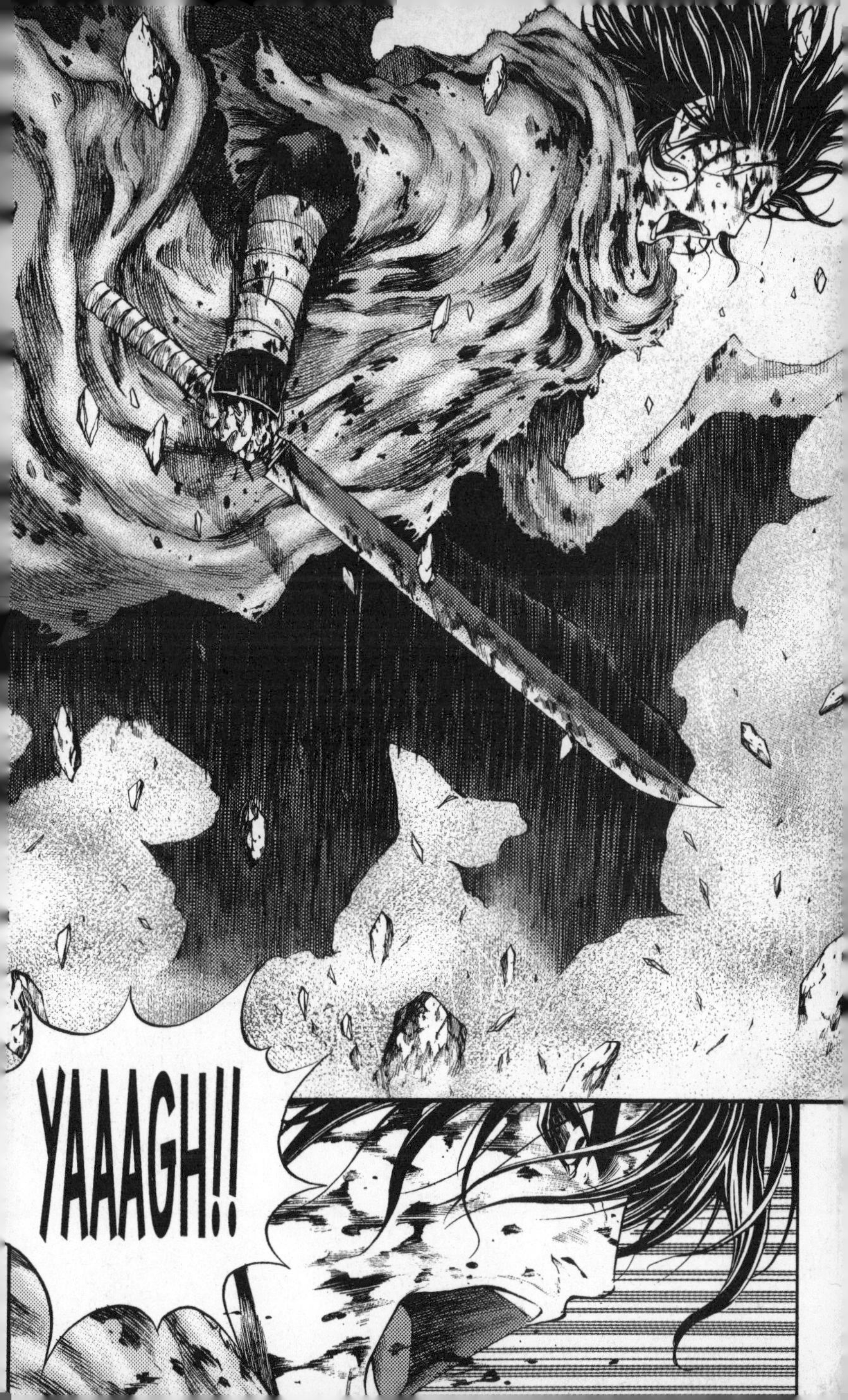
YAAAGH!!

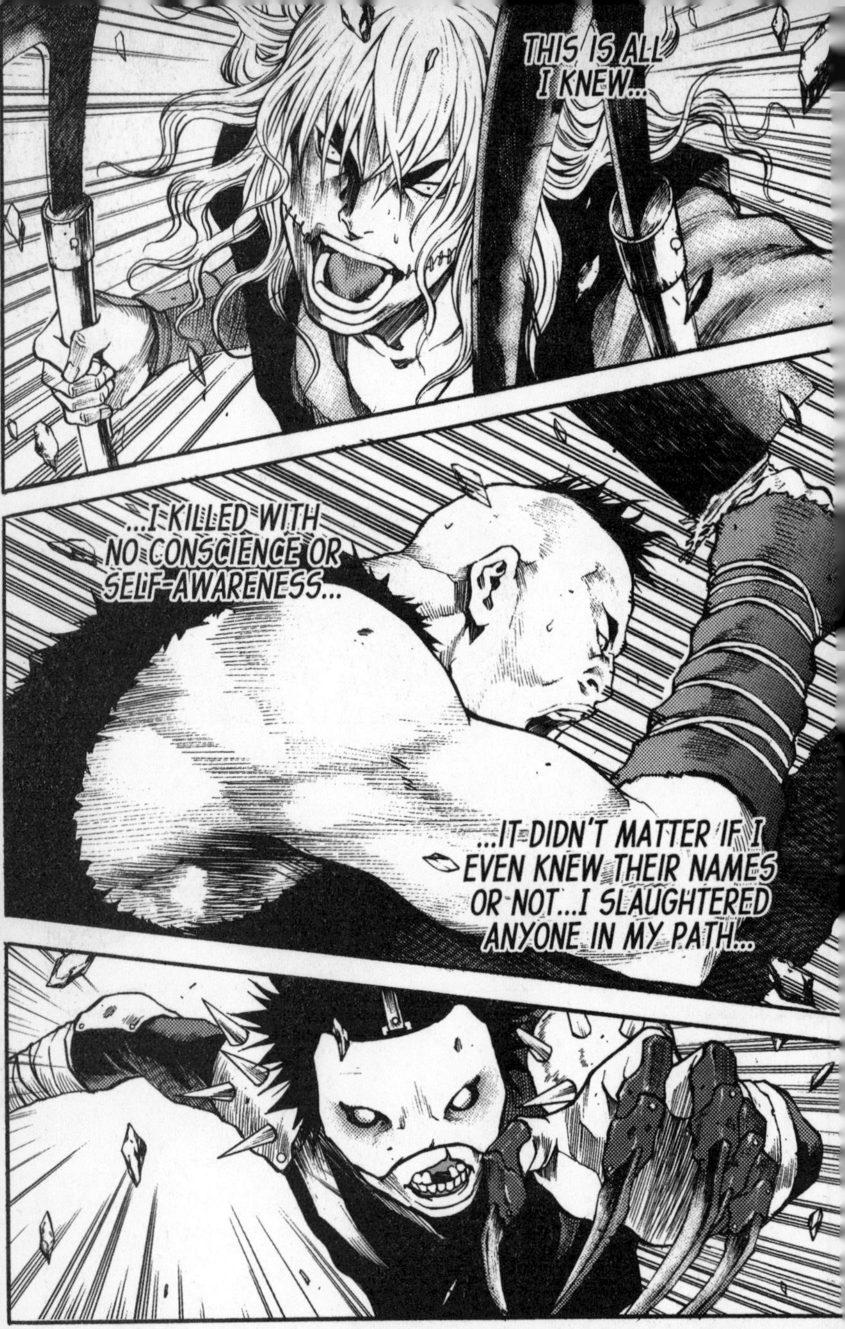
THIS IS ALL I KNEW...
...I KILLED WITH NO CONSCIENCE OR SELF-AWARENESS...
...IT DIDN'T MATTER IF I EVEN KNEW THEIR NAMES OR NOT...I SLAUGHTERED ANYONE IN MY PATH...

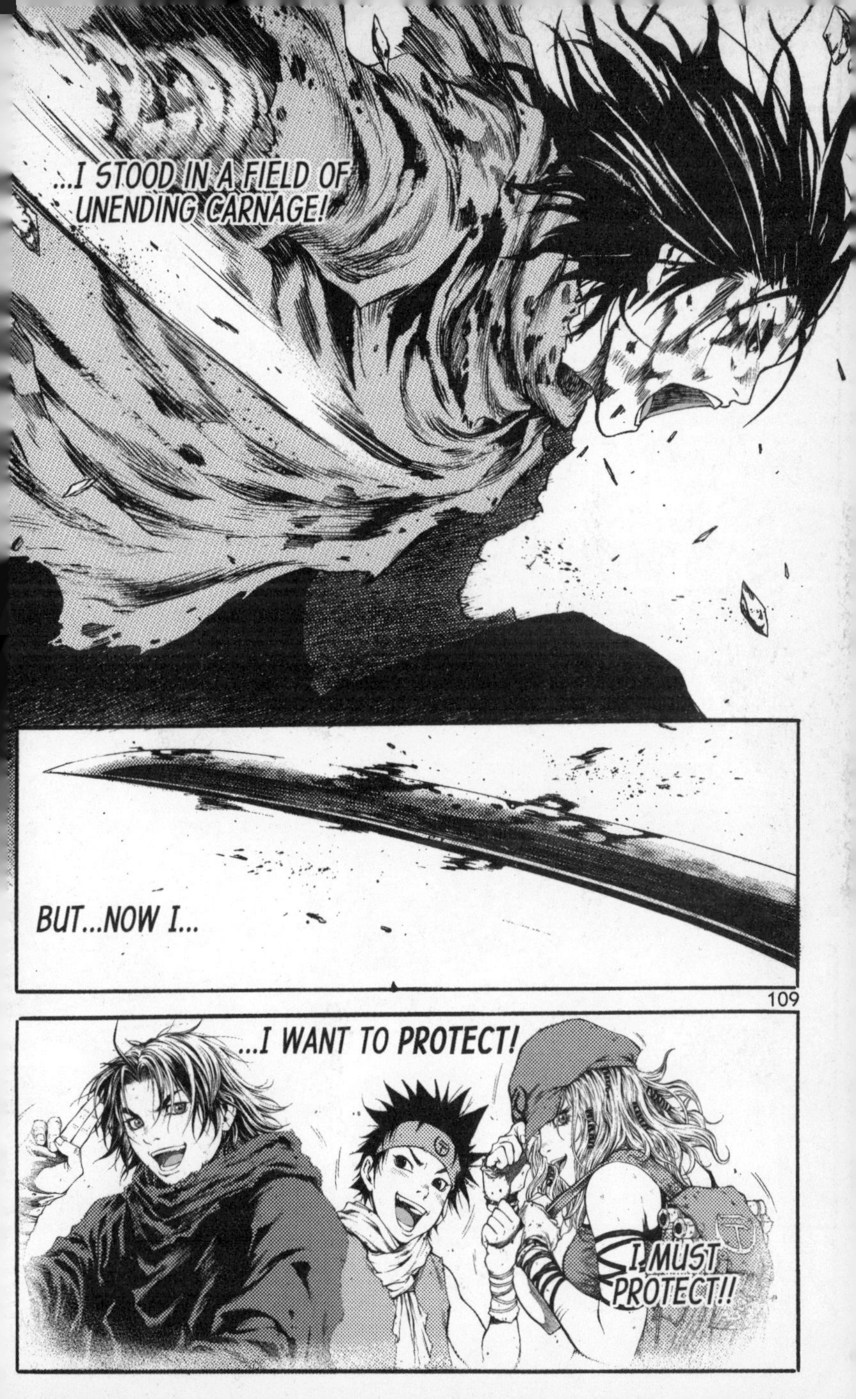
...I STOOD IN A FIELD OF UNENDING CARNAGE!
BUT...NOW I...
...I WANT TO PROTECT!
I MUST PROTECT!!

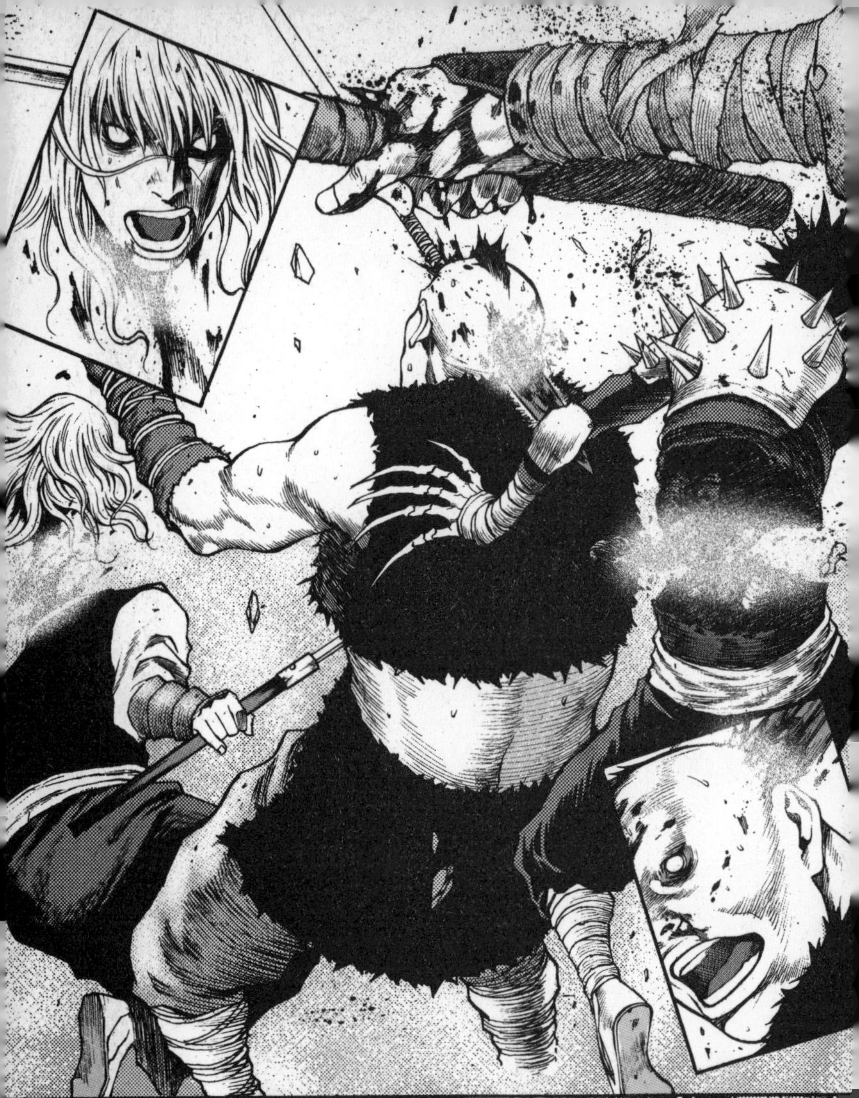
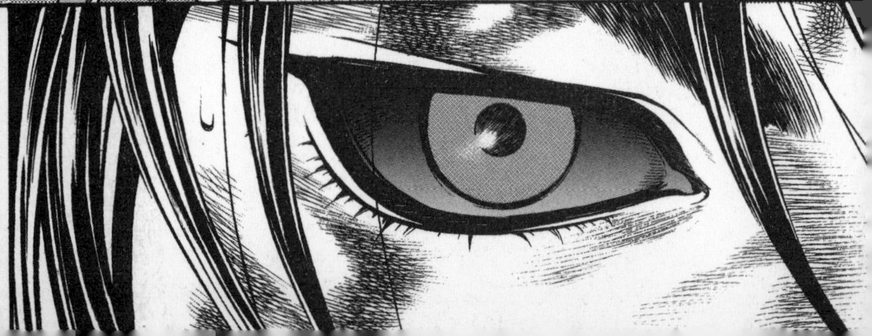

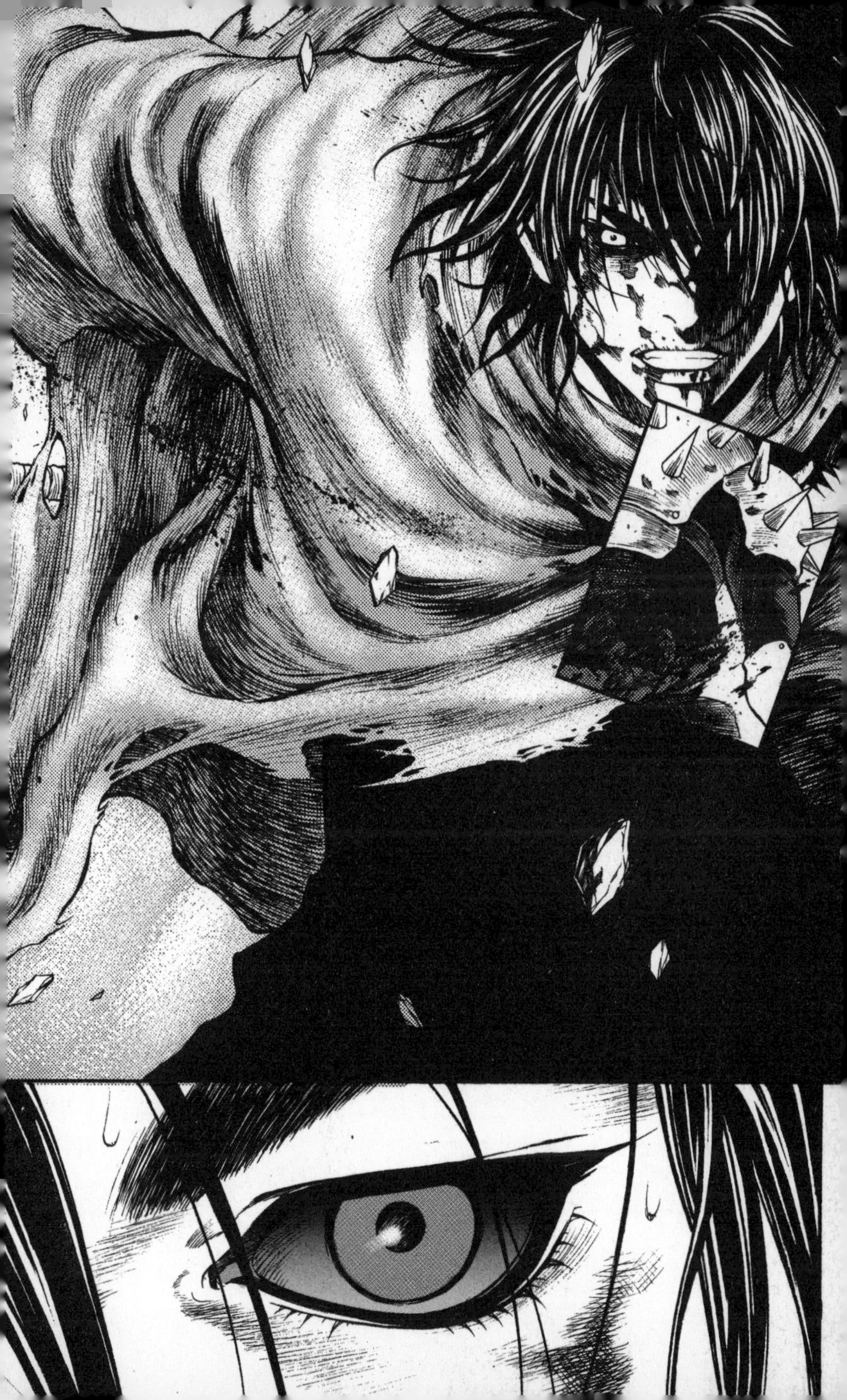

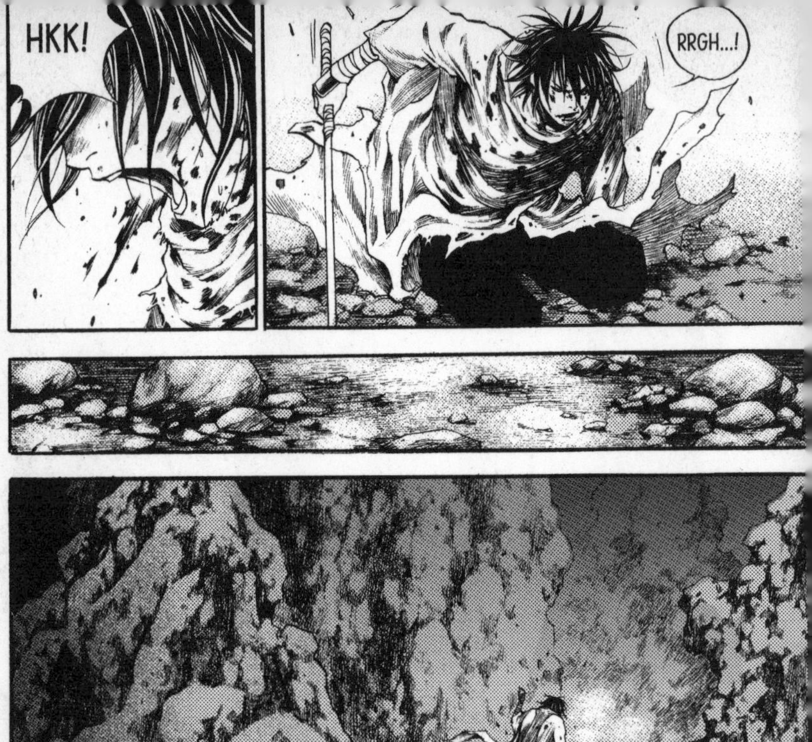
HKK!
RRGH...!



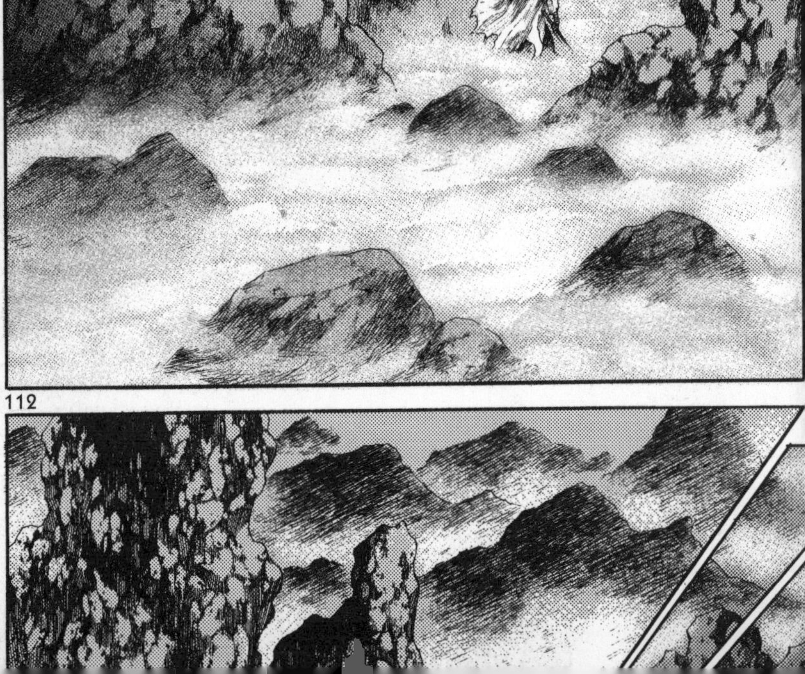

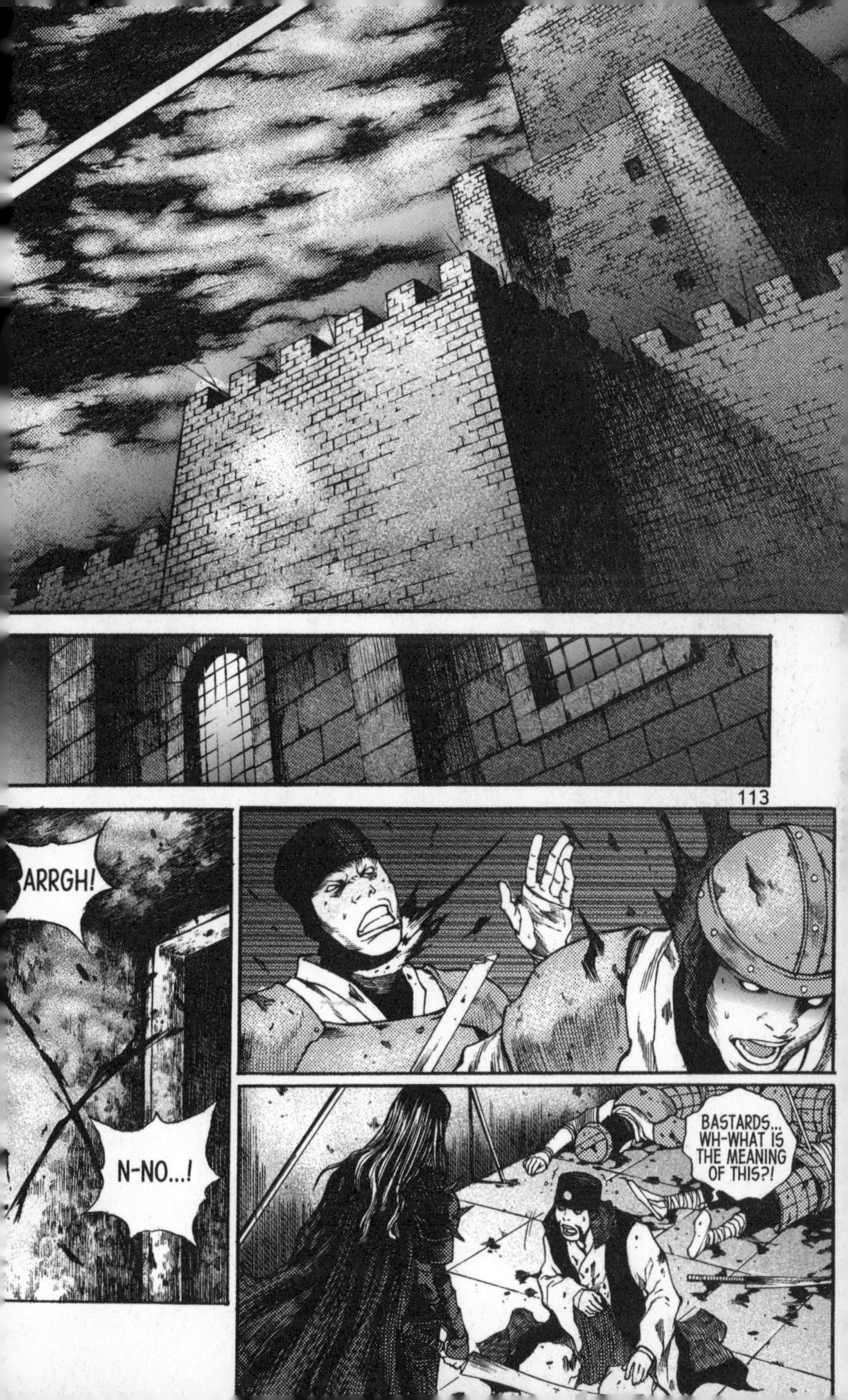
ARRGH!
N-NO...!
BASTARDS... WH-WHAT IS THE MEANING OF THIS?!

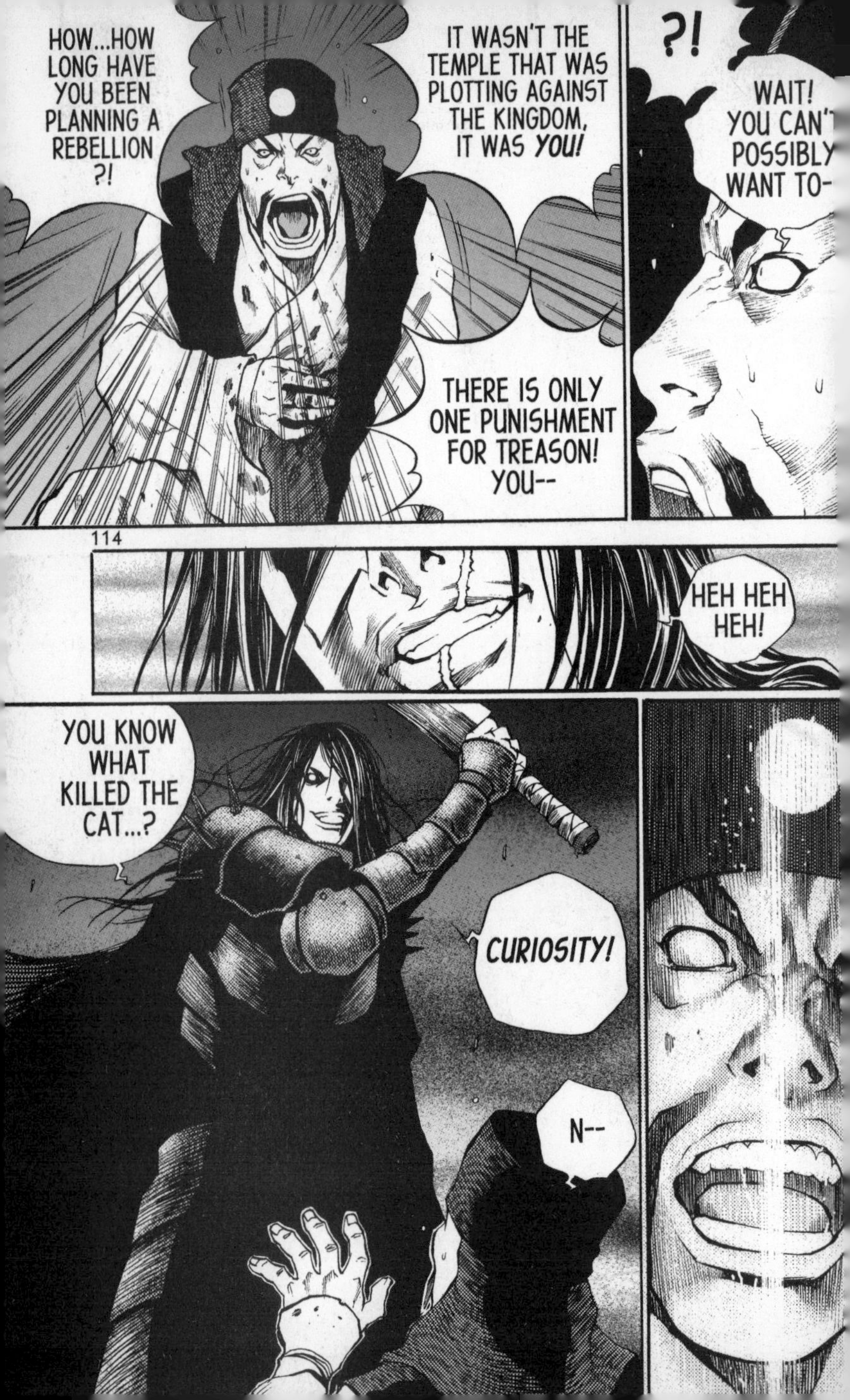

HOW...HOW LONG HAVE YOU BEEN PLANNING A REBELLION ?!
IT WASN'T THE TEMPLE THAT WAS PLOTTING AGAINST THE KINGDOM, IT WAS *YOU!*
THERE IS ONLY ONE PUNISHMENT FOR TREASON! YOU--
?!
WAIT! YOU CAN'T POSSIBLY WANT TO-
HEH HEH HEH!
YOU KNOW WHAT KILLED THE CAT...?
CURIOSITY!
N--

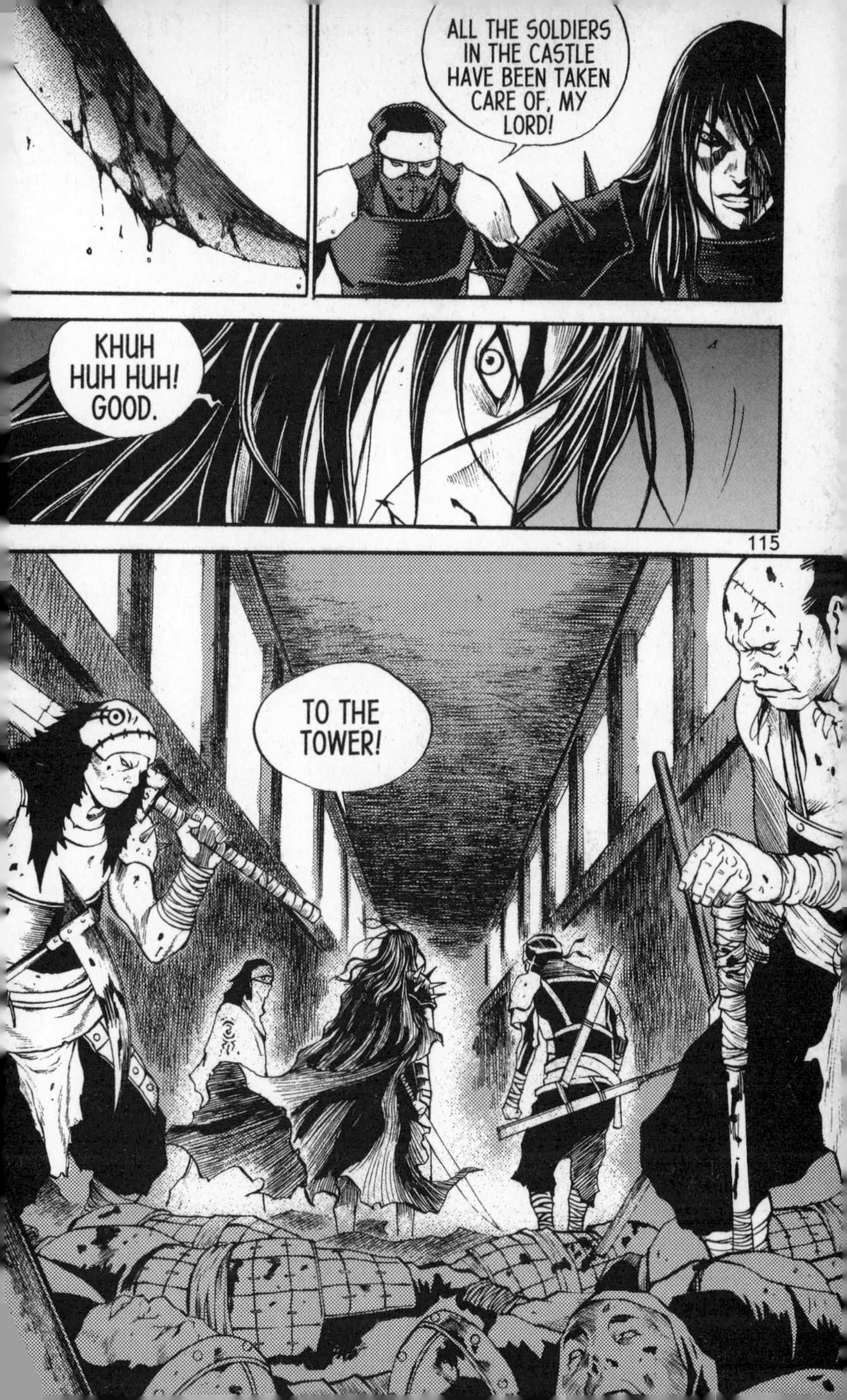
ALL THE SOLDIERS IN THE CASTLE HAVE BEEN TAKEN CARE OF, MY LORD!
KHUH HUH HUH! GOOD.
TO THE TOWER!

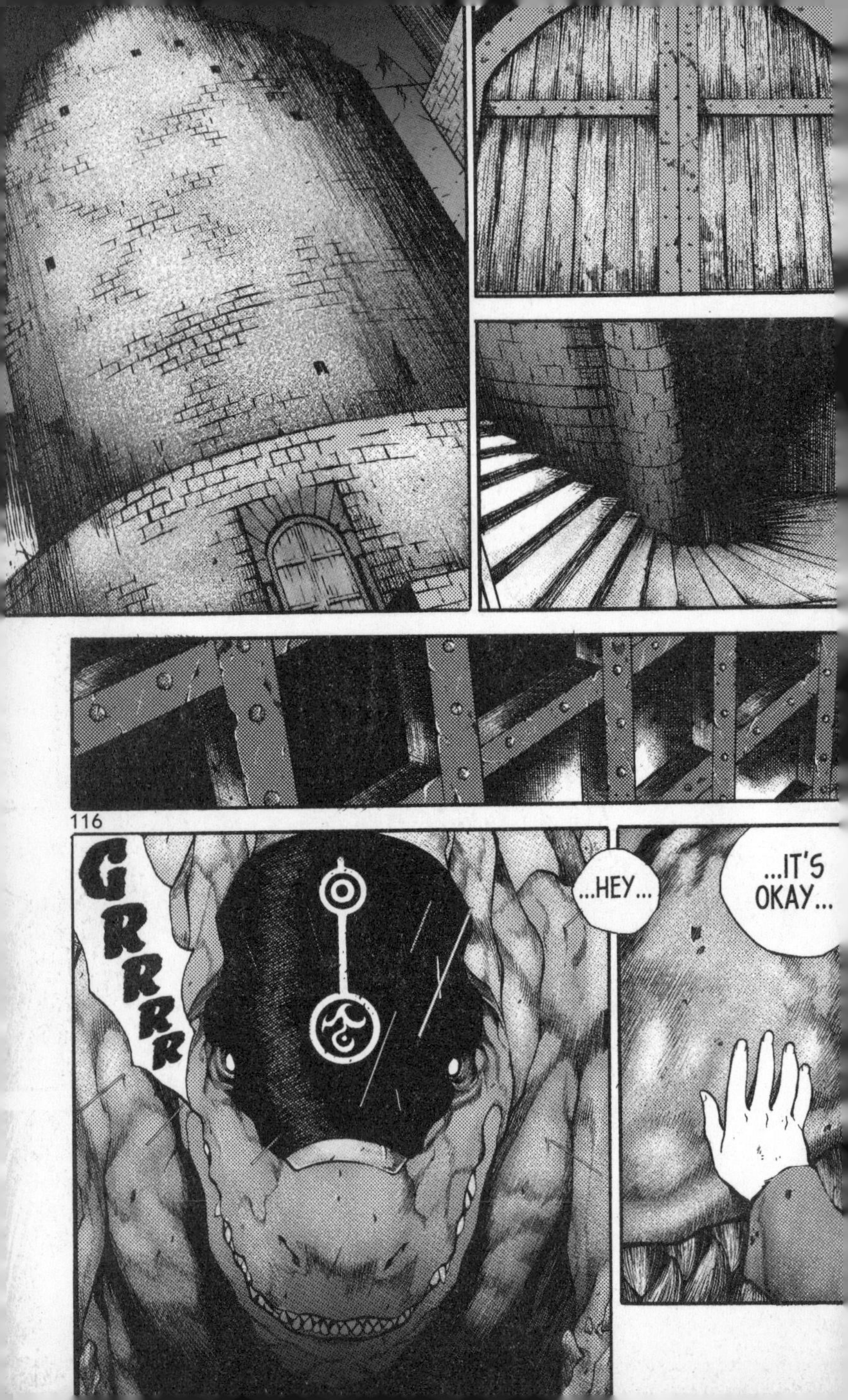
GRRRR
...HEY...
...IT'S OKAY...
116

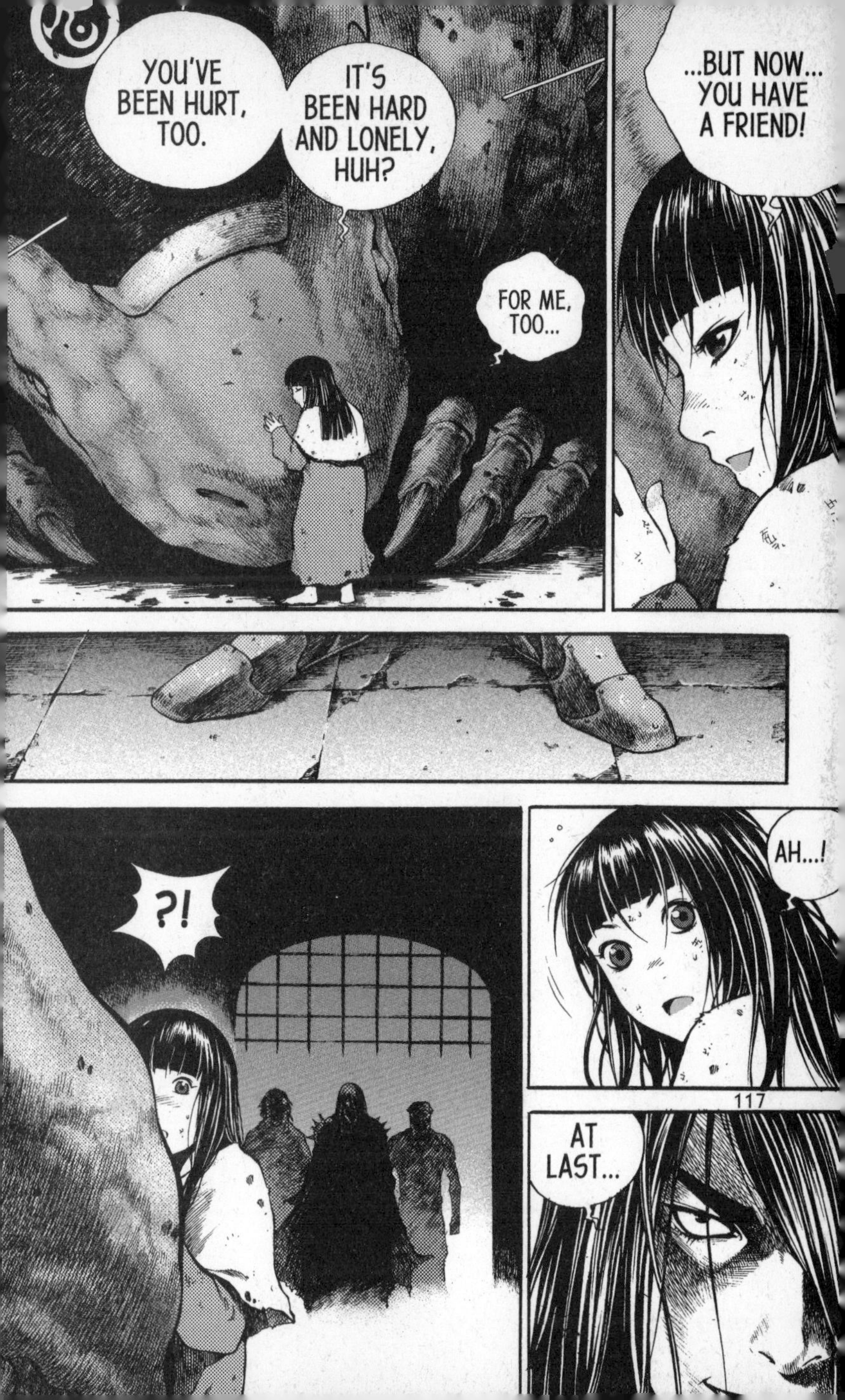
YOU'VE BEEN HURT, TOO.
IT'S BEEN HARD AND LONELY, HUH?
FOR ME, TOO...
...BUT NOW... YOU HAVE A FRIEND!
AH...!
?!
AT LAST...

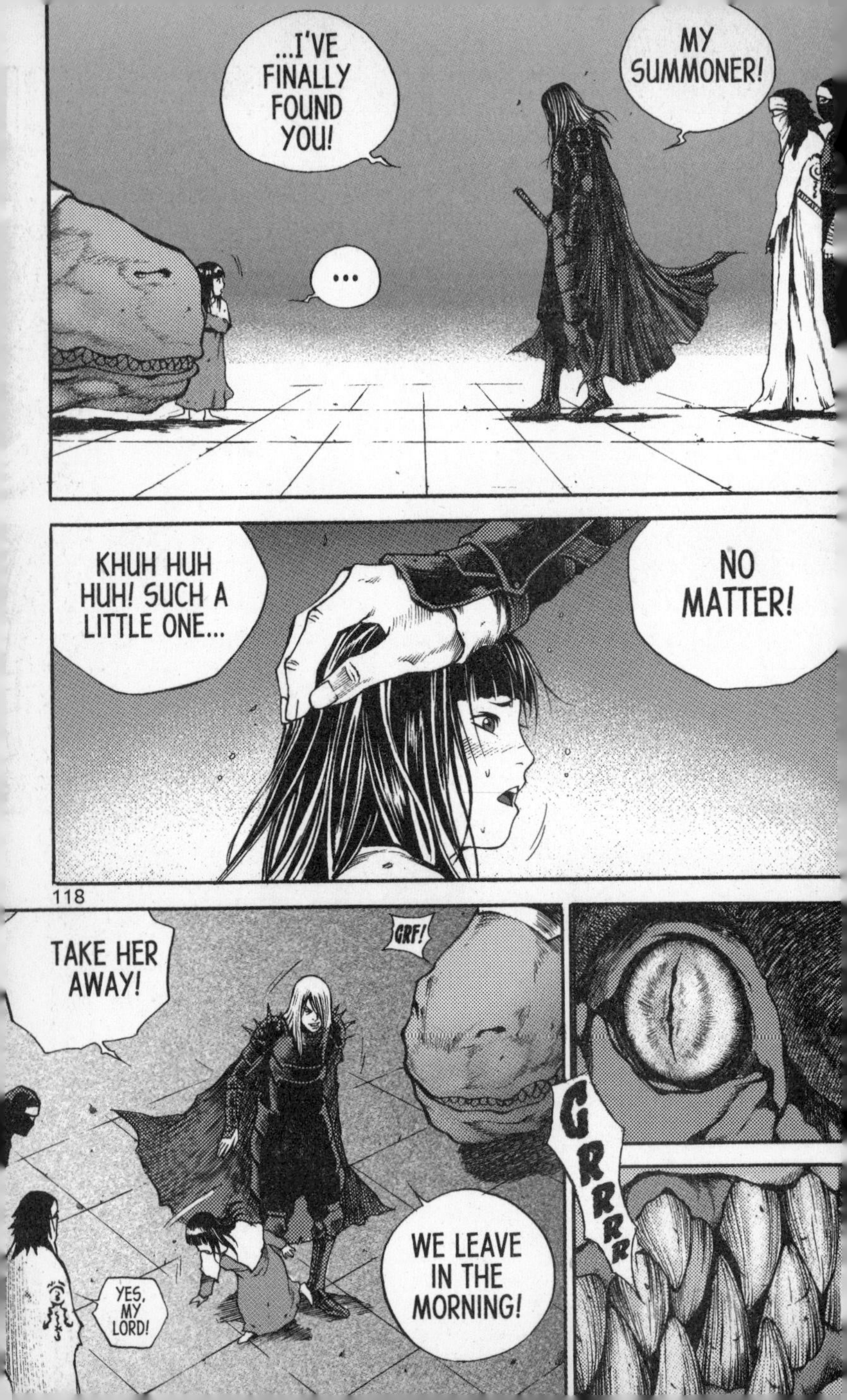
...I'VE FINALLY FOUND YOU!
MY SUMMONER!
...
KHUH HUH HUH! SUCH A LITTLE ONE...
NO MATTER!
TAKE HER AWAY!
GRF!
WE LEAVE IN THE MORNING!
YES, MY LORD!
GRRRR

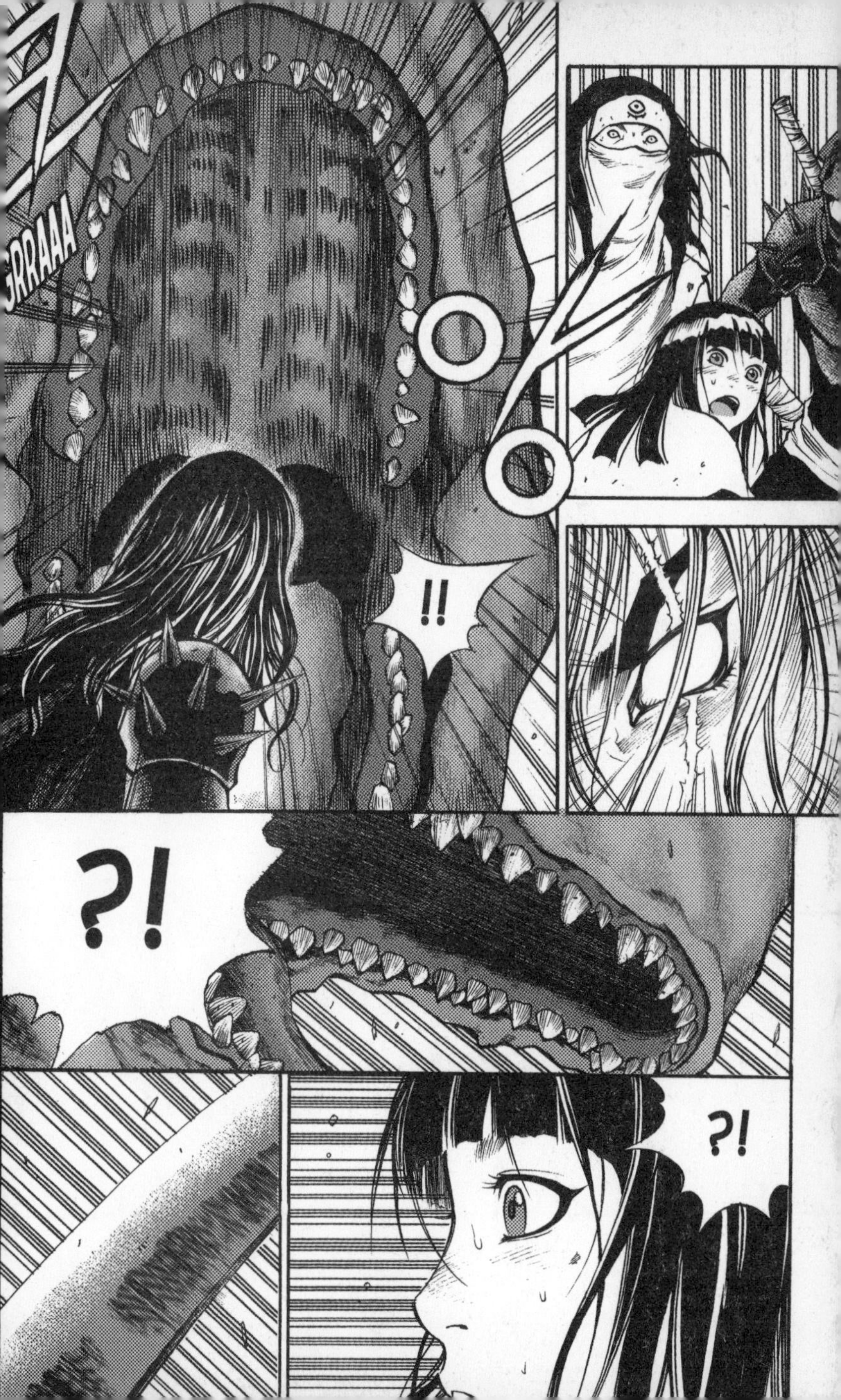
GRRAAA
!!
?!
?!

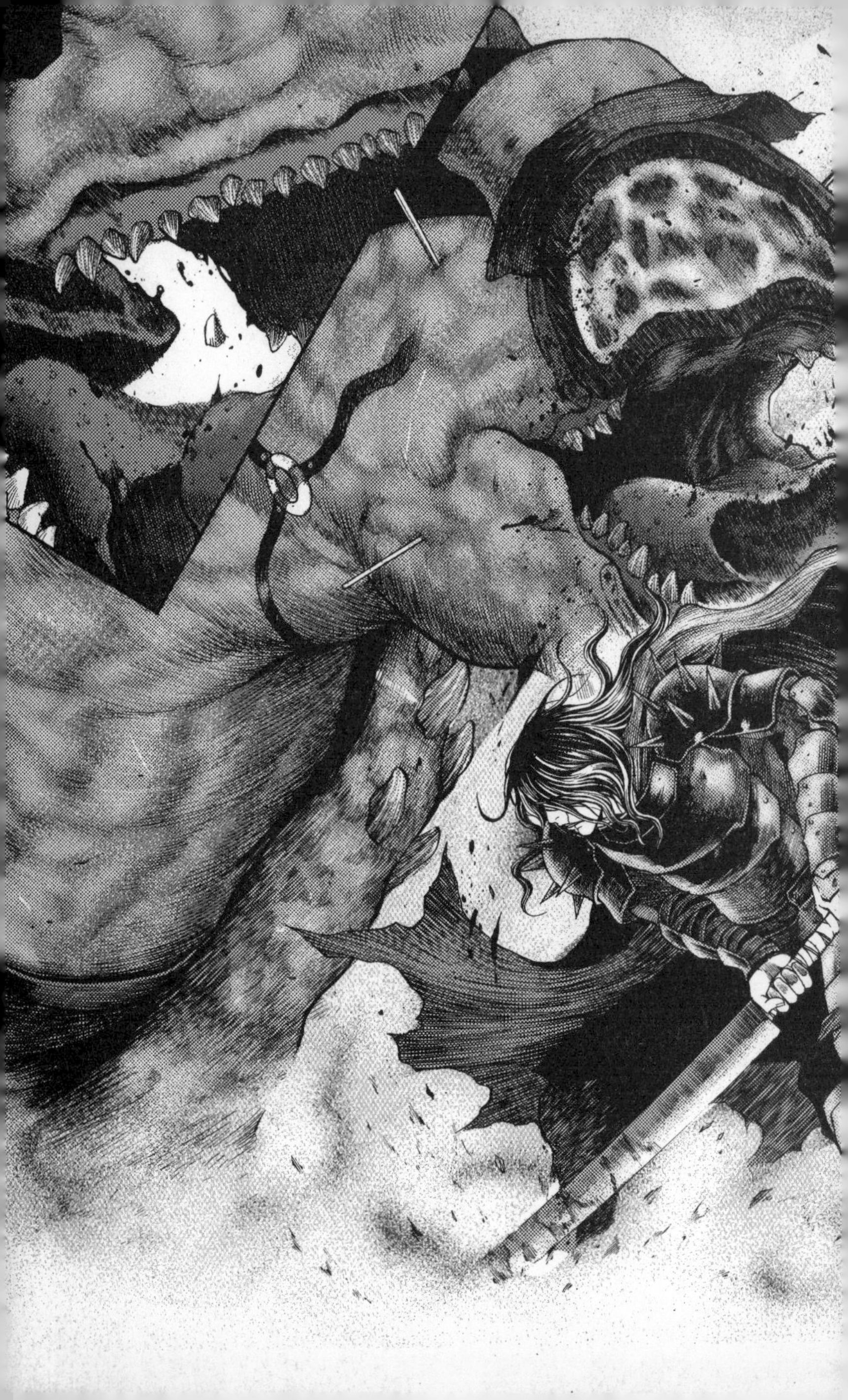

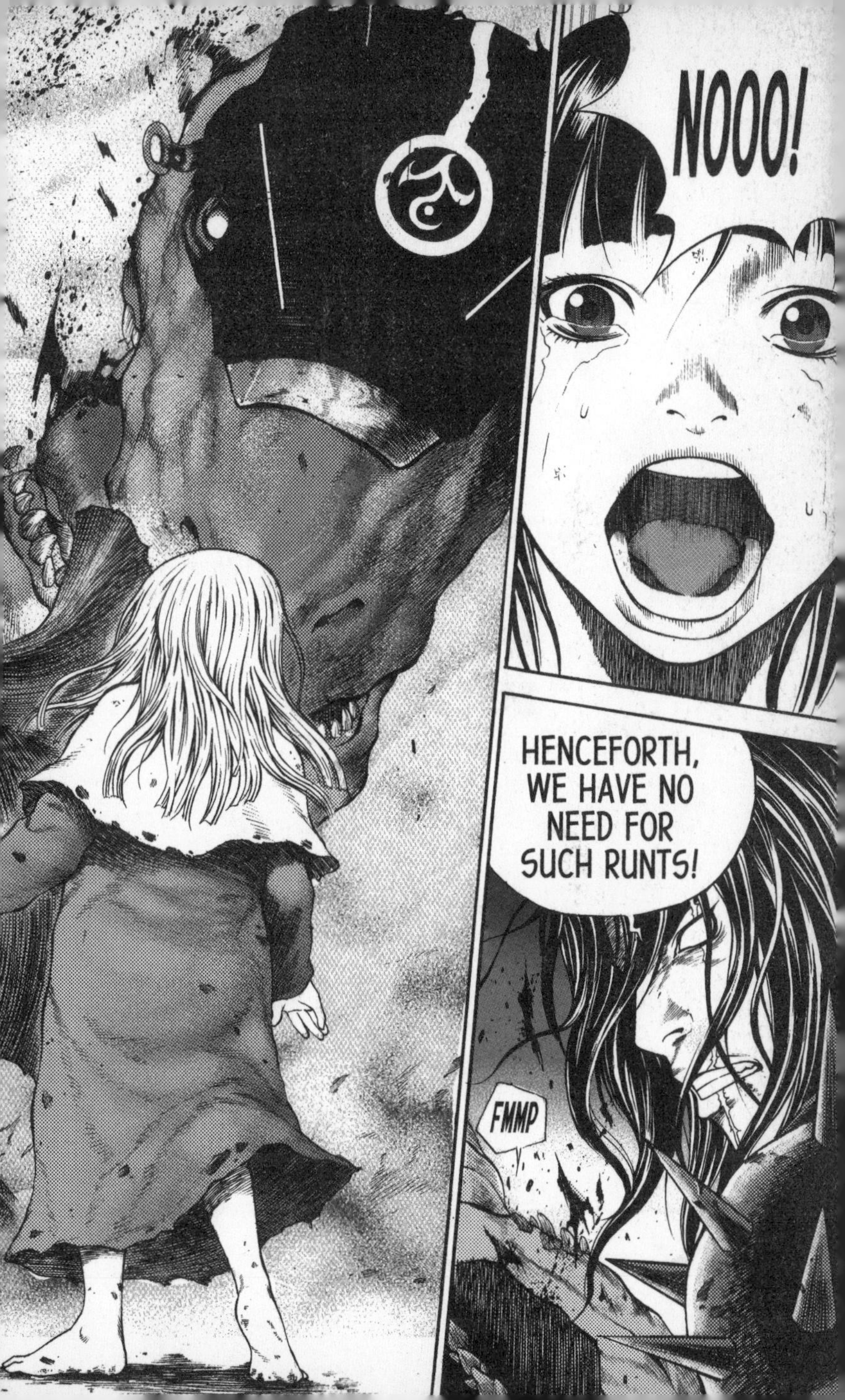
NOOO!
HENCEFORTH, WE HAVE NO NEED FOR SUCH RUNTS!
FMMP

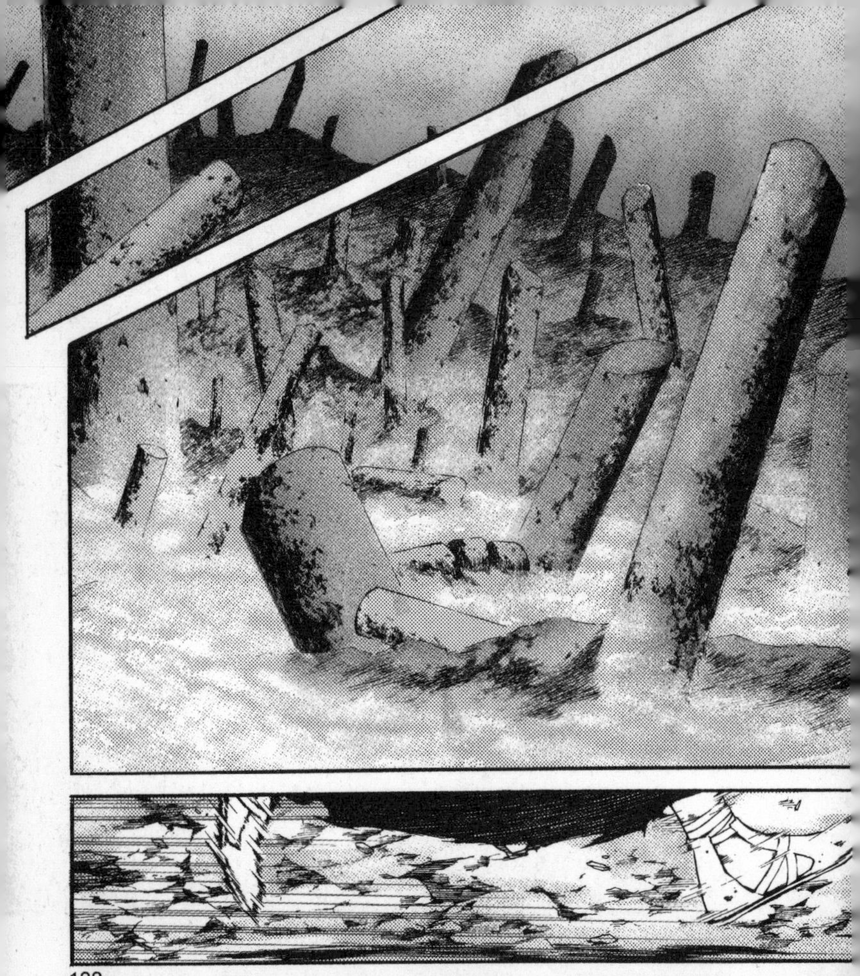



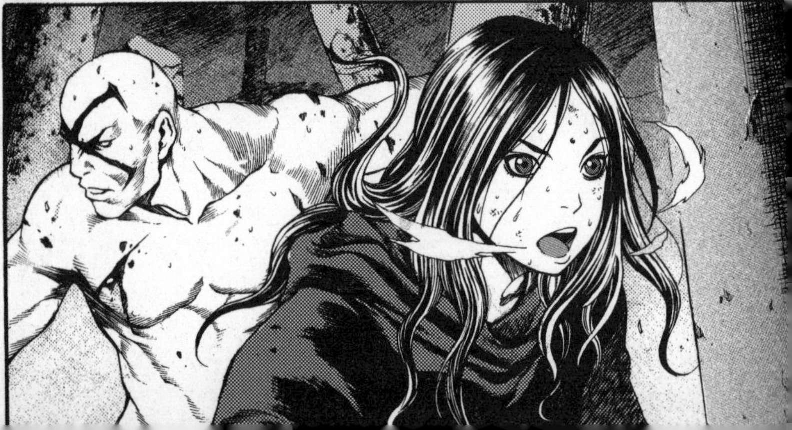

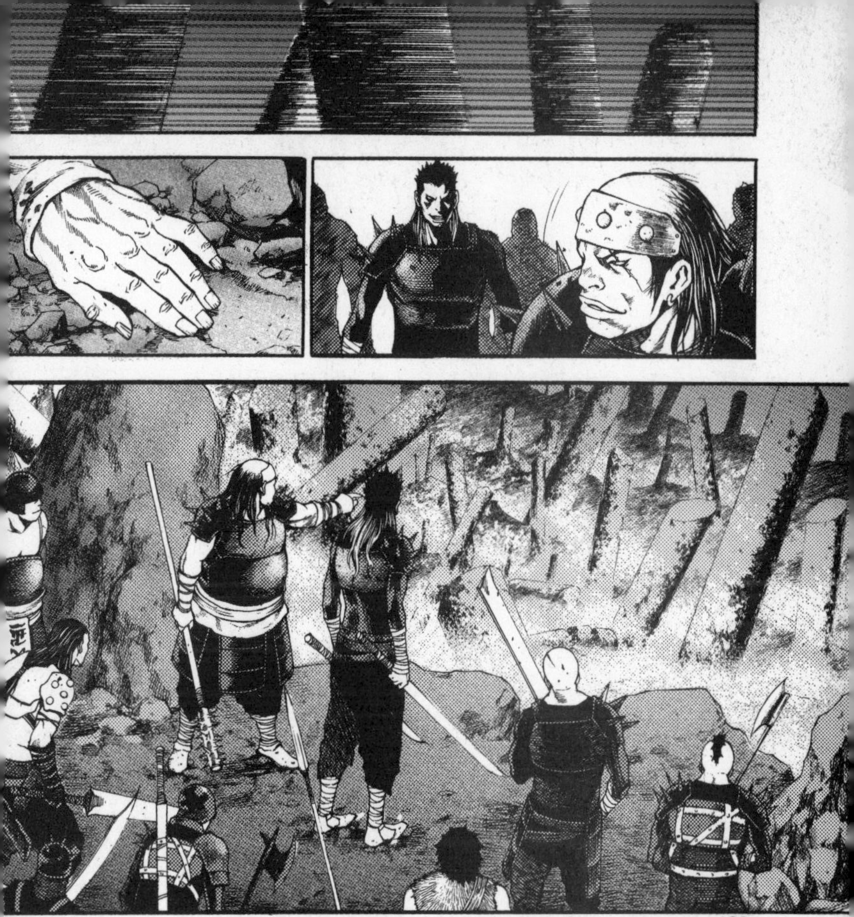



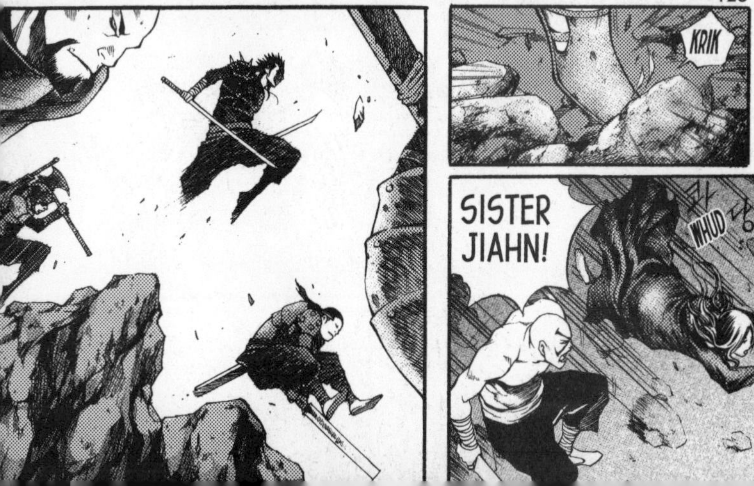
KRIK
SISTER JIAHN!
WHUD
OOF!

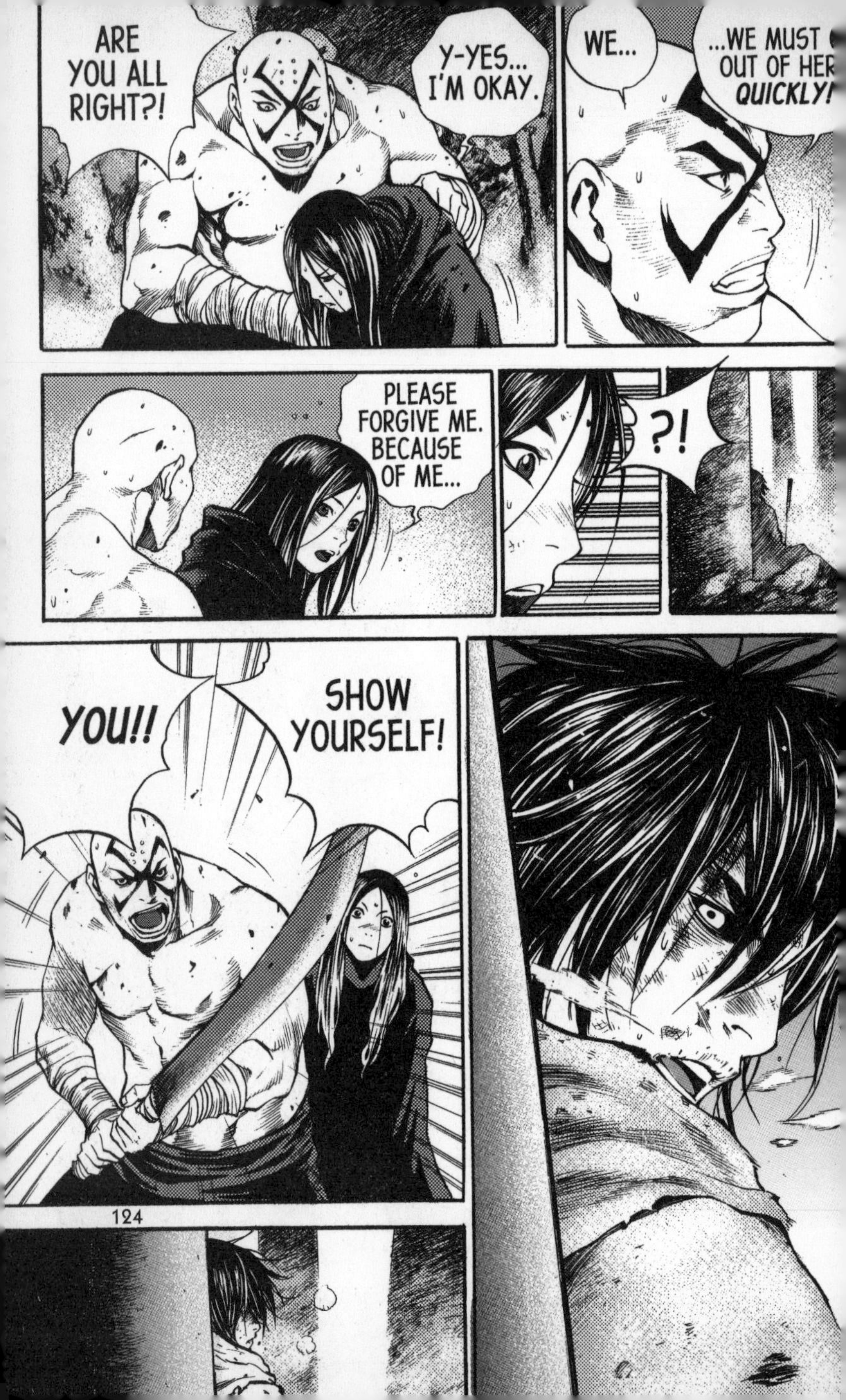
ARE YOU ALL RIGHT?!
Y-YES... I'M OKAY.
WE...
...WE MUST
OUT OF HER
QUICKLY!
PLEASE FORGIVE ME. BECAUSE OF ME...
?!
YOU!!
SHOW YOURSELF!

Banya

the explosive delivery man

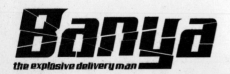

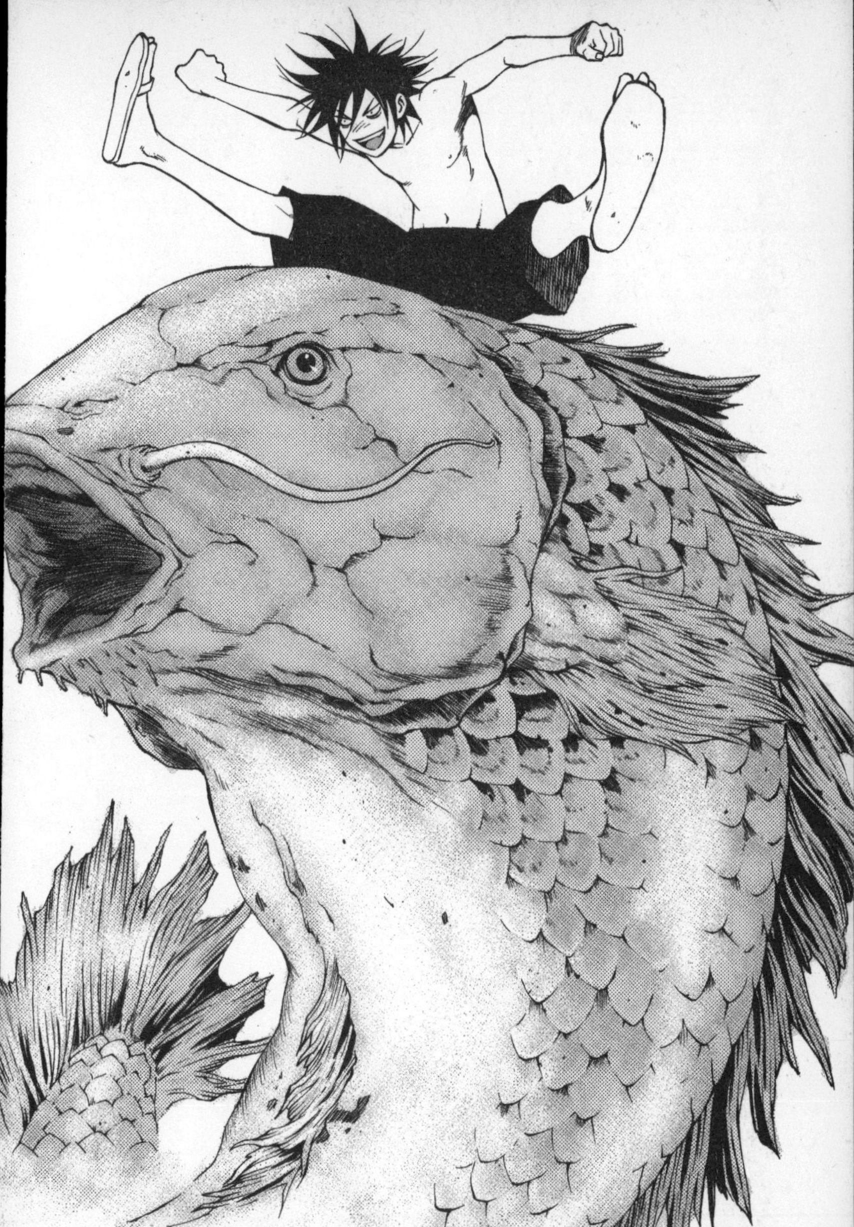

Chapter 28
**OMEN**

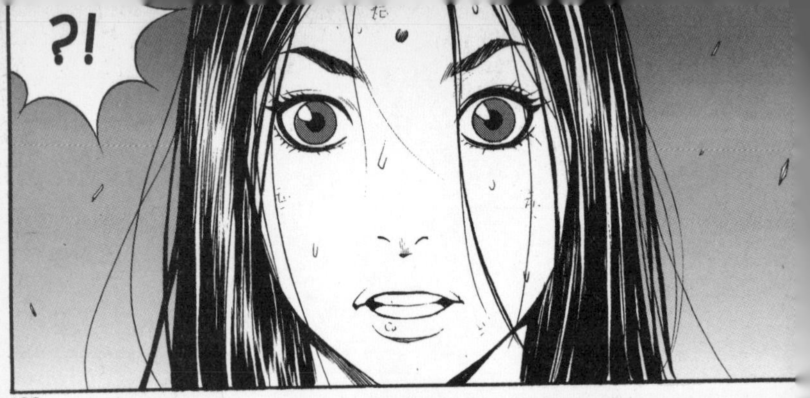
?!



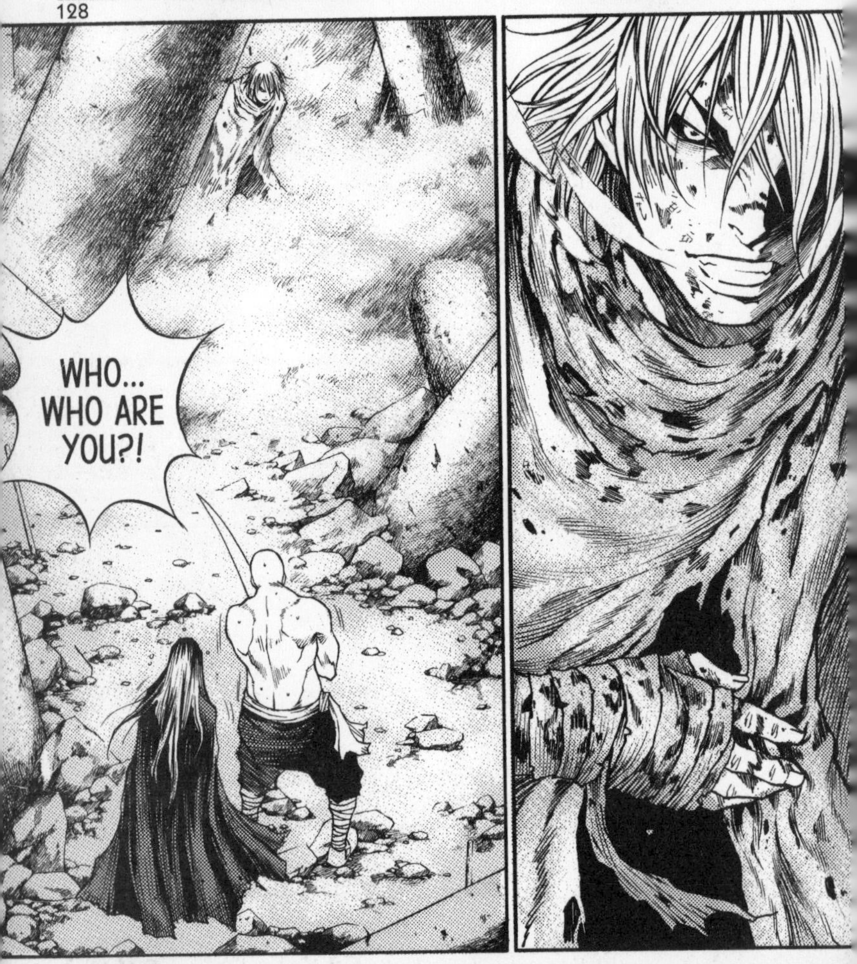
WHO...
WHO ARE
YOU?!

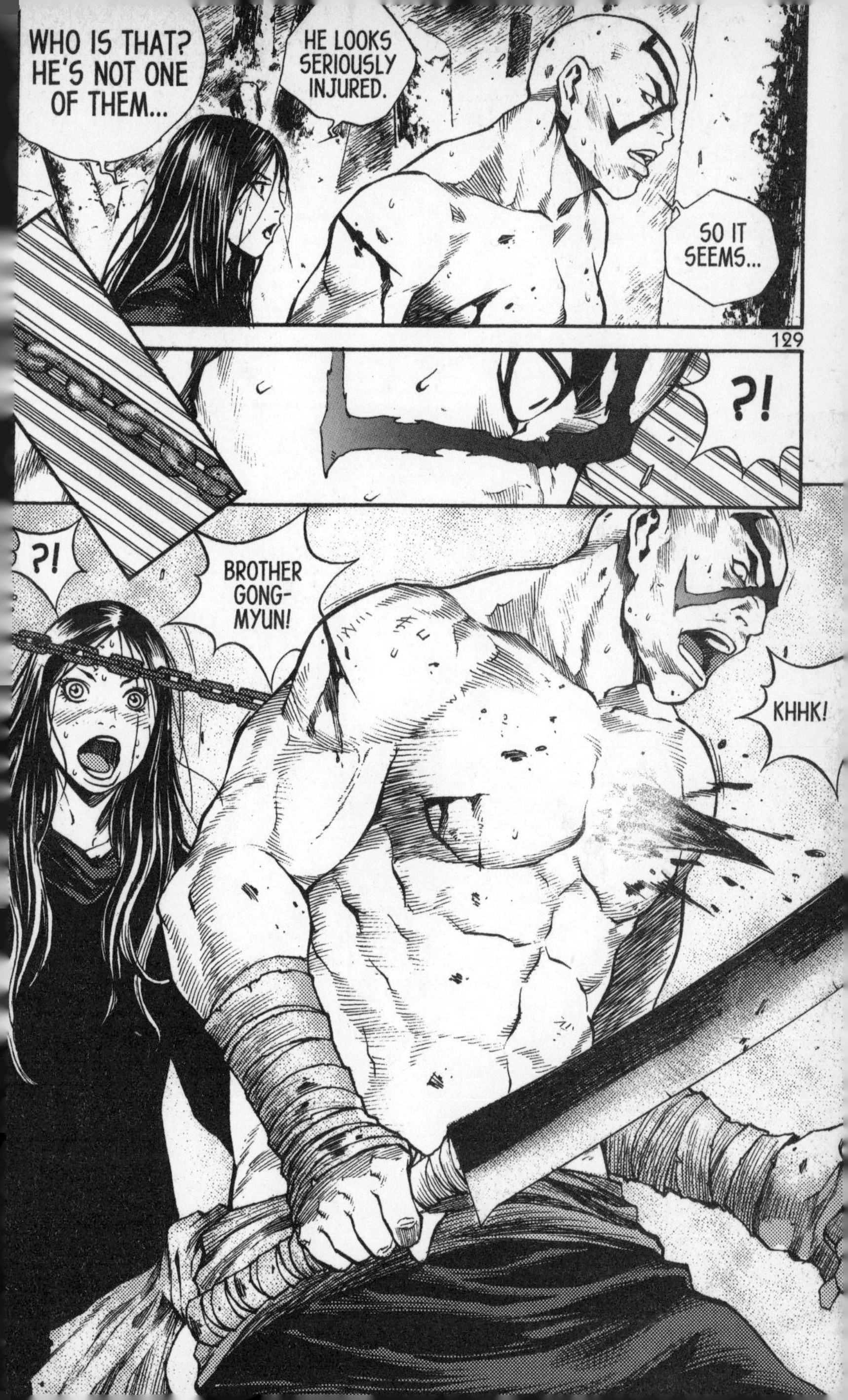
WHO IS THAT? HE'S NOT ONE OF THEM...
HE LOOKS SERIOUSLY INJURED.
SO IT SEEMS...
?!
?!
BROTHER GONG-MYUN!
KHHK!

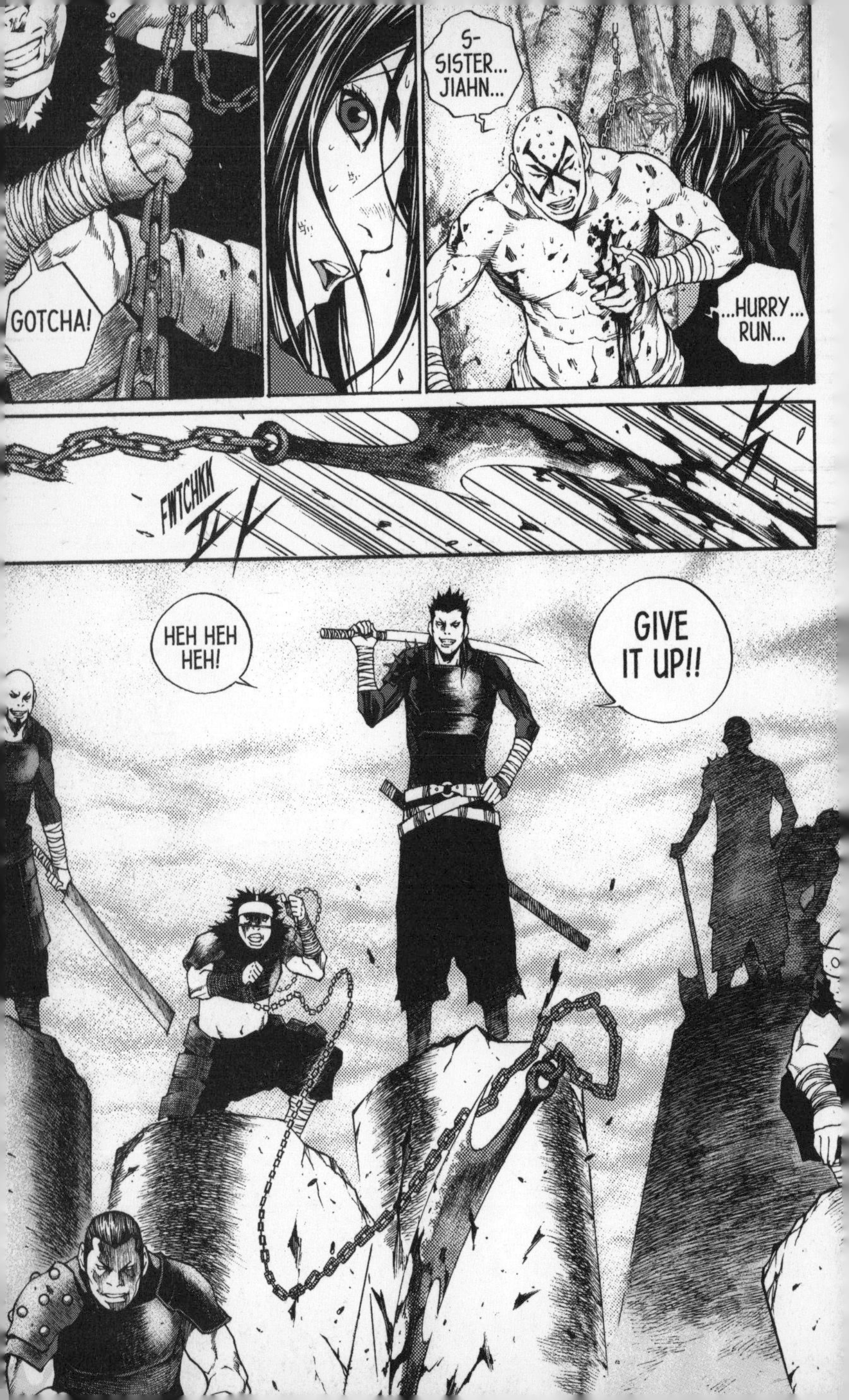
GOTCHA!
S-SISTER... JIAHN...
...HURRY... RUN...
FWTCHKK
HEH HEH HEH!
GIVE IT UP!!

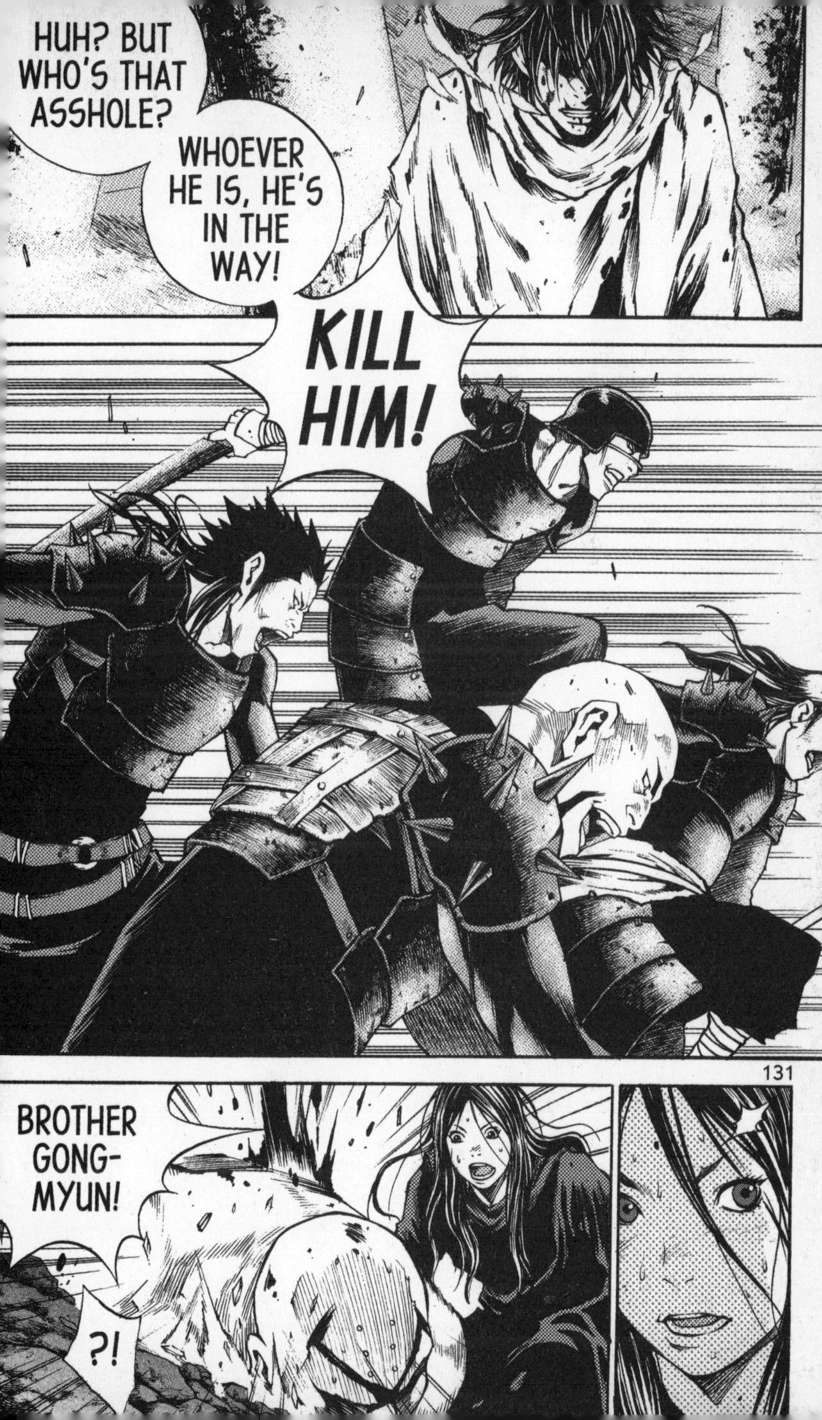
HUH? BUT WHO'S THAT ASSHOLE?
WHOEVER HE IS, HE'S IN THE WAY!
KILL HIM!
BROTHER GONG-MYUN!
?!

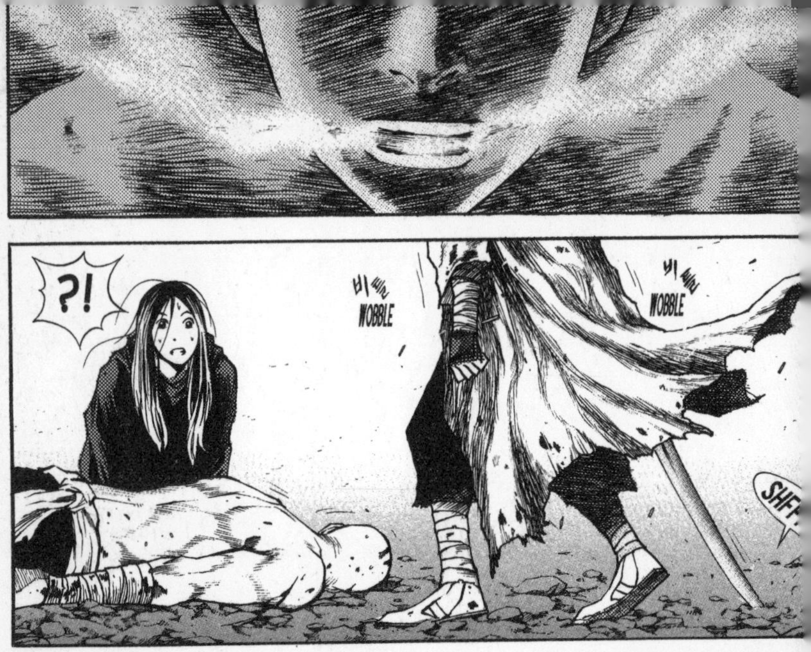
?!
비씩
WOBBLE
비씩
WOBBLE
SHFF
...?



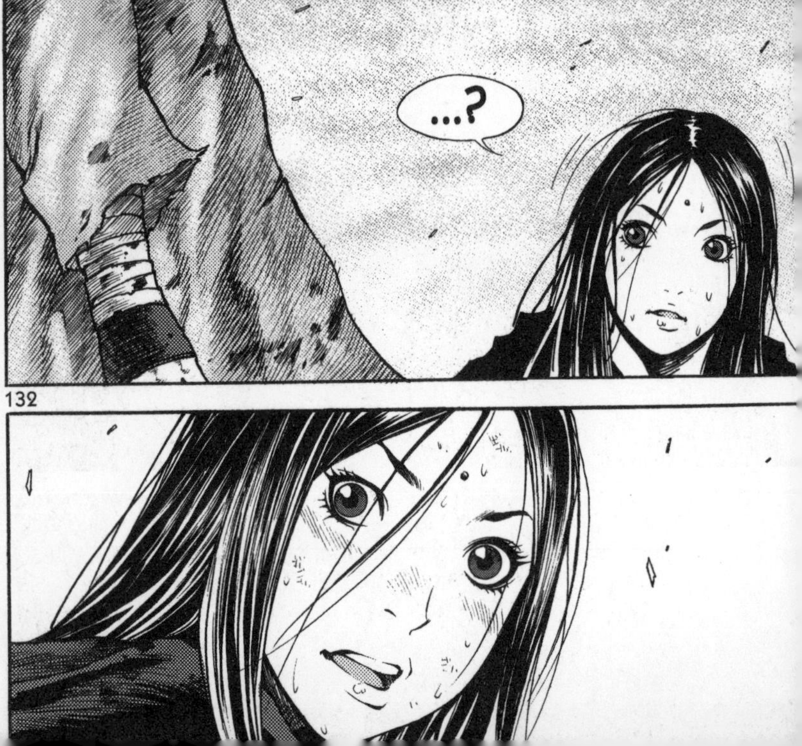

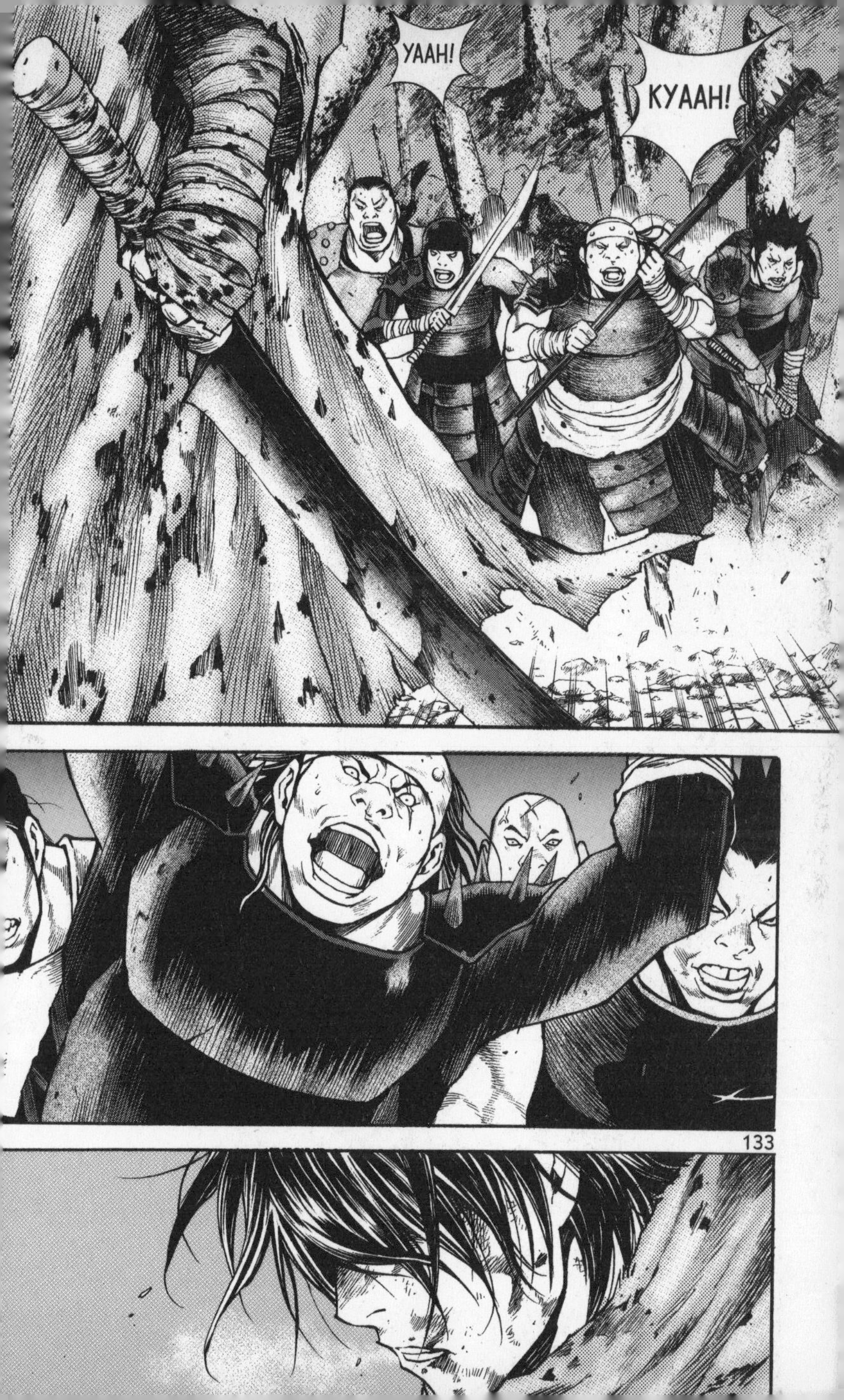
KYAAH!
YAAH!

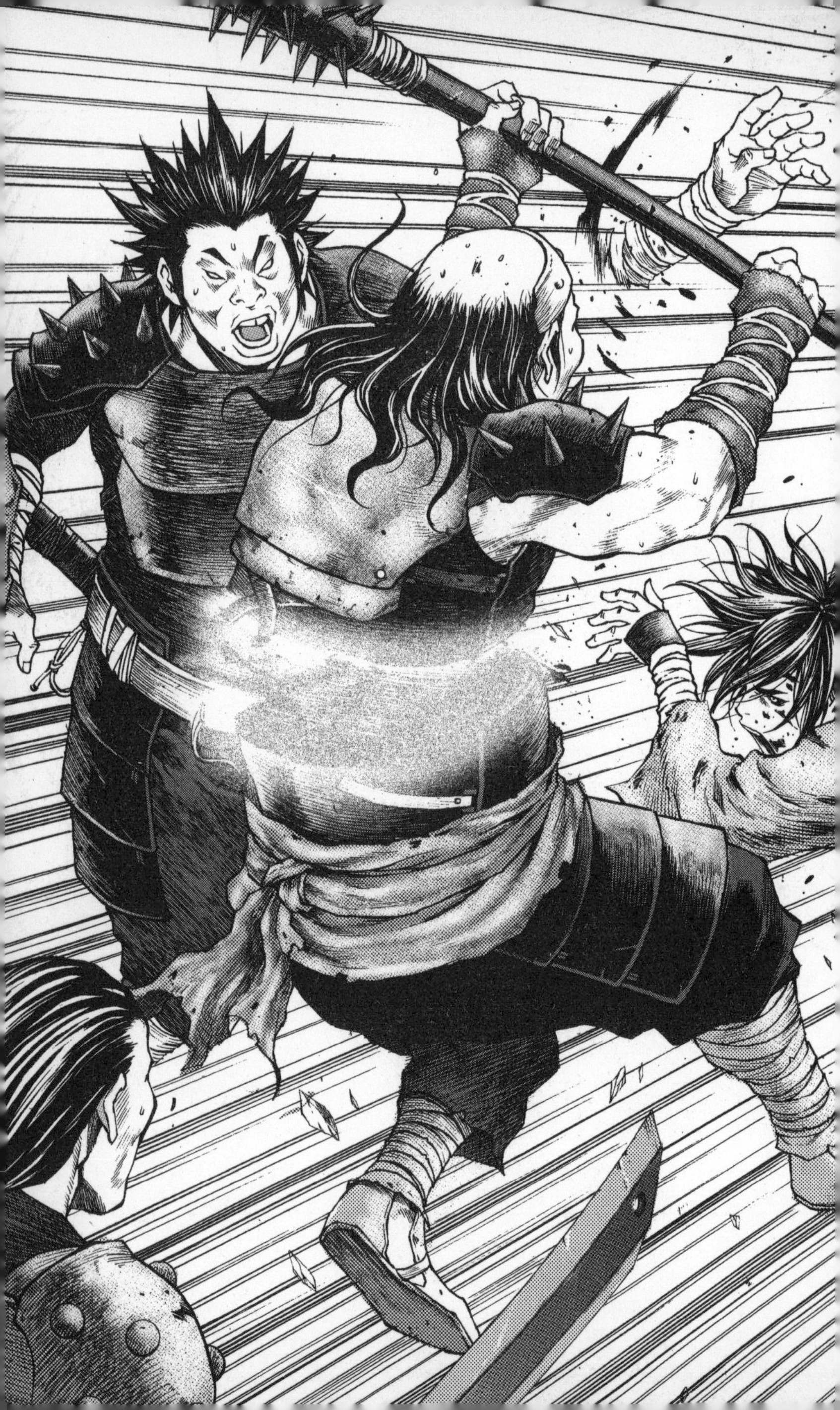

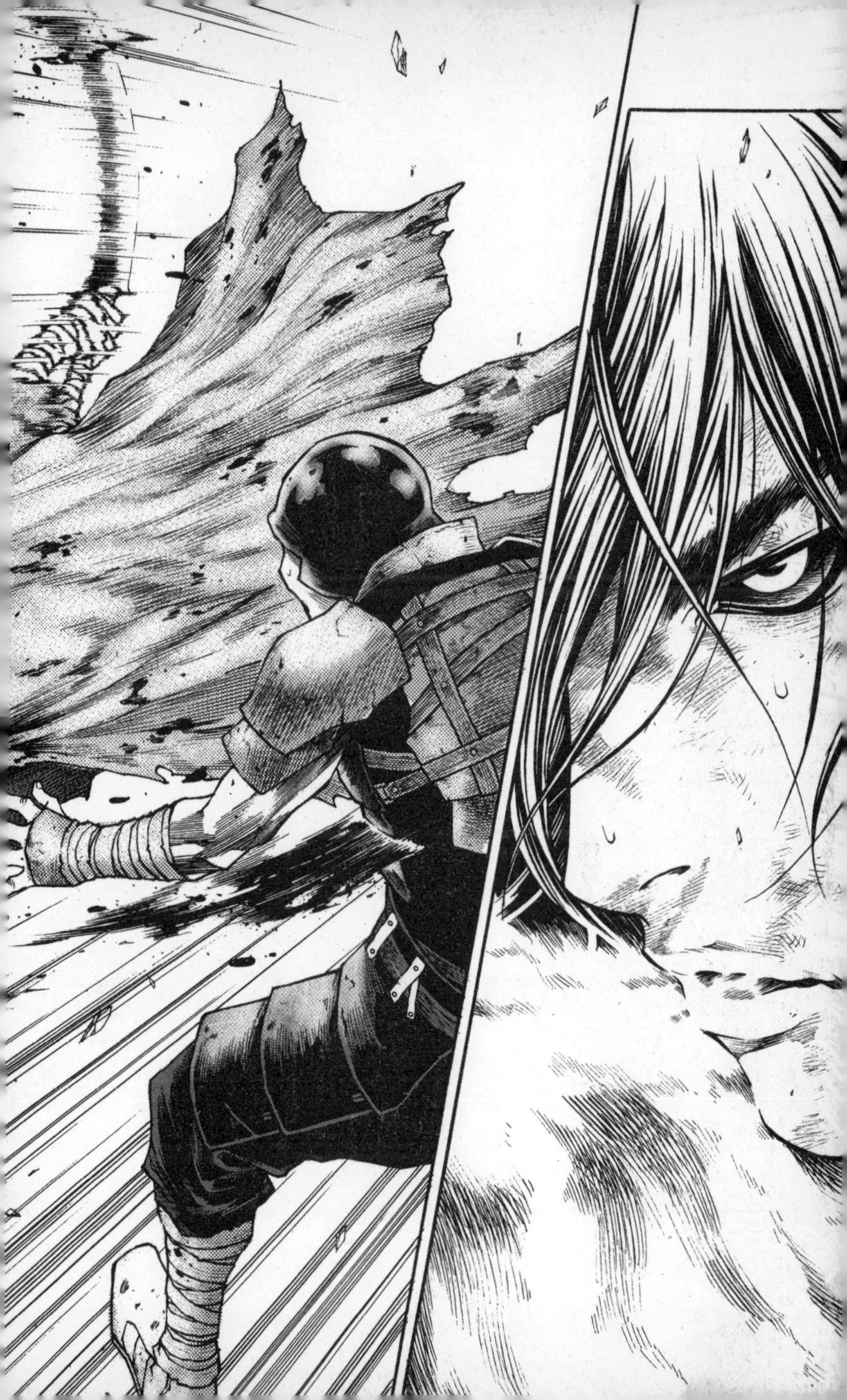

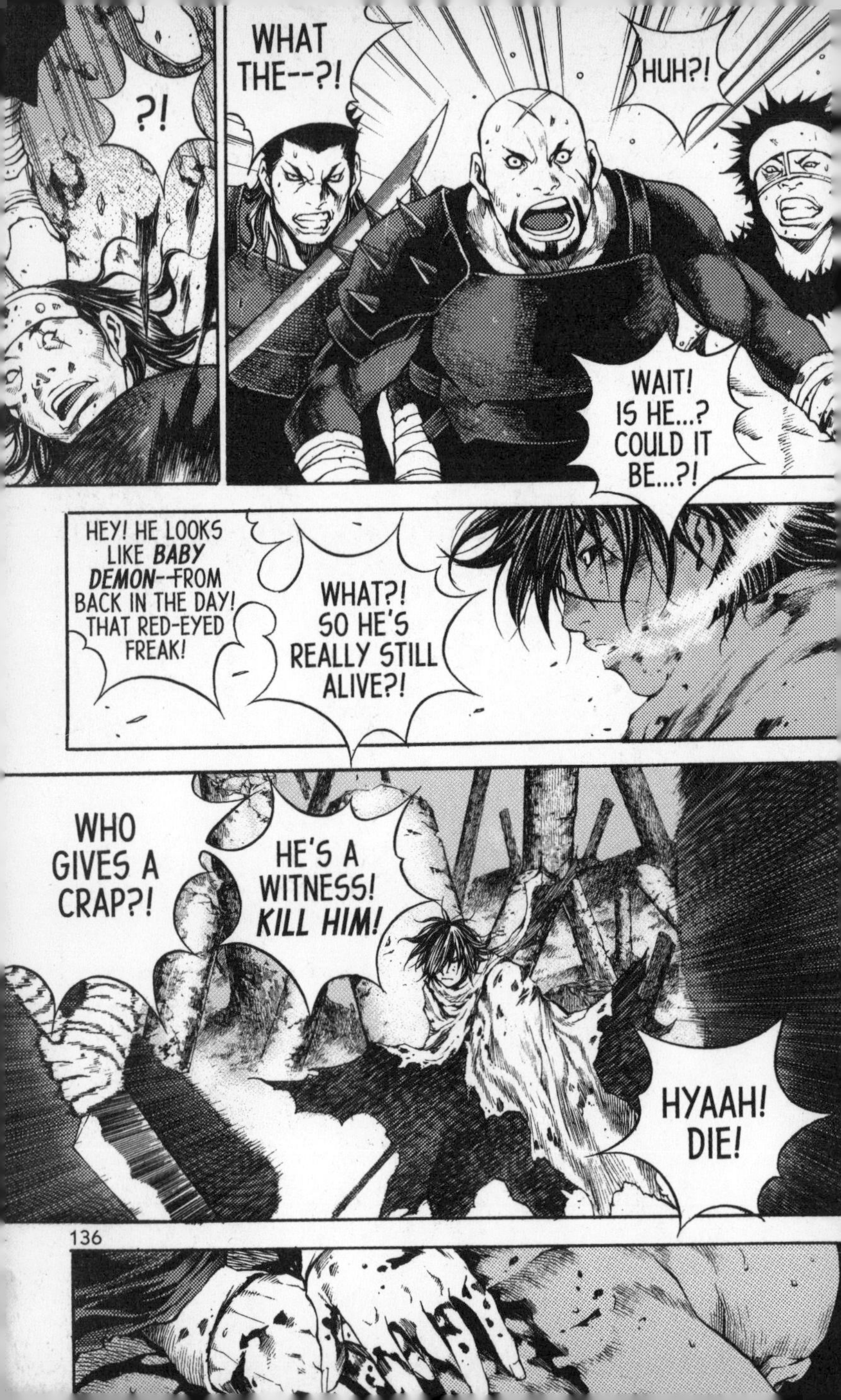
?!
WHAT THE--?!
HUH?!
WAIT! IS HE...? COULD IT BE...?!
HEY! HE LOOKS LIKE BABY DEMON--FROM BACK IN THE DAY! THAT RED-EYED FREAK!
WHAT?! SO HE'S REALLY STILL ALIVE?!
WHO GIVES A CRAP?!
HE'S A WITNESS! KILL HIM!
HYAAH! DIE!

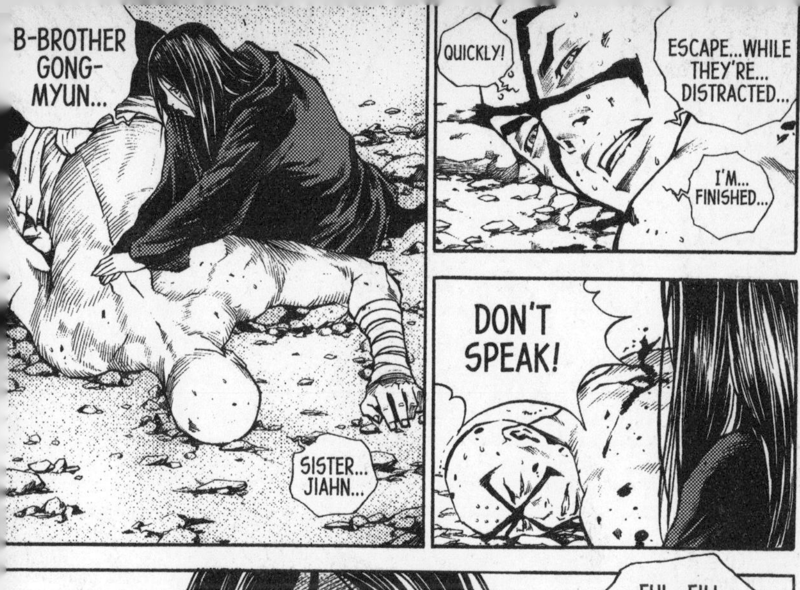
B-BROTHER GONG-MYUN...
SISTER... JIAHN...
QUICKLY!
ESCAPE...WHILE THEY'RE... DISTRACTED...
I'M... FINISHED...
DON'T SPEAK!
P-PLEASE...
FUL...FILL YOUR...DESTINY... RESCUE THE LAND...FROM... DESTRUCTION...
FMP
B-BROTHER GONG-MYUN...



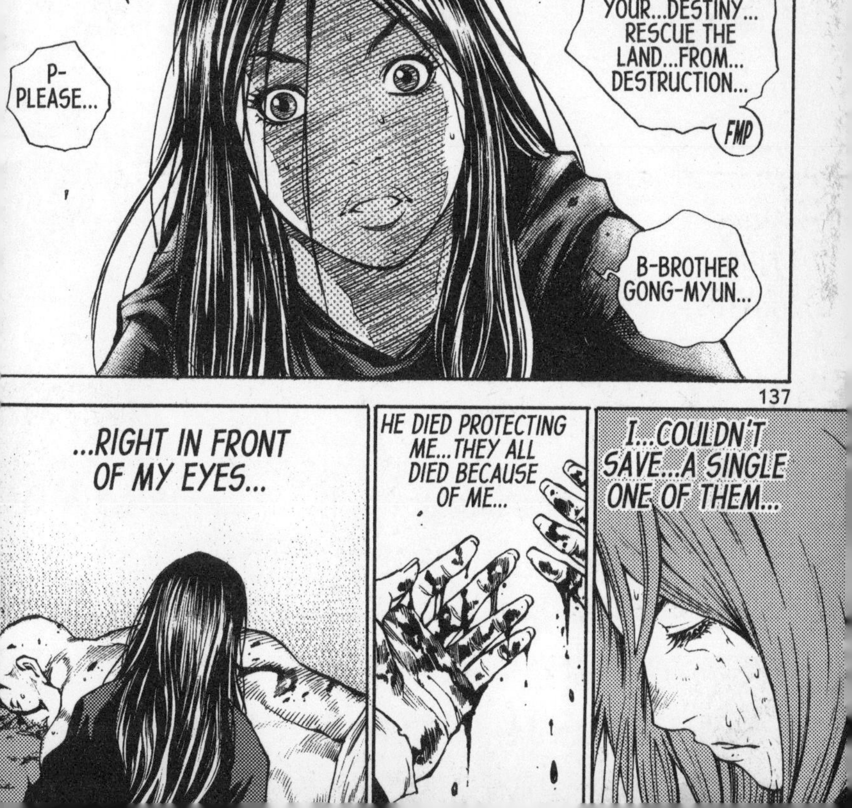
...RIGHT IN FRONT OF MY EYES...
HE DIED PROTECTING ME...THEY ALL DIED BECAUSE OF ME...
I...COULDN'T SAVE...A SINGLE ONE OF THEM...

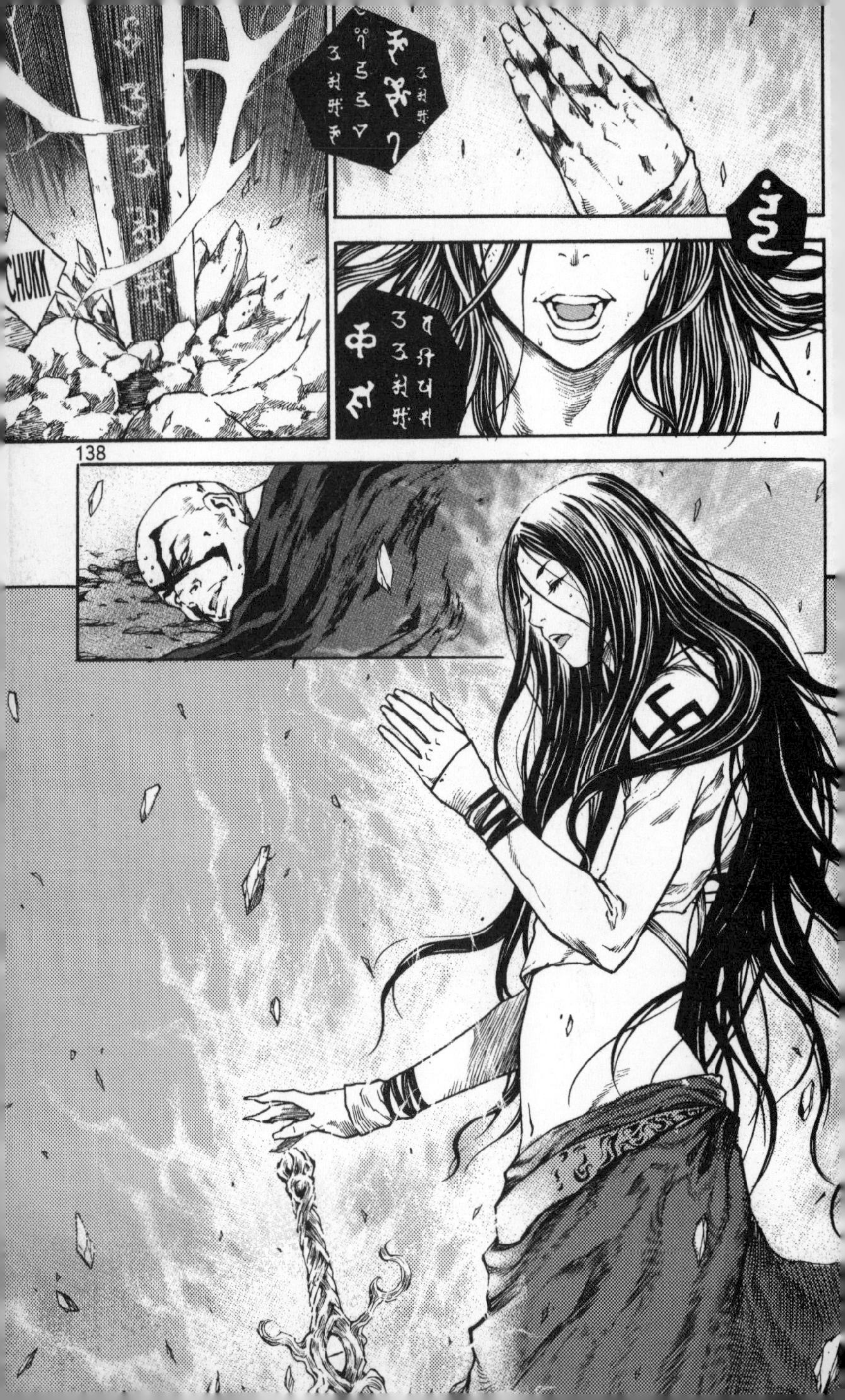
CHUKK

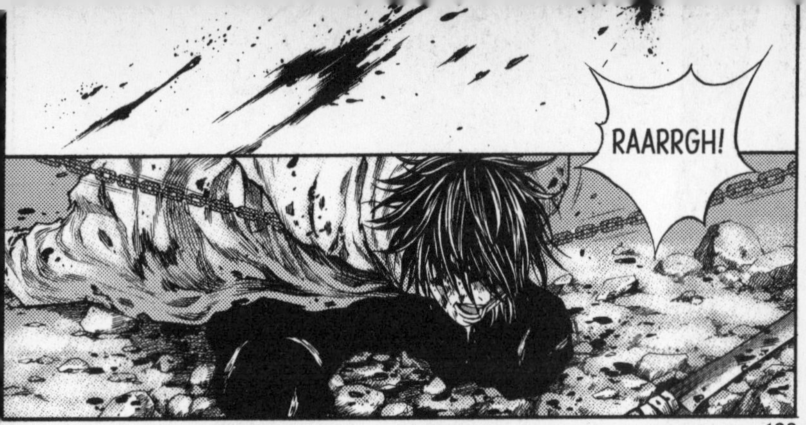
RAARRGH!



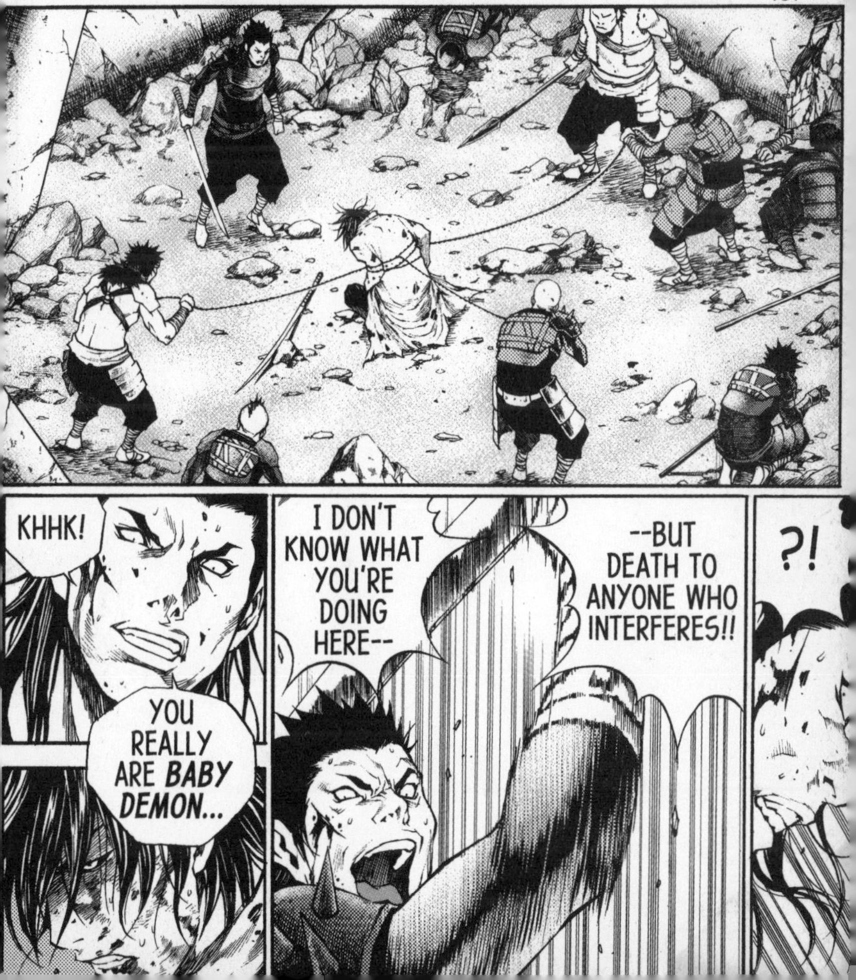
KHHK!
YOU REALLY ARE *BABY DEMON*...
I DON'T KNOW WHAT YOU'RE DOING HERE--
--BUT DEATH TO ANYONE WHO INTERFERES!!
?!

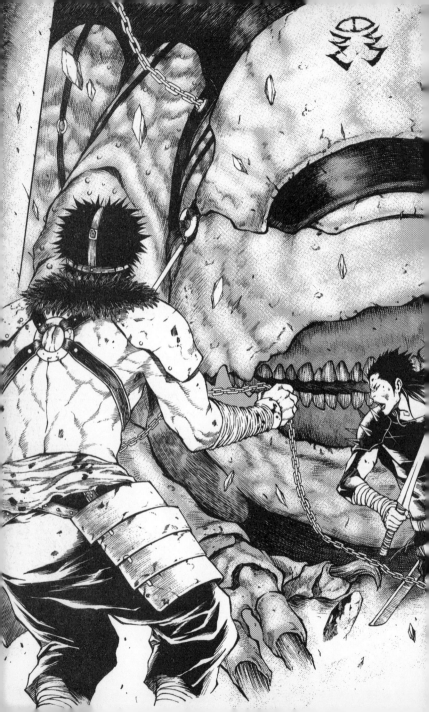

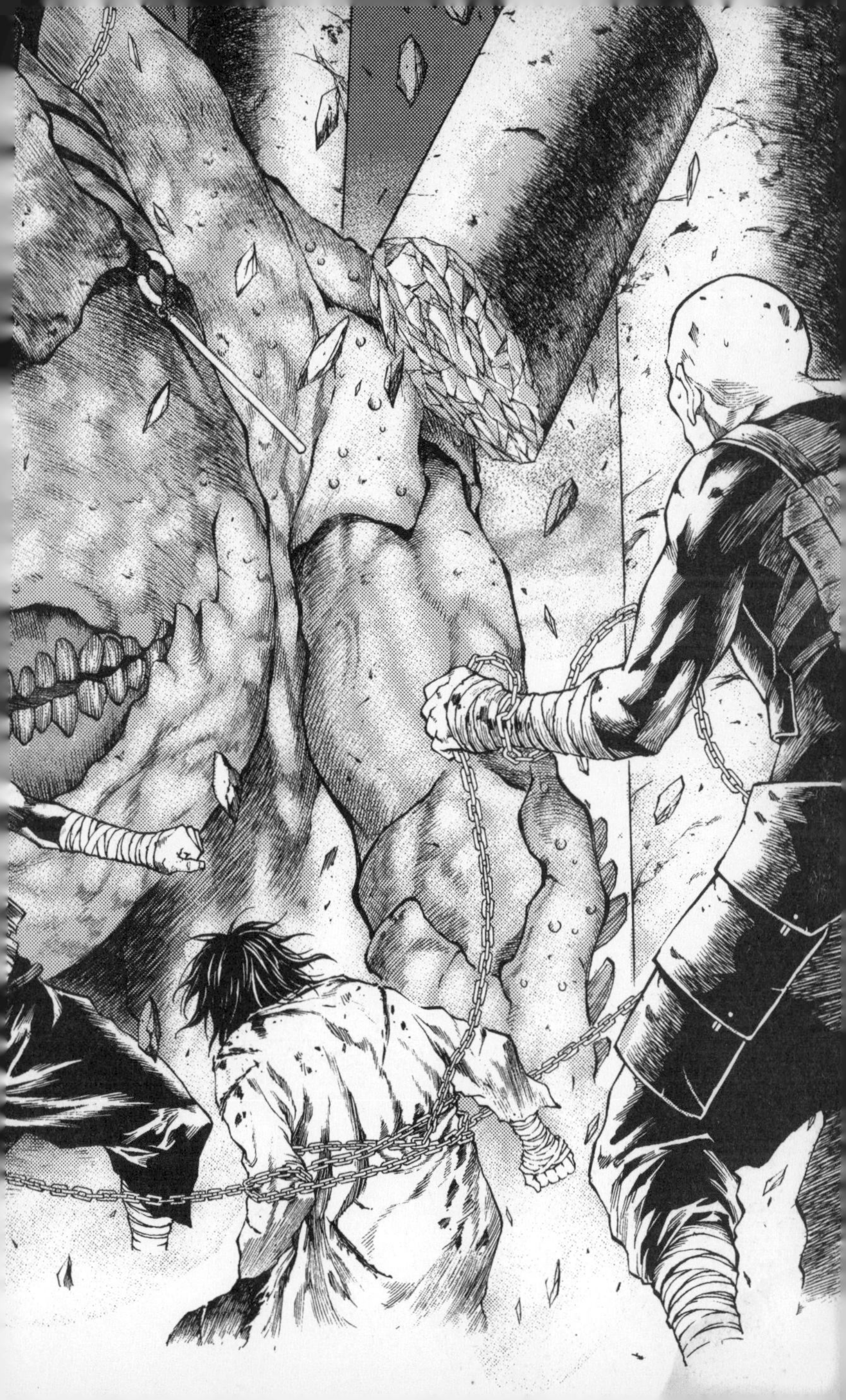

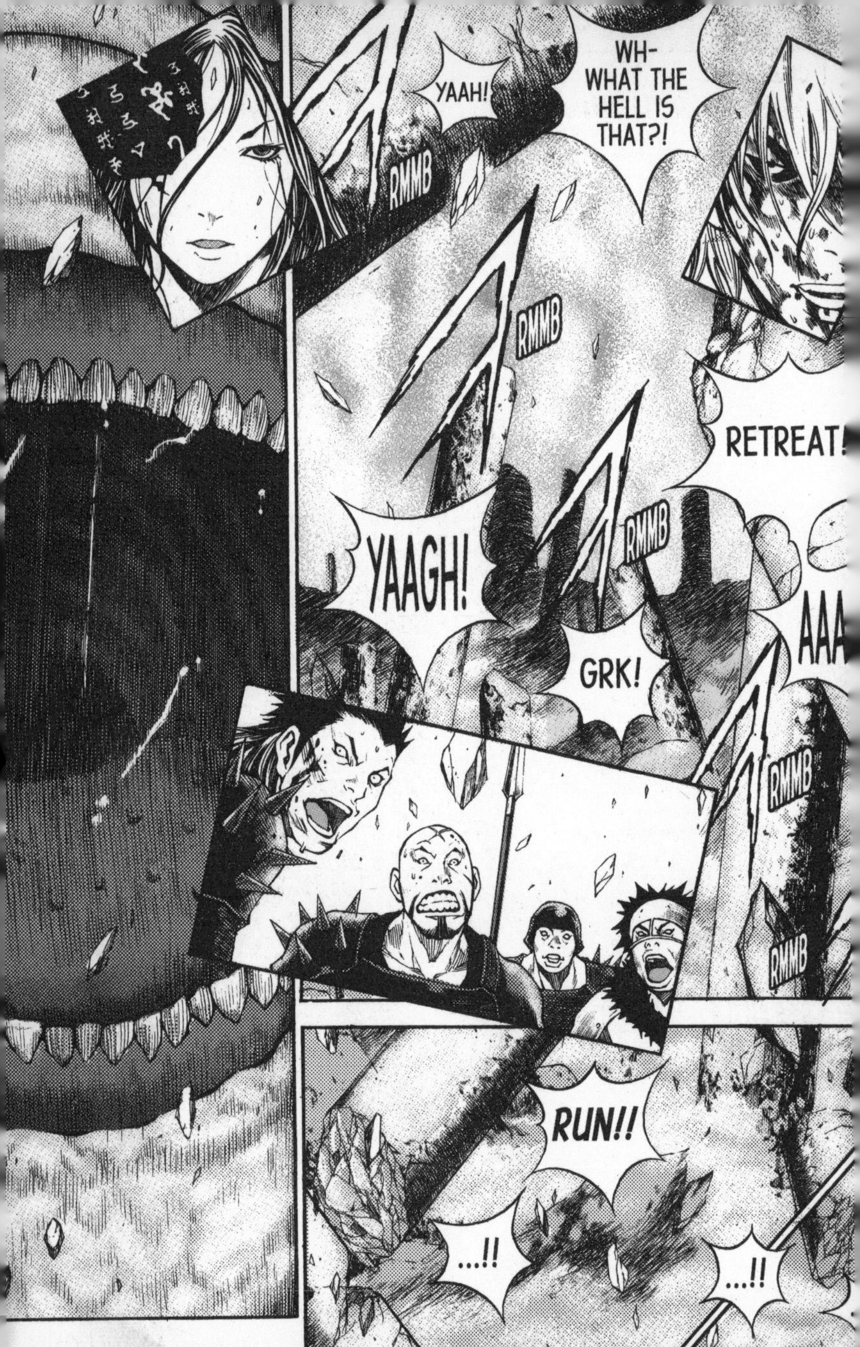
WH- WHAT THE HELL IS THAT?!
YAAH!
RMMB
RETREAT!
RMMB
AAA
RMMB
YAAGH!
GRK!
RMMB
RMMB
RUN!!
...!!
...!!

# Chapter 29
# MAN AND SWORD

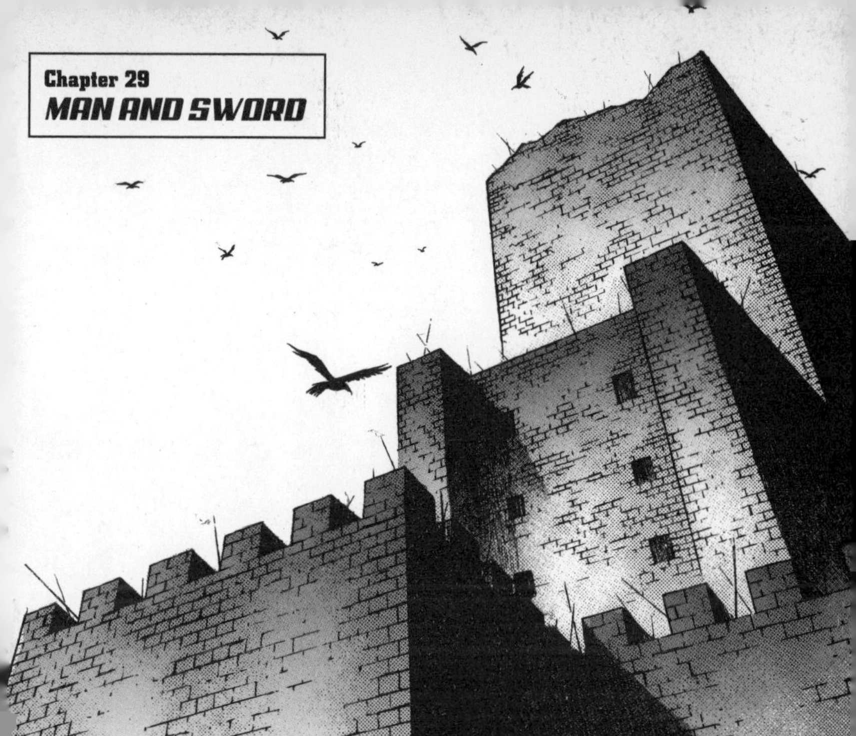

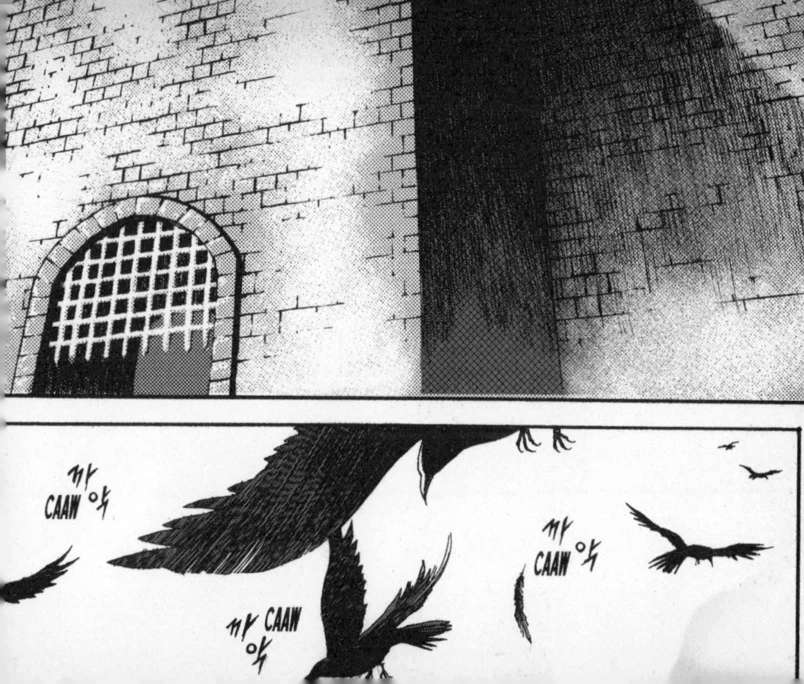
까악
CAAW
까악
CAAW
까악
CAAW

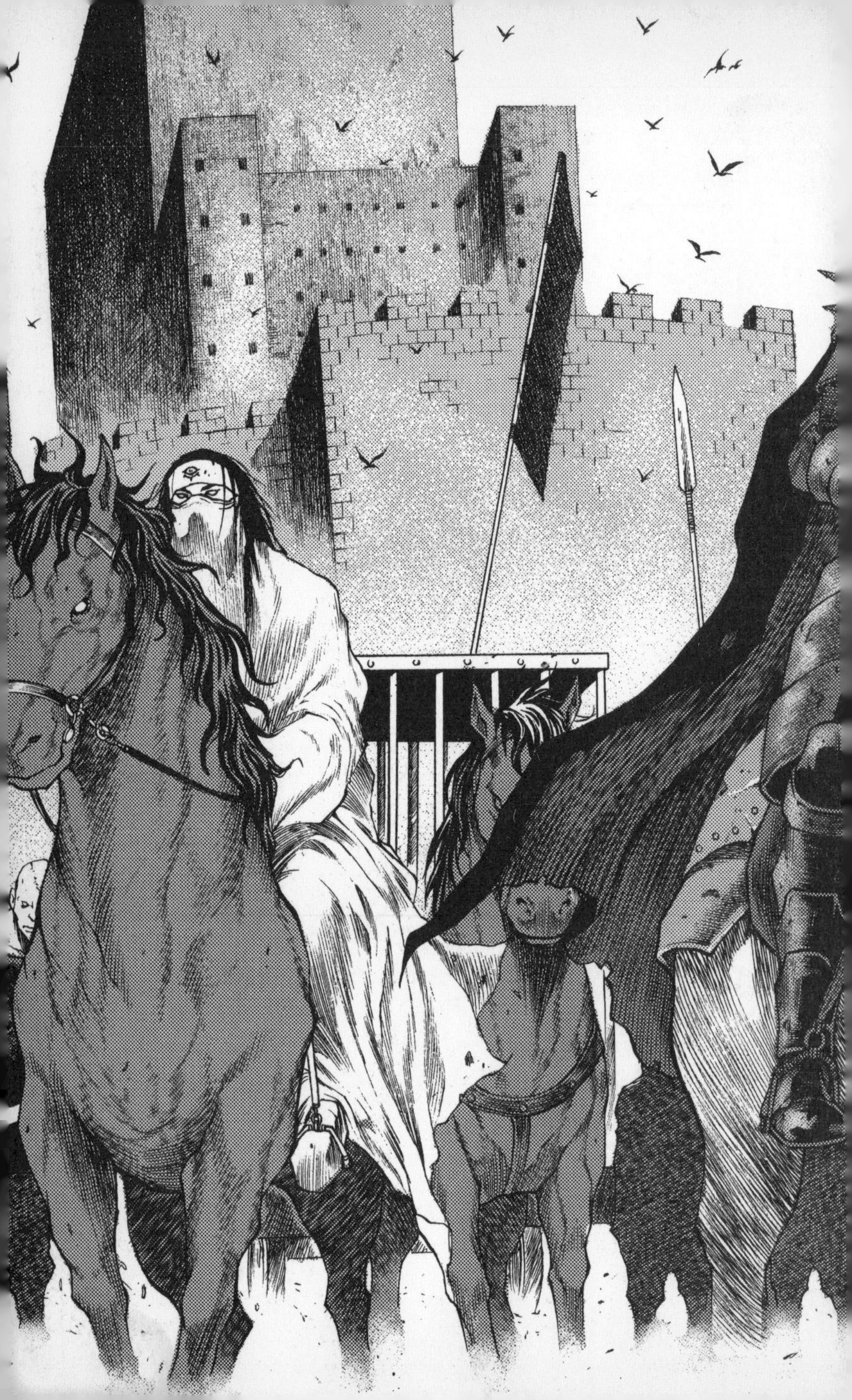

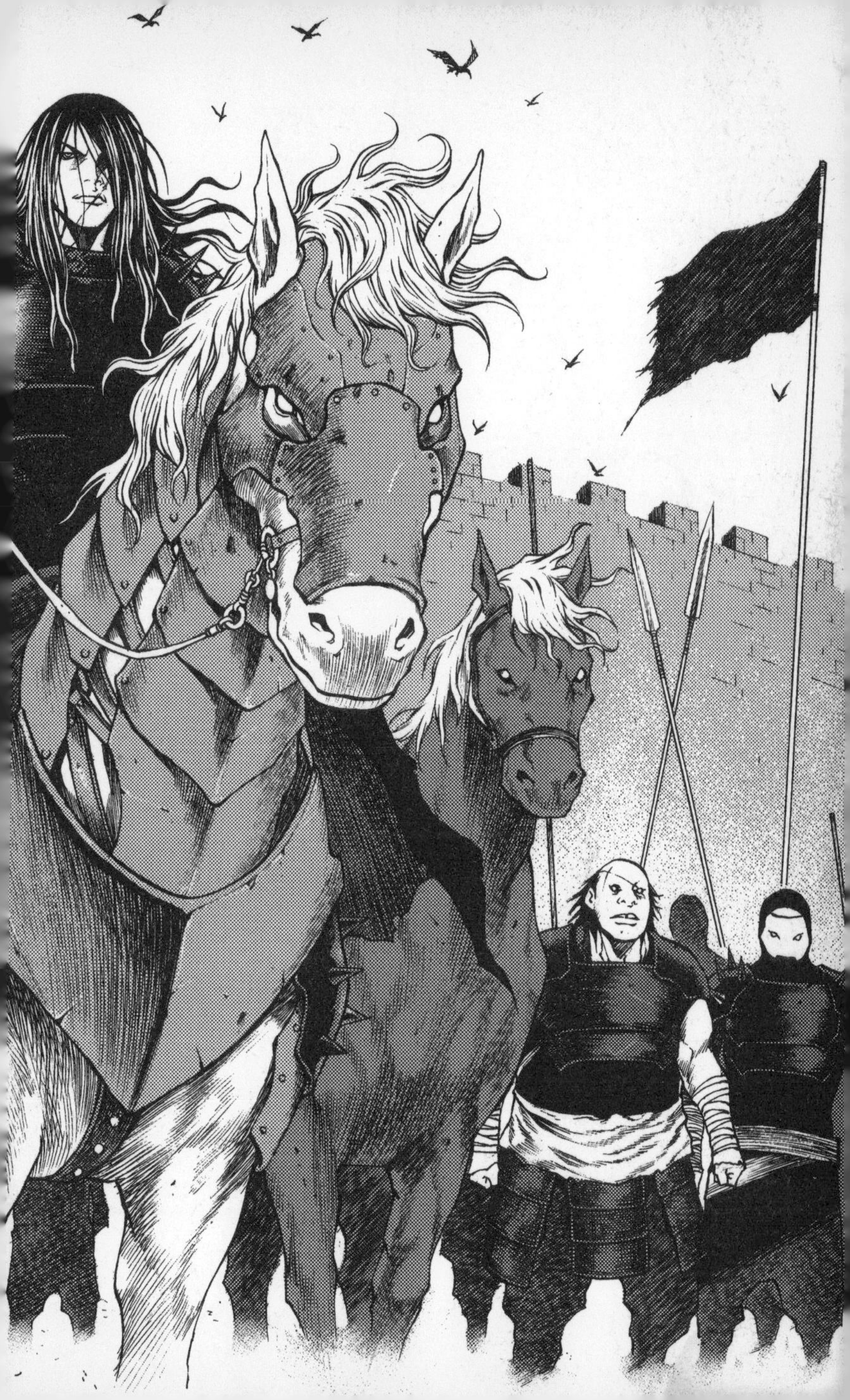

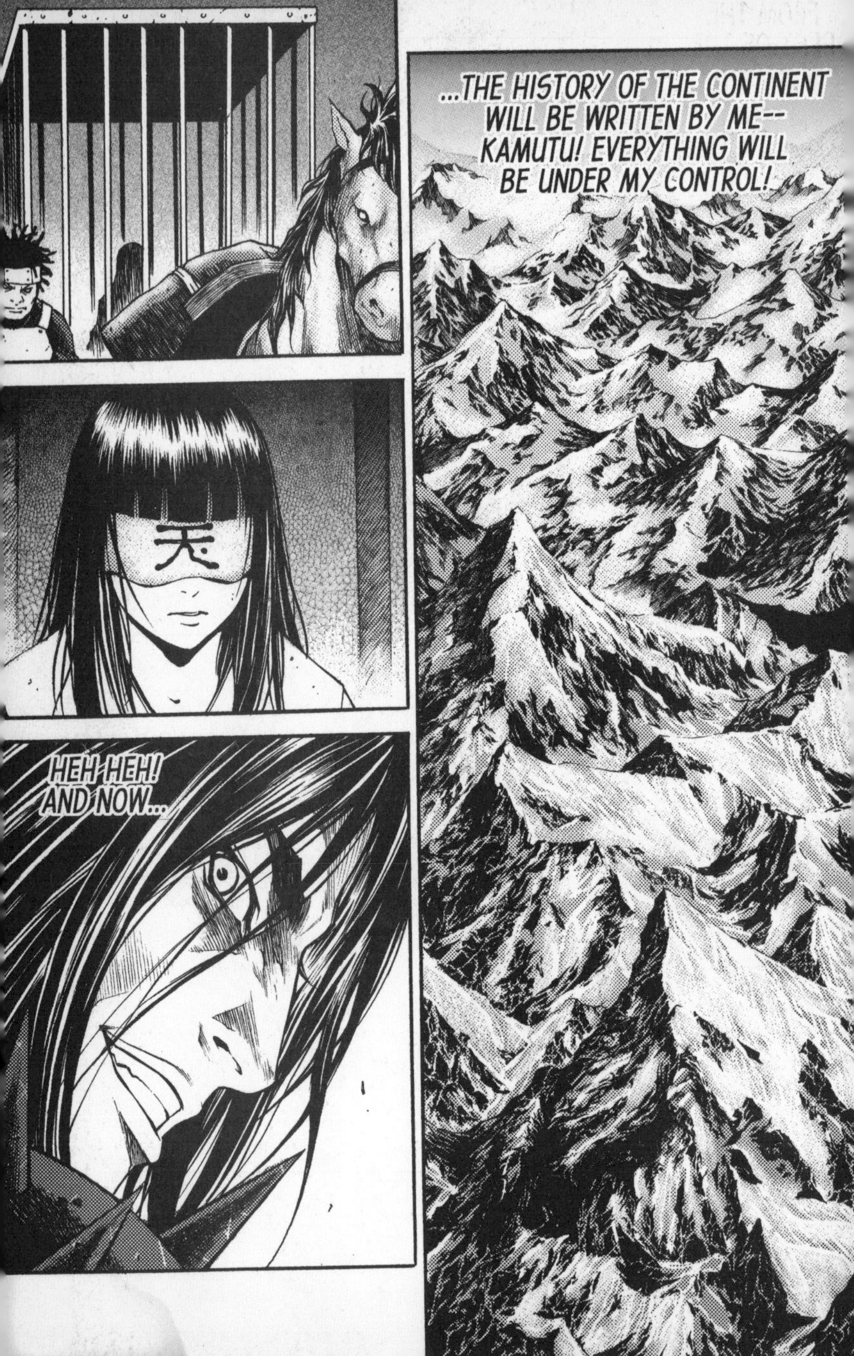
HEH HEH! AND NOW...
...THE HISTORY OF THE CONTINENT WILL BE WRITTEN BY ME-- KAMUTU! EVERYTHING WILL BE UNDER MY CONTROL!

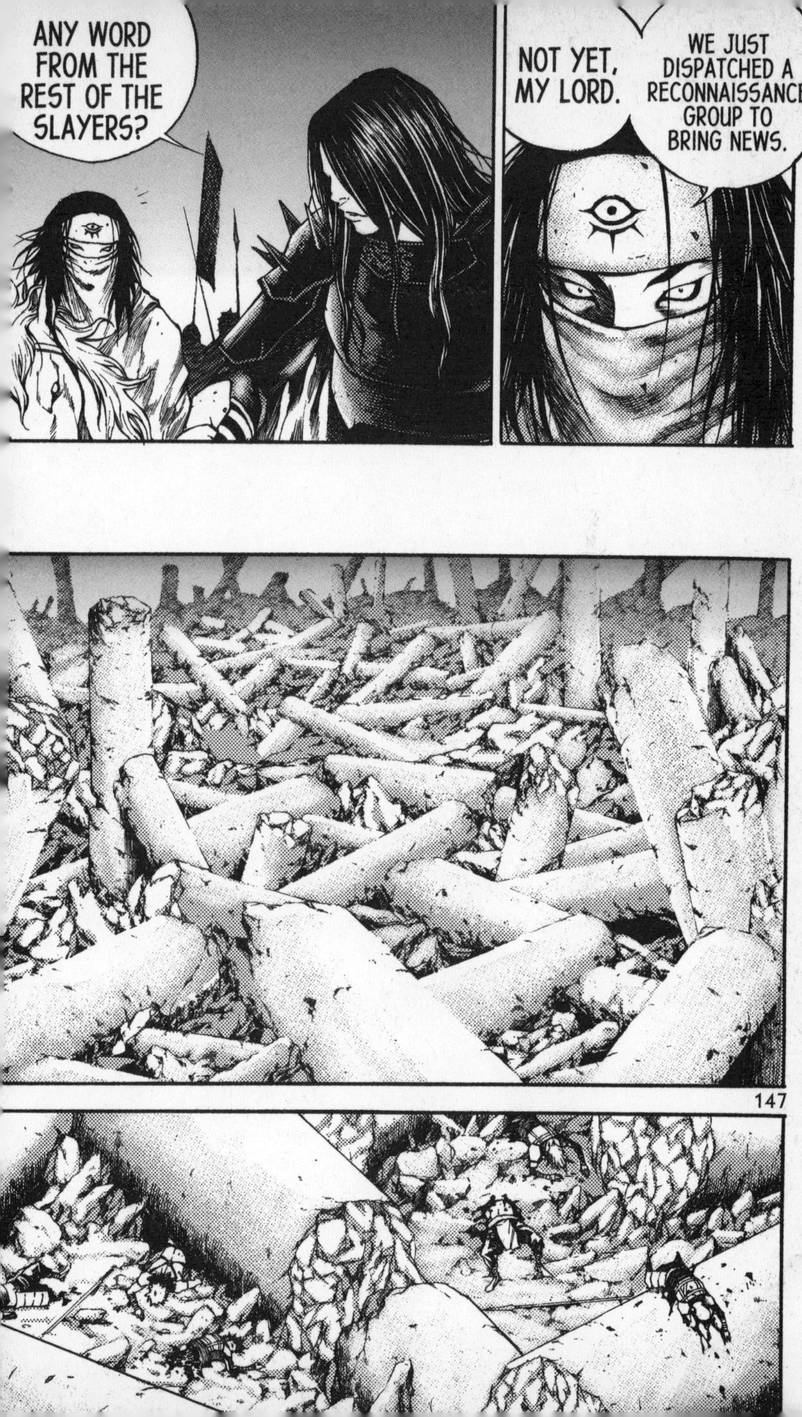
ANY WORD FROM THE REST OF THE SLAYERS?
NOT YET, MY LORD.
WE JUST DISPATCHED A RECONNAISSANCE GROUP TO BRING NEWS.

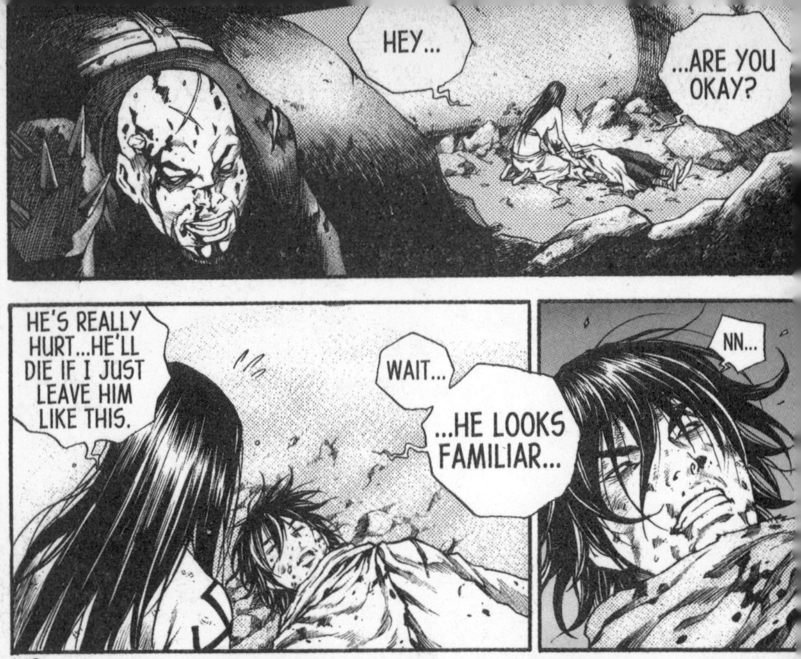
HEY...
...ARE YOU OKAY?
HE'S REALLY HURT...HE'LL DIE IF I JUST LEAVE HIM LIKE THIS.
WAIT...
...HE LOOKS FAMILIAR...
NN...



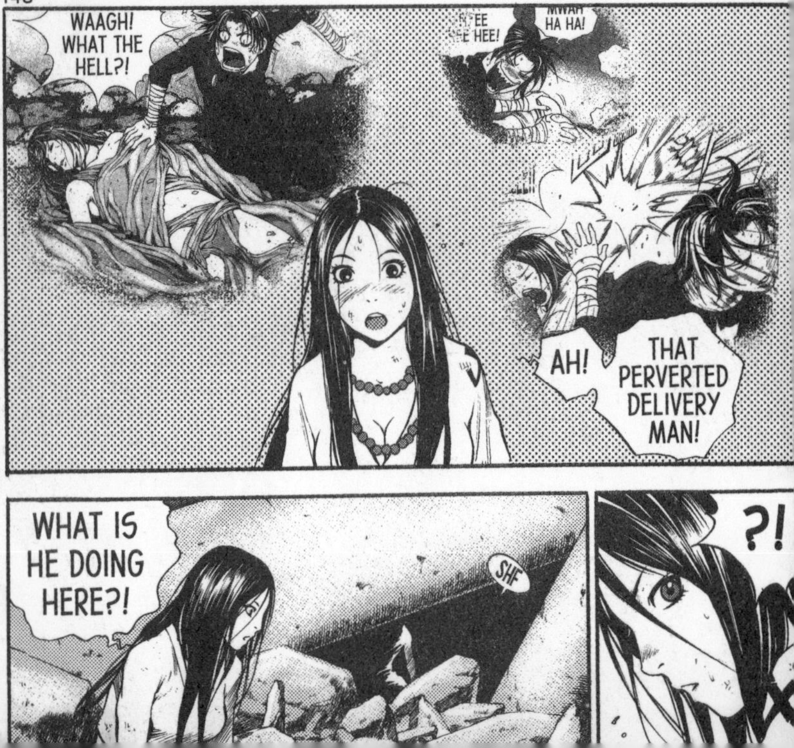
WAAGH! WHAT THE HELL?!
MWAH HA HA!
AH!
THAT PERVERTED DELIVERY MAN!
WHAT IS HE DOING HERE?!
SHF
?!

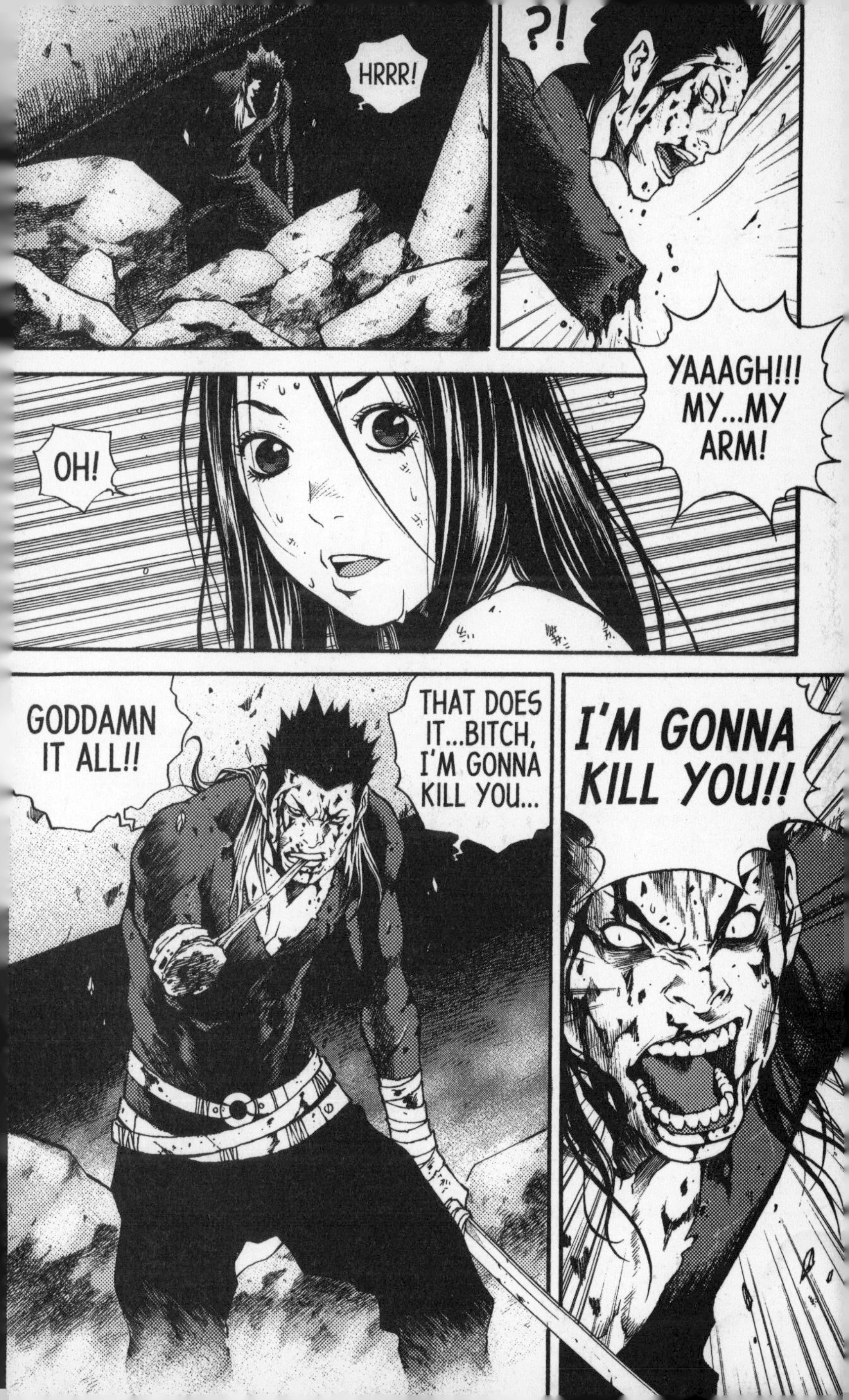
?!
HRRR!
YAAAGH!!! MY...MY ARM!
OH!
I'M GONNA KILL YOU!!
THAT DOES IT...BITCH, I'M GONNA KILL YOU...
GODDAMN IT ALL!!

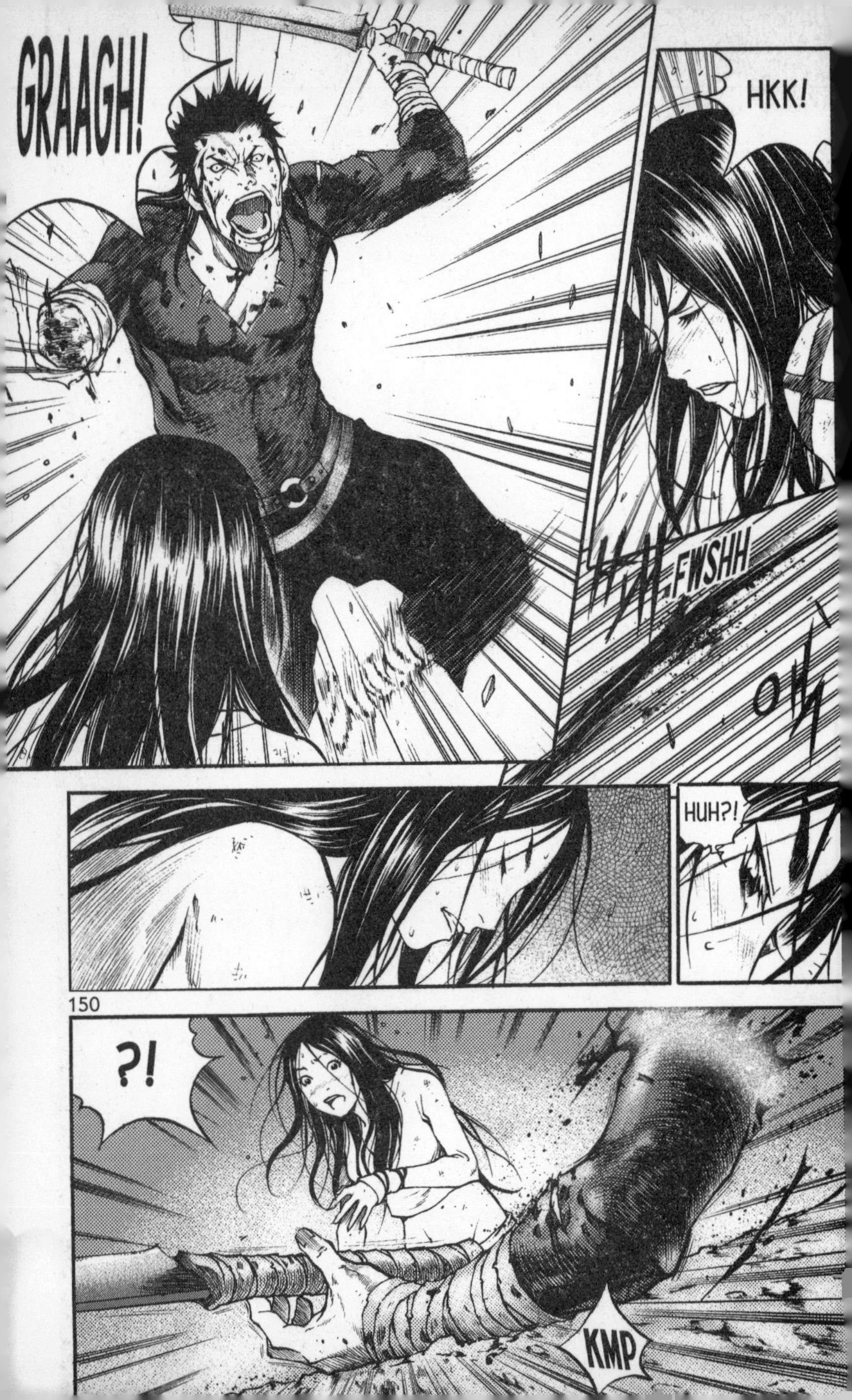
HKK!
GRAAGH!
FWSHH
HUH?!
?!
KMP

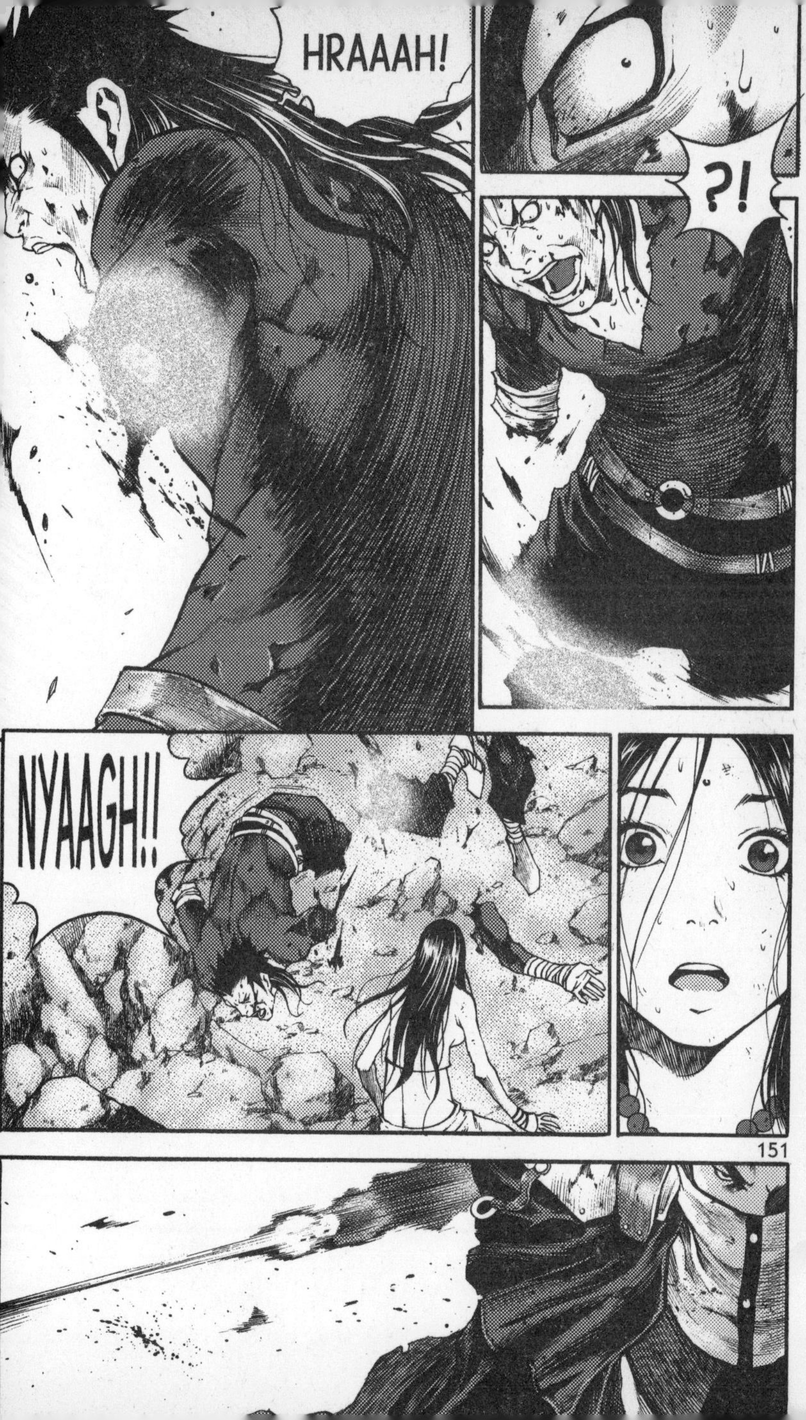
?!
HRAAAH!
NYAAGH!!

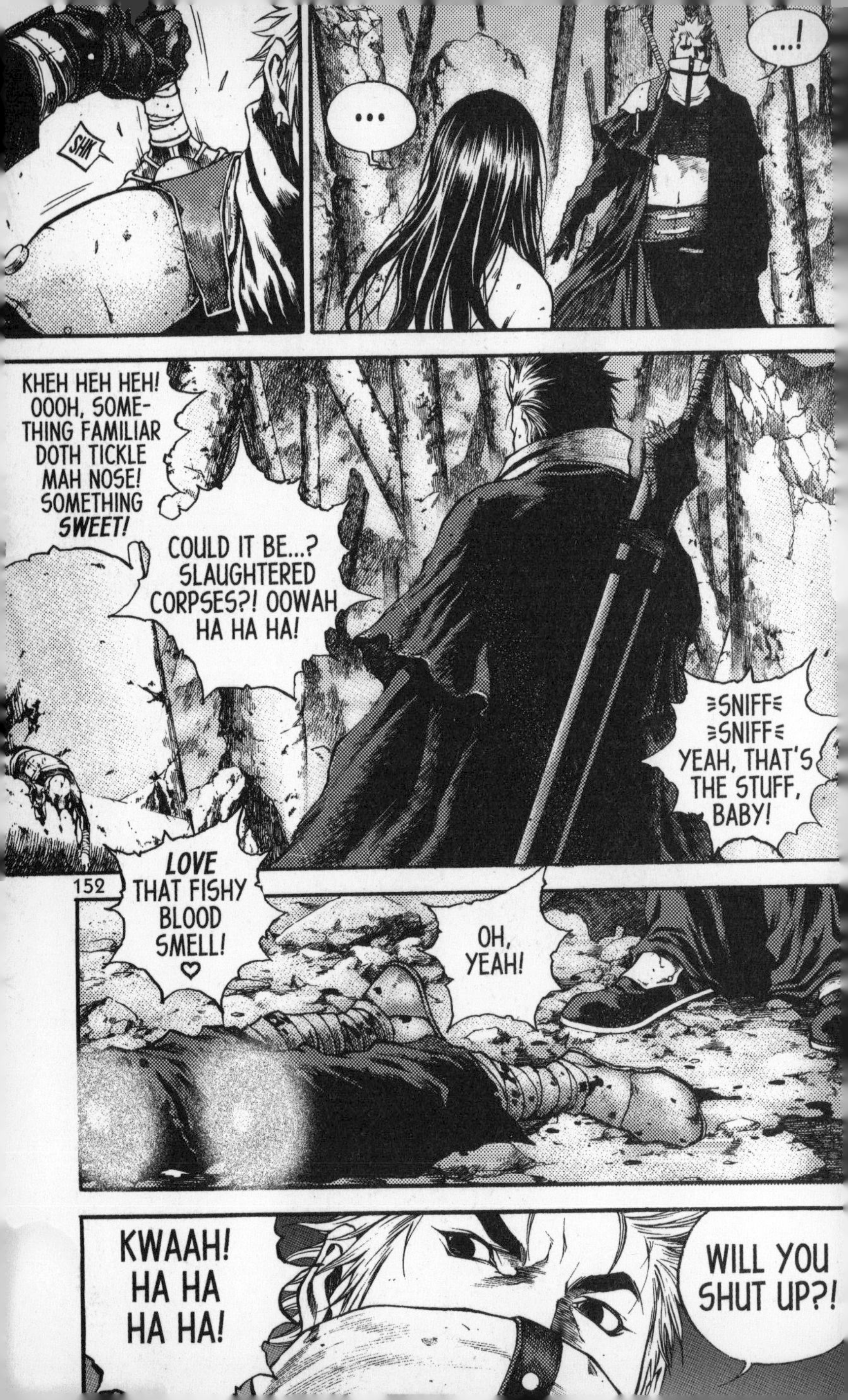
SHK
...
...!
KHEH HEH HEH! OOOH, SOMETHING FAMILIAR DOTH TICKLE MAH NOSE! SOMETHING SWEET!
COULD IT BE...? SLAUGHTERED CORPSES?! OOWAH HA HA HA!
SNIFF SNIFF YEAH, THAT'S THE STUFF, BABY!
LOVE THAT FISHY BLOOD SMELL! ♡
OH, YEAH!
KWAAH! HA HA HA HA!
WILL YOU SHUT UP?!

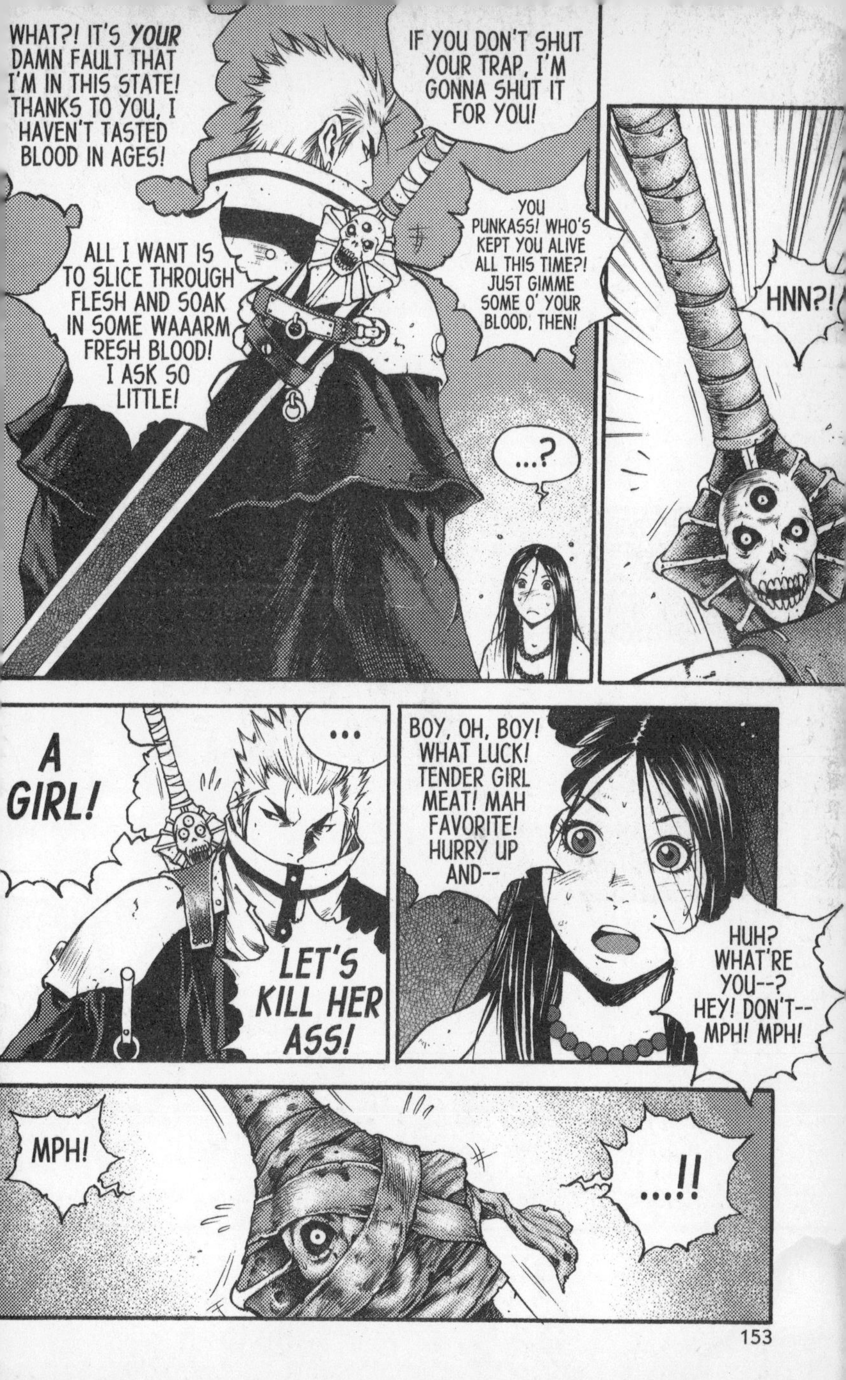
IF YOU DON'T SHUT YOUR TRAP, I'M GONNA SHUT IT FOR YOU!
WHAT?! IT'S *YOUR* DAMN FAULT THAT I'M IN THIS STATE! THANKS TO YOU, I HAVEN'T TASTED BLOOD IN AGES!
YOU PUNKASS! WHO'S KEPT YOU ALIVE ALL THIS TIME?! JUST GIMME SOME O' YOUR BLOOD, THEN!
ALL I WANT IS TO SLICE THROUGH FLESH AND SOAK IN SOME WAAARM FRESH BLOOD! I ASK SO LITTLE!
...?
HNN?!
BOY, OH, BOY! WHAT LUCK! TENDER GIRL MEAT! MAH FAVORITE! HURRY UP AND--
HUH? WHAT'RE YOU--? HEY! DON'T-- MPH! MPH!
...
A GIRL!
LET'S KILL HER ASS!
...!!
MPH!

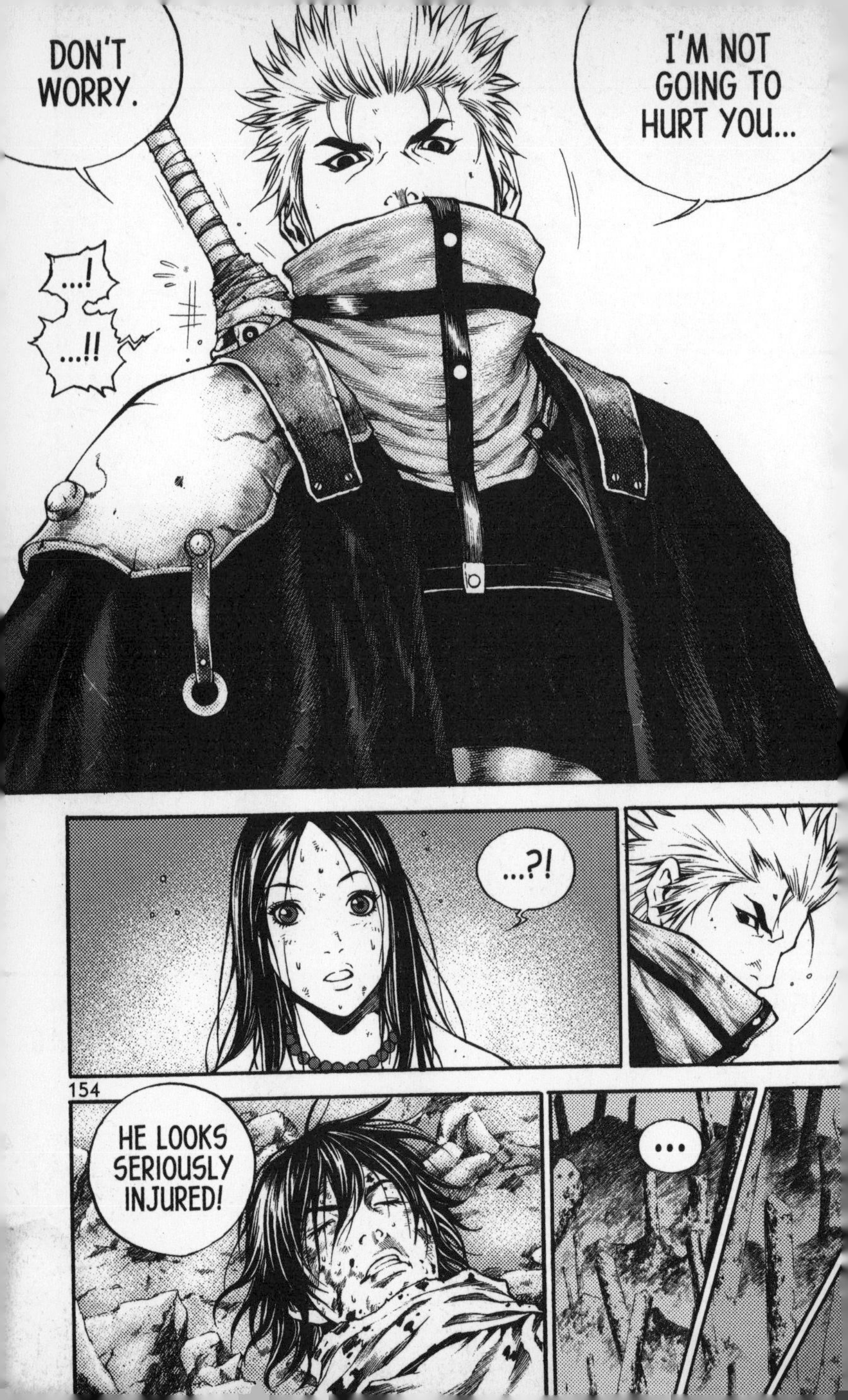
DON'T WORRY.
I'M NOT GOING TO HURT YOU...
...!
...!!
...?!
HE LOOKS SERIOUSLY INJURED!
...

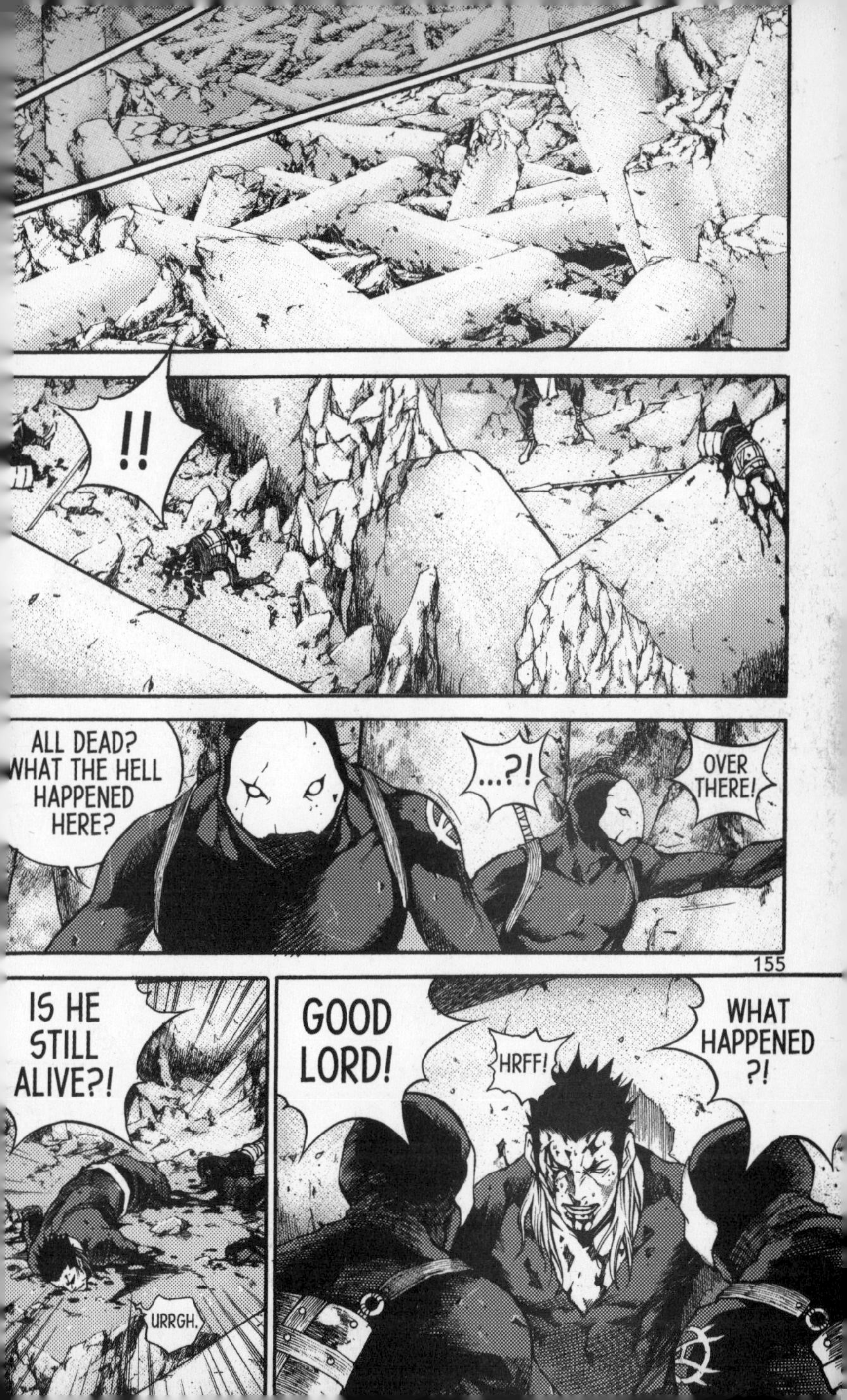
!!
OVER THERE!
...?!
ALL DEAD? WHAT THE HELL HAPPENED HERE?
WHAT HAPPENED ?!
HRFF!
GOOD LORD!
IS HE STILL ALIVE?!
URRGH.

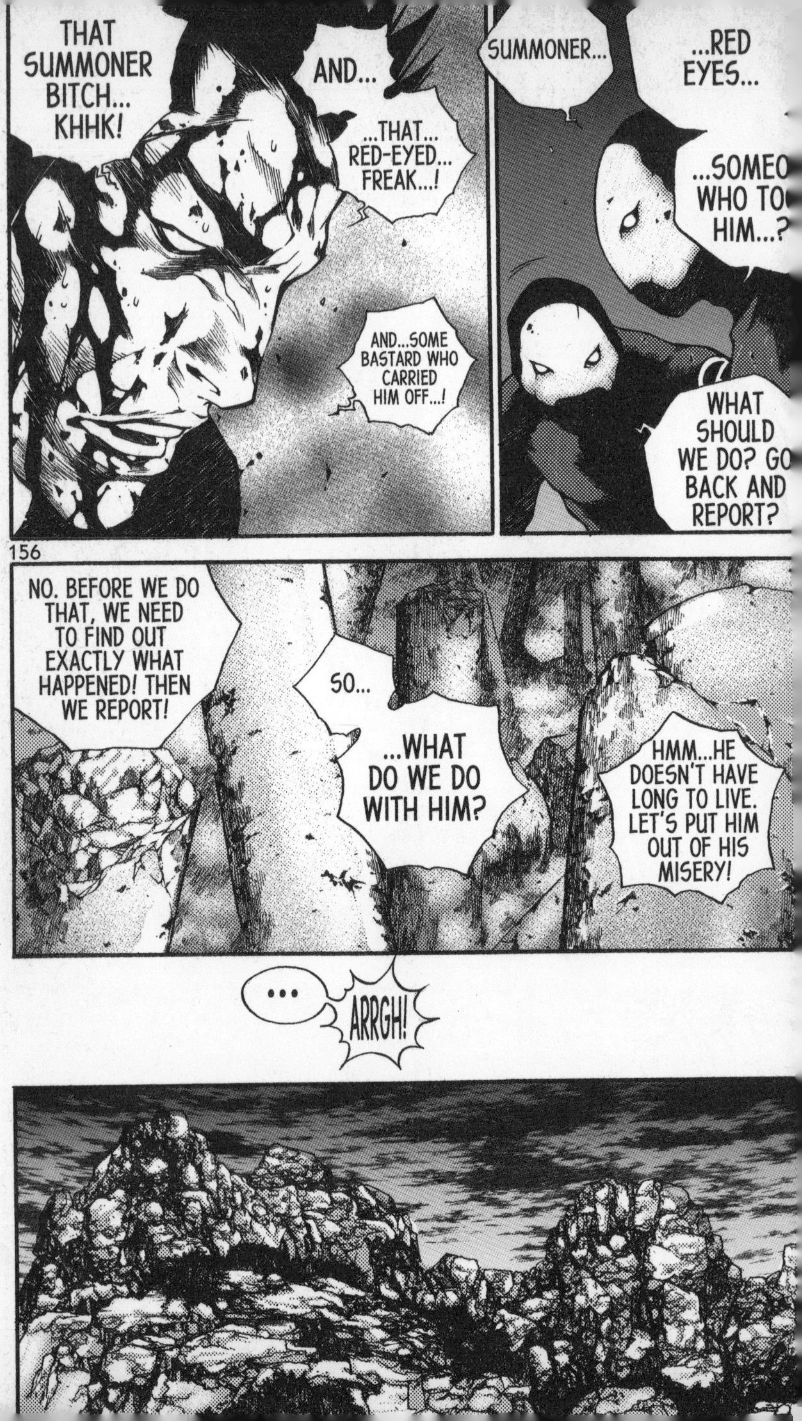
THAT SUMMONER BITCH... KHHK!
AND...
...THAT... RED-EYED... FREAK...!
AND...SOME BASTARD WHO CARRIED HIM OFF...!
SUMMONER...
...RED EYES...
...SOMEO WHO TO HIM...?
WHAT SHOULD WE DO? GO BACK AND REPORT?
NO. BEFORE WE DO THAT, WE NEED TO FIND OUT EXACTLY WHAT HAPPENED! THEN WE REPORT!
SO...
...WHAT DO WE DO WITH HIM?
HMM...HE DOESN'T HAVE LONG TO LIVE. LET'S PUT HIM OUT OF HIS MISERY!
...
ARRGH!

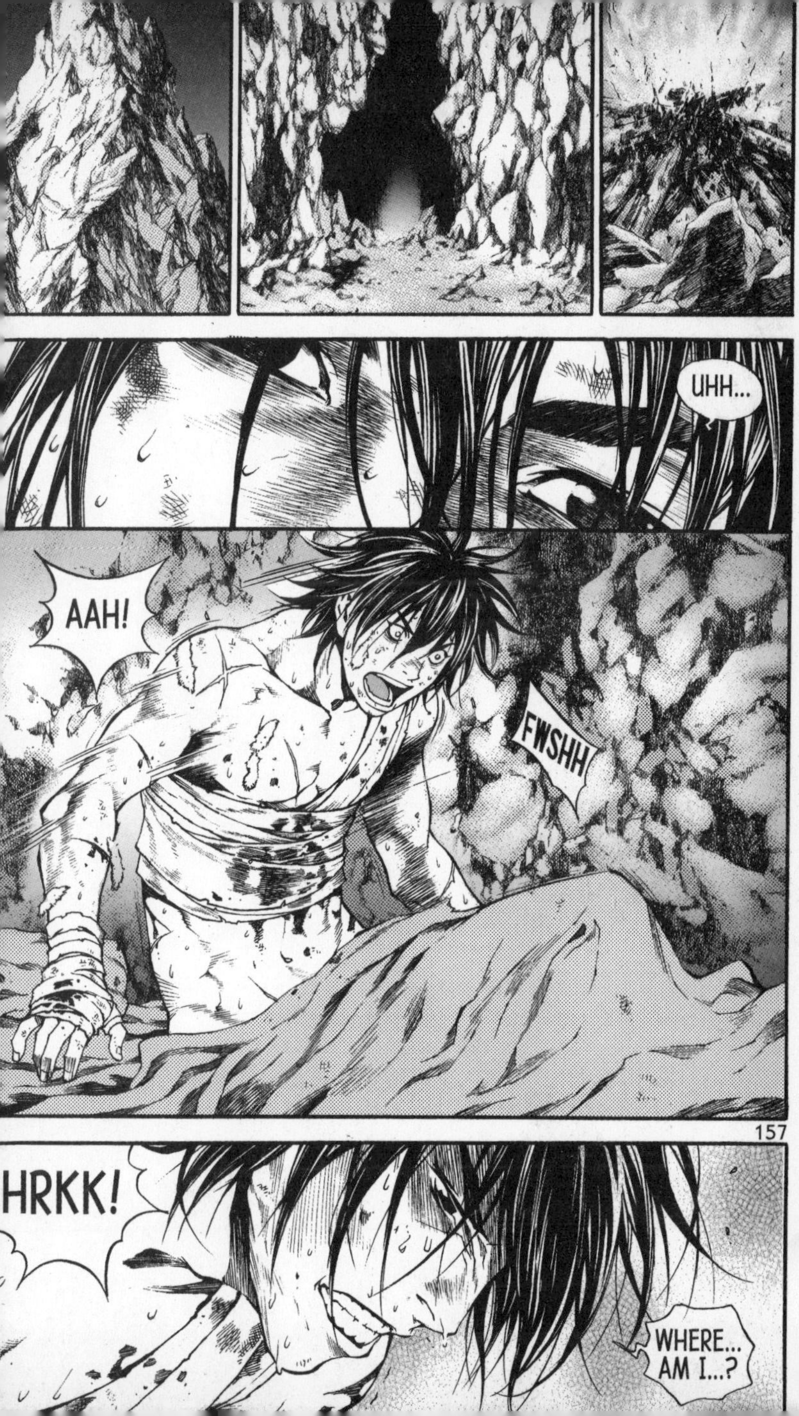
UHH...
AAH!
FWSHH
HRKK!
WHERE... AM I...?

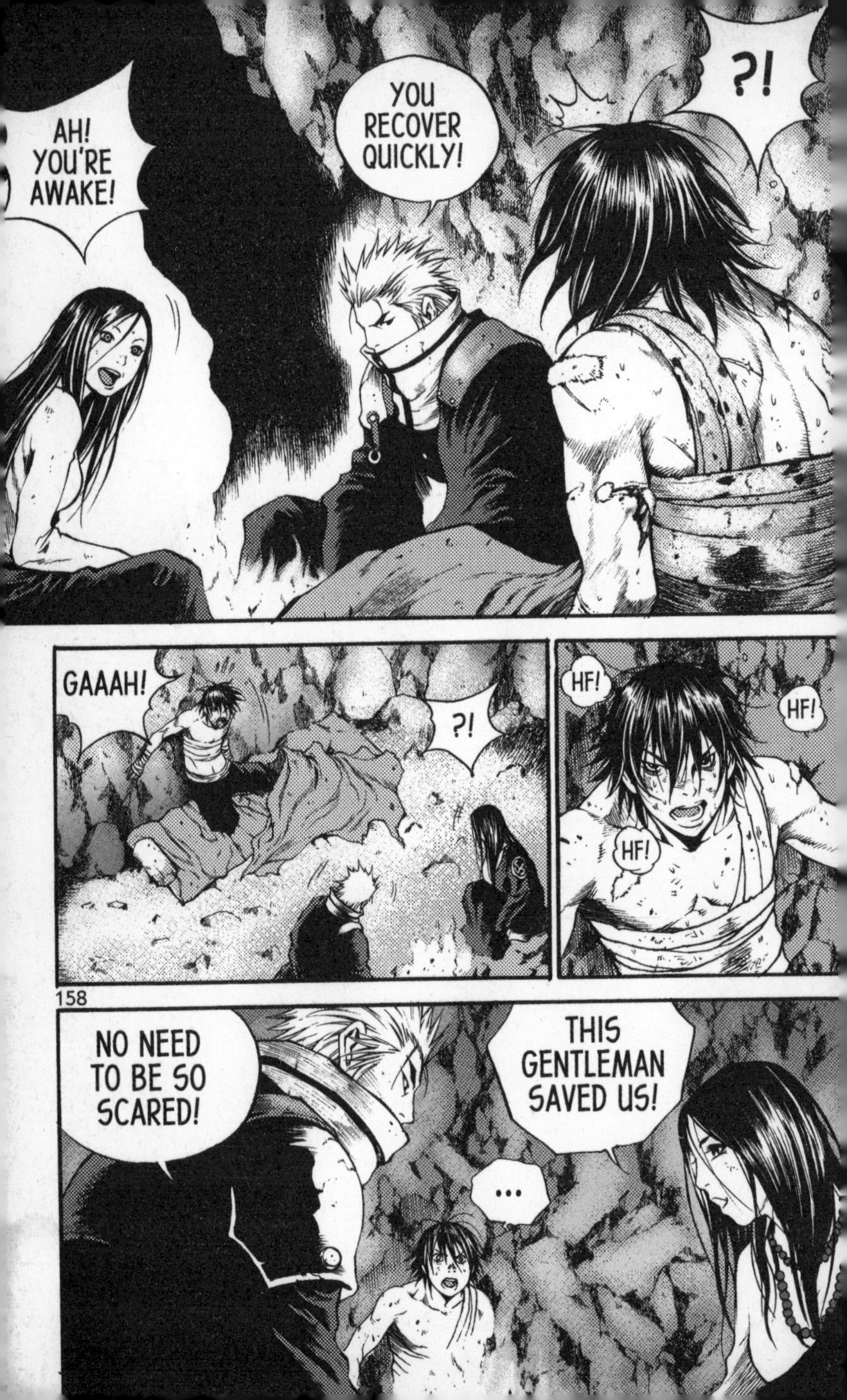
AH! YOU'RE AWAKE!
YOU RECOVER QUICKLY!
?!
GAAAH!
?!
HF!
HF!
HF!
NO NEED TO BE SO SCARED!
THIS GENTLEMAN SAVED US!
...

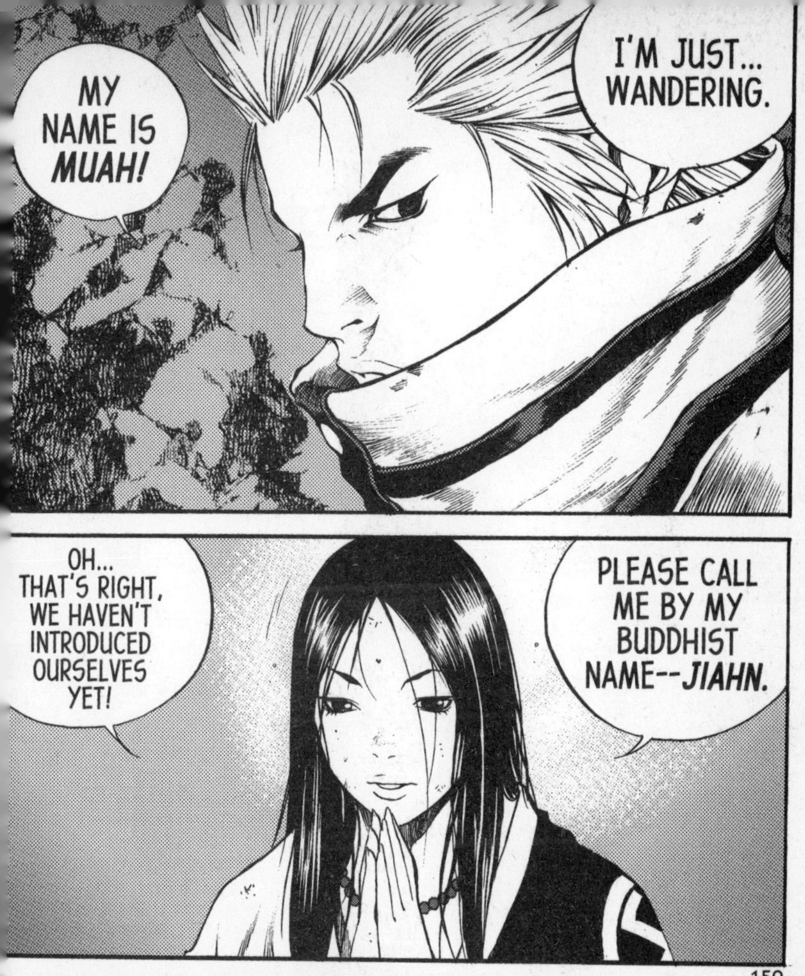
MY NAME IS *MUAH!*
I'M JUST... WANDERING.
OH... THAT'S RIGHT, WE HAVEN'T INTRODUCED OURSELVES YET!
PLEASE CALL ME BY MY BUDDHIST NAME--*JIAHN.*



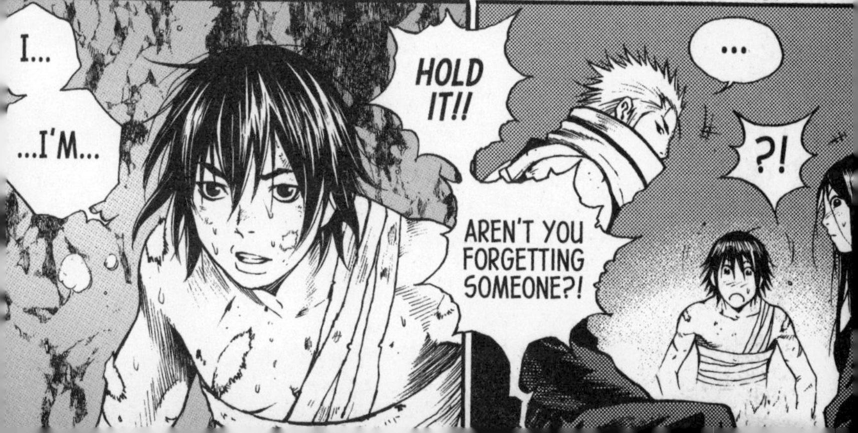
I...
...I'M...
*HOLD IT!!*
...
?!
AREN'T YOU FORGETTING SOMEONE?!

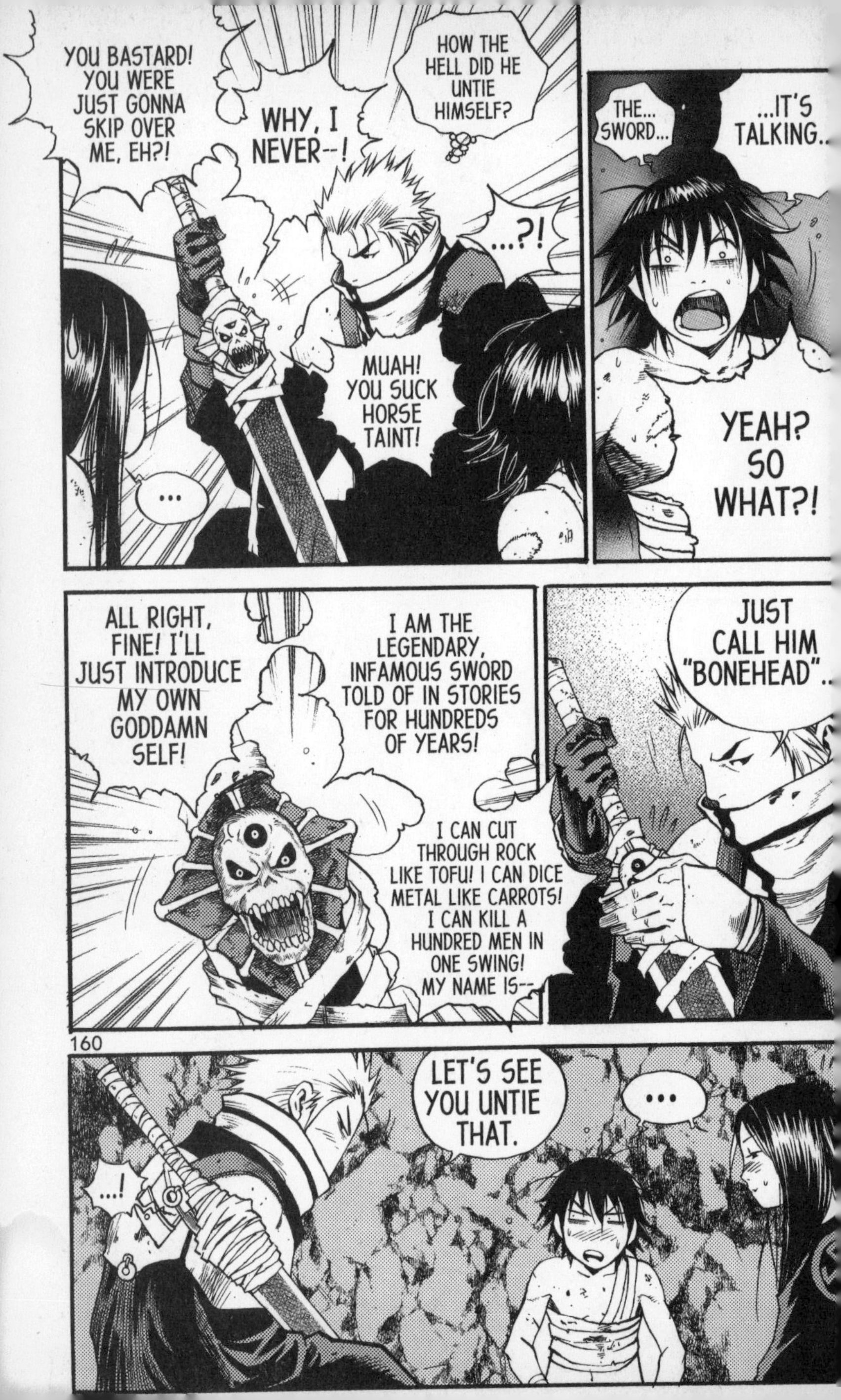

YOU BASTARD! YOU WERE JUST GONNA SKIP OVER ME, EH?!
WHY, I NEVER--!
HOW THE HELL DID HE UNTIE HIMSELF?
...?!
MUAH! YOU SUCK HORSE TAINT!
...
THE... SWORD...
...IT'S TALKING..
YEAH? SO WHAT?!
ALL RIGHT, FINE! I'LL JUST INTRODUCE MY OWN GODDAMN SELF!
I AM THE LEGENDARY, INFAMOUS SWORD TOLD OF IN STORIES FOR HUNDREDS OF YEARS!
I CAN CUT THROUGH ROCK LIKE TOFU! I CAN DICE METAL LIKE CARROTS! I CAN KILL A HUNDRED MEN IN ONE SWING! MY NAME IS--
JUST CALL HIM "BONEHEAD"..
LET'S SEE YOU UNTIE THAT.
...
...!

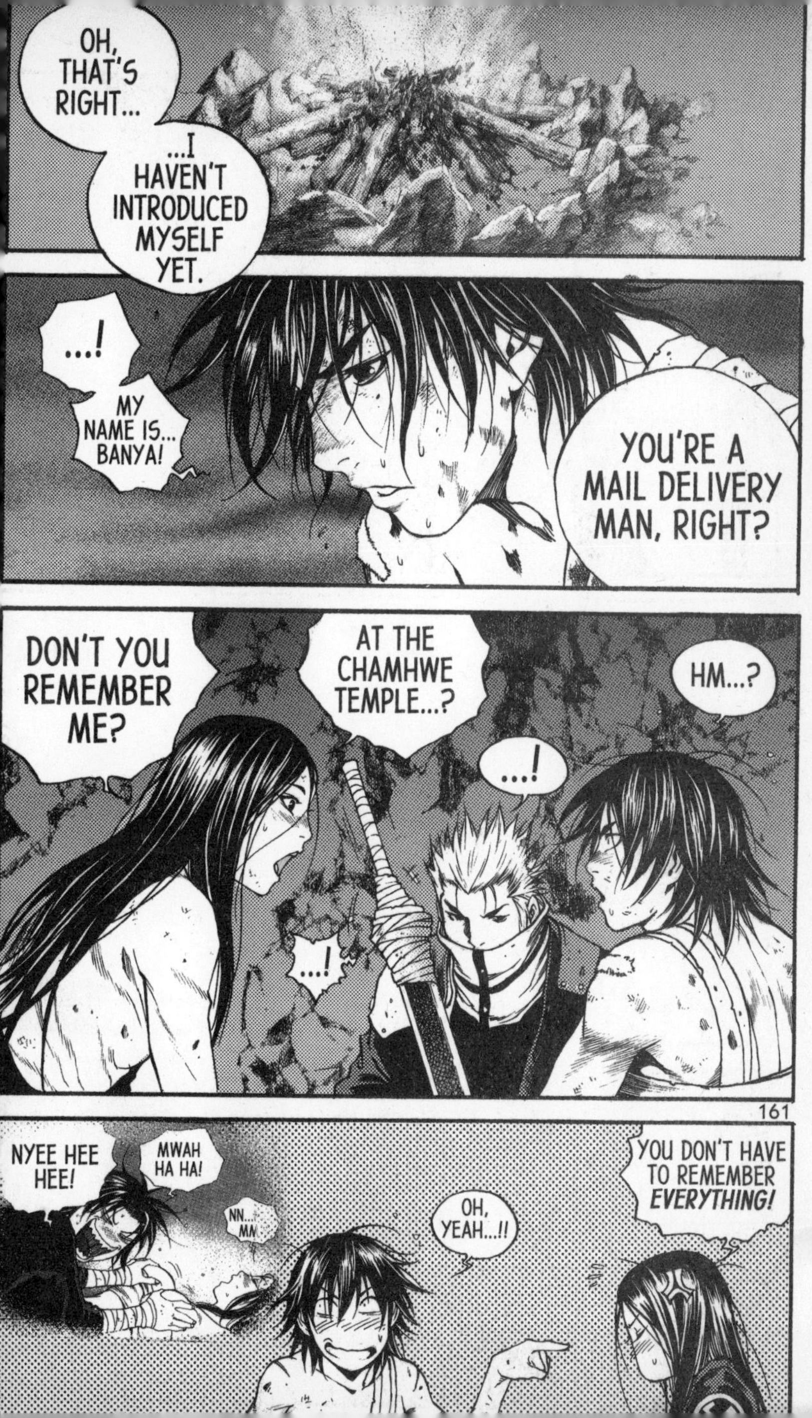
OH, THAT'S RIGHT...
...I HAVEN'T INTRODUCED MYSELF YET.
...!
MY NAME IS... BANYA!
YOU'RE A MAIL DELIVERY MAN, RIGHT?
DON'T YOU REMEMBER ME?
AT THE CHAMHWE TEMPLE...?
HM...?
...!
...!
NYEE HEE HEE!
MWAH HA HA!
NN... MN
OH, YEAH...!!
YOU DON'T HAVE TO REMEMBER *EVERYTHING!*

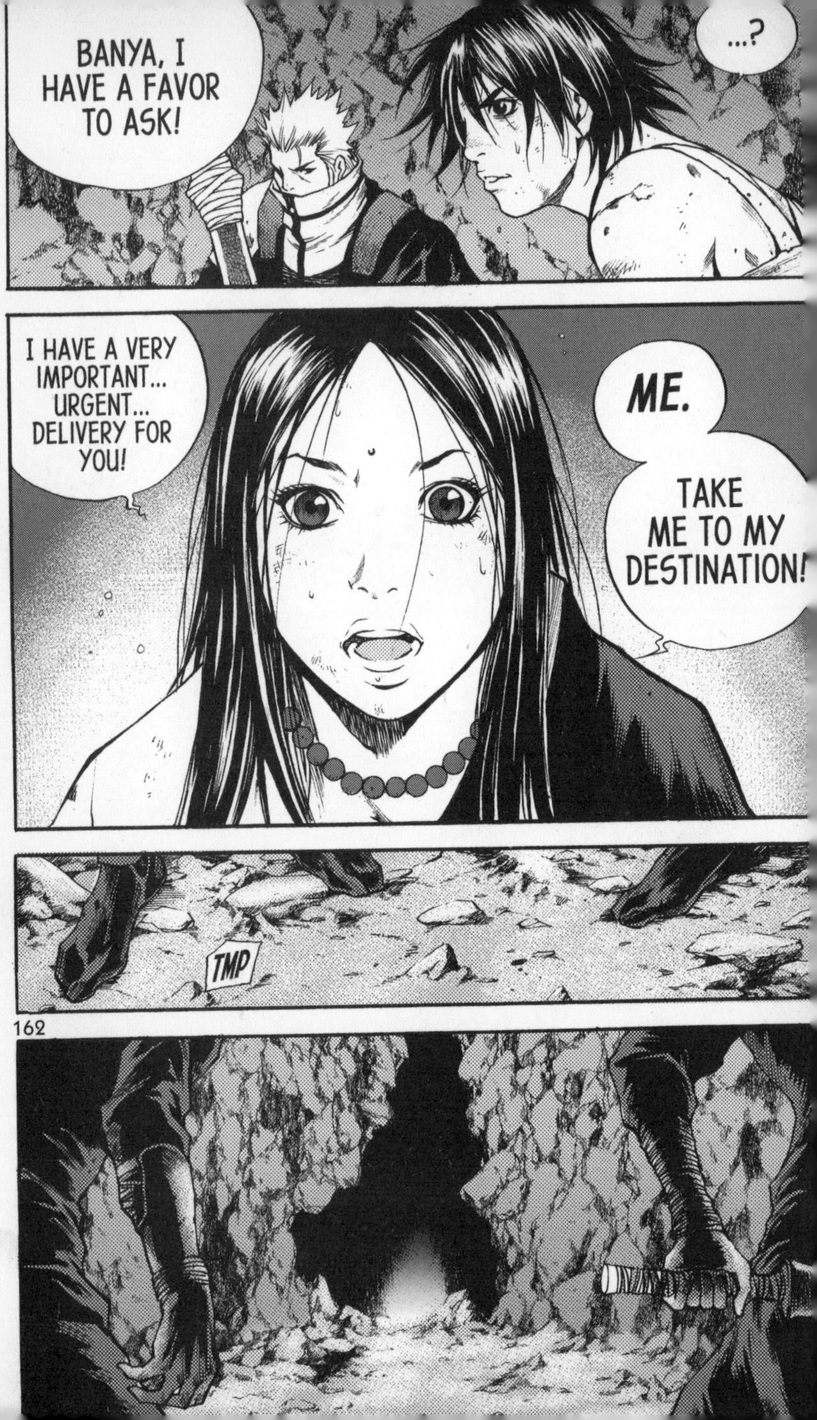
...?
BANYA, I HAVE A FAVOR TO ASK!
ME.
TAKE ME TO MY DESTINATION!
I HAVE A VERY IMPORTANT... URGENT... DELIVERY FOR YOU!
TMP

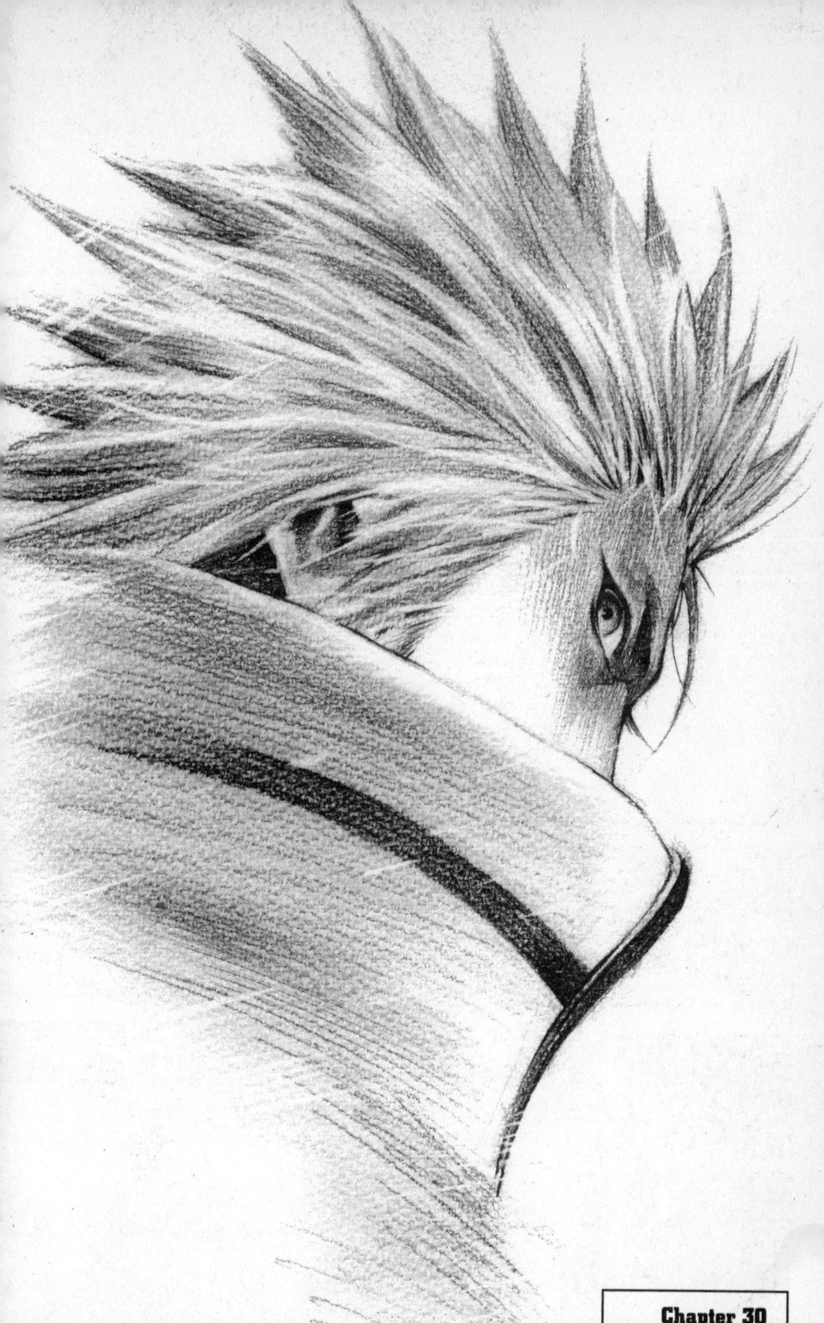

## Chapter 30
## COMPANY

THE *LAND OF DEATH* IN THE SOUTH!

PLEASE TAKE ME THERE!

...!

...

164

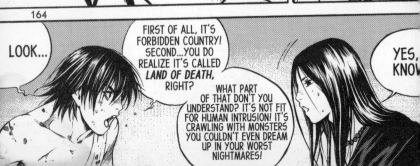

LOOK...

FIRST OF ALL, IT'S FORBIDDEN COUNTRY! SECOND...YOU DO REALIZE IT'S CALLED *LAND OF DEATH*, RIGHT?

WHAT PART OF THAT DON'T YOU UNDERSTAND? IT'S NOT FIT FOR HUMAN INTRUSION! IT'S CRAWLING WITH MONSTERS YOU COULDN'T EVEN DREAM UP IN YOUR WORST NIGHTMARES!

YES, I KNO...

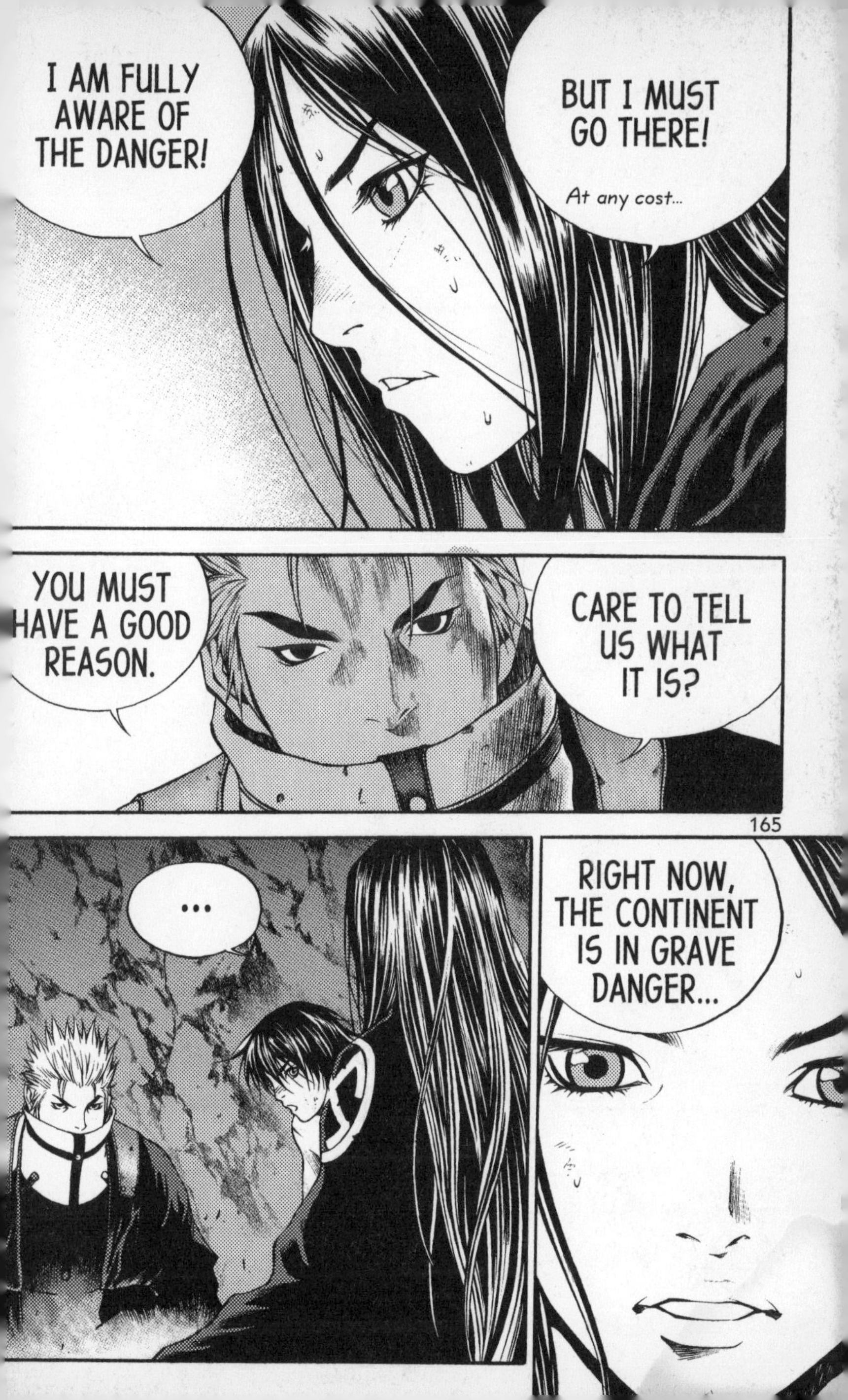
BUT I MUST GO THERE!
At any cost...
I AM FULLY AWARE OF THE DANGER!
CARE TO TELL US WHAT IT IS?
YOU MUST HAVE A GOOD REASON.
RIGHT NOW, THE CONTINENT IS IN GRAVE DANGER...
...

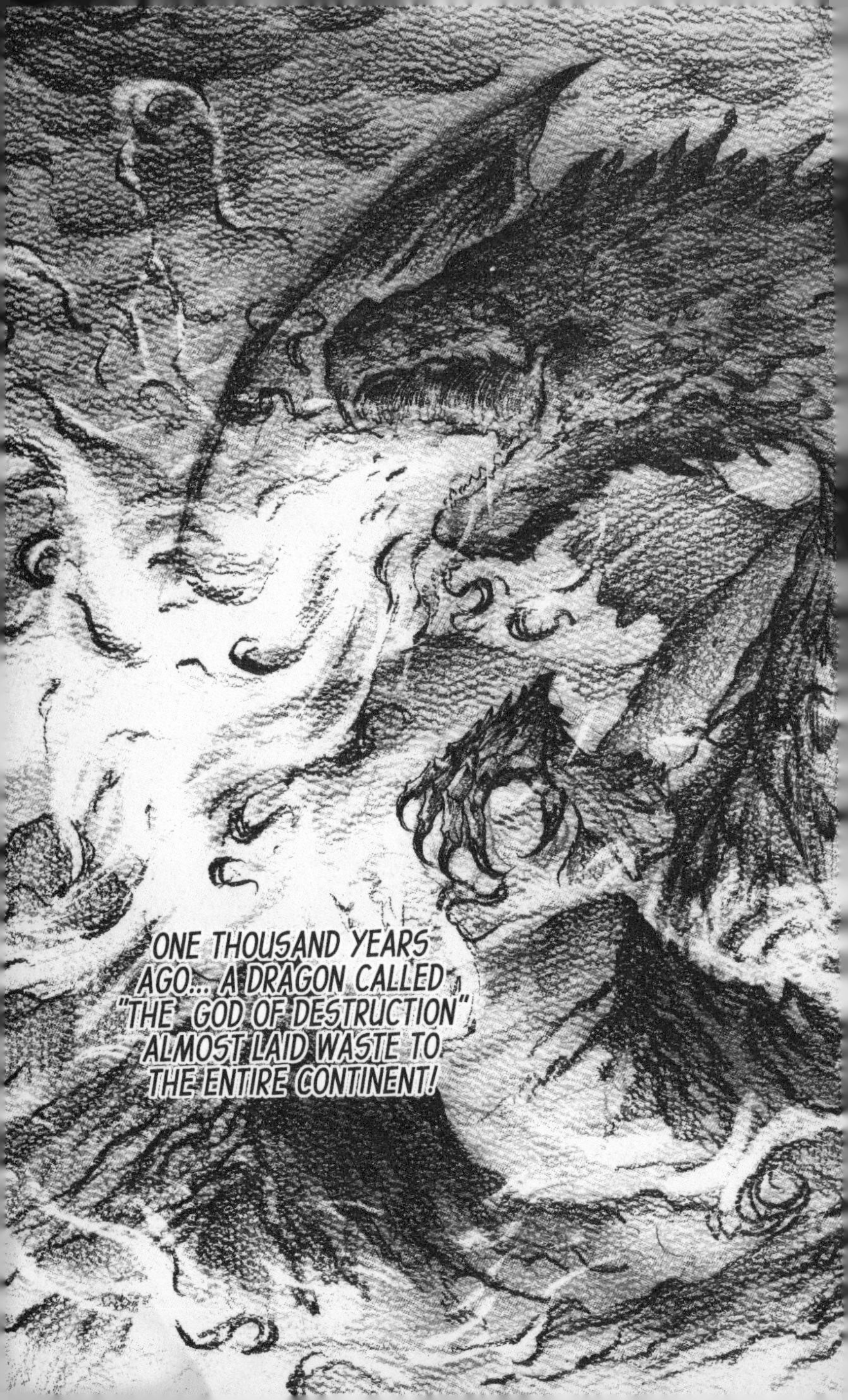
ONE THOUSAND YEARS AGO... A DRAGON CALLED "THE GOD OF DESTRUCTION" ALMOST LAID WASTE TO THE ENTIRE CONTINENT!

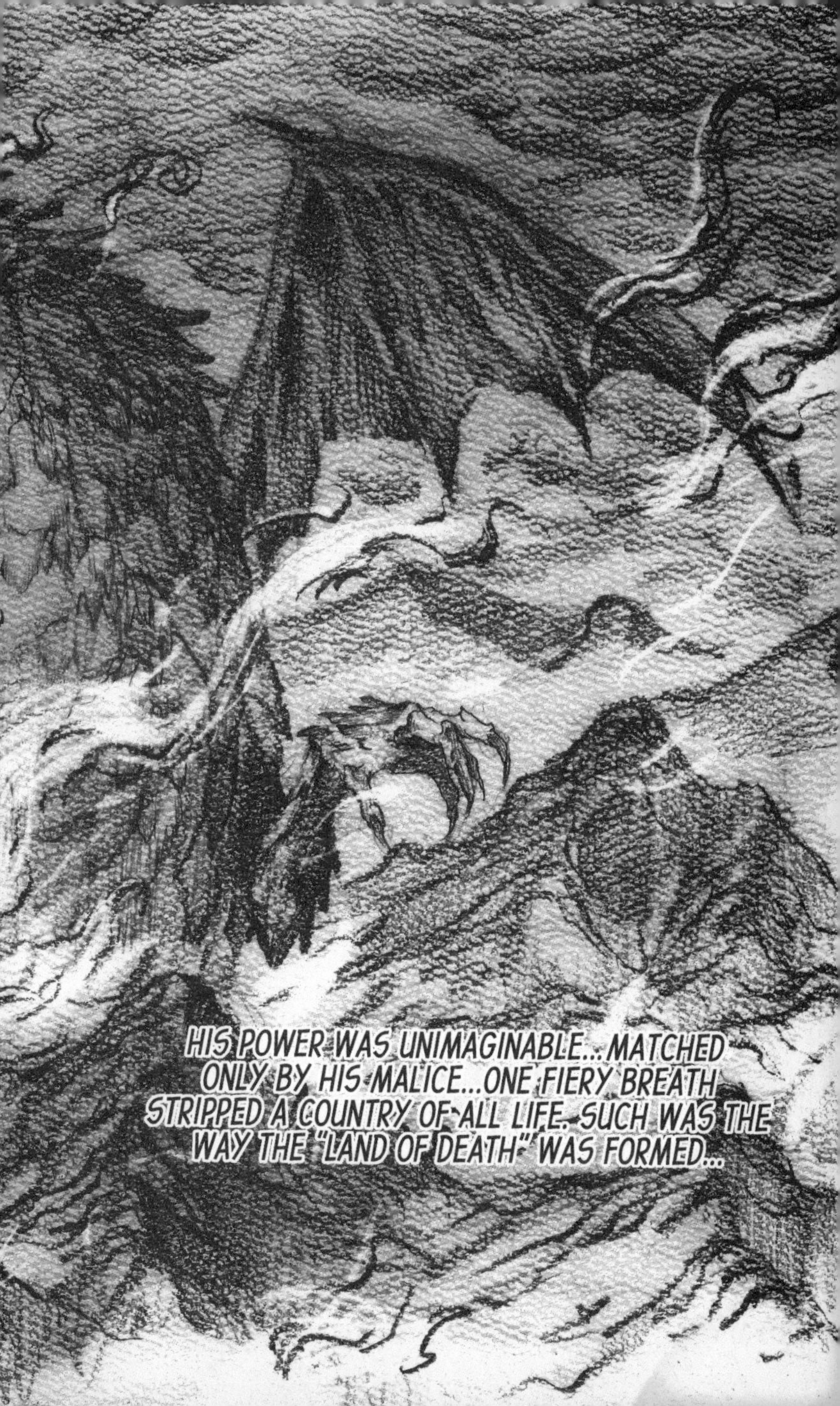
HIS POWER WAS UNIMAGINABLE... MATCHED ONLY BY HIS MALICE...ONE FIERY BREATH STRIPPED A COUNTRY OF ALL LIFE. SUCH WAS THE WAY THE "LAND OF DEATH" WAS FORMED...

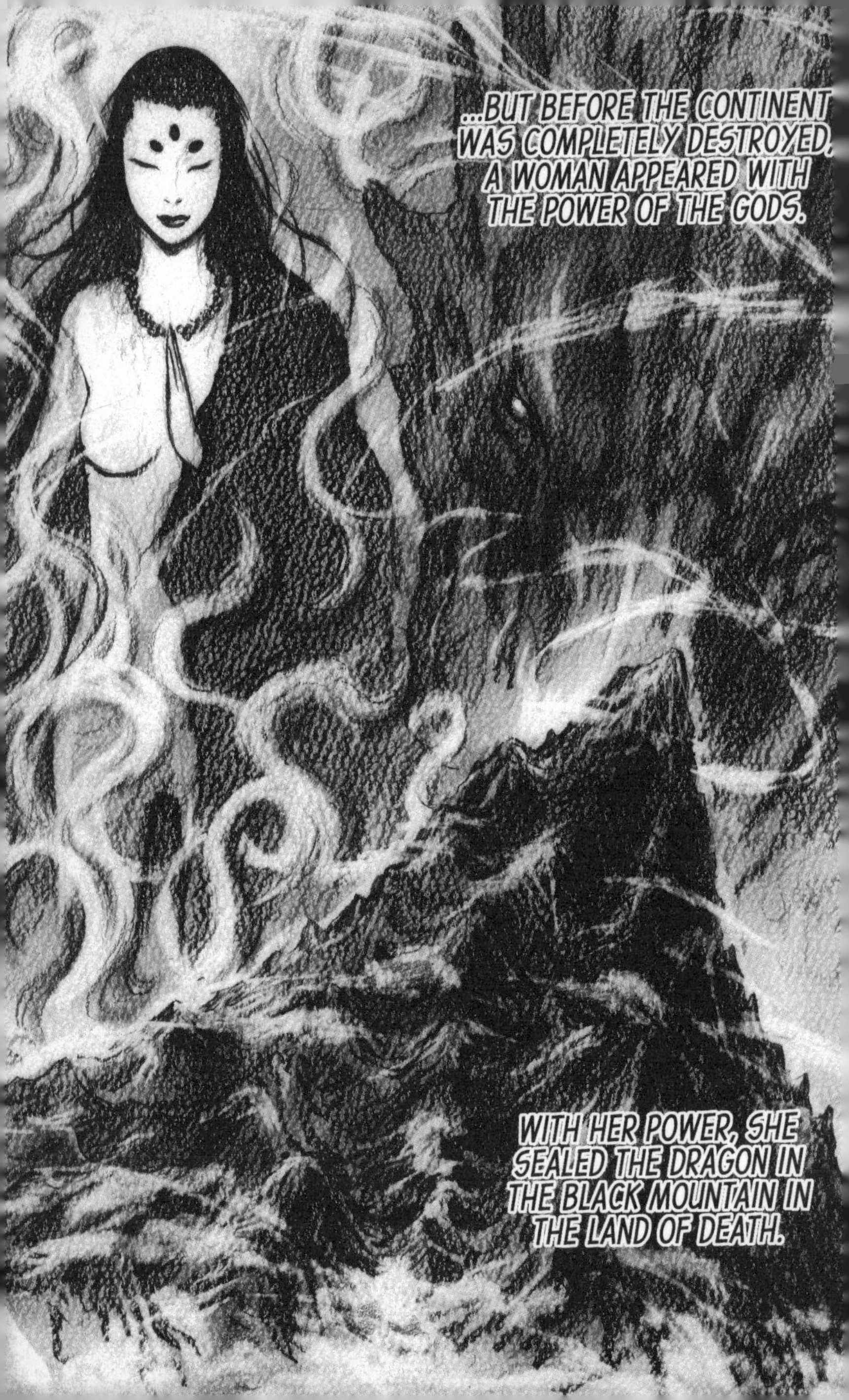
...BUT BEFORE THE CONTINENT WAS COMPLETELY DESTROYED, A WOMAN APPEARED WITH THE POWER OF THE GODS.
WITH HER POWER, SHE SEALED THE DRAGON IN THE BLACK MOUNTAIN IN THE LAND OF DEATH.

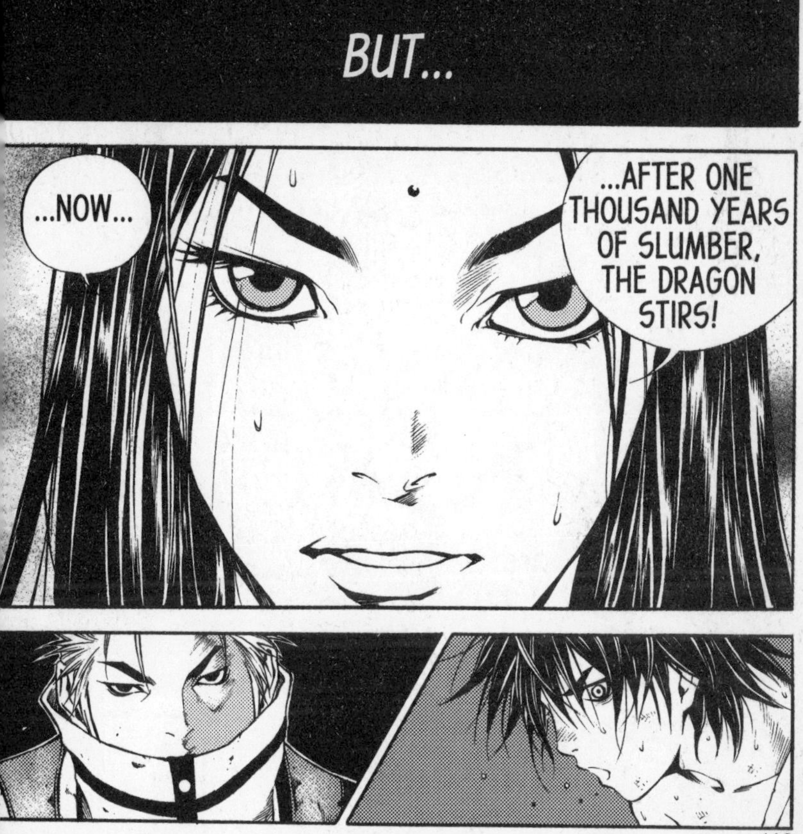
BUT...
...NOW...
...AFTER ONE THOUSAND YEARS OF SLUMBER, THE DRAGON STIRS!



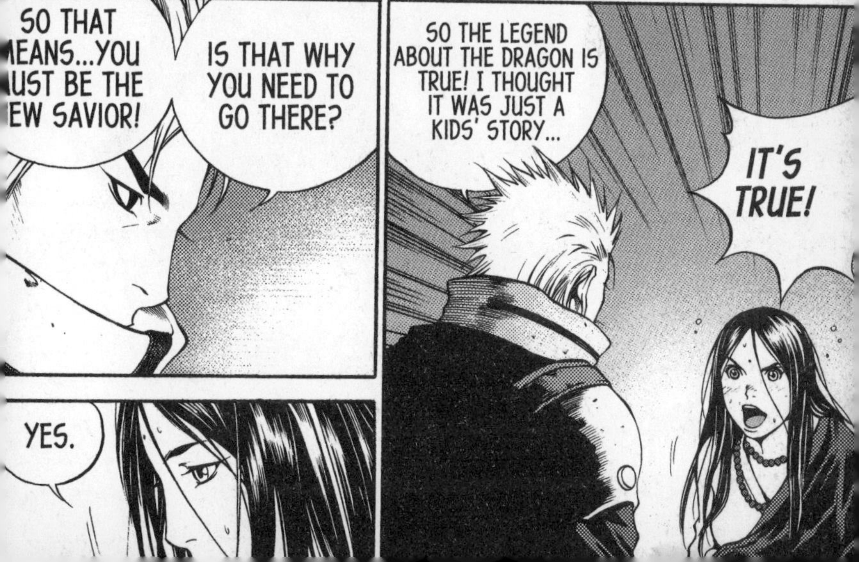
SO THAT EANS...YOU UST BE THE EW SAVIOR!
IS THAT WHY YOU NEED TO GO THERE?
YES.
SO THE LEGEND ABOUT THE DRAGON IS TRUE! I THOUGHT IT WAS JUST A KIDS' STORY...
IT'S TRUE!

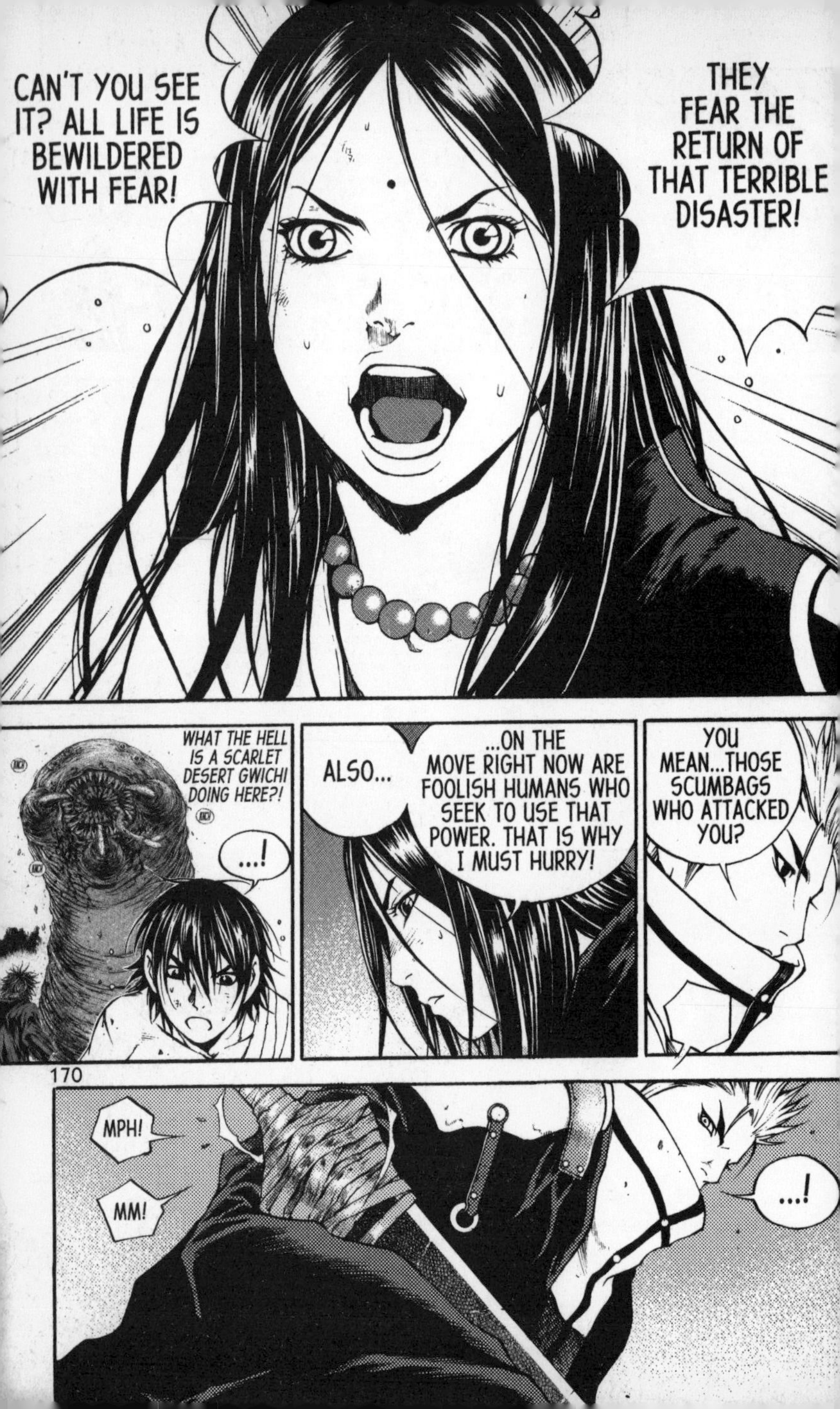
CAN'T YOU SEE IT? ALL LIFE IS BEWILDERED WITH FEAR!
THEY FEAR THE RETURN OF THAT TERRIBLE DISASTER!
WHAT THE HELL IS A SCARLET DESERT GWICHI DOING HERE?!
...!
ALSO...
...ON THE MOVE RIGHT NOW ARE FOOLISH HUMANS WHO SEEK TO USE THAT POWER. THAT IS WHY I MUST HURRY!
YOU MEAN...THOSE SCUMBAGS WHO ATTACKED YOU?
MPH!
MM!
...!

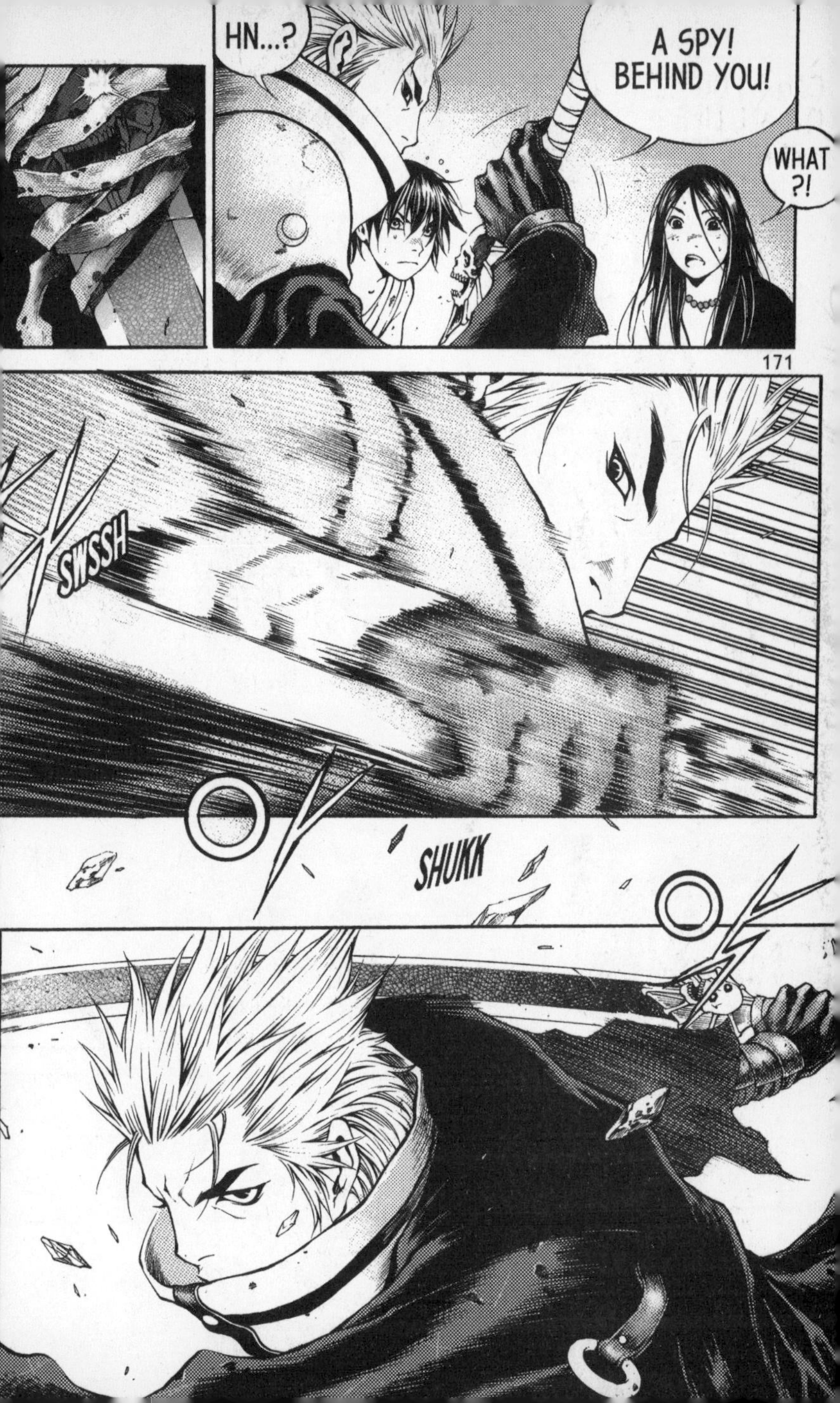
A SPY!
BEHIND YOU!
HN...?
WHAT
?!
171
SWSSH
SHUKK

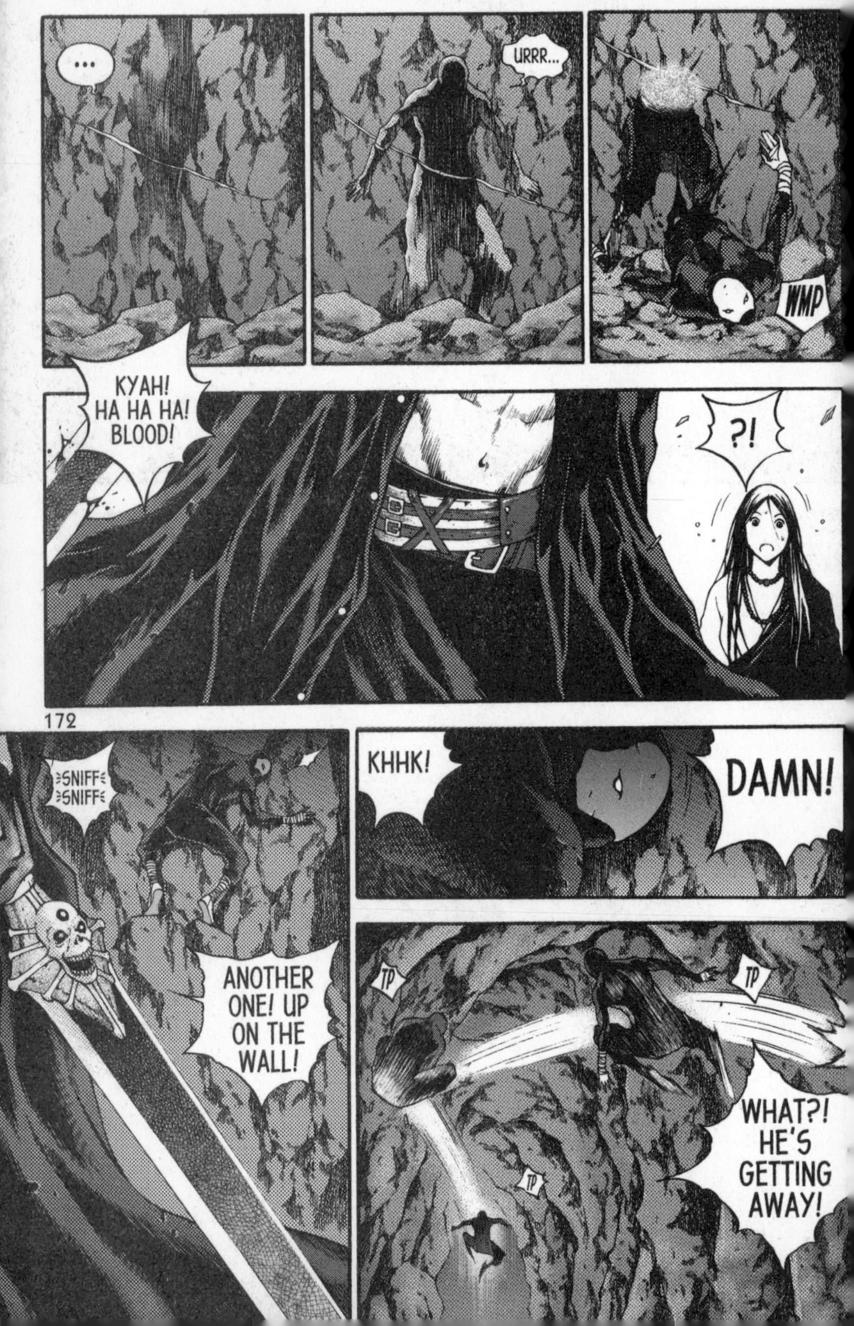
...
URRR...
WMP
KYAH! HA HA HA! BLOOD!
?!
SNIFF SNIFF
ANOTHER ONE! UP ON THE WALL!
KHHK!
DAMN!
TP
TP
TP
WHAT?! HE'S GETTING AWAY!

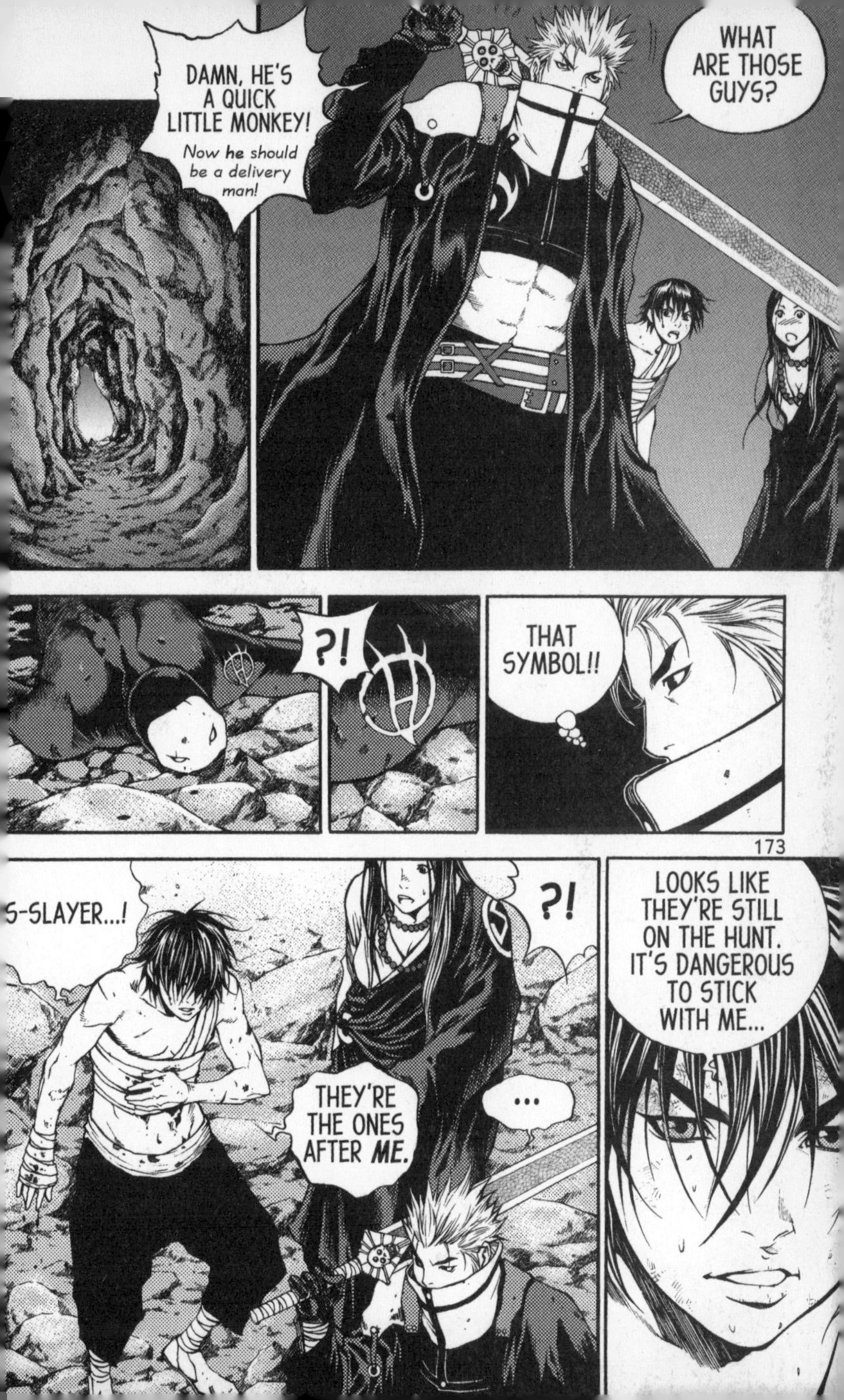
DAMN, HE'S A QUICK LITTLE MONKEY!
Now he should be a delivery man!
WHAT ARE THOSE GUYS?
?!
THAT SYMBOL!!
S-SLAYER...!
?!
THEY'RE THE ONES AFTER ME.
...
LOOKS LIKE THEY'RE STILL ON THE HUNT. IT'S DANGEROUS TO STICK WITH ME...

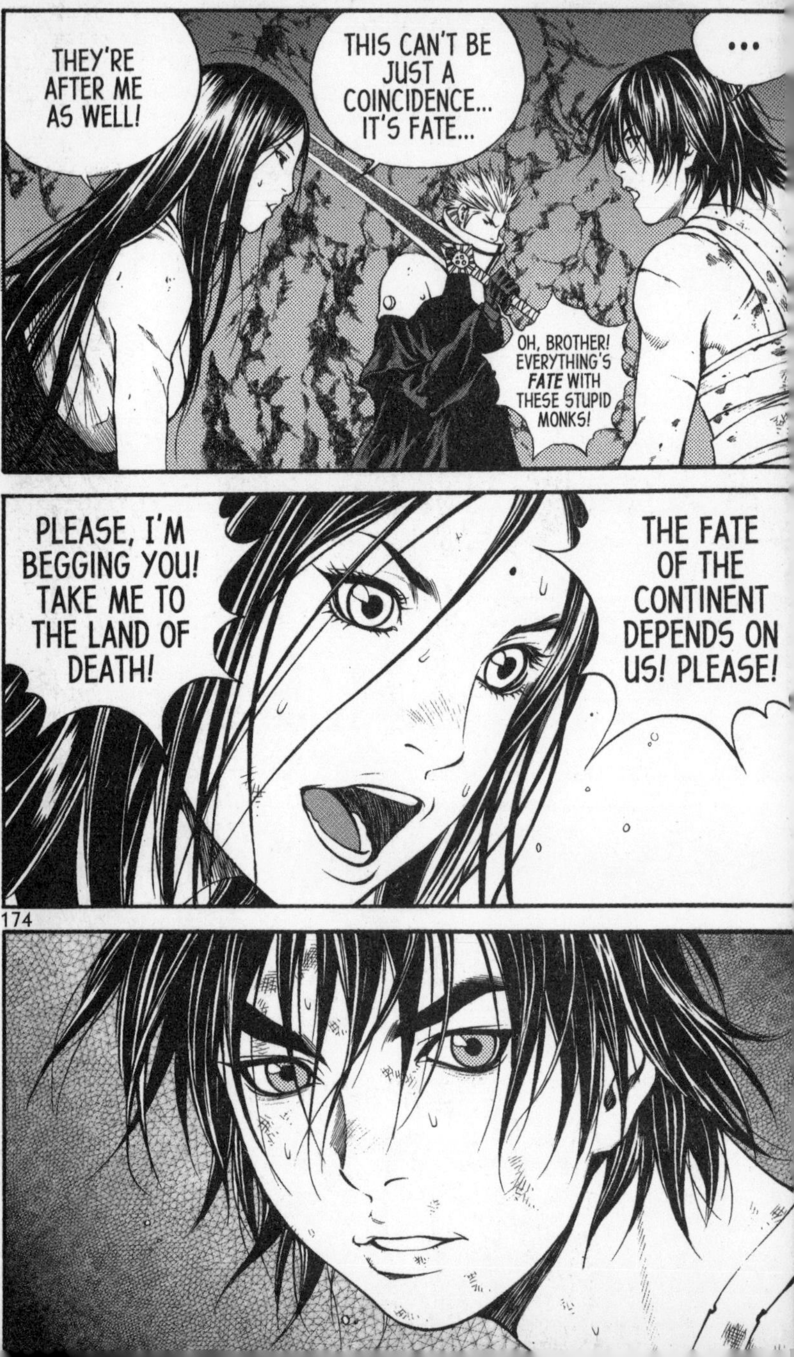
...
THIS CAN'T BE JUST A COINCIDENCE... IT'S FATE...
THEY'RE AFTER ME AS WELL!
OH, BROTHER! EVERYTHING'S FATE WITH THESE STUPID MONKS!
THE FATE OF THE CONTINENT DEPENDS ON US! PLEASE!
PLEASE, I'M BEGGING YOU! TAKE ME TO THE LAND OF DEATH!

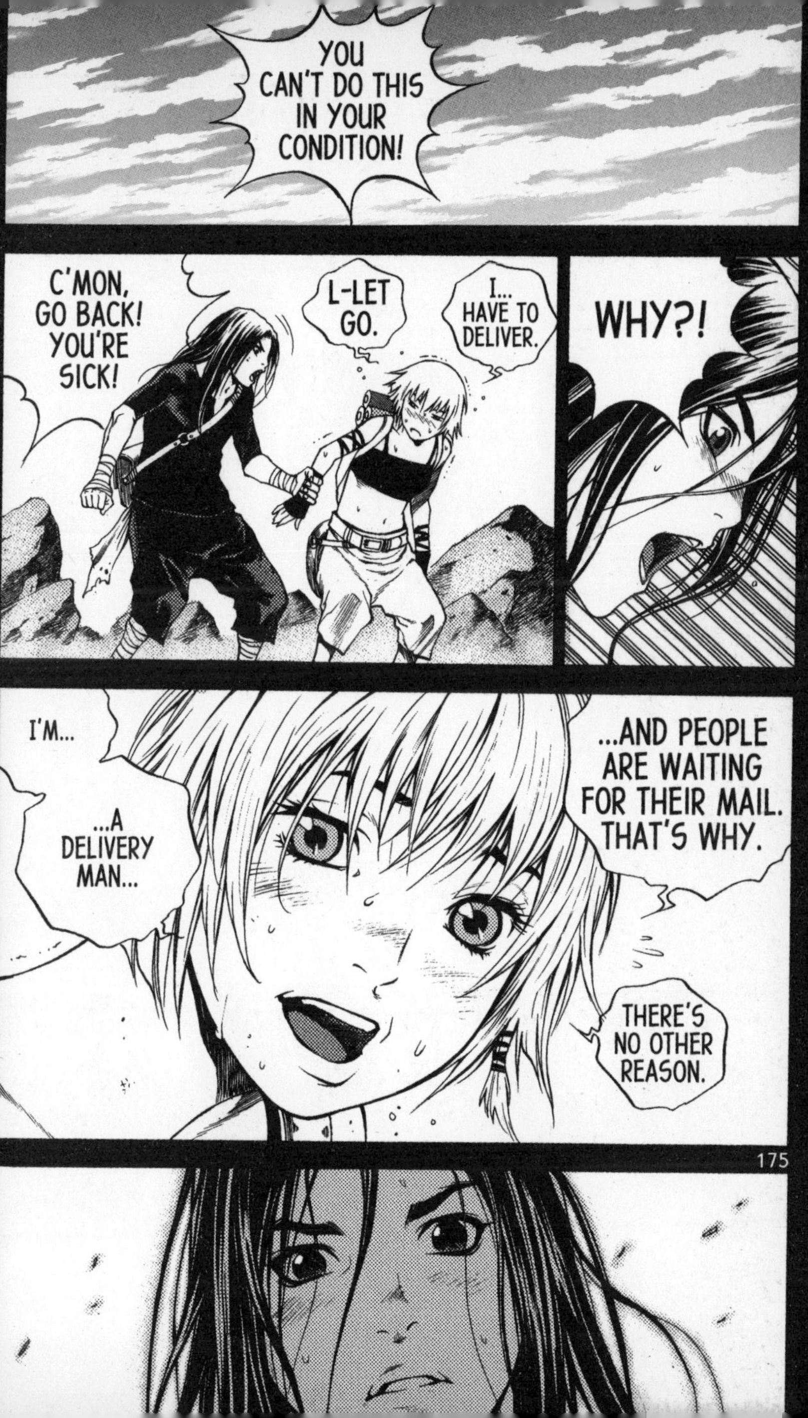
YOU CAN'T DO THIS IN YOUR CONDITION!
C'MON, GO BACK! YOU'RE SICK!
L-LET GO.
I... HAVE TO DELIVER.
WHY?!
I'M...
...A DELIVERY MAN...
...AND PEOPLE ARE WAITING FOR THEIR MAIL. THAT'S WHY.
THERE'S NO OTHER REASON.

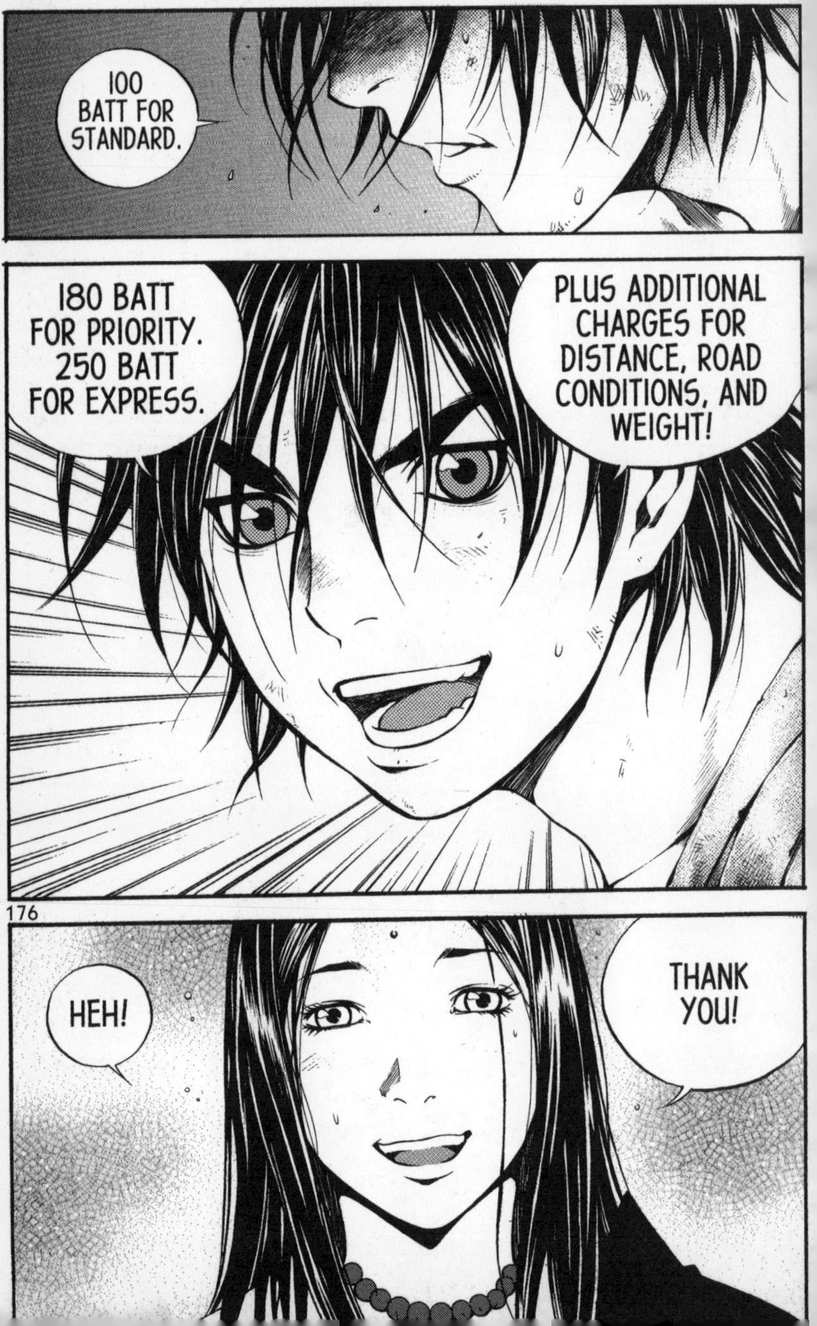
100 BATT FOR STANDARD.
180 BATT FOR PRIORITY. 250 BATT FOR EXPRESS.
PLUS ADDITIONAL CHARGES FOR DISTANCE, ROAD CONDITIONS, AND WEIGHT!
HEH!
THANK YOU!

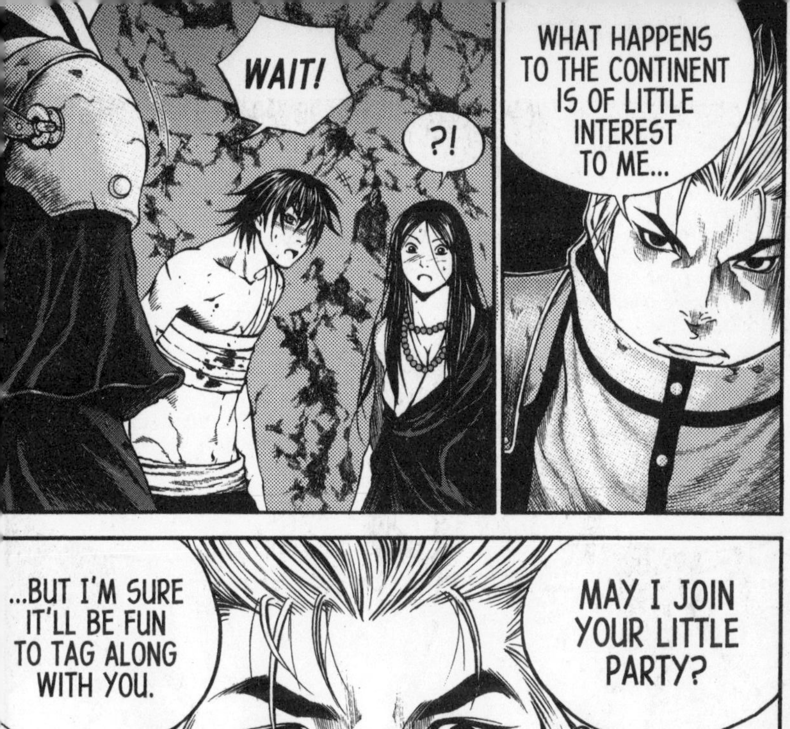
WAIT!
?!
WHAT HAPPENS TO THE CONTINENT IS OF LITTLE INTEREST TO ME...
...BUT I'M SURE IT'LL BE FUN TO TAG ALONG WITH YOU.
MAY I JOIN YOUR LITTLE PARTY?



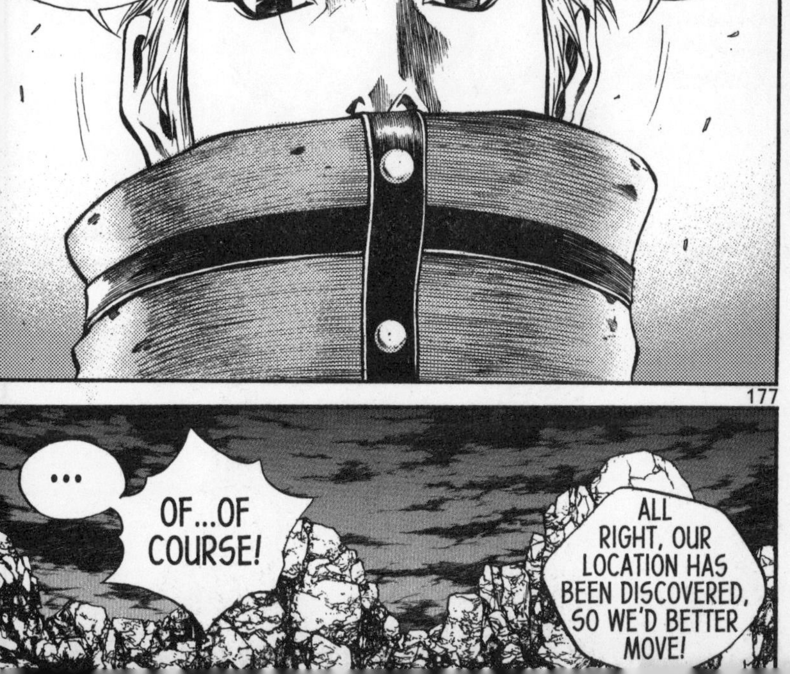
...
OF...OF COURSE!
ALL RIGHT, OUR LOCATION HAS BEEN DISCOVERED, SO WE'D BETTER MOVE!

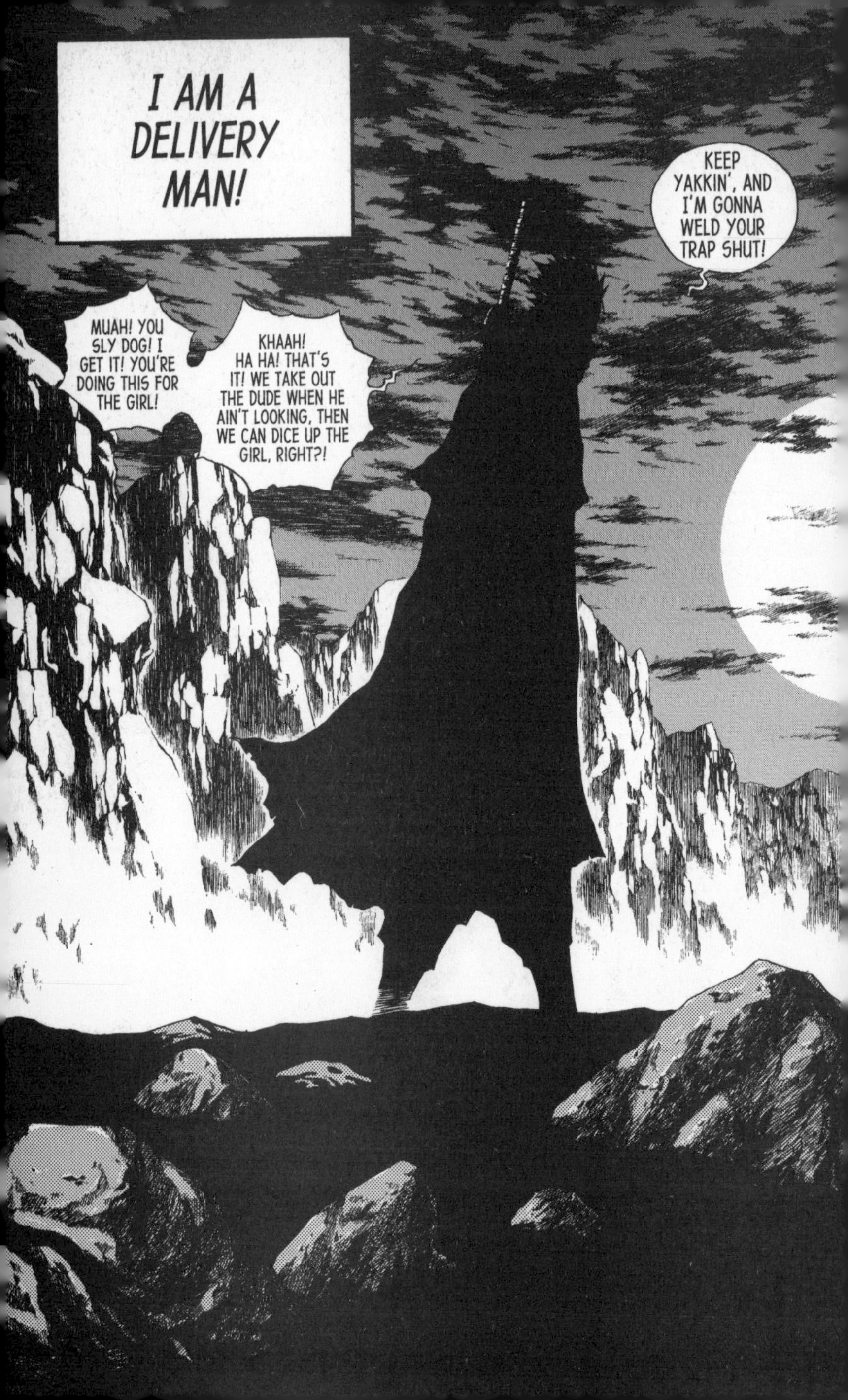
I AM A DELIVERY MAN!
KEEP YAKKIN', AND I'M GONNA WELD YOUR TRAP SHUT!
KHAAH! HA HA! THAT'S IT! WE TAKE OUT THE DUDE WHEN HE AIN'T LOOKING, THEN WE CAN DICE UP THE GIRL, RIGHT?!
MUAH! YOU SLY DOG! I GET IT! YOU'RE DOING THIS FOR THE GIRL!

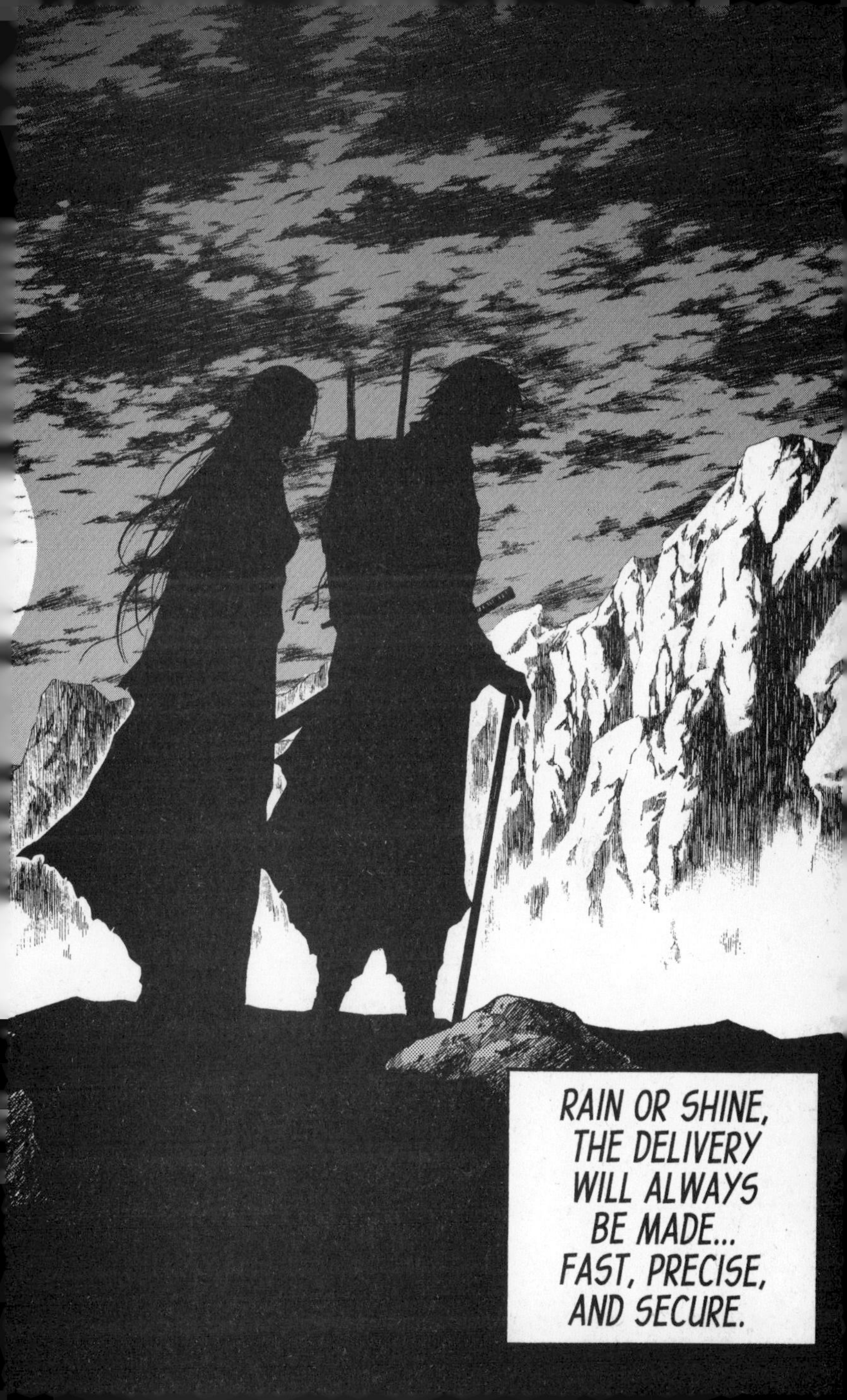
RAIN OR SHINE, THE DELIVERY WILL ALWAYS BE MADE... FAST, PRECISE, AND SECURE.

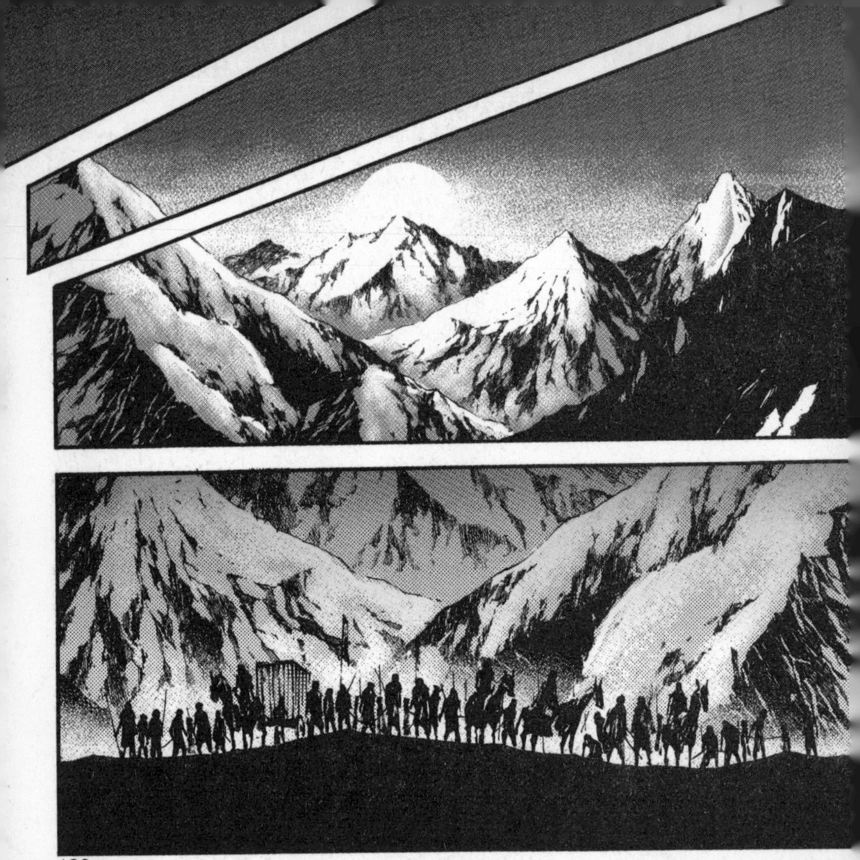



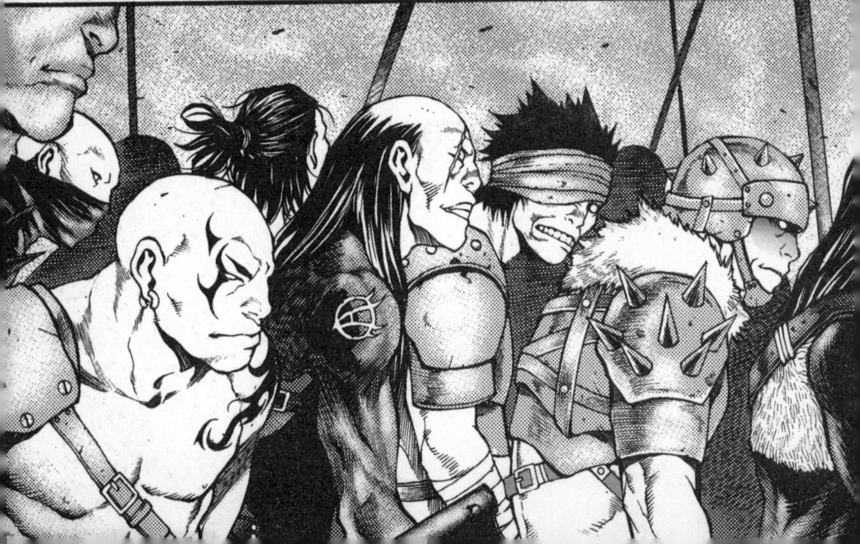

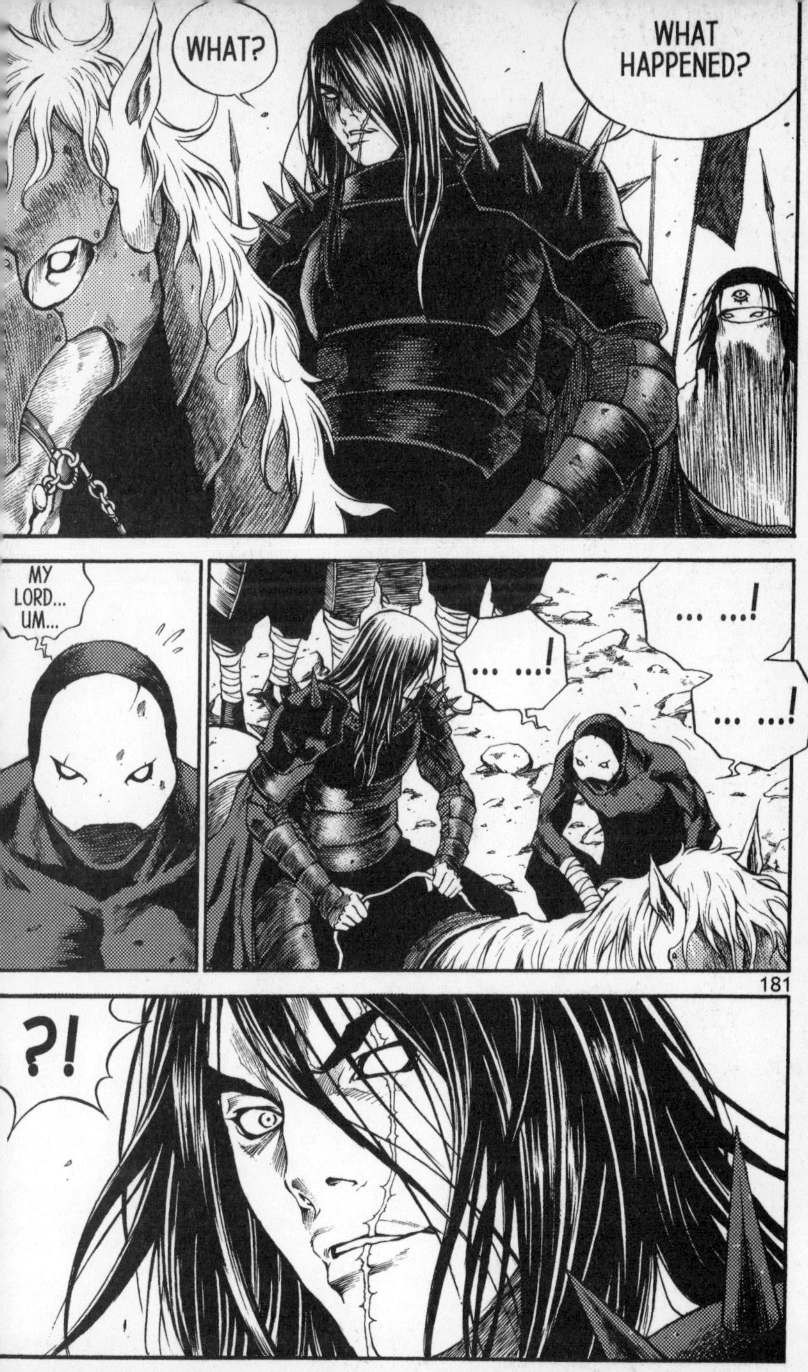
WHAT?
WHAT HAPPENED?
MY LORD... UM...
... ...!
... ...!
... ...!
?!

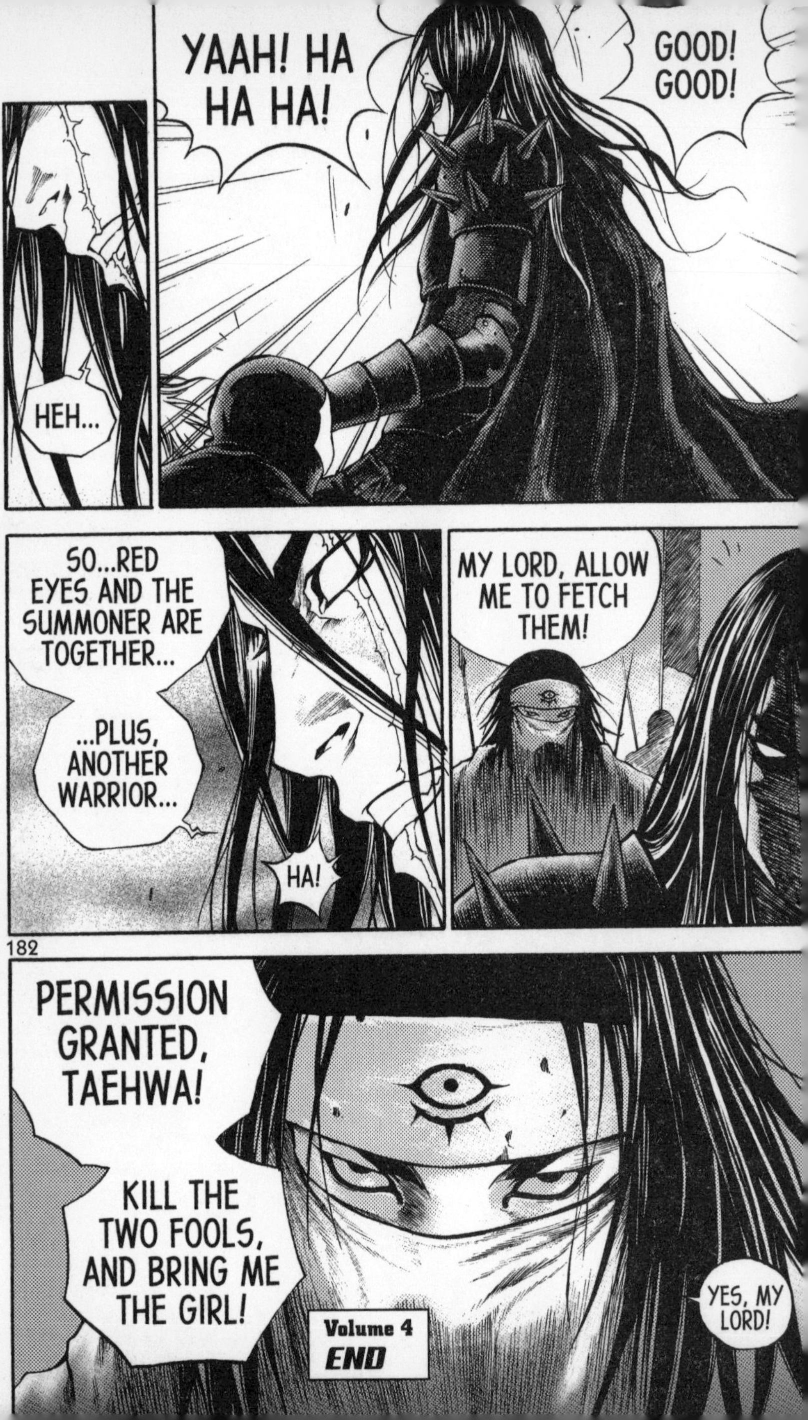
HEH...
YAAH! HA HA HA!
GOOD! GOOD!
SO...RED EYES AND THE SUMMONER ARE TOGETHER...
...PLUS, ANOTHER WARRIOR...
HA!
MY LORD, ALLOW ME TO FETCH THEM!
PERMISSION GRANTED, TAEHWA!
KILL THE TWO FOOLS, AND BRING ME THE GIRL!
YES, MY LORD!
Volume 4
END

publisher
**MIKE RICHARDSON**

editor
**PHILIP SIMON**

editorial assistant
**RYAN JORGENSEN**

digital production
**RYAN HILL**

collection designer
**M. JOSHUA ELLIOTT**

art director
**LIA RIBACCHI**

Special thanks to Michael Gombos, Dr. Won Kyu Kim, J. Myung Kee Kim, and Julia Kwon.

English-language version produced by DARK HORSE COMICS.

**BANYA: THE EXPLOSIVE DELIVERY MAN Volume 4**

DARK HORSE MANHWA
A division of Dark Horse Comics, Inc.
10956 SE Main Street
Milwaukie OR 97222

darkhorse.com

To find a comics shop in your area, call the
Comic Shop Locator Service toll-free at 1-888-266-4226

First edition: June 2007
ISBN-10: 1-59307-774-2
ISBN-13: 978-1-59307-774-7

10 9 8 7 6 5 4 3 2 1
Printed in Canada

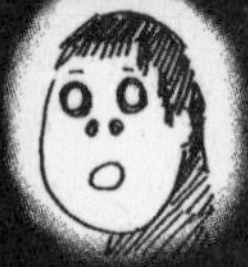

# STUDIO DIARY

BY JI-HOON, ASSISTANT ARTIST

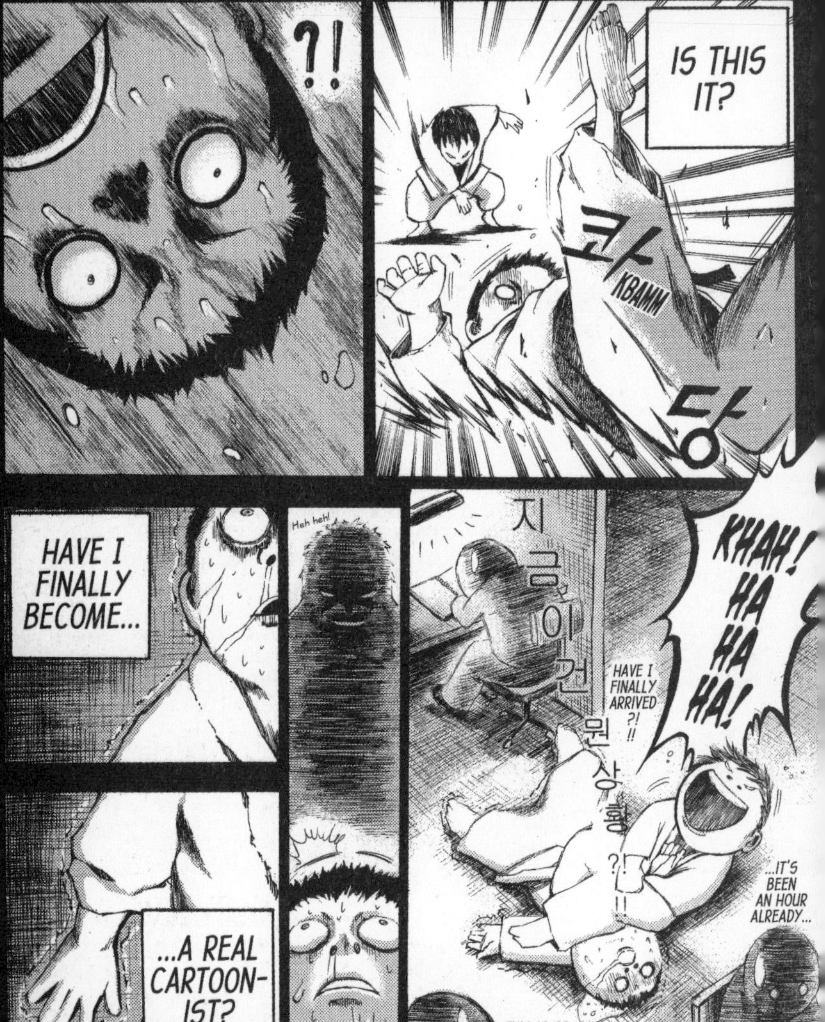
?!
IS THIS IT?
콰
KBAMM
당
HAVE I FINALLY BECOME...
Heh heh!
...A REAL CARTOON-IST?
KHAH! HA HA HA HA!
지금 이건 뭔 상황
?! !!
HAVE I FINALLY ARRIVED ?! !!
...IT'S BEEN AN HOUR ALREADY...
THIS IS SO WRONG...

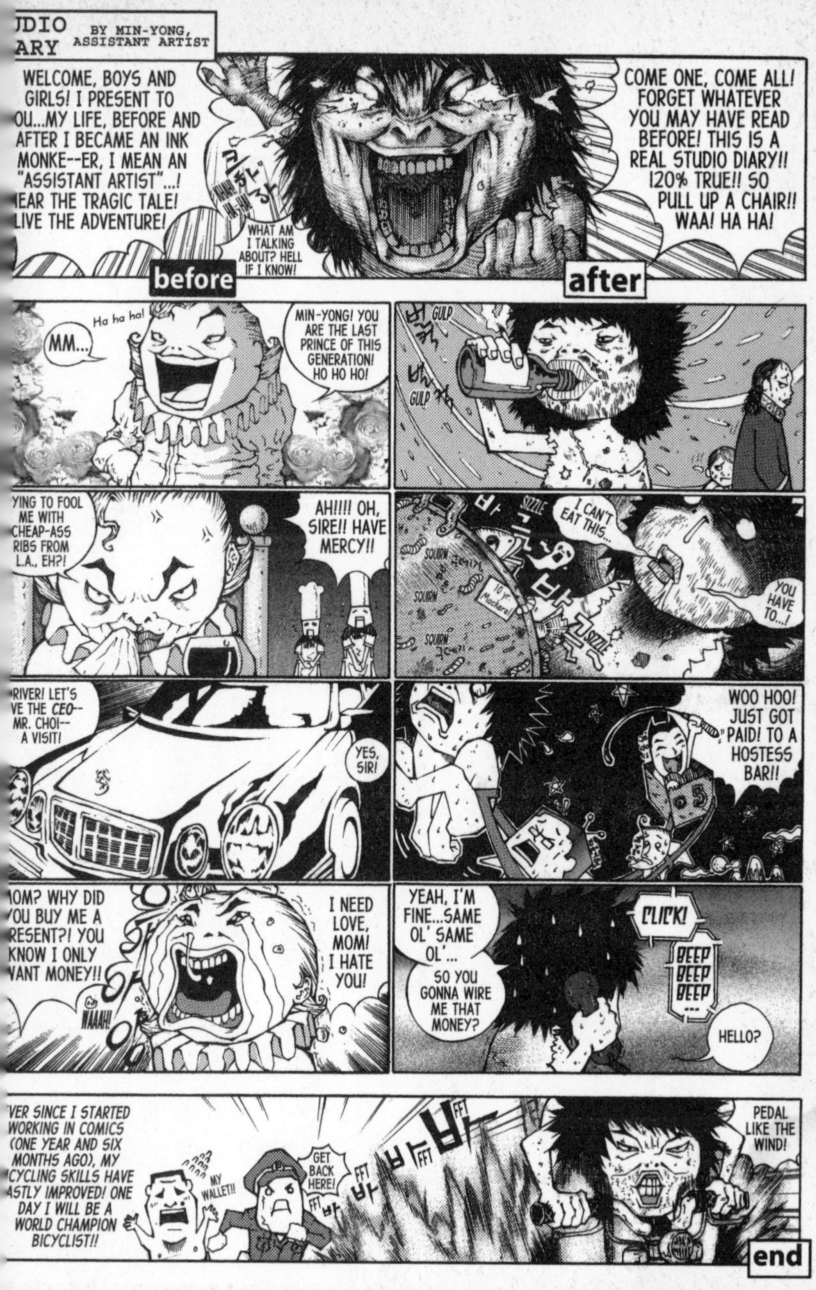

UDIO
ARY
BY MIN-YONG, ASSISTANT ARTIST
WELCOME, BOYS AND GIRLS! I PRESENT TO OU...MY LIFE, BEFORE AND AFTER I BECAME AN INK MONKE--ER, I MEAN AN "ASSISTANT ARTIST"...! HEAR THE TRAGIC TALE! LIVE THE ADVENTURE!
WHAT AM I TALKING ABOUT? HELL IF I KNOW!
COME ONE, COME ALL! FORGET WHATEVER YOU MAY HAVE READ BEFORE! THIS IS A REAL STUDIO DIARY!! 120% TRUE!! SO PULL UP A CHAIR!! WAA! HA HA!
before
after
Ha ha ha!
MM...
MIN-YONG! YOU ARE THE LAST PRINCE OF THIS GENERATION! HO HO HO!
GULP
GULP
YING TO FOOL ME WITH CHEAP-ASS RIBS FROM L.A., EH?!
AH!!!! OH, SIRE!! HAVE MERCY!!
SIZZLE
I CAN'T EAT THIS...
SQUIRM
SQUIRM
SQUIRM
10 yr. Mackerel
SIZZLE
YOU HAVE TO...!
RIVER! LET'S VE THE CEO-- MR. CHOI-- A VISIT!
YES, SIR!
WOO HOO! JUST GOT PAID! TO A HOSTESS BAR!!
MOM? WHY DID OU BUY ME A RESENT?! YOU KNOW I ONLY WANT MONEY!!
I NEED LOVE, MOM! I HATE YOU!
WAAAH!
YEAH, I'M FINE...SAME OL' SAME OL'...
SO YOU GONNA WIRE ME THAT MONEY?
CLICK!
BEEP BEEP BEEP ...
HELLO?
VER SINCE I STARTED WORKING IN COMICS (ONE YEAR AND SIX MONTHS AGO), MY ICYCLING SKILLS HAVE ASTLY IMPROVED! ONE DAY I WILL BE A WORLD CHAMPION BICYCLIST!!
MY WALLET!!
GET BACK HERE!!
FFT
FFT
FFT
FFT
PEDAL LIKE THE WIND!
end

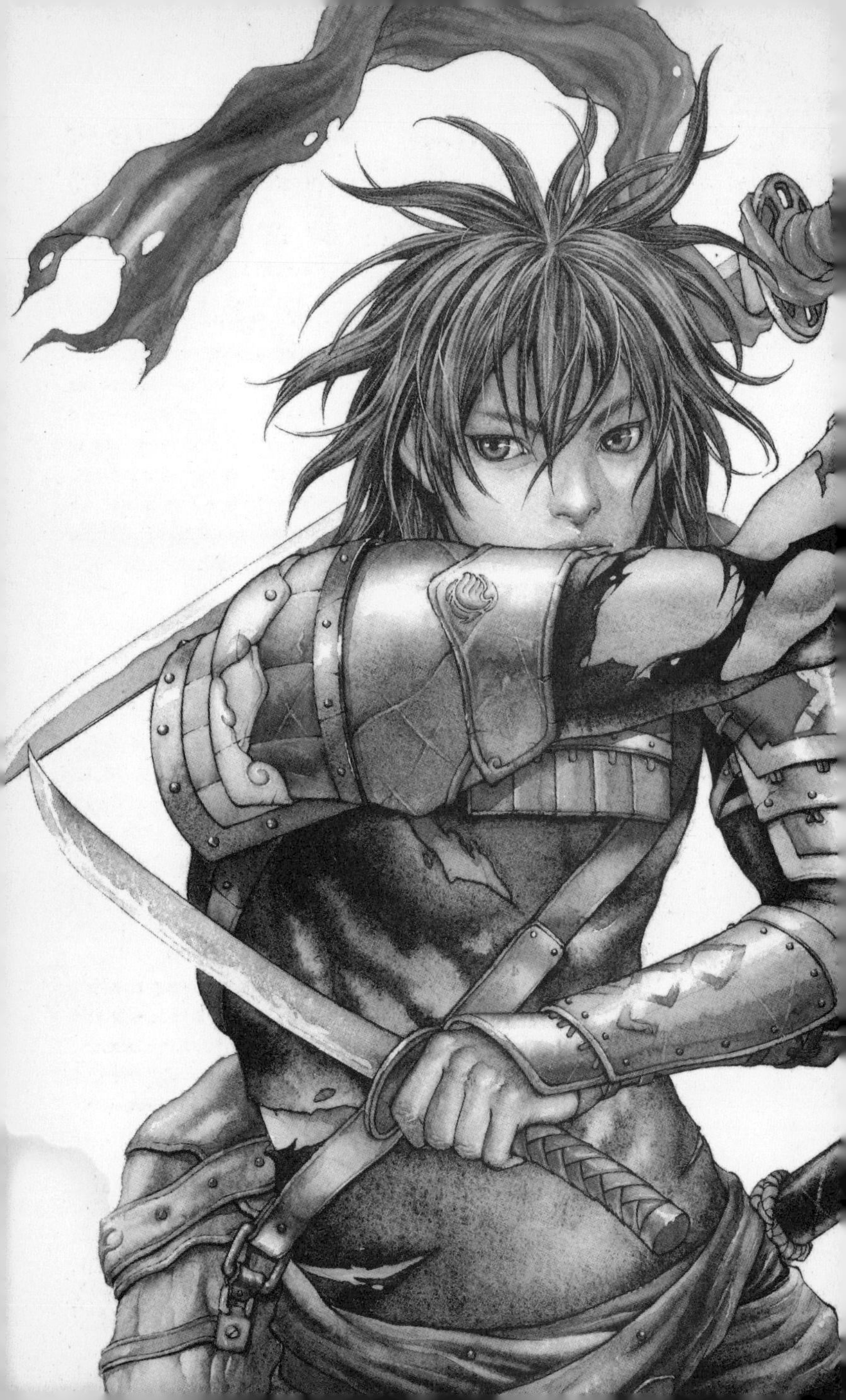

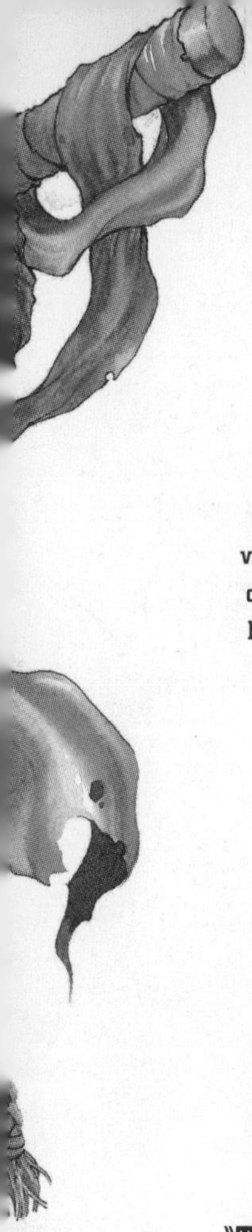

# Coming soon in
# Banya
### the explosive delivery man
## Volume 5! The Finale!

In an exciting volume of nonstop action, the story of Banya: The Explosive Delivery Man comes to an end! Banya races to deliver his most important package ever to the aptly named Land of Death—but a vicious pack of warriors and monsters, led by the villainous Kamutu, is closing in quickly. With Banya regaining more missing memories from his violent past, will he slip back into the role of a brutal killer and join Kamutu, or will his love for his friends at the Gaya Desert Post Office overcome the pull of a former life filled with bloodshed and rage?

Kim Young-Oh delivers a brilliantly illustrated climax to this action-packed series, which is filled with strange monsters, vicious swordplay, and a dash of oddball humor.

" . . . **Banya** is an engaging ride. The art is note-perfect for this kind of material, richly detailed and engaging. When the swords start swinging and the spears start flying, you know you're in very good hands. The landscapes offer varied and convincing menace, and the characters fulfill their central-casting functions with charm and specificity."
—David Welsh, *ComicWorldNews.com*

"This is a phenomenal work that I have been enjoying reading over and over again. The scenes float by like a movie in the mind. It is absorbing enough to stay on the lookout for successive volumes and to keep re-reading ones already owned."
—Matt Butcher, *IndependentPropaganda.com*

DARK
HORSE
MANHWA

## AUTHOR'S NOTE

I paid a lot for this bicycle . . .

I couldn't even pay my assistants for a few months.
Whew!
I seem to spend my comics money here . . . there . . . everywhere.
I never seem to have enough to live.

These days,
I've been really wanting a Mizuno Judo uniform.
Hmm . . . better get back to the comic so I can make more bling . . .
and watch it disappear again . . .

**Text and photograph: Kim Young-Oh**

(Assistant artists: Moon Ji-Hoon and No Min-Yong)

## Kim Young-Oh's
# Banya
### the explosive delivery man

With a worldwide war raging between humans and monsters, the young delivery men and women of the Gaya Desert Post Office do not pledge allegiance to any country or king. They are banded together by a pledge to *deliver* . . . "Fast. Precise. Secure." Banya, the craziest and craftiest of the bunch, will stop at nothing to get a job done.

**Volume 1**
ISBN-10: 1-59307-614-2
ISBN-13:978-1-59307-614-6

**Volume 2**
ISBN-10: 1-59307-688-6
ISBN-13: 978-1-59307-688-7

**Volume 3**
ISBN-10: 1-59307-705-X
ISBN-13: 978-1-59307-705-1

**Volume 4**
ISBN-10: 1-59307-774-2
ISBN-13: 978-1-59307-774-7

**$12.95 EACH!**

Previews for *BANYA: THE EXPLOSIVE DELIVERY MAN* and other DARK HORSE MANHWA titles can be found at darkhorse.com!

AVAILABLE AT YOUR LOCAL COMICS SHOP OR BOOKSTORE. To find a comics shop in your area, call 1-888-266-4226. For more information or to order direct: On the web: darkhorse.com. E-mail: mailorder@darkhorse.com. Phone: 1-800-862-0052 Mon.-Fri. 9 A.M. to 5 P.M. Pacific Time.

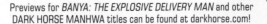

# PARK JOONG-KI'S
## S·H·A·M·A·N
# WARRIOR

One of Korea's top five best-selling manhw
titles! From the desert wastelands emerge tv
mysterious warriors, master wizard Yarong ar
his faithful servant Batu. On a grave missio
from their king, they have yet to realize t
whirlwind of political movements and secr
plots which will soon engulf them and chang
their lives forever. When Yarong is injured
battle, Batu must fulfill a secret promise to lea
Yarong's side and protect h
master's child. As Batu see
to find and hide the infan
Yarong reveals another secr
to those who have tracked hi
down to finish him off—the dead!
hidden power of a Shaman Warric

**Volume**
ISBN-10: 1-59307-638-
ISBN-13: 978-1-59307-638-

**Volume**
ISBN-10: 1-59307-749-
ISBN-13: 978-1-59307-749-

**Volume**
ISBN-10: 1-59307-769-
ISBN-13: 978-1-59307-769-

*$12.95 EACH*

Previews for *SHAMAN WARRIOR* and other DARK HORSE
MANHWA titles can be found at darkhorse.com!

AVAILABLE AT YOUR LOCAL COMICS SHOP OR BOOKSTORE. To find a comics shop in your area, call 1-888-266-4226.
For more information or to order direct: On the web: darkhorse.com. E-mail: mailorder@darkhorse.com.
Phone: 1-800-862-0052 Mon.-Fri. 9 A.M. to 5 P.M. Pacific Time.